The Corinthian Pottery

University Museum Monograph 95

THE EXTRAMURAL SANCTUARY OF DEMETER
AND PERSEPHONE AT CYRENE, LIBYA
FINAL REPORTS
Donald White, Series Editor
VOLUME VII

The Corinthian Pottery

Arcadia Kocybala

Published by
THE UNIVERSITY MUSEUM
University of Pennsylvania
Philadelphia
1999

for
THE LIBYAN DEPARTMENT OF ANTIQUITIES
As-Saray Al-Hamra
Tripoli
People's Socialist Libyan Arab Jamahiriya

Design, editing, production
   Publications Department
   The University Museum

Printing
   Science Press
   Ephrata, Pennsylvania

Endpapers taken from F. W. and H. W. Beechey, *Proceedings of the Expedition to Explore the Northern Coast of Africa from Tripoly Eastwards* (London 1828)

Library of Congress Cataloging-in-Publication Data
(Revised for vol.7)

The Extramural Sanctuary of Demeter and Persephone at
   Cyrene, Libya.

   (University Museum monograph: 52. 56. 67. 97. 95)
   Arabic and English
   Spine title: Cyrene final reports
   Excavations conducted by the University of Pennsylvania, Philadelphia and the Department of Antiquities of the People's Socialist Libyan Arab Jamahiriya.
   Two folded plans in pocket, v. 1.
   Includes bibliographic references and indexes.
   Contents: v. 1. Background and introduction to the excavations / Donald White -- v. 2. The East Greek, island, and Laconian pottery / Gerald P. Schaus -- v. 4. Excavations in the Extramural Sanctuary of Demeter and Persephone at Cyrene, Libya.
   1. Demeter (Greek deity)--Cult. 2. Persephone (Greek deity)--Cult. 3. Excavations (Archaeology)--Libya. 4. Sanctuary of Demeter and Persephone (Cyrene). 5. Cyrene (Ancient city). 6. Libya--Antiquities. I. White, Donald, 1935-   II. University of Pennsylvania. University Museum. III. Libya. Maslahat al-Athar. IV. Title. V. Title: Cyrene final reports. VI. Series. VII. Series: Univesity Museum monograph ; 52, etc.
DT239.C9E98   1984   939'.75   83-19866
ISBN 0-934718-50-4 (set)
ISBN 0-934718-51-2 (v. 1)
ISBN 0-934718-55-5 (v. 2)
ISBN 0-934718-71-6 (v. 3)
ISBN 0-934718-50-4 (v. 4)
ISBN 0-924171-17-0 (v. 5)
ISBN 0-924171-48-0 (v. 6)
ISBN 0-924171-45-6 (v. 7)

Copyright © 1999
The University Museum
University of Pennsylvania
Philadelphia
All rights reserved
Printed in the United States of America

Arcadia Kocybala received her Ph.D. in classical archaeology from the University of Pennsylvania. Her doctoral dissertation, "Greek Colonization on the North Shore of the Black Sea in the Archaic Period," was partly researched during a ten-month stay in the Soviet Union on a graduate student/young faculty exchange program. She has excavated at Gordion in Turkey and Porto Cheli in Greece, and was site cataloguer at Cyrene in Libya. With C. Canby, she published *A Guide to the Archaeological Sites of Israel, Egypt and North Africa*. In 1984, she joined the computer sciences department at the IBM Thomas J. Watson Research Center, where she is currently technical assistant to the Research Division Vice President of Services, Applications and Solutions.

Contents

TEXT ILLUSTRATIONS ix

FIGURES x

PLATES xi

BIBLIOGRAPHICAL ABBREVIATIONS xiii

MINOR ABBREVIATIONS xvi

PREFACE by Donald White . . . .

INTRODUCTION 1
   Selection and Cataloguing Procedure 2
   Clay and Glaze 2
   Shapes 3
   Dating 5
   Decorative Techniques 6
   Painters and Workshops 10
   Concentrations of Finds 11
   Pottery from Archaic Contexts 11

ALABASTRA 13

ARYBALLOI 16
   Black-Figure 16
   Warrior Aryballoi 18
   Linear Style 19
   Quatrefoil and Variant 19
   Black-Polychrome "Football" 20
   Rims/Miscellaneous 20

PYXIDES 21
   Concave-Sided Pyxides 21
   Convex Pyxides 22
   Tripod Pyxides 24
   Powder Pyxides 26

LIDS 29
   Flat, Flanged Lids 29
   Domed Lids 33
   Knobs 34

KOTYLAI 35
   Black-Figure 35
   Silhouette Style 40
   Conventionalizing 42

Linear Style 43
Black-Glazed 46

KYLIKES 48

BOWLS AND RELATED OPEN SHAPES 50

PLATES 52
Black-Figure 53
Silhouette Style 56
Linear Style 58

KOTHONS 60

OINOCHOAI 63

AMPHORISKOI 67

CLOSED SHAPES 68

KRATERS 73

RING VASE 78

MINIATURE VASES 78
Aryballoi 79
Pyxides 79
Concave Pyxides 80
Convex Pyxides 80
Tripod Pyxides 80
Powder Pyxides 81
Lids 81
Kotylai 81
Kylikes 85
Phialai Mesomphaloi 85
Bowls 85
Kana 86
Kothons 86
Oinochoai 87
Olpe 87
Hydriai 87
Kraters and Krater-Cups 94

PLASTIC VASES 94

CONCLUSIONS 97

APPENDIX I 101

APPENDIX II 111

ARABIC SUMMARY by Jamal el Harami 113

FIGURES

PLATES

Text Illustrations

Illustration 1. Black-Figure Aryballos (**15**) 16
Illustration 2. Black-Figure Aryballos (**19**) 17
Illustration 3. Black-Figure Kotyle (**110**) 36
Illustration 4. Black-Figure Kotyle (**111**) 36
Illustration 5. Black-Figure Kotyle (**112**) 37
Illustration 6. Black-Figure Kotyle (**113**) 37
Illustration 7. Black-Figure Kotyle (**115**) 38
Illustration 8. Silhouette Style Plate (**201**) 57
Illustration 9. Black-Figure Olpe? (**257i**) 69
Illustration 10. Black-Figure Olpe? (**257j**) 69
Illustration 11. Black-Figure Convex-Pyxis? (**260**) 70
Illustration 12. Black-Figure Closed Shape (**261**) 70
Illustration 13. Krater (**280**) 74
Illustration 14. Krater (**281a**) 75
Illustration 15. Krater (**281b**) 75
Illustration 16. Krater (**281c**) 76
Illustration 17. Krater (**282**) 76

Figures

Figure 1. Silhouette Style Kotyle (**134**)
Linear Style Kotylai (**147, 156**)
Black-Glazed Kotylai (**159, 161, 163, 164**)
Kylix (**175**)
Bowls (**184, 188**)

Figure 2. Black-Figure Plates (**192, 200**)
Silhouette Style Plates (**204, 205**)
Linear Style Plates (**207–210**)
Krater (**289**)
Miniature Pyxis? (**296**)
Miniature Concave Pyxis (**297**)
Miniature Convex Pyxis (**299**)
Miniature Kotylai (**304—306, 310, 311**)

Figure 3. Miniature Kotylai (**313, 314, 317, 318, 320**)
Miniature Phiale Mesomphalos (**323**)
Miniature Bowl (**324**)
Miniature Kothon (**331**)
Miniature Hydriai (**338, 339, 344, 351, 355, 356, 360, 363, 371, 376, 380**)
Miniature Krater (**389**)

Plates

Plate 1.   Alabastra (**1–7**)
Plate 2.   Alabastra (**8, 9**)
Plate 3.   Alabastra (**10–14**)
Plate 4.   Aryballoi (**15–21**)
Plate 5.   Aryballoi (**22–27**)
Plate 6.   Aryballoi (**28–32**)
Plate 7.   Aryballoi (**34–39**)
Plate 8.   Pyxides (**40–45**)
Plate 9.   Pyxides (**46–51**)
Plate 10.   Pyxides (**52–56**)
Plate 11.   Pyxides (**57–62**)
Plate 12.   Pyxides (**63–67**)
Plate 13.   Pyxides (**68–73**)
Plate 14.   Pyxides (**74–78**)
Plate 15.   Pyxides (**79–82**)
Plate 16.   Lids (**83–88**)
Plate 17   Lids (**89–95**)
Plate 18.   Lids (**96–102**)
Plate 19.   Lids (**103–109**)
Plate 20.   Kotylai (**110–116**)
Plate 21.   Kotylai (**117–122**)
Plate 22.   Kotylai (**123–130**)
Plate 23.   Kotylai (**131–137**)
Plate 24.   Kotylai (**138–147**)
Plate 25.   Kotylai (**148–156**)
Plate 26.   Kotylai (**157–164**)
Plate 27.   Kylikes (**165–171**)
Plate 28.   Kylikes (**172–176**)
Plate 29.   Bowls and Related Open Shapes (**177–183**)
Plate 30.   Bowls and Related Open Shapes (**184–190**)
Plate 31.   Plates (**191–193**)
Plate 32.   Plates (**194–196**)
Plate 33.   Plates (**197–201**)
Plate 34.   Plates (**202–206**)
Plate 35.   Plates (**207–210**)
Plate 36.   Kothons (**211–220**)
Plate 37.   Kothons (**221–227**)
Plate 38.   Oinochoai (**228–236**)
Plate 39.   Oinochoai (**237–238, 240–243**)
Plate 40.   Oinochoai (**244–251**)
Plate 41.   Amphoriskoi (**252–256**)
Plate 42.   Closed Shapes (**257a-e**)
Plate 43.   Closed Shapes (**257f-j–259**)
Plate 44.   Closed Shapes (**260–266**)
Plate 45.   Closed Shapes (**267–272**)
Plate 46.   Closed Shapes (**273–279**)
Plate 47.   Kraters (**280–284**)

Plate 48.   Kraters and Ring Vase (**285–292**)
Plate 49.   Miniature Vases: Aryballoi and Pyxides (**293–297**)
Plate 50.   Miniature Vases: Pyxides and Lids (**298–303**)
Plate 51.   Miniature Vases: Kotylai (**304–310**)
Plate 52.   Miniature Vases: Kotylai (**311–317**)
Plate 53.   Miniature Vases: Kotylai, Kylix, and Phiale Mesomphalos (**318–323**)
Plate 54.   Miniature Vases: Bowls, Kana, and Kothons (**324–329**)
Plate 55.   Miniature Vases: Kothons, Oinochoe, Olpe, and Hydriai (**330–337**)
Plate 56.   Miniature Vases: Hydriai (**338–346**)
Plate 57.   Miniature Vases: Hydriai (**347–354**)
Plate 58.   Miniature Vases: Hydriai (**355–361**)
Plate 59.   Miniature Vases: Hydriai (**362–368**)
Plate 60.   Miniature Vases: Hydriai (**369–375, 377**)
Plate 61.   Miniature Vases: Hydriai (**378–385**)
Plate 62.   Miniature Vases: Hydriai, Kraters, and Krater Cups; and Plastic Vases (**386–394**)

Bibliographical Abbreviations

This series of reports adopts the standard abbreviations used by the *American Journal of Archaeology*. The works listed below are supplementary.

Agora XII	B. Sparkes and L. Talcott, *The Athenian Agora*, vol. XII, *Black and Plain Pottery of the 6th, 5th and 4th Centuries B.C.* (Princeton 1970).
Amyx	D. Amyx, "Dodwelliana," *CSCA* 4 (1971) 1–48.
Callipolitis-Feytmans	D. Callipolitis-Feytmans, "Évolution du plat corinthien," *BCH* 86 (1962) 117–164.
Corinth VII:1	S. Weinberg, *The Geometric and Orientalizing Pottery* (Cambridge, Mass. 1943).
Corinth VII:2	D. A. Amyx and P. Lawrence, *Archaic Corinthian Pottery and the Anaploga Well* (Princeton 1975).
Corinth VII:3	G. R. Edwards, *Corinthian Hellenistic Pottery* (Princeton 1975).
Corinth XIII	C. W. Blegen, H. Palmer, and R. S. Young, *The North Cemetery* (Princeton 1964).
Corinth XV:3	A. N. Stillwell and J. L. Benson, *The Potters' Quarter, The Pottery* (Princeton 1984).
CorVP	D. A. Amyx, *Corinthian Vase-Painting of the Archaic Period* (Berkeley 1988).
The Greeks Overseas	J. Boardman, *The Greeks Overseas* (London 1980).
Délos X	C. Dugas, *Les vases de l'Heraion, Délos: Exploration archélogique de Délos faite par l'École française d'Athènes* (Paris 1928).
Délos XVII	C. Dugas, *Les Vases Orientalisants de Style non Mélien, Délos: Exploration archélogique de Délos faite par l'École française d'Athènes* (Paris 1935).
Fairbanks	A. Fairbanks, *Catalogue of the Greek and Etruscan Vases in the Museum of Fine Arts, Boston I, Early Vases Preceding Athenian Black-figured Ware* (Cambridge, Mass. 1928).
Final Reports III	S. Lowenstam et al., *The Extramural Sanctuary of Demeter and Persephone at Cyrene, Libya* III (Philadelphia 1987).

GkV	J. L. Benson, *Die Geschichte der korinthischen Vasen* (Basel 1953).
Hopper	R. Hopper, "Addenda to Necrocorinthia," *BSA* 44 (1949) 162–257.
Lo Porto	F. G. Lo Porto, "Ceramica arcaica dalla Necropoli di Taranto," *ASAtene*, N. S. 21–22 (1959–1960) 7–230.
Mégara Hyblaea	G. Vallet and F. Villard, *Mégara Hyblaea* II, *La céramique archaïque* (Paris 1964).
NC	H. Payne, *Necrocorinthia* (Oxford 1931).
Perachora I	H. Payne et al., *Perachora: The Sanctuaries of Hera Akraia and Limenia*, vol. I (Oxford 1940).
Perachora II	T. J. Dunbabin, ed., *Perachora: The Sanctuaries of Hera Akraia and Limenia*, vol. II (Oxford 1962).
Schaus, *Final Reports* II	G. P. Schaus, *The Extramural Sanctuary of Demeter and Persephone at Cyrene, Libya* II: *The East Greek, Island, and Laconian Pottery* (Philadelphia 1985).
Stucchi, *L'Agora d Cirene*	S. Stucchi, *L'Agora di Cirene* I: *I lati nord et est della platea inferiore* (Rome 1965).
Tocra I	J. Boardman and J. Hayes, *Excavations at Tocra 1963–1965, The Archaic Deposits* I, BSA suppl. vol. 4 (Oxford 1966).
Tocra II	J. Boardman and J. Hayes, *Excavations at Tocra 1963–1965, The Archaic Deposits* II *and Later Deposits*, BSA suppl. vol. 10 (Oxford 1973).
Ure, *AFR*	P. Ure, *Aryballoi and Figurines from Rhitsona in Boeotia* (Cambridge 1934).
Warden et al., *Final Reports* IV	P. G. Warden, A. Oliver, P. Crabtree, and J. Monge, *The Extramural Sanctuary of Demeter and Persephone at Cyrene, Libya* IV: *The Small Finds, Glass, Faunal and Human Skeletal Remains* (Philadelphia 1990).
White, *First Report*	D. White, "Excavations of the Demeter Sanctuary at Cyrene 1969. A Preliminary Report," *LA* 8 (1971) 85–104.
White, *Second Report*	D. White, "Excavations in the Demeter Sanctuary at Cyrene 1971. Second Preliminary Report," *LA* 9–10 (1972–1973) 171–195.
White, *Third Report*	D. White, "Excavations in the Sanctuary of Demeter and Persephone at Cyrene 1973: Third Preliminary Report," *AJA* 79 (1975) 33–48.
White, *Fourth Report*	D. White, "Excavations in the Sanctuary of Demeter and Persephone at Cyrene. Fourth Preliminary Report," *AJA* 80 (1976) 165–181.

White, *Fifth Report*	D. White, "Excavations in the Sanctuary of Demeter and Persephone at Cyrene. Fifth Preliminary Report," *LA* 13–14 (1976–1977) 289–312.
White, *Final Reports* I	D. White, *The Extramural Sanctuary of Demeter and Persephone at Cyrene, Libya* I: *Background and Introduction to Excavations* (Philadelphia 1984).
White, *Final Reports* V	D. White, *The Extramural Sanctuary of Demeter and Persephone at Cyrene, Libya* V: *The Site's Architecture, its First Six Hundred Years of Development* (Philadelphia 1993).

Minor Abbreviations

A.f.	Animal frieze	LC	Late Corinthian
Bldg	Building	MC	Middle Corinthian
cm.	centimeters	MPD	Maximum Preserved Diameter
D	Diameter	MPDim	Maximum Preserved Dimension
EC	Early Corinthian	MPH	Maximum Preserved Height
Est	Estimated	MPL	Maximum Preserved Length
F.o.	Filling ornament	MPW	Maximum Preserved Width
H	Height	r.	right
Inv. No.	Inventory Number	Sb.	Sherd box
l.	left	Th	Thickness
L	Length		

Editor's Preface

When the sanctuary's East Greek, Island and Laconian Archaic wares were published 14 years ago, G. Schaus suggested that any final conclusions as to when its grounds were first occupied would have to wait until the publication of the Attic Black Figure and Corinthian pottery.[1] In the event, the earliest examples of the Attic wares turned out to be no earlier than the very early sixth century B.C.[2] and thus had no particular impact on the issue of the cult site's earliest occupancy. This created an expectation that the last of the site's big accumulations of archaic pottery, the Corinthian, would settle once and for all the question of whether worship of Demeter and Persephone had taken root on the south slope of Wadi Bel Gadir thirty years after the traditional 631 B.C. foundation date for the city or was instead more or less contemporary with it. As matters have turned out, despite the fact that the Corinthian pottery does not begin until ca. 600 B.C.,[3] the issue lives on, in somewhat enfeebled form, in a small number of pre-foundation date lamps, East Greek terracotta figurines,[4] and miscellaneous small finds.[5] For all practical purposes, however, the matter can be regarded as largely settled. While it is hard to imagine a sanctuary functioning in any kind of normally organized manner without pottery, the presence of other objects reliably attributed to the final quarter of the seventh century and earlier seem to signal some type of late seventh century B.C. activity that may have preceded the erection of the first permanent stone buildings, which probably do date to 600 B.C. In this regard it was very helpful that the outlines of Arcadia Kocybala's conclusions, including her basic chronology, were available in time for inclusion in the final analysis of the site's earliest architectural phase.[6]

The author gained an extensive first-hand acquaintance with the Wadi Bel Gadir sanctuary while serving as the Pennsylvania project's cataloguer during the 1978 season; she returned a year later to study the Corinthian material as a member of the 1979 study season team. A relatively short time after the final study season in 1981, she left archaeology to join the business world. It understandably required a very special effort to divide her time between a demanding career with IBM and the detailed analysis, research, and eventual writing-up of the present report. Given the fact that the Corinthian imports represent the largest percentage of all of the wares found in the sanctuary[7] as well as a real cornerstone for the dating of many of the architectural elements of the sixth century precinct, the Pennsylvania Expedition and I in particular owe Dr. Kocybala a major debt of gratitude for her important contribution. It should be pointed out that the lapse of more than eight years between her submission of the text and the appearance of this volume was caused by circumstances beyond the control of the author. I also wish to take this occasion to thank once again Karen Vellucci and the other members of the University of Pennsylvania Museum's publication staff for their contributions to the production phase of this volume. I also wish to thank Dr. Jamal el Harami for contributing the Arabic summary. And, as always, Dr. Kocybala joins me and all past members of the expe-

---

1. Schaus, *Final Reports* II, 4.

2. M. Moore, *Final Reports* III, 1.

3. See, in addition, infra.

4. Still awaiting final publication, but see J. Uhlenbrock, "History, Trade and the Terracottas," *Expedition* 34, nos. 1-2 (1992), 17-18.

5. P. G. Warden, *Final Reports* IV, 3, 10, no. 26, 36, no. 234, 61-2, nos. 457-73.

6. Dated ca. 620 to 500 B.C. in deference to the chronological issues just referred to, D. White, *Final Reports* V, 5-41, 187-95.

In a double issue of *Expedition*, sub-titled *Gifts to the Goddesses: Cyrene's Sanctuary of Demeter and Persephone* and written for a non-specialist audience, the question of a pre-construction phase of activity was ignored and the sanctuary's origin dated to "about a generation after the initial foundation of Cyrene." See D. White, "The Sanctuary's History and Architecture," *Expedition* 34, nos. 1-2 (1992), 7.

7. To say nothing of perhaps one of the most difficult classes of pottery to clean owing to the extreme fragility of its sherds and fugitive character of its painted decoration. See G. Schaus, "Pottery from the Sanctuary—a Question of Function," *Expedition* 34, nos. 1-2 (1992), 27; T. Fuller, *Final Reports* III, 5. See also infra, n. 1.

dition's staff together with the current director of the University of Pennsylvania Museum, Dr. Jeremy Sabloff, in thanking Dr. Fadel Ali Mohammed, Director-General of the Department of Antiquities and his various colleagues for enabling our work to take place in the first place.

Donald White
1999

Editor's Note: The complete manuscript for this volume was submitted to University Museum Publications of the University of Pennsylvania Museum in 1991. For reasons beyond the control of the author, no references to publications after 1991 could be included.

Introduction*

Corinthian pottery represents a substantial, perhaps even the most sizable, portion of the imported archaic Greek wares uncovered at the extramural Sanctuary of Demeter and Persephone at Cyrene.[1] The material, with its markedly broad range of types and quality, provides insight into both the early history of the sanctuary and the nature of the export wares of this major Greek pottery center.

At the Cyrene sanctuary, vases of Corinthian manufacture span nearly two centuries: beginning about 600 B.C., growing in volume throughout the sixth century, and continuing sporadically not only into the fifth, but also into the early part of the fourth century B.C. The ceramic finds at each end of this long chronological span are not numerous. The pieces attributed to the Early Corinthian period are comparatively few, and some of these have been only tentatively assigned. Although the Middle Corinthian period is far better represented, the majority of our pottery belongs to the Late Corinthian I and II periods. More moderate in volume, the pottery of the Late Corinthian II/III period consists mainly of miniatures. Only a score of vases can be assigned to the Late Corinthian III period, and several of our miniature black-glazed hydriai may be as late as the fourth century B.C. Our latest and seemingly anomalous find is a black-glazed echinus bowl of the first half of the fourth century B.C.

Our assemblage, consisting of both full-size and miniature vases, is quite diverse. The products of archaic Corinthian workshops, which occur in varying quality and quantity, include vases decorated in black-figure, linear style, silhouette, black-polychrome, black-glaze, conventionalizing, and red-ground techniques. Toward the end of the archaic period, reflecting the changes in Corinthian pottery manufacture, there is a decrease both in the variety of the decorative techniques and in the size of the vases.

The study and publication of the Corinthian pottery was expected to hold much promise for resolving the chronological question of the foundation of the Demeter Sanctuary at Cyrene.[2] Although it can solidify the conclusions drawn by the study of the Attic,[3] East Greek, and Laconian pottery,[4] that pottery imports begin in the early sixth century, the Corinthian pottery does not hold the key to solving the question of the date of the foundation of the sanctuary for one major reason: the generally poor state of preservation of the surviving pottery. Not only is the pottery very fragmentary, with most of the vases reduced to sherds, but the soil conditions at the extramural sanctuary at Cyrene have further exacerbated the state of preservation by leaving a layer of lime and soil encrustation, which often, even after cleaning, results in a soil-stained surface without painted decoration.[5] Thus, this local problem has been added to the inherent qualities of Corinthian pottery—a fabric that can often be friable and a glaze that does not adhere well.[6]

Despite these difficulties, significant information can be derived from the Corinthian pottery in relation to the sanctuary from a chronological, historical, and perhaps even a social perspective. Moreover, the

---

* Editor's note: Throughout this introductory chapter, the author refers to archaeological contexts that have some particular relevance to her discussion. Many, but not all, are discussed at greater length in *Final Reports* I and V. Rather than burdening the notes of this introductory chapter with a large number of references to these more general studies, it is suggested that those who wish to pursue contextual matters further refer to "Appendix I: Dates of Archaeological Contexts Organized by Area, Trench, Stratum, and Classes of Objects," *Final Reports* V, 187–195.

1. An indication of the volume of Corinthian imports can be obtained from the results of the 1978 cubic meter test made in the F14/G14 grid backfill, wherein imported fine wares constituted 37% of the pottery. In this fine ware category, plain black glaze was the most numerous (37.24%), followed by Corinthian (25.26%) and Attic (21.85%) as well as much smaller percentages of East Greek, Island, and Laconian pottery. On the cubic meter test, see D. White, "Cyrene's Sanctuary of Demeter and Persephone: A Summary of a Decade of Excavation," *AJA* 85 (1981), 26; Schaus, *Final Reports* II, xxi; *Final Reports* III, ix.

2. I wish to thank Donald White, the director of the excavations, for inviting me to publish the Corinthian pottery, for his hospitality during two summers at Cyrene, and for his assistance in providing certain requested research materials during the preparation of the manuscript.

3. Moore, *Final Reports* III, 1–4.

4. Schaus, *Final Reports* II, 93 ff.

5. T. Fuller, *Final Reports* III, 4–5.

6. On Corinthian clay and glaze, see M. Farnsworth, "Corinthian Pottery: Technical Studies," *AJA* 74 (1970), 9–20; *Perachora* II, 133–134; and *CorVP*, 535–539.

pottery provides some interesting new material for Corinthian vase-painting in general and adds to our knowledge of certain vase-painters in particular.

Although our discussions and conclusions are based primarily on the catalogued pottery, they are supplemented by the uncatalogued material as much as possible.

Selection and Cataloguing Procedure

Nearly 400 pieces are included in our catalog from the more than 5100 fragments retained from the excavations.[7] That is, our catalog contains less than 8% of the Corinthian pottery that was available for study from the seven seasons of excavation of the sanctuary.[8] Although this may appear to the reader as a disappointingly small percentage, it does, nevertheless, represent the best-preserved Corinthian pottery from the site.

The criteria for selecting the pottery for the catalogue were threefold: (1) state of preservation, (2) representative of the types of pottery found at the site, and (3) interest for the study of Corinthian vase-painting. As noted above, the Corinthian material is generally fragmentary and poorly preserved. There are relatively few complete vases and only a somewhat larger number of nearly complete vases. These, however, are almost exclusively miniatures, mainly black-glazed hydriai and pattern-decorated kotylai, as well as one or two instances of other miniature shapes.[9] There are only three nearly complete full-size vases: an LC linear-style lid (**94**), a mended LC black-figure alabastron (**10**) whose painted decoration has worn off, and a small LC II/III broad-bottomed oinochoe (**246**). Otherwise, our catalog contains body fragments, rims, bases, and various combinations of bodies, bases, necks, rims, handles, and shoulders.

Every shape identified among the finds from the sanctuary occurs in the catalog.[10] Depending on the state of preservation, some shapes are better represented than others. For example, miniature black-glazed hydriai are more fully documented than miniature kotylai, with 25% of the hydriai published and only a little over 1% of the kotylai. Where the shapes are more commonly decorated in black-figure, such as alabastra and plates, these vases are also proportionally better represented in the catalog.

The Corinthian pottery from the sanctuary includes a wide range of decorative styles, and all of these have been presented in the catalog. From the perspective of intrinsic interest for figured vase-painting, there is a relative preponderance of black-figure fragments. The sampling in our catalog should, nonetheless, give the reader a fair notion of the range and quality of the Corinthian pottery imported into the Sanctuary of Demeter and Persephone at Cyrene.

In our catalog, the examples are arranged by shape. The miniature vases are discussed in a separate section and they, too, are arranged by shape. An introduction, summarizing the finds, precedes the catalog entries for each shape. Within each shape section, the pieces are arranged according to their decorative style in approximate chronological order. Black-figure pieces are usually treated first. Each catalog entry is identified by its context (area, trench, stratum) and by either an inventory number (Inv. No.)[11] or a sherd box number (Sb.) along with a hyphenated digit to differentiate the individual fragments from the same box.[12] A description and the dimensions of each piece are given. Comparanda are cited wherever possible, but are not intended to be exhaustive. Occasionally, drawings are included for poorly preserved black-figure fragments to supplement the photographs in the plates. Due to the paucity of intact vases, there are a limited number of profile drawings.[13]

Clay and Glaze

Corinthian clay has the reputation of being easily identifiable, though it is often characterized by rather subjective terms to indicate hue and color.[14]

---

7. Retention procedure explained by D. White in Schaus, *Final Reports* II, xxi. The fragments appear to represent about 5000 different vases; all possible joins were made.

8. A preliminary review of the Corinthian pottery was made during the summer of 1978, while the author was site cataloguer, and was examined again during the study season in the summer of 1979.

9. These include aryballoi (**293–295**), a pyxis (**299**), a phiale (**323**), a bowl (**325**), kana (**326–327**), a kothon (**331**), an oinochoe (**332**), and a krater-cup (**391**).

10. See section on Shapes below.

11. An annual inventory number was generally given only to those pieces that were relatively well preserved.

12. Most of our pottery is identified with a sherd box number.

13. Profile drawings of fragments, however, have also been included.

14. See Farnsworth, *AJA* 74:1 (1970), 11; *CorVP*, 535–537.

The clay of the fragments contained in the catalog ranges from various tones of buff (creamy, ivory, pale yellow, pinkish, deep, tan), to buff with pale orange or pale pink core, and to light green. The quality among our fragments varies from a fine, well-levigated clay to a somewhat coarser consistency. There are occasional instances of lime inclusions.

The black glaze,[15] when preserved, is either a blackish brown, a dark brown, or sometimes a maroon brown. Occasionally, it has fired red or has a metallic quality. It is rarely black and nearly always matte. Where the glaze is more thickly applied, it is often crazed, and where thinly applied, it ranges from brown to yellow. The added red on our fragments ranges to purple. Added white, used primarily for subsidiary decoration, is less often preserved, frequently appearing as a discoloration on the fragment.

Shapes

A broad range of shapes, characteristic of the Corinthian repertoire, is represented at the Demeter and Persephone Sanctuary.[16] The vase forms include containers for perfume-oil (alabastra, aryballoi, amphoriskoi) and scented liquid (kothons), cosmetic or trinket boxes (various types of pyxides), drinking cups (kotylai and kylikes), and vessels for pouring (oinochoai of various types, olpai, hydria), and storage and mixing (amphorai and kraters), as well as serving (plates and bowls).[17] The order of their presentation in our catalog basically adheres to the sequence originally used by Payne in the Necrocorinthia Catalog and followed in other studies of Corinthian pottery as, for example, those by Hopper[18] and Amyx and Lawrence.[19]

The vase shapes found at the sanctuary are thus presented as follows:

alabastra
aryballoi
pyxides (concave, convex, tripod, and powder)
lids
kotylai
kylikes
bowls and related open shapes
plates
kothons (exaleiptra)
oinochoai
amphoriskoi
closed shapes
kraters
ring vase
plastic vases

Our vessels fall into two size categories: full and miniature in the ratio of 2:1. In the full- or standard-size vase category, large shapes, both open and closed, are far less common than smaller shapes. For the large shapes, there are only a dozen kraters and one hydria. Among the smaller closed shapes, there are a significant number of unidentifiable vases, numerous aryballoi, an appreciable number of oinochoai, some amphoriskoi, a number of alabastra, a couple of small amphorai, one olpe, and a single ring vase. The smaller open shapes have a much stronger representation, with an exceedingly high number of kotylai (some of very broad dimension), a large quantity of pyxides of various type, and a good selection of kothons, as well as a lesser number of kylikes, plates, and bowls. The miniature vases, which constitute a considerable quantity, essentially replicate the full-size shapes, with the exception of plates[20]; among the miniatures, however, there are also a few kana and phialai.

To give a more comprehensive picture of the nature of the Corinthian imports and the quantity of each vase form, we tabulated the actual number of pieces and percentages of both catalogued and uncatalogued fragments for each shape retained from the excavations. Given the odds of retention, these figures obviously can only give an approximation of the volume of the vase types found at the sanctuary. Nonetheless, the relative proportions should be approximately correct.

The full-size imported vases, amounting to two-thirds of all the Corinthian pottery unearthed at the sanctuary, are considered first. The percentages for each shape are based on the total number of full-size vase fragments (over 3400).

The most common vase and, in fact, virtually ubiquitous is the kotyle. Kotylai constitute nearly 50% of the full-size pottery fragments retained from the

---

15. See Farnsworth, *AJA* 74:1 (1970), 18–20; *CorVP*, 537–539.

16. Interestingly, there are no identifiable examples of kalathoi from the excavations of the sanctuary.

17. Among the Attic black-figure and black-pattern wares, basically the same types of shapes (kraters, oinochoai, plates, numerous and various cups, kothons) occur in some quantity, with the understandable exception of a much larger number of amphorai as well as more full-sized hydriai. There are relatively few oinochoai, lekanides, alabastra, and lekythoi. There is a similar pattern among the East Greek, Island, and Laconian imports, where we also see a large number of cups, as well as kraters, jugs, plates, and aryballoi. The exception here is the larger number of dishes.

18. *BSA* 44 (1949); *Perachora* II.

19. *Corinth* VII:2; Amyx, *CorVP*, 436ff.

20. There are also no miniature alabastra, which do not appear to have been a miniature shape.

excavation of the sanctuary.[21] They range in size from some very large examples, with diameters of over 20 cm., to rather small vases, only somewhat larger than miniatures. Dating from MC to LC III, they are decorated in black-figure, linear (most frequently), silhouette, black-glaze, and conventionalizing styles.

After the kotylai, pyxides are the most common vases, though numerically far below kotylai, i.e., about 11% of the finds. The four major types are represented in the following descending order of frequency: convex, tripod, powder, and concave pyxides. Like the kotylai, they range in date from MC to LC III. The pyxides are predominantly decorated in the linear and white style, but include black-figure, except on the powder pyxides, and conventionalizing floral patterns on the convex pyxides.

Next in quantity are various types of closed vases whose identification is not certain, such as tentatively assigned olpai, amphorai, convex-pyxides, oinochoai, and a flat-bottomed aryballos, as well as a couple of recognizable vases (a hydria and a lekythos). As a group, these closed shapes constitute less than 10% of the finds. Their chronological range is also from MC to LC III. They are decorated in black-figure, linear style, black-glaze, conventionalizing florals, red-ground, and black-glaze.

Aryballoi constitute the next most frequent group, accounting for over 8% of the ceramic finds. Ranging in date from possibly EC, but at least MC, through LC, the aryballoi occur in a variety of styles: black-figure, linear, warrior, quatrefoil, and football types. Interestingly, almost all of our aryballoi are of the round variety.[22]

Kothons or exaleiptra follow in terms of quantity, forming less than 8% of the finds. Dating from MC to LC II, they occur in both the more frequent round and the far less common rectangular section; several of the latter belong to Amyx's Winchester Group. Although most of the kothons are decorated in the linear style, including white style, there are some examples in black-figure.

Pyxis lids of both flat and domed type along with knobs comprise the next most numerous type, under 6% of the finds. Flat lids are twice as common as the domed types. The flat lids range in date from EC to LC II and exhibit more diverse decoration, including black-polychrome, black-figure, silhouette, red-ground, and linear style. The domed lids date to LC and are invariably decorated in the linear style.

Identifiable oinochoai are not very frequent, just over 2% of the finds. There are certain examples of broad-bottomed, conical, and small cylindrical oinochoai, but most of the fragments cannot be precisely attributed to specific oinochoe types. Our oinochoai, ranging in date from MC to LC II/III, are decorated in black-figure, linear style, and black-glaze. There are also a few black-glazed oinochoe lids.

Plates, though not numerous (almost 2% of the full-size pottery), span the EC through the LC II periods. They include two very unusual examples, which are probably EC; a number of black-figure pieces, of which at least three belong to the Chimaera Group; some silhouette style; and a couple of linear-style examples. Pieces of one of the silhouette plates (**201**) were found in three different areas of the site.

Kylikes are also not common (less than 2%), and date from late MC to LC I/II. About half of all the fragments are in black-figure, and a substantial portion of these can be attributed to LC "bird cups." There are also some examples decorated in the silhouette style.

The other shapes, each constituting less than 1% of the retained full-size pottery finds, include bowls/lekanoid vases, amphoriskoi, alabastra, and kraters. In addition, there are a few plastic vases and one ring vase. The bowls are predominantly black-glazed and LC in date, with one example dating to the first half of the fourth century B.C. The lekanoid vases, occurring in black-figure and the linear style, date from MC through LC III. Our amphoriskoi are all late MC and decorated in black-figure. Although our alabastra are limited in quantity, they are among our earliest imports and range in date from EC to LC. The alabastra are predominantly decorated in black-figure, but also include a few examples in the linear style and one in the warrior style. Our krater fragments, even fewer in number, are almost exclusively in black-figure and date from MC to LC I. One or two black-glazed kraters are also represented among the finds. Plastic vases are very rare with two, possibly three, MC fragments preserved.

Miniature vases are very well represented, forming about one-third of all the finds retained from the excavation of the sanctuary. Because of their size, they are better preserved than the full-sized vases. Miniature kotylai, mainly decorated with linear patterns,[23] constitute the bulk (82%) of all the miniatures. The next most common miniature shape is the black-glazed hydria (over 12%). The remainder of just over 100 examples, in descending order of frequency, consists of pyxides (convex, tripod, powder, and concave), bowls, kothons, lids, kylikes, oinochoai, aryballoi, krater-cups, phialai, kana, and an

---

21. In fact, kotylai, both full-size and miniature, constitute nearly 60% of the total number of fragments retained from the excavations; miniatures account for over 27% of this total.

22. Identifiable flat-bottomed types are limited to one uncatalogued black polychrome "football" fragment, two miniatures (**294**, **295**), and possibly one closed shape (**264**).

23. There are a small number of black-glazed examples.

olpe. Except for the miniature hydriai, there is, in fact, a rather similar pattern of popularity between the full-size and miniature classes of pottery in certain of the vessel forms; namely, kotylai, pyxides, and kothons. The miniatures date to the second half of the sixth century and the early part of the fifth century B.C. Some of the hydria may be as late as the fourth century B.C. Our miniatures are decorated in both black-glaze and linear-style patterns.

Dating

The following dates have been adopted for the chronology of our pottery[24]:

EC	620/15–595/590 B.C.
MC	595/90–570 B.C.
LC I	570–550 B.C.
LC II	550–500 B.C.
LC III	after 500 B.C.

The poor state of preservation of the pottery, in particular, has impeded our ability to assuredly date a rather significant portion of the fragments.[25] As a result, a fair quantity of fragments are in our questionable category; that is, they are only tentatively assigned to a particular period or, in the case of late finds, broadly assigned to the Late Corinthian period without further differentiation.

EARLY CORINTHIAN

Only a very small number of our pottery finds, less than a dozen, can be attributed to the Early Corinthian period. Of this number, three black-figure alabastra (**1–3**) and three black-polychrome flat lids (**83–85**) can be confidently assigned. The remainder, consisting of fragments of a black-figure (**4**) and a linear-style alabastron (**12**), a black-figure aryballos (**15**), and two plates (**207, 208**), may be of EC date. Of the over 5000 fragments of Corinthian pottery examined, these few vases, which can be dated to the late seventh or early sixth century B.C., constitute our only evidence for dating the foundation of the sanctuary to ca. 600 B.C. None comes from an undisturbed archaic context. In fact, with two exceptions (**12, 208**), all these EC pieces were found in the constructional backfill of the middle sanctuary retaining wall.

MIDDLE CORINTHIAN

With the Middle Corinthian period, corresponding approximately to the first quarter of the sixth century B.C., there is an expansion in both the volume and range of pottery imports. This can be seen in the increase in absolute numbers, represented shapes, and decorative techniques. Of our catalogued entries, at the maximum some 130 fragments may be MC (i.e., one-third of our catalog), at the minimum about 70. In other words, some 60 fragments are questionably MC, either MC or LC I, or transitional MC/LC I. The quantity of uncatalogued fragments ascribable to the MC period could not be determined.[26]

Our MC vases include warrior and quatrefoil aryballoi, black-figure and small silhouette-style kotylai, black-figure and silhouette-style plates, black-figure kothons, black-figure oinochoai and closed vases, black-figure amphoriskoi and kraters, and one black-figure lid fragment, as well as a couple of plastic vases. More tentative are some black-figure alabastra and aryballoi along with some linear-style and a few black-glazed vases that may be LC I. In any case, the majority of the firmly attributed MC fragments are decorated in black-figure.

Although there is a wider distribution of MC vase fragments in the sanctuary, nearly 60% of the catalogued MC fragments were found in the backfill of the middle sanctuary retaining wall. One fragment (**282**) from a black-figure krater was found in an undisturbed archaic level; eight catalogued fragments were found in largely undisturbed archaic levels.[27]

LATE CORINTHIAN

The Late Corinthian period (LC I–III), beginning in the second quarter of the sixth century and continuing into the fifth century B.C., has the largest representation in the catalog: over 60% of the entries date to this long period. Mainly because of their poor state of preservation, about one-third of these pieces could only be identified as LC without further breakdown. The wide variety of styles and shapes among the full-size vases include black-figure, warrior, and quatrefoil aryballoi; linear style pyxides and lids, black-figure tripod pyxides, as well as white style and conventionalizing convex pyxides; black-figure, linear style, black-glazed, silhouette style, and conventionalizing kotylai; black-figure and silhouette style kylikes; black-glazed bowls; linear style kothons and

---

24. This is basically Amyx's scheme (*CorVP*, 428).

25. This is in addition to certain types of pottery that generally cannot be dated with accuracy.

26. Presumably, a significant portion of the some 240 uncatalogued black-figure fragments could be MC, as could some of the uncatalogued sherds in other styles.

27. These include five black-figure kotylai (**111, 112, 115, 123, 125**), two black-figure kylikes (**165, 166**), and one silhouette-style plate (**206**).

oinochoai; and red-ground closed vases. In addition, during this period, the miniature vases form a very large group, constituting one-quarter of our catalog.[28]

More than half of the catalogued LC pottery was found in the backfill of the middle sanctuary retaining wall. Seven pieces, including four miniatures[29] and three standard-size vases[30] were uncovered in undisturbed archaic levels; 35 pieces, including 16 miniatures, were uncovered in largely undisturbed archaic levels.[31]

Close to half of our catalogued pottery, most of it consisting of full-size vases, dates to the LC I and II periods. During this period, the second quarter through the second half of the sixth century B.C., there is a significant increase in the number of linear style vases (convex, powder and tripod pyxides; flat and domed lids; kothons; closed vases and oinochoai; kotylai of various size; and miniatures), which constitute over one-half of our catalogued finds of this period, and a marked decrease in the number of black-figure vases (alabastra, aryballoi, tripod pyxides, kotylai, kylikes), which constitute about 12% of the LC finds.

The vases attributable to LC I and LC I/II are decorated in black-figure, linear, and white style, black-glaze, silhouette, warrior, conventionalizing, and red-ground. Among the shapes, there are aryballoi, alabastra, kotylai, convex and tripod pyxides, kylikes, plates, kothons, and closed vases. The datable LC II (second half of the sixth century B.C.) vases are painted in a more limited scope of techniques: linear, black-glaze, and conventionalizing floral style. The shapes include powder pyxides, lids, kotylai, kothons, small broad-bottomed oinochoai, closed vases, and miniatures, particularly kotylai.

During the late archaic to the early classical period, LC II/III, the repertoire of shapes and decorative techniques is further reduced to some linear style and black-glaze kotylai, linear style pyxides, a few conventionalizing closed vases, and a large number of miniatures, decorated with linear patterns (primarily kotylai) or with black-glaze (mostly hydriai).

The classical period proper (LC III) is represented by a small number of vases. Aside from some miniatures, the following catalogued fragments are dated to this period: a black-glazed kotyle (**163**), a semi-glazed kotyle (**164**), a conventionalizing convex pyxis (**51**), a linear-style lekanis (**181**), and a black-glazed lekythos (**279**). Our other fifth-century finds included miniature black-glazed hydriai, a few of which may be as late as the fourth century B.C. Our latest Corinthian fragment belongs to a black-glazed echinus bowl (**187**) of the first half of the fourth century B.C.

Decorative Techniques

The Corinthian pottery from the Sanctuary of Demeter and Persephone displays a broad range of decorative techniques—black-figure, black-polychrome, linear style, warrior style, silhouette style, red-ground, black-glaze, and conventionalizing—in varying quantity. Because of our pottery's fragmentary nature and poor state of preservation, however, a relatively small number of our catalogued, but nearly half of the uncatalogued, finds could not be identified or assigned with certainty.[32] This pertains especially to the kotylai, where almost one-half of the fragments could not be ascribed with certainty; there are indications that presumably a majority of these questionable fragments were decorated in the linear style. The following discussion of decorative techniques is based mainly on our catalogued pottery but is supplemented by the 50% of the uncatalogued pottery that can be identified.

LINEAR STYLE

Vases in the linear style form the largest portion (22%) of all the identifiable full-size Corinthian pottery finds from the sanctuary, owing to the large number of kotylai where patterns appear as the favorite decoration. The percentage is probably greater,

---

28. Or 40% of the LC catalogued pieces.

29. Lid (**303**) decorated with patterns, black-glazed trefoil-mouth oinochoe (**332**), and two black-glazed hydriai (**370, 371**).

30. Two small kotylai (**156, 157**) and a powder pyxis bottom (**80**).

31. Quatrefoil aryballos (**32**), linear-style lid (**94**), a black-figure lid (**89**), 2 linear-style closed vases (**275, 277**), linear-style powder pyxis lid (**77**) and bottom (**78**), linear-style powder pyxis lid (?) (**73**), 2 black-glazed kotylai (**158, 161**), black-figure kylix (**168**), 2 black-figure tripod pyxides (**55, 59**), white-style

tripod pyxis (**62**), small black-glazed bowl (**186**), red-ground closed shape (**268**), a small linear-style broad-bottomed oinochoe (**245**), a conventionalizing convex pyxis (**51**), and an aryballos (**36**); the 16 miniature finds consist of 1 concave pyxis (**297**), a flat-bottomed aryballos (**294**), 4 pattern-decorated kotylai (**304, 310, 311, 314**), a black-glazed bowl (**325**), 8 black-glazed hydriai (**335–339, 357, 376, 383**), and a kanoun (**326**).

32. Included in this category of uncatalogued fragments whose decorative style could not be ascertained precisely are aryballoi rims (over 100), plate rims (over 40), kothon body and base fragments (125), miscellaneous body fragments of closed and open shapes (560), and kotylai fragments (850).

since a significant portion of the unidentifiable kotylai fragments are probably also decorated in the linear style. Included in this group are vases in the white style, such as convex and tripod pyxides, kothons, and one plate.[33] Linear-style decoration is found mainly on kotylai, followed by pyxides (especially powder pyxides, but also on convex or globular pyxides, tripod pyxides, and to a lesser extent on concave pyxides), domed and flat pyxis lids, unidentified closed shapes, aryballoi, oinochoai, as well as on a few bowls, plates, and alabastra; that is, the linear style is found on every shape except amphoriskoi, kylikes, and kraters. Pattern decoration also occurs on our miniature vases, specifically on kotylai, pyxides, lids, and one kanoun. Mainly as a result of their poor state of preservation, linear-style vases are not as well represented in the catalog as the black-figure pieces, with only 13% of all the identifiable linear style finds appearing in the catalog.

Our vases exhibit the painted patterns common to the Corinthian linear style, such as horizontal bands of varying thickness, concentric rings, outlined tongues, dotted bands (single, double- and triple-dot), vertical and horizontal zigzags (particularly in the handle-zones of kotylai), maeanders, cones, triangles, and hooks. In addition, there are some more unusual linear motifs.

The linear-style vases have a long duration, beginning perhaps in Early Corinthian and continuing into Late Corinthian II–III. There are three linear-style pieces that may date to EC: an alabastron shoulder-body fragment (**12**) and two very unusual burnt plate fragments (**207**, **208**), each preserving the rim as well as part of the floor and foot. Although there are no definitely ascribable MC linear-style pieces, there are a few which have been dated to MC or LC, such as an aryballos fragment (**27**), two flat lids (**92**, **93**), a white-style plate (**209**), a concave pyxis (**40**), and a tripod pyxis (**61**). Thus, the major portion of our linear-style pottery dates to the LC I and II periods. The pieces datable to LC II/III include mainly small and miniature kotylai, but also a small cylindrical oinochoe, a miniature kanoun, a domed lid, and a tripod pyxis. Our latest linear-style piece is a LC III lekanis (**181**).

About half of our linear-style catalog entries were found in the backfill of the middle sanctuary retaining wall. By contrast, only three pieces were uncovered in undisturbed archaic levels: two small LC II/III kotylai (**156**, **157**) in F14/G14, 1, 4 and one LC(?) powder pyxis (**80**) bottom in D16/17, 1, 4. A higher number, 13 pieces, were found in largely undisturbed archaic levels: two (an LC oinochoe?, **275**, and an LC I white-style tripod pyxis, **62**) in D12/13, A, 3; one (an LC II/III miniature kotyle, **314**) in C13 1 4a; eight in D12/13, B, 4 (three miniature LC II kotylai, **304**, **310**, **311**; an LC II small broad-bottomed oinochoe, **245**; an LC powder pyxis lid, **77**; an LC powder pyxis bottom, **78**; an LC miniature concave pyxis, **297**; and an LC white-style closed vase, **277**); one (a nearly complete flat lid, **94**) in C13/D13, 1, 6; and one (an LC powder pyxis lid, **73**) in E11, 3, 3. These finds in undisturbed and largely undisturbed archaic levels are supplemented by the uncatalogued finds that are noted in the shape introductions in the catalog.

Corinthian pottery decorated in the linear style has not received the same study as black-figure. While the bulk of our linear-style pottery, consisting in large part of kotylai, is prosaic and routine, there are a number of pieces which are most attractive and elaborately decorated. In this category, for example, there are several LC II rectangular kothons (**214–216**) and powder pyxis lids (**66–68**) as well as a flat lid (**98**), which are related to Amyx's Winchester Group. A small LC II plate (**210**) and a kotyle fragment (**147**) also belong in this category. All the aforementioned pieces, with the exception of one unstratified kothon (**214**), were found in the backfill of the middle sanctuary retaining wall.

There are a significant number of miniatures with pattern decoration, the mass of which (94%) are kotylai. The other shapes include pyxides, lids, kothons, two kana, and one aryballos. The miniatures dates to LC II–III.

BLACK-FIGURE

The proportion of black-figure fragments to all the finds retained from the excavation is rather small—about 10%. Every vase shape in our catalog, with the exception of powder pyxides and domed pyxis lids, occurs in black-figure.[34] Black-figure pieces constitute over one-quarter of our catalog (104), which contains 30% of all the black-figure vase fragments retained from the excavations. For a number of shapes, such as alabastra, tripod pyxides, plates, identifiable oinochoai, and kraters, a majority of the black-figure finds appear in the catalog. For other shapes, such as kotylai, closed vases, kylikes, amphoriskoi, aryballoi, kothons, and convex pyxides, the proportion of black-figure examples in the catalog, compared to the known finds, is much smaller because they are more poorly preserved.

In general, the black-figure pieces have not fared well in the soil of the sanctuary: even some of the fragments in our catalog no longer preserve their

---

33. White-style vases are not easily recognizable from fragments.

34. Although the concave pyxis entries in our catalog are both in the linear style, there is a very poorly preserved example in black-figure among the uncatalogued finds.

paint. On these, and on many of the uncatalogued black-figure finds, only the incision marks and occasionally "shadows" of the original decoration now remain.

Our black-figure pieces range in date from Early Corinthian to Late Corinthian I. There are only five black-figure fragments, four alabastra (**1–4**), and one aryballos (**15**) that can be attributed to the Early Corinthian period, and two of these are questionable (**4** and **15**). The majority of our catalogued black-figure fragments appear to be Middle Corinthian (60%),[35] while the rest are Middle Corinthian/Late Corinthian or Late Corinthian I. Middle Corinthian black-figure appears on alabastra, aryballoi, amphoriskoi, closed vases, a few kothons, kotylai, kraters, oinochoai, and plates. Our MC/LC and LC I vases include an alabastron, aryballoi, kotylai, kraters, kylikes, and lids, as well as convex and tripod pyxides.

Given the state of preservation of our black-figure pieces, judgments regarding the quality of these Corinthian imports must be made with a degree of caution. The general impression, which may in large part be due to their poor state of preservation, is that on the whole the quality was average to mediocre. The only counterbalance is a relatively small portion of very fine pieces.[36] In fact, our black-figure pottery is not unlike the range of the Corinthian pottery at Tocra, characterized as "good, bad and indifferent."[37]

Although a relatively small number of pieces can be attributed to recognized vase-painters, our Corinthian black-figure is generally represented by the stock repertoire of animal frieze decoration on such shapes as alabastra, aryballoi, amphoriskoi, closed shapes, kotylai, and plates. Here and there, we may point to some unusually better examples that cannot be attributed to recognized painters' hands. Among the alabastra, **3** has an exceptionally fine lion head, and **8**, our best-preserved example of this shape, has a neatly and rather elaborately incised lion. There is also a convex pyxis with part of a fine griffin head (**42**) and a double-frieze kotyle with a distinctively drawn siren (**110**). In addition, there are notable fragments of plates belonging to the Chimaera Group, kraters related to the circle of the Painter of Munich 237 or Louvre E 627 and the Detroit Painter, as well as some closed vases attributable to the circle of the Dodwell Painter, which are discussed below.

Exclusive of vases with warrior frieze decoration, examples decorated with human figures are rare: hoplites appear on four of our kraters (**280–283**); one of our aryballoi has part of a hoplite combat (**17**), and another has a komast (**22**).

There are also some rather bad or particularly odd black-figure pieces, e.g., an "uncorinthian" aryballos (**21**) with feline and sphinx, two flat lid fragments (**88, 89**) with unusual horizontal lotuses, and a black-figure kylix (**176**) with a feline paw.

Close to half of our catalogued black-figure fragments were found in the backfill of the middle sanctuary retaining wall. There is only one fragment (**282**) from an undisturbed archaic level (E11, 2, Pit 3) that belongs to an MC krater showing a strong connection to the Painter of Munich 237 and the Painter of Louvre E 627. However, 11 pieces (belonging to kotylai, kylikes, tripod pyxides, and one lid), dated from MC to LC I, were found in largely undisturbed levels: five (three kotylai, **111, 112, 123**; and two kylikes, **165, 168**) in D12/13, A, 3; two (a kotyle, **125**, and a kylix, **166**) in D12/13, A, 4; one (a large kotyle, **115**) in D12/E12, D, 3; one (a tripod pyxis, **59**) in D12/E12, D, 4; and two (a tripod pyxis, **55**, and a flat lid, **89**) in E11, 3, 3.

In contrast, among the uncatalogued black-figure fragments, four were found in undisturbed archaic levels[38] and a proportionally high number (nearly 50) in largely undisturbed archaic levels; over half of these belong to kotylai.[39]

BLACK-GLAZE

Next in popularity are black-glazed vessels, which, exclusive of the miniatures, constitute 8.4% of the finds retained from the excavations. Aside from the kotylai, which make up almost 90% of the black-glazed pottery, there are, in descending order of frequency, only a limited number of black-glazed vessels—bowls, oinochoai, closed vases, oinochoe lids, and kraters—and a small number of examples of each shape.

The earliest of our black-glazed vases are MC, represented by a few pieces, such as conical oinochoai (**235, 236**) and possibly two oinochoe lids (**250, 251**).

---

35. About one-quarter of these, however, are only tentatively assigned to the Middle Corinthian period.

36. This is in contrast to the Attic black-figure, see Moore, *Final Reports* III, 1, 5.

37. *Tocra* I, 21.

38. Two kotyle fragments: one in D16/17, 1, 4, the other in C13, 1, 4b; two kylix fragments, both in C13/D13, 1, 7.

39. Kotylai: D12/13, B, 4 (1 rim, 2 body fragments), D12/13, A, 3 (6 body fragments), D12/13, A, 4 (10 body fragments), E11/12, Pit Area (2 body fragments), D12/E12, D, 3 (1 body fragment), D12/13, F, 3, including burnt section (6 body fragments), D13/E13, 1, 4 (1 body fragment with a bird), and C13/D13, 1, 4 (rim fragment with a lotus-and-bud chain in the handle-zone); closed vases: 1 each in D12/13, B, 4; D12/13, A, 3; E11/12, Pit Area, 3; E12/13, C, 4; D12/E12, D, 3; and C13, 1, 4a; kylikes: D12/13, A, 3 (3 fragments), D12/E12, D, 3 (1 fragment); flat lids: 1 each in D12/13, A, 3 and D12/13, A, 4; aryballoi: 1 each in E11, 3, 3 and D12/13, B, 4; alabastra: 1 fragment in D12/13, B, 4; plates: 1 fragment in D12/E12, D, 3; oinochoai: 1 fragment in D12/E12, D, 3; and 1 questionable amphoriskos fragment in E11, 3, 3.

Black-glazed vases continue into LC as illustrated by several kotylai of Palmer's group ii (**159**) and iii (**160, 161**), small broad-bottomed oinochoai (**247, 248**), bowls (**183–186**), and a krater (**290**). Our latest examples include an LC III lekythos (**279**) fragment and an echinus bowl (**187**) of the first half of the fourth century B.C. In addition, there is an interesting semi-glazed black-glazed hydria fragment (**274**) and an LC III semi-glazed kotyle (**164**).

The black-glazed miniatures display slightly more variety in shapes, though with a preponderance of hydriai, which form over 80% of all the black-glazed miniatures (264). The other shapes consist of a comparatively small number of kotylai (20), bowls (19), followed by oinochoai (4), krater-cups (3), as well as one phiale, kothon, and olpe. These miniatures date to LC II through III, with some of our hydriai dating to the late fifth and even fourth century B.C.

Aside from the miniatures, which are discussed in their respective section, less than 40% of the black-glazed vase fragments were found in the constructional backfill of the middle sanctuary retaining wall. Just three uncatalogued kotyle fragments were uncovered in undisturbed archaic levels.[40] Moreover, only a few of our catalogued black-glazed vases were found in largely undisturbed archaic levels: a small LC II bowl (**186**) from D12/13, B, 4[41]; an LC II kotyle (**161**) from C15/16, 1, 4–2, 5; and a large LC kotyle (**158**) from E11/12, Pit Area, 3. By comparison, however, a significant number of uncatalogued pieces (nearly 50) were found in largely undisturbed archaic levels.[42]

SILHOUETTE STYLE

The silhouette style occurs on a relatively small number of vases, which can be dated from MC to LC I.[43] This decorative technique is confined to kotylai, plates, kylikes, and a few lids. A total of 68 silhouette-style fragments, 21 of which are in our catalog, have been retained from the excavation. The majority (70%) of these fragments belong to kotylai. The kotyle series, including miniatures with "running dogs" (**134–139**), covers the MC and LC periods. The group of late MC plates (**201–206**) with silhouette animal friezes is fairly well represented. There are also some kylikes (**174, 175**) with silhouette friezes that represent a further deterioration of the LC "bird cups." An unusual fragment belongs to a lid (**90**) with a frieze of debased figures.

The majority of our catalogued entries are from the backfill of the middle sanctuary retaining wall. None of our catalogued, but three of our uncatalogued, pieces come from undisturbed archaic levels; these three fragments, belonging to two kotylai and one plate, were found in C13 1 4b. Although one catalogued fragment, that of a plate (**206**), was found in a largely undisturbed archaic level (D12/13, B, 4), eight of our uncatalogued pieces were uncovered in largely undisturbed archaic contexts.[44]

WARRIOR STYLE

The warrior style, with a total of only 30 identifiable fragments, is almost exclusively represented on MC and LC aryballoi (**23–26**); about 10% of all our aryballos fragments belong to this type. There is only one example of a warrior alabastron (**11**).

Over half of these fragments come from the backfill of the middle sanctuary retaining wall. None of the five catalogued pieces, but four uncatalogued aryballos fragments, were uncovered in largely undisturbed archaic levels.[45]

CONVENTIONALIZING

In this category, we have included fewer than 20 pieces, belonging to convex pyxides (**50, 51**), closed vases (**270–273**), and kotylai (**140–143**), decorated with floral patterns that are generally unincised. These vases are dated to LC II and LC III. The cups belong to the type known as "lotus kotylai." Particularly unusual, however, is a LC I/II oinochoe fragment (**231**) with lotus-and-bud frieze. Most of these pieces were found in the backfill of the middle sanctuary retaining wall.[46]

---

40. One each in C12/D12, G, 3; C13, 1, 4b; and F14/G14, 1, 6. See also introduction to black-glazed kotylai.

41. A number of miniature hydriai as well as a miniature bowl were also found here.

42. See *infra* n. 312 in black-glazed kotylai section.

43. There is also a silhouette-style miniature kylix (**322**), which is LC II.

44. These fragments consist of one kylix from D12/E12, D, 3; one lid (?) from C13, 1, 4a; and six kotylai, including two full-size (one each from D12/E12, D, 3 and from D12/13, F3) as well as four miniatures (one each from E11, 3, 3; E11/12, Pit Area, 3, D12/E12, D, 3, and C13, 1, 4a).

45. Two were found in D12/13, A, 3, one was found in E11/12, Pit Area, 3, and another was found in C13, 1, 4a.

46. One uncatalogued lotus kotyle was found in a largely undisturbed archaic level (D12/13, F, 4).

BLACK-POLYCHROME

There are a small number of fragments (14) and only three shapes that are decorated in the black-polychrome technique. Most numerous, with a total of eight, are flat lids, four of which have been catalogued (**83–86**). Such lids are generally dated to EC and would, thus, be among our earliest finds. **85** with white dot rosettes in panels, is particularly interesting. There are also a few "football" aryballoi, such as **35**. In addition, two concave-sided pyxides among the uncatalogued finds were originally decorated in this technique. Hesitatingly, we have also included in this category what may be an alabastron fragment (**266**) and two miniature flat-bottomed aryballoi, one of which (**294**) was found in a largely undisturbed archaic level (D12/E12, D, 3).

Two uncatalogued fragments, from a lid and from a concave pyxis, were also found in largely undisturbed levels.[47] Half of the finds, including the four catalogued lids, are from the backfill of the middle sanctuary retaining wall.

RED-GROUND

A total of four LC red-ground vases, all included in our catalog, have been identified.[48] The flat lid fragment (**95**), preserving concentric bands and a band of tongues, is quite unique. The other fragments belong to closed vases, two probably to small-panel amphorai or possibly olpai. With the exception of the fragment with a swan (**267**), they are, unfortunately, poorly preserved. Male heads are discernible in the panels of the other two closed vase fragments (**268, 269**); the former was found in a largely undisturbed archaic level.

Painters and Workshops

Only a very small fraction (35 pieces) of the Corinthian pottery can be attributed or related to recognized painters or workshops. The attributions are mainly for our black-figure pieces, but some non-figured fragments can also be ascribed to workshops.

Not only is the proportion of black-figure among the Corinthian pottery imports relatively small (about 10%), much of it, regrettably, is poorly preserved. Given these constraints, attributions of the fragments included in our catalog to recognized painters or groups are limited. Beside the indistinguishable examples of the fairly typical output of Corinthian black-figure painters, there are some notable exceptions. Prominent are at least three MC plates (**192–194**)[49] that can be attributed to the Chimaera Group: **194** is by the Painter of the Copenhagen Sphinxes, while the other two (**192, 193**), with virtually identical and most unusual floral designs on the interior, are unlike the work of any of the recognized painters of this group. Among the plates, there is also a fragment with a more standard animal frieze (**191**), which is broadly related to the Carrousel Painter.

There are at least two closed vases (**257, 258**) and one pyxis (**43**) that are related to the Geladakis Painter, either by him or by a painter very close to him. In addition, there are a number of pieces (**259–263**) among the closed shapes that can be placed in the circle of the Dodwell Painter, and two of these (**260, 263**) seem Geladakian.

Three of our black-figure krater fragments (**280–282**), with remains of combat scenes, show a close relationship to both the Painter of Munich 237 and the Painter of Louvre E 627. In addition, another fragment (**283**), with riders, appears to belong to the circle of the Detroit Painter.

Several of our tripod pyxides belong to significantly lesser LC I painters. There is a pyxis (**58**) that can be attributed to Amyx's Long Duck Painter, and several pyxides (**52–55**) may be associated with Benson's *Gruppe der traurigen Sirene* (Sad Siren Group). Two other tripod pyxis fragments (**59, 60**), decorated with lotus chains, can be attributed to Benson's TP Workshop.

Our only warrior alabastron fragment (**11**) apparently belongs to Amyx's Late Warrior Frieze Vases.

Two of our quatrefoil aryballoi (**29, 30**) show similarities in the drawing of the lotuses with the quatrefoils on the aryballoi of the Liebieghaus Group, though no fragments of handles with female heads in outline, characteristic of the group, have been uncovered.

Among the late workshops of the conventionalizing or Benson's orientalizing style, there are fragments attributable to two workshops: Dot-cluster Workshop (**51**, LC III convex pyxis) and the LC II Arc-palmette Workshop (**272**, a closed vase).

In addition, a number of our linear-style kothons (**214–216**) and powder pyxides (**66–68**) as well as perhaps a flat lid (**98**), with their attractive, elaborate pattern decoration and mouldings, can probably be ascribed to Amyx's Winchester Group.

---

47. The lid was found in E11, 3, 3 and the pyxis in E11, 2, 3 "Pit."

48. Fragments of only a single red-ground vase, a pyxis, were found at Tocra (*Tocra* II, 8, no. 1857, pl. 3).

49. **195** also appears to be related to the Chimaera Group.

Finally, one of our plastic vases (**392**) belongs to Ducat's "Groupe de Mégara Hyblaea."

The majority of these attributable pieces were found in the backfill of the middle sanctuary retaining wall.

Concentrations of Finds

Overall, finds of Corinthian pottery, particularly kotylai, are fairly well distributed throughout the excavated areas of the sanctuary. The largest source of our finds, consonant with the densest concentrations of other imported wares, is the constructional backfill of the early imperial (first half of the first century A.D.) middle sanctuary retaining wall (T10).[50] Half of our catalogued entries come from this area and more than 40% of our uncatalogued pottery (over 2100 fragments). With the exception of kylikes and kraters, both of which occur in small quantity, the percentage of finds of all other vase shapes from the sanctuary in this backfill area is approximately in the 40% range. The chronological range of our pottery from this area is EC to LC II–III. In fact, most of our EC pottery fragments were found here.

Then there is a dramatic drop with D12/13, B, 4,[51] a largely undisturbed archaic level that was excavated in 1971, yielding the second-largest concentration of finds, consisting of about 240 pieces, 17 of which are in our catalog. The full-size pottery from this level, ranging in date from MC to LC II/III, consists primarily of fragments of kotylai, but also some sherds of pyxides, kothons, and aryballoi, as well as one cylindrical oinochoe and one alabastron. A significant portion of the finds from this context are small and miniature Late Corinthian II–III vessels (kotylai, hydriai, bowls, pyxides) in a relatively complete state of preservation. The earliest fragment belongs to a late Middle Corinthian silhouette plate (**206**), while the majority of the pottery is Late Corinthian II.

An adjacent area, D12/13, A, 3, also a largely undisturbed archaic level, was comparatively rich in Corinthian pottery, yielding over 120 fragments.[52] Here the finds included MC/LC and LC black-figure kotylai and kylikes, and other full-size and miniature kotylai, as well as small numbers of pyxides, kothons, aryballoi, and closed shapes.

There are only two other areas where the term concentration can be applied, and both of these are fills. The first is E10/11 (Area 1), 1, 3, excavated in 1969, which is a dump of the imperial period, predating the third century A.D. earthquake,[53] from which there were some 115 retained finds, including kotylai, kothons, pyxides, closed vases, aryballoi, and plates. These pieces range in date from MC to LC II. Two adjoining pieces of a silhouette plate (**201**) fragment found here were uncovered in two other locations in the sanctuary (D12/E12, D (Balk), 2 and F11, 1, 2). The other is E11, 1, 2, excavated in 1971, also a fill associated with the 262 A.D. earthquake,[54] which yielded about 100 fragments, including kotylai, kylikes, various types of pyxides, kothons, aryballoi, a plate, a krater, and our only ring vase. Here, too, the pottery dates from MC to LC II. Aside from these contexts, one cannot speak of concentrations of finds.

Pottery from Archaic Contexts

Finds of Corinthian pottery from archaic contexts are quite limited, and their chronological range extends from Middle Corinthian to Late Corinthian II/III, with a significantly larger quantity of fragments datable to Late Corinthian. There are two types of archaic deposits at the sanctuary: those that are undisturbed by later intrusions, which are relatively few in number, and those that are largely undisturbed occupation levels.

Just over 1% of our pottery comes from undisturbed archaic levels, and most of it is fairly uninteresting. Only eight of our catalogued entries were found in levels undisturbed by later intrusions.[55] With one exception, a Middle Corinthian black-figure krater (**282**), these catalogued pieces (**332**, a black-glazed miniature trefoil oinochoe; **303**, a nearly complete miniature linear-style lid; **80**, a powder pyxis bottom; **156**–**157**, two small linear-style kotylai; and **370**–**371**, two miniature black-glazed hydriai) date to the Late Corinthian period, and five of them are

---

50. Includes F12/G12, 1, 2; F13/G13, 1, 2; F13/G13, 2, 2; F14/G14, 1, 2; and F14/G14, 1, 3. See White, *Final Reports* I, 38, 83 ff.

51. See White, *Second Report*, 181–182; White, *Final Reports* I, 78; White, *Final Reports* V, 30.

52. White *Final Reports* V, 50–51.

53. White, *Final Reports* I, 69, 115; Schaus, *Final Reports* II, xxii; White, *Final Reports* III, xi–xii; White, *Final Reports* V, 123.

54. Schaus, *Final Reports* II, xxii; White, *Final Reports* V, 122.

55. C11, 2, 5 (**332**), C13, 1, 4b (**303**), D16/17, 1, 4 (**80**), E11, 2, 3 (**282**), F14/G14, 1, 4 (**156**, **157**), and F14/G14, 1, 5 (**370**, **371**).

Late Corinthian II/III. In addition, 57 of our uncatalogued fragments, including 18 miniatures, were found in undisturbed archaic levels.[56] These include the following full-size vase fragments: 18 kotylai, 5 kothons, 4 pyxis lids, 4 kylikes, 3 pyxides, 2 plates, 1 closed vase, and 2 aryballoi. The miniature vases consist of 14 kotylai, 3 hydriai, and 1 lid. These uncatalogued pieces range in date from late Middle Corinthian and Late Corinthian I to Late Corinthian II/III.

The percentage of pottery from largely undisturbed levels is greater, over 13% (about 680 pieces). Three-quarters of the full-size vases (ca. 460) are kotylai fragments. Other vase shapes that occur in more than a dozen examples each are aryballoi, convex pyxides, lids, kothons, and closed vessels. There are also some tripod and powder pyxides, as well as a few kylikes, plates, and oinochoai. Nearly one-third of these fragments from largely undisturbed archaic levels are miniatures, and most are kotylai. The catalogued pieces found in largely undisturbed archaic levels number 43, with concentrations in D12/13, A, 3 (8) and D12/13, B, 4 (17) where eleven are miniatures (mainly hydriai and kotylai). Other contexts include C13, 1, 4a; D12/E12, D, 3; D12/13, F, 3; E11, 3, 3; and E11/12, Pit Area, 3. These catalogued pieces, ranging in date from Middle Corinthian through Late Corinthian II/III, include eight miniature black-glazed hydriai, seven full-size and four miniature kotylai, three kylikes, three tripod pyxides, four lids, three closed vases, and two aryballoi, as well as single examples of a full-size and miniature pyxis, a small and miniature bowl, a cylindrical oinochoe, a silhouette plate, a powder pyxis bottom, a miniature aryballos, and a miniature kanoun. In general, these fragments are not noteworthy. Of more than passing interest are a number of black-figure kotylai (**111**, **112**, **115**, **123**); two black-figure kylikes (**165**, **166**); two black-figure tripod pyxides, one (**55**) with traces of a siren, the other (**59**) with alternately reversed lotuses attributable to the TP Workshop; a black-figure lid with an unusual horizontal lotus (**89**); a large black-glazed or black-figure kotyle (**158**); and a red-ground closed vase (**268**). The uncatalogued finds from largely undisturbed archaic levels appear to cover the same time span, and are noted in the introductions to the shapes.

---

56. These levels are: E11, 2, 3 (1 aryballos rim, 1 concave pyxis fragment, 1 closed vase fragment, 2 kothon fragments); C12/D12, G, 3 (1 quatrefoil aryballos fragment, 1 black-glazed kotyle fragment, 1 small kotyle base, 1 kylix fragment, 3 miniature kotyle fragments); C13, 1, 4b (1 tripod pyxis, 1 small flat lid, 1 black-figure kotyle, 2 silhouette kotylai, 1 black-glazed, 5 miscellaneous kotylai fragments, 2 miniature kotylai, 1 kothon fragment, 1 silhouette plate); C13/D13, 1, 7 (1 knob, 1 lid, 2 black-figure "bird" kylikes, 1 plate, 1 kothon, 1 miniature lid, 7 miniature kotylai); D16/17, 1, 4 (1 powder pyxis, 1 black-figure kotyle, 1 large kotyle base, 2 kotylai handles, 1 kylix, 2 miniature kotylai); E15, 1, 4 (molded knob); F14/G14, 1, 4 (kothon handle); F14/G14, 1, 5 (2 black-glazed miniature hydriai, 2 small pattern kotylai); F14/G14, 1, 6 (1 black-glazed kotylai); D12 Balk, 5 (1 miniature black-glazed hydria).

Catalog

Alabastra (1–14)

Our catalog contains 14 fragments, which largely illustrate the distinguishable alabastron finds from the sanctuary. Although alabastra are decidedly rare,[57] our examples range from the EC through the LC period. In fact, a number of these fragments are among the earliest pieces of Corinthian pottery known from the site.

Best represented, by 10 fragmentary examples, are black-figure alabastra;[58] **1** with the lower body of a winged creature and **2** with the upper part of a swan can definitely be attributed to the EC period. The fragment with the very fine, but incomplete, lion head (**3**) should be EC, while the encrusted fragment (**4**), with part of a cock, may be EC. Particularly noteworthy among the other black-figure entries is the late MC or LC I fragment (**8**) with its neatly incised lion. The LC period is also represented by several pieces, including a fragment of a warrior alabastron (**11**), which should be categorized among Amyx's Late Warrior Frieze Vases,[59] and a small, almost complete LC alabastron whose surface decoration has virtually disappeared. In addition, there is one fragment of a linear-style alabastron (**12**) in the catalogue that is probably EC.[60] The two rim fragments (**13**, **14**) appear to be MC.

Half of the alabastron fragments retained from the excavation, including the three attributed EC black-figure examples in the catalog, were found in the backfill of the middle sanctuary retaining wall. Only one piece, a black-figure neck-upper body fragment, unfortunately encrusted and unidentifiable, was found in a largely undisturbed archaic level (D12/13, B, 4).

Finds of alabastra, including EC ones, are paralleled at Tocra where they are also not common, but found in a more complete state than at Cyrene.[61]

1   Pl. 1   Sb. 443–2   F13/G13 Wall Test
Lower body fragment. Light green clay. Worn black glaze, somewhat metallic, dull where thin. Added red worn.
MPH: 0.036; MPW: 0.039

Lower part of bird or winged creature, probably with outspread wing, to l. Added red on wing section. F.o. of incised, crisscross "plus" rosette. Ring of dots on base, possibly part of a dot rosette.

The fragment belongs to a small EC alabastron, Payne's Group A,[62] more commonly decorated with tongues on the base,[63] and presumably to his group with sirens. For the type, see *NC*, no. 338, pl. 17,6, with bearded siren from Olbia; Dugas, *Délos* X, p. 29, no. 410; *Perachora* II, pl. 59, no. 1526, with bearded siren; and *Corinth* VII:1, pl. 28, 195. For EC alabastra with dots or dot rosette on the base, rather than tongues, see *NC*, no. 267, pl. 17,1; *Tocra* II, pl. 1, nos. 1832, 1838; *Corinth* XIII, pl. 18, 129–135; *Corinth* VII:1, pl. 28, no. 196; *Perachora* II, pl. 59, no. 1523.

EC

2   Pl. 1   Sb. 536–2   F12/G12 1 2
Upper body fragment, preserving three-quarters of rim, neck, handle, and upper body. Light green buff clay. Very worn black glaze, generally crazed where preserved, but brown in spots. Added red worn.
MPH: 0.0454; MPW: 0.0384; D: 0.0302 (rim)

---

57. Only 14 other fragments were identified, all poorly preserved: 8 rims (4 with neck and handle), 3 lower body-bases, and at least 3 body sherds.

58. Only three other sherds of black-figure are among the uncatalogued finds (two upper body fragments, one with a neck, and one lower body/base fragment). The neck-upper body fragment, noted above, was found in a largely undisturbed archaic level (D12/13, B, 4).

59. *CorVP*, 156.

60. Two other linear-style fragments were identified, both burnt. One, found in E13/F13, 1, 1, preserved tongues on the neck, four bands on the body, and concentric bands around the base.

61. *Tocra* I, 21, nos. 26–27; *Tocra* II, nos. 1832, 1835, pl. 1.

62. *NC*, 281–2.

63. See also Ure, *AFR*, 9 (Group A) with ring of large dots on base.

Trace of tongue rosette on top of rim. Dots around edge of rim. Barely visible vertical stripe down handle. Shadows of tongues on neck. Part of swan with head to l. and outspread wings. Added red on wing section. F.o. of incised crisscross "plus" rosette (left of head) and eight-petaled incised rosette below handle.

The subsidiary decoration on the rim, neck, and handle places the fragment in Payne's EC Group A. For a similar swan, see *Délos* X, pl. 29, no. 388 (EC).

EC

3   Pl. 1   Sb. 61–2   E12   1   3

Body fragment. Buff clay. Black glaze worn, ranges from metallic to grayish brown where dilute. Encrusted.
MPH: 0.0396; MPW: 0.0326

Head of lion to l., with hatched ruff separated from crosshatched mane by incised wavy line. Undulating double incised line along edge of ruff next to face. Incised brow and two concentric circles for the eye. Double incised line for jaw. Apparently large, thick tongue and trace of incision for tooth(?). F.o. of small incised blob rosette.

Although this particular combination of crosshatched mane and hatched ruff is a characteristic feature of EC lions,[64] it does continue on some MC lions.[65] Among the many EC alabastra with lions whose ruff and mane are rendered in this manner, there is usually only a single incised line along the edge of the ruff near the face,[66] not a wavy double incised line as on our lion. Futhermore, the corners of the eyes are commonly incised, whereas in our example the eye is rendered merely by two concentric circles.

There appears to be no exact analogy for the incised drawing on our lion's head, but it reflects something of the style of the Columbus Painter.[67]

EC

4   Pl. 1   Sb. 516–24   F14/G14   1   2

Body fragment. Buff clay. Black glaze dull, worn, and crazed. Trace of added red. Heavily encrusted.
MPH: 0.051; MPW: 0.019

Cock to r. Hackle rendered by vertical hatching. Added red on wing.

Cocks, often in a heraldic pose, are a favorite motif on EC alabastra[68] but continue on those of the MC period.[69] From our fragment, the composition on the alabastron cannot be determined. It may possibly belong to Payne's Group A of alabastra with cocks flanking various central motives.[70]

EC/MC

5   Pl. 1   Sb. 516–12   F14/G14   1   2

Body fragment. Deep buff clay. Black glaze worn. Added red. Surface worn and encrusted.
MPH: 0.0246; MPW: 0.022

Part of lion head to r.(?).

The representation on this fragment is very difficult to identify. Assuming it is part of the ruff and mane of lion to r., the vertical hatching is for the mane,[71] and a strip of added red separates the mane from the ruff, which is also vertically hatched. On the right of the fragment, the area of black glaze, inscribed by a curved incised line, would be part of the lion's head. Oddly, there is no incision to mark the features of the face, as one would expect. Usually the incision on the face starts near the ruff. However, one might compare the lion on an alabastron from the Potters' Quarter at Corinth where there is an interval between the eye and brow and the ruff.[72] The interpretation of this fragment is problematic.

MC?

6   Pl. 1   Sb. 484–1   G12   1   2

Body fragment from a large alabastron. Buff clay on surface with pale orange core. Black glaze almost entirely worn off. Surface worn.
MPH: 0.0842; MPW: 0.0574

Part of outspread wing of avian.

Creatures with outspread wings were common on large alabastra in the EC[73] and MC periods.[74]

Probably MC

7   Pl. 1   Sb. 501–2   F14/G14   1   Test mixed with some St 2

Upper body fragment from a large alabastron. Tan-gray clay. Glaze worn, black to reddish brown where preserved. Added red worn. Surface worn and slightly encrusted.
MPH: 0.0428; MPW: 0.035

Tips of tongues on neck. Three bands above frieze. In frieze, part of palmette with trace of red on one of the petals. F.o. of dots and crisscross incised rosette.

The decoration possibly consisted of two confronted figures with a floral ornament between, as in *Délos* X, pl. 30, 436 or Ure, *AFR*, pl. IX, 50.259 (Group IV.iv.c.).

MC?

8   Pl. 2   Sb. 419–12   F13/G13   2   2

Fragment, preserving most of base (partially restored in plaster), less than one-half of lower body, and part of body frieze. Buff clay. Firm black glaze, somewhat worn on the bands, brown where dilute. Added red (purple). Mended.

---

64. Noted by Benson, *Corinth* XV:3, 93, no. 421 (an aryballos).

65. As on the winged lions depicted on the alabastra attributed to the Erlenmeyer Painter (J. L. Benson, "The Erlenmeyer Painter," *AK* 7 [1964], pl. 23, nos. 1, 2, 4); on the lions on two pyxides by the Honolulu Painter (D. A. Amyx, "The Honolulu Painter and the 'Delicate Style,'" *AK* 5 [1962], pl. 1, 2 and pl. 2, 1–2); and on a lion depicted on an aryballos by the Riehen Painter (P. Lawrence, "Notes on the Chimaera Group," *AJA* 66 [1962], pl. 55, fig. 6).

66. See *Perachora* II, pl. 59, no. 1543; *Corinth* XV:3, pl. 23, no. 456; *Délos* XVII, pl. 57, no. 61; *NC*, pl. 15, 9, pl. 17, 2, 7, 12; and the alabastra of the EC Columbus Painter (D. A. Amyx, "The Alabastron of Oinanthe," *AM* 76 [1961], 13, no. 1, pl. 6,1, no. 2, pl. 6, 2, and no. 5, pl. 7, 1; *CorVP*, pl. 35, 1–4); *CVA* Stockholm, pl. 3, nos. 1–2.

67. See *CorVP*, 85, pl. 35.

68. See *CorVP*, 83 (Cock Painter), pl. 34, 2. Cf. also *Tocra* II, pl.

1, no. 1832; *Corinth* XV:3, pl. 24, no. 461 (with crosshatched hackle), no. 462; *Délos* XVII, pl. 56, no. 46; S. P. Boriskovskaia, "Gruppa Rannekorinfskikh Alabstrov," *Khudozhestvennaia Kul'tura i Arkheologiia Antichnogo Mira* (Moscow, 1976), 63, fig. 4.

69. See Benson, *Antike Kunst* 7 (1964), pl. 25 nos. 2–8.

70. *NC*, 282 (Payne's Group A; cocks: various central motives), pl. 17, 4 (no. 269).

71. For a vertically hatched mane on an alabastron with two confronted lions by the EC Dolphin Painter, see *NC*, pl. 17, 3.

72. *Corinth* XV:3, pl. 23, 455B.

73. For example, the alabastra of the Panther-Bird Group (*CorVP*, 93–94, pl. 43, 1–2).

74. For example, the alabastra of the Hermitage Painter (*CorVP*, 152, pl. 58, 2) and the Erlenmeyer Painter (Benson, *AK* 7 [1964], 72–81; *CorVP*, 160 ff.).

MPH: 0.082 MPW: 0.0953

Frieze: forepart of lion to r. (part of head, chest, shoulder, and forelegs preserved); lower part of wing and tail of avian to r.; lower forelegs of feline to l.; lower edge of outspread wing. Added red on chest and belly of lion and on tail and wing section of avian. F.o. of dots, incised blob rosettes, and double-centered rosette. Three black bands below frieze. On base: multi-petaled tongue rosette and two concentric circles around a central dot.

This is the best-preserved example of this shape, which has retained its decoration, from the sanctuary. It is noteworthy for its ample and careful incision work, particularly on the lion: curved lines on the muzzle, unusual, short slanted lines on the chest; the hatched ruff ending in a point; markings inside the jaw; the patterning on the mane, reminiscent of crosshatching, but recalling bows.

Although there is no exact analogy for our alabastron, for a similar style, see *NC*, pl. 36, 8 and 12 (both LC I)[75] and W. Moon, *Greek Vase-Painting in Midwestern Collections*, no. 9, p. 13, dated MC. The latter, an alabastron in the Putnam Museum, has very similar f.o., and the cock exhibits to some degree the same varied patterning of the hatching as on our lion.

Certain features—for example, flattened base, the concentric bands below the frieze, the f.o. of dots, bordering a figure, crisscross rosettes, and the double-centered rosette—place this fragment in Ure's Group IV.iv.c. (i.e., from the group c graves, dated ca. 590–570).[76] The rather elaborate decoration on the bottom with a multi-petaled tongue rosette is not so common on late alabastra, where concentric circles are more frequent.

Late MC or LC I

9   Pl. 2   Sb. 528–7   F12/G12   Tunnel A

Body fragment from a large alabastron. Buff clay. Dull black glaze fired reddish brown to black, and flaking. Added red (purple) worn. Surface soil-stained.
MPH: 0.0538; MPW: 0.0315

Four bands above frieze. Part of outspread wing of avian, which extends into banded zone. Added red on top wing section.

The presence of multiple bands bounding the frieze on top indicate a rather late date. See *NC*, 319, fig. 159, pl. 36, nos. 3, 9; Ure, *AFR*, 31–32.

LC I

10   Pl. 3   Inv. No. 71–819   E11   3   2

Almost complete small alabastron. Mended from several fragments, some restoration in plaster, and large piece missing from body. Buff clay. Black glaze fugitive except for a few tiny patches on handle, body, and base. Surface worn and soil-stained.
H: 0.0913; D: 0.035 (rim); D: 0.05 (max)

Staining reflects to some degree original areas of glazed decoration, such as the band around the edge of the rim, tongues on neck, and banding above and below body frieze. In frieze: faint traces of lion to r., including crosshatched (?) mane, short incised arcs to indicate body markings, and ear. Incised blob rosette to r. of lion. Curved vertical incisions behind lion's head.

Although the decoration is barely discernible, the traces of subsidiary decoration together with the shape indicate an LC date.[77]

LC I

11   Pl. 3   Sb. 40–7   E11   1   2

Body fragment. Light buff clay with slight greenish tinge. Black glaze worn. Added red (purple) overpainted. Surface worn and encrusted.
MPH: 0.044; MPW: 0.05

In warrior frieze: two warriors to r., legs and round shields preserved. Added red on shield centers. F.o. of groups of dots, resembling dot rosettes, between the warriors. Bands below frieze.

The fragment belongs to a warrior alabastron with two friezes, as in *Délos* X, pl. 31, no. 458.[78] Amyx has attributed the Delos vase to his grouping of Late Warrior Frieze Vases.[79]

LC I, Late Warrior Frieze Group

12   Pl. 3   Sb. 375–1   C11   1   3   North of Wall

Fragment, preserving shoulder, part of handle, and upper body. Light greenish buff clay. Black glaze worn and ranges to red. Encrusted.
MPH: 0.0386; MPW: 0.0374

Tongues on neck. On body: thin and broad band, double-dot band, and two narrow bands below. Three vertical stripes on handle.

This is the only catalogued example of a linear-style alabastron from the sanctuary. Such small alabastra where the decoration consists of bands alternating with double dot bands, as in our example, are ascribed mainly to the EC period.[80] For the type, see *Corinth* XV:3, pl. 63, no. 1559 (EC); *Mégara Hyblaea*, pl. 39, 4 (Transitional).

EC ?

13   Pl. 3   Sb. 189   E10 Bldg   1   2

Fragment, preserving about one-half rim, complete neck and handle. Buff clay. Worn black glaze. Encrusted.
MPH: 0.044; MPW: 0.06; Est D: 0.065 (rim)

On top of rim: two concentric black bands around mouth, multi-petaled tongue rosette, and two concentric black bands at edge. Row of black dots around edge of rim. Tongues on neck. On handle: vertical zigzag between two vertical stripes.

The subsidiary pattern decoration of tongues on the rim, dots around the edge of the rim, and tongues on the neck is characteristic of alabastra of both the EC and the MC periods. With the main decorative zone missing, more precision in dating is not possible. Given the diameter of the rim (6 cm.), however, the fragment obviously belongs to a large vase.

Probably MC

14   Pl. 3   Sb. 531–1   F13/G13   1   Wall surface

Fragment, preserving about one-third rim, chipped along edge, complete neck and handle. Buff clay. Black glaze worn and brown were dilute. Surface worn and slightly encrusted.
MPH: 0.0473; MPW: 0.046; Est D: 0.06 (rim)

On top of rim: multi-petaled tongue rosette between two concentric bands and band around mouth. Traces of dots along edge of rim. Paint on handle worn off. Tongues on neck. Band below.

MC?

---

75. *NC*, 319 where both are grouped under "More careful versions of the same style."

76. Ure, *AFR*, 23, 32–33. See also *NC*, 319 (LC Group B).

77. *NC*, 319, fig. 159.

---

78. See also *NC*, 319, nos. 1228–1232, dated probably LC.

79. *CorVP*, 156 (no. 3).

80. *NC*, 2840 no. 376, fig. 121B (Group C I), on p. 283. See also *Corinth* XV:3, no. 1559, pl. 63, especially n. 1 for references to additional examples.

Aryballoi (15–39)

Aryballoi were among the more common dedications at the sanctuary. The 25 examples in our catalogue represent black-figure, linear-style, warrior, quatrefoil, and 'football' aryballoi, all types that are similar to those found at Tocra.[81] Dating from possibly EC to LC I, most are small, round aryballoi.[82]

Nearly 260 other fragments were retained from the excavations, including over 100 rims, which could not be assigned to particular types, and almost 100 body fragments of different aryballoi.[83] For the most part, these sherds seem to be LC in date.

Over half of all our fragments were found in the backfill of the middle sanctuary retaining wall. A relatively significant number of uncatalogued fragments (22) were found in largely undisturbed archaic levels[84] as were two of our catalogued examples: 32, a LC quatrefoil aryballos, and 36, presumably also LC, unfortunately with no preserved decoration. Furthermore, two uncatalogued sherds were found in undisturbed archaic levels.[85]

BLACK-FIGURE

There are 8 examples of black-figure aryballoi in our catalog. In addition, 17 other fragments were identified among the finds retained from the sanctuary.[86] These were all generally worn or encrusted, not unlike several of the examples included here. For the black-figured pieces, in particular, their fragmentary preservation and lack of indicative subsidiary decoration on the rim, shoulders, handle, and bottom, often preclude definitive attribution to a particular shape or class, as defined by Payne.

The earliest of our pieces is the heavily encrusted fragment with a cock (15), which may be EC. The fragments attributed to the MC period belong to aryballoi with animal friezes (16, 18, 19, 20), common in this period, as well as to a more exceptional example (17), with part of a hoplite combat. For the LC period, there is a fragment with a padded dancer (22)[87] and another odd, almost "uncorinthian" fragment (21) with a feline and a sphinx.

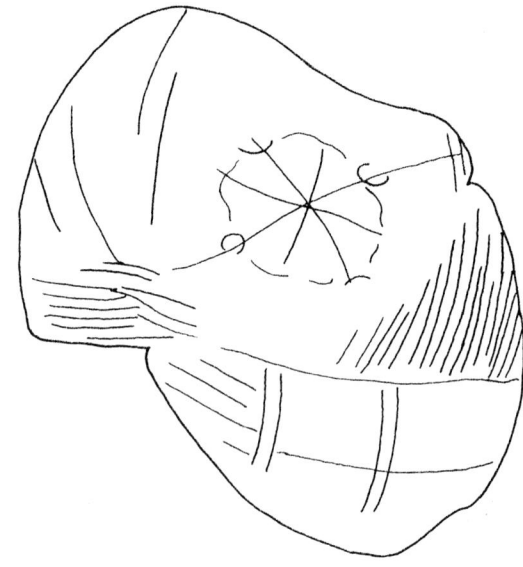

Illustration 1 (15)

15   Pl. 4; Ill. 1.   Sb. 296–3   F13/G13   1   2
Body and shoulder fragment. Buff clay. Glaze worn and fired red. Added red flaked. Mended from two joins. Surface extremely worn and heavily encrusted.
MPH: 0.0355; MPW: 0.051

Traces of petals on shoulder. Cock with closed wing to r., added red on wing cap and tail feathers. Vertical incised hatching on neck. Wing cap divided by vertical double incised line, intersected by a horizontal incised line, and separated from tail feathers by another vertical double incised line. Incised rosette with two tiny circles on periphery at opposite sides of one of incised spokes of rosette.

---

81. *Tocra* I, 22, 29–30, pls. 8–9.

82. The only possible example of a flat-bottomed aryballos is **264** in the section on closed shapes. There are, in addition, two complete LC II miniature flat-bottomed aryballoi (**294, 295**).

83. The 257 uncatalogued finds comprise: 107 rims, 98 body fragments, 17 shoulder-body, 20 lower body/base fragments, 15 neck or neck-shoulder fragments. Three of the fragments were burnt. On the fragments where the shoulders were preserved (37), tongue decoration appeared on 16. The shape also occurs in a few miniature examples.

84. E11, 3, 3 (worn black-figure base with an incised blob); D12/13, B, 4 (severely worn black-figure body sherd, a quatrefoil body fragment, a neck, and a rim); D12/13, A, 3 (neck-shoulder, 2 warrior aryballoi body fragments, and an unidentified body); E11/12, Pit Area, 3 (3 fragments of 1 war-

rior aryballos, 2 fragments of 1 quatrefoil aryballos, and 1 rim with concentric bands; D12/E12, D, 3 (a rim with outline rosette and diagonal lines on the edge, probably MC); D12/13, F, 3 (a rim); D12/13, F, 4 (3 fragments of 1 quatrefoil aryballos and 1 rim); C13/D13, 1, 5 (body with fugitive glaze); C13/D13, 1, 6 (2 rims); C13, 1, 4a (2 joining fragments of 1 warrior aryballos, 1 burnt rim with tongue rosette on top, 1 neck fragment).

85. E11, 2, 3 (an encrusted rim) and C12/D12, G, 3 (quatrefoil aryballos body fragment).

86. These included 14 body, 1 shoulder-body, and 2 lower body/base fragments.

87. This is the only sherd of this type identified among the finds.

For a similar type, see *Perachora* II, pl. 63, no. 1609, dated EC, with two sets of double incised lines on the wing, as in our example; *Corinth* XV:3, pl. 23, no. 422, ascribed to Payne's Group E and dated EC.
EC ?

16   Pl. 4   Sb. 288–2   F13/G13 1 2

Fragment, preserving about one-quarter of neck, one-third of shoulder, and part of body. Buff clay. Black glaze slightly worn and crazed. Added red. Slightly soil-stained.
MPH: 0.049; MPW: 0.0615; MPL: 0.0542

Black tongues on shoulder. Four black concentric bounding lines above frieze. Frieze: panther to l., with part of head and elongated torso preserved. Added red on neck, underbelly (?) and between the two anterior incised body markings. F.o. of incised rosette, double-centered incised rosette, incised blobs, and dots.

Probably from a round aryballos, shape B1, as *Corinth* XV:3, pl. 37, no. 798 (MC). There are, however, usually double or at most triple bounding lines above the frieze on aryballoi.[88] The incision is quite sloppy.
MC

17   Pl. 4   Sb. 288–8   F13/G13 1 2

Body and shoulder fragment. Light green clay. Worn black glaze. Added red and white. Soil-stained.
MPH: 0.034; MPW: 0.0515; MPL: 0.0392

Hoplite to r., with crested helmet. Left arm holds shield and right arm raised (holding spear?). Added red on shield, helmet, and chest (cuirass?). White dots along shield rim. No trace of f.o.

The chest and arm of the hoplite are both clumsily and disproportionately incised. The representation is apparently part of a hoplite combat scene, characteristic of the EC Warrior Group.[89] Our fragment, however, among other traits, does not preserve the thick filling ornament characteristic of that group, but the white dot decoration appears on the aryballoi of the Käppeli Painter of the Warrior Group.[90] The shields of the hoplites on an aryballos in Lucerne (Käppeli 408) have white dots around the edge (*CorVP*, pl. 47, 5) as does the shield on our fragment. Aside from the subject and the white dots, a stylistic connection cannot be made with the Warrior Group. White dots were also a feature of the Lion Group.[91] It is unfortunate that our piece is so fragmentary and lacking in subsidiary decoration.

For a related type, see *CVA* Robinson Collection, pl. 14, 9 (Group E).[92]
MC?

18   Pl. 4   Sb. 61–4   E12 1 3

Lower body and base fragment of a round aryballos. Light green clay. Fugitive black glaze. Encrusted.
MPH: 0.028; MPW: 0.038; MPD: 0.046

A.f.: forelegs and part of rear paw of feline to l.; unidentified incised decoration (stag horn?) to l. of legs. F.o. of incised rosettes and dot. Two bands below frieze. Tongue rosette at base and small depression in center of base.

Spacing between the forelegs, broad enough to accommodate a rosette,[93] suggests a striding position for the feline. However, the rear paw, so close to the front leg, would almost indicate a crouching or seated pose, as that of the sphinxes on an EC aryballos by the Duel Painter.[94] In that case, the positioning of the forelegs is difficult to explain. The f.o. appears to have been rather thick.
MC ?

19   Pl. 4; Ill. 2   Sb. 200–2   F11 2 3B

Body fragment, probably from a rather large thin-walled aryballos. Buff clay with a pale pink core. Worn black glaze, ranges to a reddish brown. Surface heavily worn and encrusted.
MPH: 0.04; MPW: 0.0508; MPTh: 0.0024

A.f.: animal to l., part of haunch and rear leg preserved; feline to r., hindquarters and trace of recurved tail preserved. Rather thick f.o. of incised rosettes, incised fillers, and dots.
MC ?

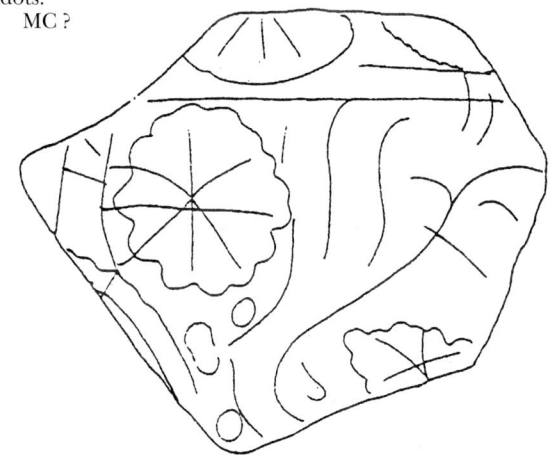

Illustration 2 (19)

20   Pl. 4   Sb. 294–2   F13/G13 1 2

Body and shoulder fragment. Light green clay. Fugitive black glaze. Trace of added red.
MPH: 0.026; MPW: 0.044; MPTh: 0.0027

Two thin bounding lines above frieze. A.f.: animal (goat?) of heavy proportion and short curved tail to r. Trace of red on belly. F.o. of blobs and dot.
MC ?

21   Pl. 4   Sb. 486–1   F14/15 1 1 and
                                    F15 1 2

Shoulder and body fragment. Deep buff clay. Black glaze, somewhat worn. Added red. Soil-stained. Mended from two joins: sphinx fragment found in F14/15, 1, 1, panther fragment found in F15, 1, 2.
MPH: 0.036; MPW: 0.05; MPTh: 0.0034

Double-dot band on shoulder. A.f.: feline to l., sphinx to r. F.o. of blobs with cross incisions, dots, and two unusual irregularly shaped discs with an incised circle divided into quadrants by a cross incision whose lines extend beyond the circle. Added red on wing of sphinx.

Incision work on this piece is unparalleled and totally unconventional, as if in imitation of Corinthian, particular-

---

88. Cf. *CVA* Copenhagen, pl. 11, 4–6, an MC flat-bottomed aryballos with four lines above frieze.

89. *NC*, 288. See also D. Amyx, "Observations on the Warrior Group," *CSCA* 2 (1969), 1–26; *CorVP*, 95–98.

90. *CorVP*, 114.

91. See *CorVP*, 118.

92. Hopper, 182 (9).

93. On aryballoi, for felines, such a space is generally decorated with a small blob rosette or dots. For an exception, see *Corinth* VII:2, pl. 5, 29. Rosettes do, however, occur more commonly between the forelegs of goats or horses.

94. D. Amyx, "Observations on the Warrior Group," *CSCA*, 2 (1969), pl. 2, 1–2; *CorVP*, pl. 44, 2a–b.

ly the body markings on the feline and the rendering of the wings of the sphinx. The incisions on the f.o. are sloppy. The two crossed circles can be paralleled by a similar ornament, more neatly rendered, which is part of a floral complex on an aryballos from Corinth (C–71–298) of late MC or early LC date.[95] The double-dot band above the frieze, though not without parallel, is quite rare on aryballoi; the frieze is usually bounded by bands above and below.[96]
LC ?

22   Pl. 5   Sb. 443–3   F13/G13   Wall Test
Lower body fragment. Buff clay with two lime inclusions. Dull black glaze. Added red. Slightly encrusted.
MPH: 0.0224; MPW: 0.04; MPTh: 0.0027
Frieze: foot of padded dancer to r., torso, legs, and hand of komast to l. Added red on garment. Two incised lines on bottom edge of garment. No f.o.
Komasts or padded dancers are known on EC through LC aryballoi.[97] The pose of two confronted dancers occurs on an MC aryballos from Taranto, but with f.o. which our example lacks.[98] In fact, almost all aryballoi with this subject have f.o.
LC

WARRIOR ARYBALLOI

The four warrior aryballoi in our catalog are quite standard. The earliest, **23**, where the warriors have recognizable features, is MC. The others are typical of the LC aryballoi of this style, though **24** is slightly better. Over 25 fragments of other warrior aryballoi were identified among the finds, most probably LC in date.[99] Several of these were found in largely undisturbed archaic levels.[100]

23   Pl. 5   Sb. 134   D16/17   1   1
Two fragments. Buff clay. Black glaze slightly worn, brown where thin. Added red overpainted, now worn. Surface somewhat worn and encrusted.
(a) Preserves complete rim, chipped on edge, neck, handle, shoulder, and upper body. Mended from two joins.
MPH: 0.037; MPW: 0.054; MPTh: 0.0028
Traces of three concentric rings on top of rim and dots around edge. Two horizontal lines on handle. Tongues on shoulder. Two bounding lines above frieze. Frieze: part of warrior to r., head, upper part of shield, and spear remain. F.o. not preserved.
(b) Body fragment, mended from two joins.
MPH: 0.0345; MPW: 0.0442; MPTh: 0.0026
Frieze: two warriors to r., with spears held forward. Hailstorm f.o. Two bounding lines below frieze. Trace of ring (?) around bottom.

All three warriors have helmets and recognizable features, hold spears to the front, and carry large shields with three closely set vertical incisions down the center. The left side of the shield is black, while the right side was originally overpainted with red.
The fragments are characteristic of Ure's class IV.vi.b, dated ca. 600–590.[101] Similar examples, particularly in the rendering of the shield (three vertical incisions in the center, black on the left and red on the right side), but without the hailstorm f.o. have been found at the North Cemetery at Corinth and dated to MC.[102]
MC

24   Pl. 5   Inv. No. 71–98   F16   1   2
Fragmentary round aryballos. Missing most of rim and neck. Buff clay. Black glaze worn. Neck and handle mended. Surface discolored, worn, and encrusted.
MPH: 0.055; MPW: 0.051
White, *Second Report*, 176 n.25, pl. 86f.
Traces of bands on inward sloping rim. Trace of black band on handle. Tongues on shoulder. Shadows of two bounding lines above and below frieze. Frieze: procession of five warriors to r., carrying large round shields with incised circle inside the rim. Spears not preserved. Features of warriors recognizable. No trace of f.o.
Because of its poor state of preservation, it is difficult to assign this aryballos with any certainty to either Ure's class IV.iv.b or IV.iv.c. The fact that the features, particularly the outline of the helmet and the eyes, are visible, may place the piece in the former class. The concentric circles of the shields are rather carefully incised. Aryballoi of this type are quite common, especially in the LC period.[103]
MC/LC I

25   Pl. 5   Sb. 516–15   F14/G14   1   2
Fragment, preserving part of body and base. Buff clay with pinkish orange core. Glaze ranges from black to reddish brown. Encrusted. White lime inclusion in wall.
MPH: 0.031; MPW: 0.0414
Part of warrior to r., carrying large shield. Bounding line below frieze. Concentric bands around bottom. Center of shield may have originally been overpainted in red. The sloppy rendering places this fragment in Ure's class IV.iv.c.[104] For comparable examples, see *Tocra* I, pl. 9, nos. 52–53.
LC

26   Pl. 5   Sb. 520–10   F14/G14   1   3
Fragment, preserving lower body and base. Light gray clay. Fugitive black glaze. Added red. Encrusted.
MPH: 0.0304; MPW: 0.0576
Frieze: parts of two warriors, carrying shields with added red in center. Four concentric bands on bottom.
Similar to preceding.
LC

---

95. Henry S. Robinson, "Excavations at Corinth: Temple Hill, 1968–1972," *Hesperia* 45 (1976), 216, pl. 55.

96. Cf. *Délos* X, pl. 27, nos. 343, 345, 2 LC flat-bottomed aryballoi.

97. For EC, see *CorVP*, 101–114; for LC, see *NC*, 320.

98. Lo Porto, fig. 94k.

99. Twenty-six body fragments.

100. Two body fragments in D12/13, A, 3; three fragments from one aryballos in E11/12, Pit Area, 3; and two joining fragments of one aryballos in C13, 1, 4a.

101. Ure, *AFR*, 38–39.

102. *Corinth* XIII, 113 and n. 72 for other references, pl. 19, 142-d, pl. 21, nos. 147–13, 147–14.

103. For example, see *Délos* X, pl. 24, nos. 279, 285, 287, 294, 296–8; *CVA*, Robinson Collection, pl. XIV, 12.; *CVA* Heidelberg, pl. 12, 12; *Corinth* XIII, pl. 21, 147–11.

104. Ure, *AFR*, 39, pl. VIII, 86.72–3.

LINEAR STYLE

Aryballoi in the linear style are rather poorly represented in the sanctuary. In addition to the two in our catalog, about a dozen other fragments have been identified.[105] These, with the exception of one sherd which had a dotted band, all appear to have horizontal monochrome bands, as our catalogued examples.

27 Pl. 5   Sb. 296–1   F13/G13 1 2
Lower body and base fragment of round aryballos. Buff clay. Worn black glaze. Encrusted.
MPH: 0.03; MPW: 0.047; MPTh: 0.0035
Four horizontal black bands on body. Dot rosette on base. Aryballoi decorated with horizontal bands, either monochrome or alternating red and black, occur from the EC through the LC periods.[106]
For similar examples of the late MC and LC periods found at Corinth, see *Corinth* XIII, pl. 21, no. 147-18, with rosette on bottom, but with alternating red and black bands on body (late MC); *Corinth* VII:1, pl. 43, nos. 365–366, dated LC. No. 366 has all black bands on body, as on our fragment. The rosette mentioned for these examples, however, may not be our type of rosette, which seems to be quite unusual.[107]
MC or LC

28 Pl. 6   Sb. 103–3   E11/12 Pit 2
Fragmentary round aryballos. Missing most of rim, about half of upper body, most of lower body, and base. Light green clay. Fugitive black glaze. Large lime inclusion on shoulder where clay has broken off. Soil-stained and encrusted.
MPH: 0.046; MPW: 0.053; MPTh: 0.003
Band on top of rim. Tongues on shoulder. Five bands on body. Trace of tongue or rosette on base.
Similar to preceding.
LC

QUATREFOIL AND VARIANT

Quatrefoil aryballoi are represented by five fragments in our catalog. Two (**29** and **30**), judging from the preserved lotuses, are MC and show similarities to the drawing seen on the aryballoi of the Liebieghaus Group. The others are common examples of the popular LC quatrefoil aryballoi, best represented by **32**, found in a largely undisturbed archaic level. **34** is notable for being our only example of a sixfoil aryballos.

Over 30 other quatrefoil aryballos fragments have been identified. A few of these were also found in largely undisturbed archaic levels.[108]

29 Pl. 6   Sb. 515–10   F14/G14 1 2
Fragment, preserving incomplete base and part of lower body. Light greenish clay. Black glaze fugitive and crazed in preserved patches. Mended from three joins, one of which (upper left) was found in Stratum 3. Encrusted.
MPH: 0.026; MPW: 0.07; MTh: 0.004
On base: upper part of vertical lotus of a quatrefoil. Elongated outlined leaves and center of upper part of lotus consisting of four arcs and eight (?) outlined petals or tongues. Round depression with a tiny protuberance in center of base. Concentric ridges on interior.
The fact that the lotus is, apparently, rather carefully drawn would indicate a relatively early date.[109] Despite its poor state of preservation, what remains of the lotus recalls the quatrefoil renderings on the aryballoi of the Liebieghaus Group. For an example, see *CVA* Copenhagen, pl. 8, nos. 4–5 (NM ant. 393)[110] and also *CVA* Copenhagen, pls. 9, 3. The Liebieghaus Group aryballoi usually have a female head in outline on the handle; however, there are no examples of such handles from the sanctuary.[111]
MC

30 Pl. 6   Sb. 419–9   F13/G13 2 2
Fragment, preserving part of base and lower body. Light greenish clay. Black glaze almost entirely worn off, crazed where preserved. Added red (purple), worn. Encrusted.
MPH: 0.024; MPW: 0.072; MTh: 0.0047
Part of upper section of lotus from a quatrefoil. Two elongated leaves, one in added red, the other in black. Petals rendered as three tongues with double outlines. Larger central tongue in added red. Thin line and crosshatching below. Small lightly incised circle in center of bottom.
The crosshatching beneath the tongues is rather unusual, as this zone generally contains arcs, zigzags, or other patterns. For a rather close parallel for our lotus, see Lo Porto, fig. 77, an MC aryballos with an elaborate floral complex, attributed to the Liebieghaus Group.[112]
MC

31 Pl. 6   Sb. 419–6   F13/G13 2 2
Bottom fragment. Buff clay. Black glaze worn, crazed or brown where dilute.
MPH: 0.0206; MPW: 0.0626
Upper part of lotus from a quatrefoil. Two elongated solid leaves with dilute outlines. Petals rendered as three elongated outlined tongues: center tongue black and broad, side tongues vertical lines. Horizontal zigzag with three horizontal lines above and two below. For a close parallel, but without the thicker central tongue, see Ure, *AFR*, pl. X, no. 86.198 (group c), and the related *CVA* Copenhagen, pl. 9, 16 (LC I).
LC

---

105. Eight were body fragments (one of which was burnt), two were lower-body/base fragments, and two were shoulder-body fragments.

106. See *NC*, p. 291; Lo Porto, 97, fig. 71c (EC); Ure, *AFR*, 26–27, pl. IV, no. 87.2 (group b) with alternating red and black bands and tongues on shoulder and tongue rosette on bottom.

107. Another aryballos base fragment from F13/G13, 1, 2 also has a rosette on the underside.

108. D12/13, B, 4 (body fragment); E11/12, Pit Area, 3 (2 fragments of one aryballos); D12/13, F, 4 (3 fragments of 1

aryballos).

109. Cf. *NC*, 147–8, fig. 54 C or D for the form of the lotus, and under no. 485. Also see *CVA*, Heidelberg, pl. 12, 1 (EC).

110. For additional references, see Comments under NM ant. 393.

111. In addition to the references to be found above, see *CorVP*, 164–165.

112. See *Corinth* VII:2, 32, no. 85.

32   Pl. 6   Inv. No. 77-1278   C13   1   4a
Fragmentary. Pinkish buff clay. Glaze fired red and worn. Mended from several fragments, pieces still missing from body. About one-third of mouth broken off. Surface worn, soil-stained, and encrusted.
H: 0.064; D: 0.064
Concentric bands on top and bands around edge of rim. Traces of dots on shoulder. Standard late quatrefoil design on body[113] with four oval outlined leaves, central elipse, and traces of crosshatching between the leaves. On underside, traces of arcs and petal tongues of lotus.

Among the most ubiquitous of LC aryballoi at many sites, this is the only nearly complete example found at the sanctuary, where the type is also quite common. These LC aryballoi are well represented in many collections, such as *CVA* Heidelberg, pl. 13, nos. 1-4, 7; *CVA* Copenhagen, pl. 9; *CVA* Karlsruhe, pl. 42, 6-7. For the Tocra examples, see *Tocra* I, 22, 30, pl. 9, nos. 79 and 81 (Type II).

This example was found in a largely undisturbed archaic level, which also yielded two joining fragments of a warrior aryballos, presumably LC, and two other aryballos fragments: a burnt rim, with a tongue rosette on the top, and a neck.
LC I

33   Sb. 515-1   F14/G14   1   2
Fragment, preserving one-quarter rim, handle, and less than one-half of shoulder. Pinkish buff clay. Glaze fired reddish-orange.
MPH: 0.0383; MPW: 0.0633
Concentric bands on top and around edge of rim. Tongues on shoulder. Part of elongated outlined leaf preserved and small section of crosshatching below. Vertical stripe on either side of handle, and two horizontal bands on handle.
LC

34   Pl. 7   Sb. 488-1   F15   1   2
Body fragment. Pale yellow buff clay. Worn black glaze. Added red. Encrusted.
MPH: 0.039; MPW: 0.038
Part of sixfoil with outlined leaves. Added red center in one of the preserved leaves and apparently a painted center in another. Other leaves seem to have double outlines.[114] A dot rosette, consisting of a black dot surrounded by smaller dots (10 visible), in center of sixfoil pattern.
For the type, see *Délos* X, pl. 22, no. 187; *CVA* Copenhagen, 30, pls. 10, 18-20 (dated MC).[115]
LC

BLACK-POLYCHROME "FOOTBALL"

The "football" aryballoi were definitely rare. The one example in our catalog with double-incised verticals is supplemented by three other fragments retained from the excavations.[116]

35   Pl. 7   Sb. 520-11   F14/G14   1   3
Body fragment. Pinkish buff clay. Black glaze severely worn. Orange discoloration on left side of fragment, where possibly originally overpainted with red.
MPH: 0.029; MPW: 0.042
Double incised vertical lines on body.
Presumably, this fragment belongs to the type illustrated in Ure, *AFR*, pl. IV, 99.52, 99.50 (group c).[117]
LC

RIMS/MISCELLANEOUS

As mentioned above, a very large number of rim fragments, over 100, were found. Most were not well preserved. Where the decoration remained, 34 had concentric bands,[118] nine had tongue rosettes,[119] similar to our catalogued examples (**38**, **39**), and two had reserved rosettes on the top of the rim. The latter recall **37**, with its outline rosette and crosshatching around the edge, dated to MC, and displaying similarities to the rims of the Liebieghaus Group.

36   Pl. 7   Inv. No. 71-372   D12/13   A   3
Fragmentary round aryballos. About one-half of rim broken off and few small fragments missing from body, otherwise almost complete after mending. Light green clay. Glaze fugitive. Surface worn.
H: 0.066; D: 0.065
Rim slopes downward toward mouth. No decoration preserved on spherical body. The shape is not unlike *CVA* Copenhagen, 25, fig. 45 (NM ant. 1359), pls. 9, 11-12, an LC quatrefoil aryballos.
This aryballos comes from a largely undisturbed archaic level, which yielded two warrior aryballos body fragments, probably LC, a neck-shoulder, and an unidentified aryballos body fragment.
LC?

37   Pl. 7   Sb. 420-3   F13/G13   2   2N
Fragment, preserving over two-thirds rim and tiny portion of neck. Light green clay. Worn black glaze. Slightly encrusted.
MPH: 0.013; D: 0.046 (rim)
Reserved rosette (originally 10 petals?) on top of rim. Crosshatching on edge of rim.
This combination of a reserved rosette on top of the rim and crosshatching on the edge of the rim is seen on the aryballoi of the Liebieghaus Group. See *Corinth* VII:2, 32, no. 85, pl. 14; *CVA* Copenhagen, pl. 8, 4-5 (NM ant. 393).
The lotuses on two of our earlier quatrefoil aryballoi (**29** and **30**) also exhibit similarities to the drawing of the lotuses on the aryballoi of this group.
MC

---

113. *NC*, 320-1, fig. 162.

114. See Ure, *AFR*, 45, and pl. X, 86.199 for a cinquefoil.

115. For a septafoil with a dot rosette in center, see *Corinth* VII:1. pl. 43, no. 364, dated LC.

116. One of these has part of a flat-base.

117. Double-incised verticals on the body, without added red, also occur on aryballoi from grave 89 (group a), cf. pl. IV, 89.5.

118. One with concentric bands on the top had dots around the edge.

119. Two of these had dots around the edge.

38   Pl. 7   Sb. 520–15   F14/G14 1 3

Fragment, preserving complete rim except for a few missing chips, wide strap handle, and most of neck. Light green clay. Worn black glaze. Encrusted.

MPH: 0.0212; D: 0.042 (rim)

Rosette of 26 tongues on top of rim and dots around edge of rim. Traces of horizontal stripes on handle.

The combination of tongue-rosette on top of rim and dots around edge occurs on aryballoi from the EC to LC periods, particularly those decorated in the black-figured technique.

MC or LC

39   Pl. 7   Sb. 200–1   F11 2 3B

Fragment, preserving complete rim except for a few missing chips, wide strap handle, neck, and part of shoulder adjacent to handle. Light green clay. Worn black glaze. Encrusted.

MPH: 0.036; D: 0.0644 (rim); W: 0.034 (handle)

Black ring around mouth. Tongue rosette on top of rim. Decoration on edge of rim not preserved. Horizontal zigzag on handle. Tongues on shoulder.

This fragment appears to be from a rather large aryballos. **19**, a black-figure aryballos body fragment, was found in the same location, but the clay is quite different.

MC ?

Pyxides (**40–82**)

Pyxides were very popular dedications at the sanctuary, especially throughout the LC period. Our catalogue contains 43 examples, representing a number of common types: concave-sided (2), convex-sided or globular (10), tripod (14), and powder (17) pyxides.[120] The pieces span the sixth century and continue into the fifth century B.C., with the earliest datable to the MC period and the latest to the LC III period, as represented by a fragment of convex pyxis (**51**) with an ivy pattern in the "conventionalizing" style.

Pyxides decorated in black-figure are not numerous, with a total of 11 fragments in the catalog.[121] The MC period is illustrated by a fragment of a convex pyxis (**42**) with part of a griffin. There is also a MC/LC convex pyxis (**43**) that is closely related to the Geladakis Painter. The other black-figure examples, datable to the MC/LC or LC period, occur on tripod pyxides and include representations of sirens with outspread wings, which can be associated with Benson's *Gruppe der traurigen Sirene* (Sad Siren Group).[122]

Pyxides decorated in the linear style predominate, especially among the convex and powder forms. Most of the pieces belong to the LC period. The linear-style and white-style fragments are not particularly noteworthy, with the exception of some of the powder pyxides with their elaborate mouldings and patterns. Almost half of these catalogued examples were found in the constructional backfill of the middle sanctuary retaining wall. A number were found in largely undisturbed archaic levels, while only one was found in an undisturbed archaic level.[123]

The majority of our fragments belong to pyxides of standard size, which range from large to small, but the form also occurs in miniature.[124] The flat flanged and domed lids, which correspond to the types represented here, are discussed in the following section. With one possible exception (**63** and **94**), there are no matches between the fragmentary lids and pyxides.[125]

Over 300 other fragments were retained from the excavations.[126] There appears to be a similar preponderance of linear-style pyxides among these uncatalogued sherds. Of all the finds, both catalogued and uncatalogued, convex-sided pyxides were the most numerous, followed by tripod then powder pyxides, while concave-sided pyxides were the least frequent.[127]

CONCAVE-SIDED PYXIDES

Remarkably, these are relatively rare at the sanctuary. Fewer than 20 fragments were retained from the excavations, two of which are included in the catalogue.[128] Three sherds were found in largely undis-

---

120. The figure in parentheses indicates the number of examples of each type in the catalog.

121. The uncatalogued black-figure sherds are equivalent in number, consisting of fragments of 1 concave, 5 convex, and 5 tripod pyxides.

122. *GkV*, 55, no. 93. See also *CorVP*, 327 (Sad Siren Group).

123. These are all noted in the text below.

124. See section on miniatures.

125. The only other probable match is a powder pyxis lid (**77**) and bottom half (**78**).

126. Over half of these uncatalogued sherds were found in early Imperial constructional backfill of the middle sanctuary retaining wall. Finds in largely undisturbed or undisturbed archaic levels are noted below in their respective sections.

127. The total number for each type, including the catalogued and uncatalogued fragments is as follows: convex pyxides—186, tripod pyxides—83, powder pyxides—72, and concave-sided—19.

128. The rather poorly preserved uncatalogued sherds include 1 with traces of black-figure decoration (E12/13, C, Polygonal Wall) and 2 with double-incised verticals on the side walls, found in D12/E12, D, 3 and E12/13, E, 2. All 3 may be MC or earlier. Interestingly, only 7 fragments (38.8%) come from the F13/G13 area. Nearly half of the finds were found in the E area.

turbed archaic levels[129] and one was found in an undisturbed archaic level.[130]

Both catalogued examples are fragmentary, retaining only the linear decoration around the base. Consequently, they cannot be accurately dated or identified.

40   Pl. 8   Sb. 421–3   F13/G13 2 2
Fragment, preserving over one-quarter of base and part of wall. Buff clay. Black glaze, flaking on interior and brown where thin. Added red (purple).
MPH: 0.0314; MPW: 0.0735; Est D: 0.09 (base)
On exterior: thin glazed band, broad purple band, two thin black bands, and very short rays at base. On interior: black ring on floor (flaked glaze) and trace of black band on side wall. Underside unglazed and with wheel marks.
For a possible type, see *Tocra* I, 23, 31, pl. 13 nos. 161, 164, 166.
MC/LC?

41   Pl. 8   Sb. 104   E11/12 Pit Area 2
Fragment, preserving over one-half of base and part of lower wall. Light yellow-green clay. Worn black glaze. Mended from two joins (one found in E11/12, Pit Area, 2, the other in E11/12, Balk, 2). Soil-stained and encrusted.
MPH: 0.022; D: 0.0908 (base)
On exterior: traces of three bands and very short black rays around base. On interior floor: traces of concentric bands concentric bands.
LC ?

CONVEX PYXIDES

Convex pyxides are represented by 10 catalogued examples, numerically not a reflection of the frequency of the type. Undoubtedly, the convex-sided[131] or globular pyxides were the most prevalent form of this shape, occurring both in the standard, some being quite large, and smaller size.

In fact, over 175 other fragments were retained from the excavations, predominantly of pyxides with vertical rims and upright cylindrical handles[132] and, less commonly, with flat rims and no handles.[133] Nearly one-quarter of these fragments belong to smaller-sized pyxides. About 45 of the fragments retained traces of tongues on the shoulder. In addition, five of the sherds preserved remains of black-figure decoration, and four were of the "conventionalizing" floral type with lotus-and-bud in the body frieze, analogous to our catalogued piece (**50**). Presumably, a significant portion of these sherds belong to linear- or white-style pyxides of the LC period. Unfortunately, few fragments retained the body decoration. Only one sherd showed traces of being burnt. Quite a few fragments (14) were found in largely undisturbed archaic levels.[134]

Our catalogued pieces range in date from MC through LC III, and most were found in the backfill of the middle sanctuary retaining wall.[135] Two are decorated in the black-figure technique: the MC piece, **42**, with its fine griffin head, is especially noteworthy, and **43** is closely related to the Geladakis Painter. The others, mainly in the linear or white style, are LC. **45** stands out for its neat style. Two (**49, 50**) belong to smaller-sized pyxides. Our latest piece (**51**), a "conventionalizing" LC III fragment with an ivy pattern from a pyxis with a flat rim, found in a largely undisturbed archaic level (E11, 3, 3), may be attributed to the Dot-cluster Workshop.

This group of pyxides is also well represented at Tocra[136] and generally in a more complete state than our examples. There is a broad correspondence in the types occuring both at Tocra and Cyrene.

42   Pl. 8   Sb. 287–1   F13/G13 1 2
Shoulder and body fragment. Buff clay. Worn black glaze, crazed where preserved. Added red (purple) worn.
MPL: 0.072; MPW: 0.0746; Th: 0.0053
On shoulder: outlined tongues with alternating two reserved, black, and red centers (..BR..BR..) and short black lines between outlines; red band and thin black band; double-dot band bordered by dilute lines above and below. A.f.: band (glaze gone): part of wing of avian; head of griffin or griffin-bird to l. Added red on neck and head of griffin, and dot of added red on wing of avian. F.o. of incised rosettes.
This is rather careful work also characterized by a substantial use of added red. The ears of the griffin, however, extend into the banding above the frieze. For a more com-

---

129. E11/12, Pit Area, 3 (base with rays and concentric circles on the interior), D12/13, B, 4 (base), D12/E12, D, 3 (body fragment with double-incised verticals).

130. Unfortunately, an undistinguishable body fragment from E11, 2, 3.

131. On the shape, see *CorVP*, 449–451 (convex-sided without handles) and 449–450 (convex-sided with upright handles).

132. Attributable to this type were 85 fragments of standard-size (41 rim-shoulder, 30 rim-shoulder-handle, 10 shoulder-handle, and 4 handle fragments) and 34 fragments of small-size (10 rim-shoulder, 19 rim-shoulder-handle, 3 rim, 2 shoulder-handle fragments). The rims are of the short vertical variety, characteristic of the convex pyxides with handles.

133. Only 7 flat rims were definitely identified among the standard-sized pyxides and 3 among the smaller size.

134. E11, 3, 3 (2 shoulder fragments with tongues, 1 shoulder-handle fragment from a small pyxis); D12/13, B, 4 West (7 vertical rim-shoulder fragments, 5 of which have tongues); D12/E12, D, 3 (vertical rim-shoulder fragment with tongues from a small pyxis); D12/13, F, 3 (severely worn vertical rim-shoulder fragment); D12/13, F, 4 (vertical rim-shoulder-handle fragment of a small pyxis); and D13/E13, 1, 4 (vertical rim-shoulder fragment with linked dots from a small pyxis). Three of the 10 miniature convex pyxis fragments were also found in largely undisturbed archaic levels (D12/13, B, 4 Middle; D12/E12, D, 3; and D12/13, F, 4).

135. 58% of the uncatalogued globular pyxis fragments retained from the excavations were also from this area.

136. *Tocra* I, pls. 10–13; *Tocra* II, nos. 1850–1860.

plete and similar pyxis, dated to MC, see *Tocra* I, pl. 10, no. 133, where griffin-birds flank a flying bird.
MC

43   Pl. 8   Sb. 528–2   F12/G12   Tunnel A
Shoulder and body fragment. Buff to pinkish clay. Dull black glaze, worn in places. Added red. Soil-stained.
MPL: 0.0577; MPW: 0.0565
On shoulder: outlined tongues with black centers; double-dot band bordered by red lines above and below. A.f.: narrow black band, above rear of animal, probably a goat, with curved tail to l.; f.o. of round blob and a dot. Unusual triple-arc incisions on top of animal's back.
The same type of circular tail occurs on a goat from a pyxis in San Simeon (5492), attributed to the Geladakis Painter.[137]
This and the preceding example follow the standard syntax of tongues on the shoulder, a double-dot band, and animal frieze on body.[138]
MC/LC, Close to the Geladakis Painter

44   Pl. 8   Sb. 16   E10/11 (Area 1)   1   3
Shoulder and body fragment. Buff clay. Flaking metallic black glaze. Added red (purple). Soil-stained and slightly encrusted.
MPL: 0.065; MPW: 0.087; MTh: 0.005
Trace of black band at base of neck. On shoulder: band of alternating reserved and group of three black tongues with individual outlines (.BBB.BBB); two thin black bands; double-dot band bordered by dilute lines above and below; red band (overpainted); two thin lines. On body: part of lotus-and-bud chain with added red on buds.
For a similar type, but without the double-dot band, see *Tocra* I, pl. 13, 147. See also *Délos* X, pl. 32, 506, for a lotus-and-bud chain on the body.
LC

45   Pl. 8   Sb. 421–5   F13/G13   1   2 and
                                        F13/G13   2   2
Fragment, preserving more than one-third of shoulder and part of upright cylindrical handle. Light green clay. Severely worn black glaze. Added red (purple). Surface worn, chipped, and flaking. Mended from three joining fragments (fragment with part of handle found in F13/G13, 1, 2, while the other two were found in F13/G13, 2, 2). Soil-stained.
MPL: 0.066; MPW: 0.163; MTh: 0.0058; MPH: 0.041 (handle)
Fragment belongs to a pyxis with vertical rim (broken off) and upright cylindrical handles (only part of one remains). Raised ridge at base of rim. On shoulder: group of lines (two red and one black); band of alternating black and red tongues with individual outlines in dilute glaze; narrow maeander band (paint ranges from black to yellow), bordered by thin black line above and red line below. Decoration in body frieze not preserved.
The fragment is unusual in having a maeander band below the shoulder tongues, the position commonly occupied by a double-dot band. The style is neat.
LC

46   Pl. 9   Sb. 516–3   F14/G14   1   2
Fragment, preserving part of shoulder and body. Pale buff clay. Black glaze, mostly worn. Added red, worn. Encrusted.

MPL: 0.053; MPW: 0.598
On shoulder: alternating black and red tongues with individual outlines, bordered by black band above and below; alternating red and brown bands.
LC

47   Pl. 9   Sb. 520–2   F14/G14   1   3
Fragment, preserving part of vertical rim, shoulder, and upright cylindrical handle. Buff clay with orangey-pink core. Black glaze, flaking and ranging from black to red to orange. Added red (purple). Chipped on rim and shoulder.
MPH: 0.054; MPW: 0.0876
Black glaze on rim, thinly applied. On shoulder: alternate glazed and red tongues with individual outlines, bordered by glazed bands above and below; double-dot band borderd by thin red line above and below. Black glaze on handle.
This fragment apparently belongs to a white-style pyxis. Similar examples have been found in Corinth.[139]
LC

48   Pl. 9   Sb. 288–24   F13/G13   1   2
Fragment, preserving base of neck, root of upright cylindrical handle, part of shoulder and body. Deep buff pinkish clay. Black glaze, brown where thin. Added red (purple).
MPL: 0.086; MPW: 0.086; MPTh: 0.004
Red at base of neck. On shoulder: alternating red and black tongues with individual outlines, bordered by black band above and below; double-dot band flanked by red band above and below; thin black band; body reserved; thin red line on belly.
Similar to preceding.
LC

49   Pl. 9   Sb. 520–14   F13/G13   1   2
Fragment, preserving part of shoulder, base of neck, and vertical cylindrical handle. Creamy buff clay. Flaking black glaze. Added red (purple). Encrusted.
MPL: 0.037; MPW: 0.0564
Black glaze at base of neck. On shoulder: remains of band of tongues with individual outlines; alternating red and black lines. Body reserved. Traces of black glaze on handle.
This fragment belongs to a small white-style pyxis with a vertical neck and handles on shoulder.
LC

50   Pl. 9   Sb. 419–16   F13/G13   2   2
Fragment, preserving about one-third rim, part of shoulder and body, and vertical cylindrical handle. Buff clay. Black glaze, brown where thin. Added red, ranges to purple.
MPL: 0.036; MPW: 0.0595; Th: 0.0022
Black glaze on vertical rim. On shoulder: band of diagonal black tongues, bordered by red band above and three black lines below. On body: chain of widely spaced buds connected by diagonal links in dilute paint, with purple on buds and red blobs on vertical stems. Trace of red band below frieze.
This fragment also belongs to a small pyxis with vertical rim and handles on shoulder. For a somewhat similar bud frieze on a flat rim pyxis but without the links, see *Tocra* II,

---

137. *CorVP*, pl. 89, 1a–b, p. 214 (no. 19). I wish to thank Patricia Lawrence for her comment that our piece looks like the Geladakis Painter.

138. For other examples, see *CVA* Copenhagen, pl. 14; *Tocra* I, pl. 11, nos. 134–136, pl. 12, no. 141.

139. C. K. Williams II and Joan E. Fisher, "Corinth 1970: Forum Area," *Hesperia* 40 (1971), pl. 8, no. 35; see also Mary Thorne Campbell, "A Well of the Black-figured Period at Corinth," *Hesperia* 7 (1938), 593, fig. 16, no. 128. From Isthmia, see Paul Clement and Margaret MacVeagh Thorne, "From the West Cemetery at Isthmia," *Hesperia* 43 (1974), pl. 85, no. 12.

12, pl. 3, no. 1854, identified as "conventionalizing style," probably early fifth century.
LC II/III

51   Pl. 9   Sb. 49–1   E11 3 3

Rim and shoulder fragment of a flat rim pyxis. Pale pinkish buff clay. Black glaze worn and ranges to an orange where dilute or worn off. Added red (purple). Mended from two joins. Encrusted.

MPL: 0.051; MPW: 0.074; Th: 0.004

Band on inner edge of flat rim. On rim: one black and one red band. On shoulder: wavy ivy leaf garland with alternating heart-shaped leaves and berry clusters. The stems of both the leaves and berry clusters are curved.

Similar examples have been found at Corinth and attributed by Benson to the LC III Dot-Cluster Workshop (see *Corinth* XV:3, pl. 46, no. 1049, and pl. 48, no. 1155). Such ivy patterns with berry clusters also occur on Corinthian white-ground lekythoi of the second half of the fifth century.[140]

LC III, Dot-cluster Workshop

TRIPOD PYXIDES

There are 14 catalogued examples of tripod pyxides, most of which date to the LC period. Nine are in the black-figure technique,[141] while the others are in the linear style. A fairly common type, a siren with outspread wings on the foot, is represented by four fragmentary examples (**52–55**),[142] two of which seem to be of somewhat better quality (**52, 53**).[143] The renderings of the sirens differ to some degree in all our examples, as they do in most published examples. The presence or absence of sad expressions on our fragments notwithstanding (complete faces are lacking), they may be generically connected to Benson's *Gruppe der traurigen Sirene* (Sad Siren Group).[144] Where preserved, the projecting rims (**53, 55**) are horizontally grooved on the exterior. Interestingly, this type does not occur at Tocra. There are also LC black-figure fragments with swans (**56, 57**) and one with a bird (**58**) that is attributable to the Long Duck Painter, whom Amyx has characterized as "inconsequential."[145] Two other LC I fragments (**59, 60**), decorated with alternately reversed lotuses, may be attributed to the TP workshop. With one exception (**58**), all the black-figure pieces have a rather high, straight foot and a relatively shallow bowl.

The fragmentary linear-style examples, spanning the LC period, usually have low feet and very deep bowls. They are generally in a neat style, and among them, **61**, appears to belong to a more carefully painted pyxis.

Of the catalogued pieces, three (**55, 59, 62**), all dated to LC I, were found in largely undisturbed archaic levels, while half were found in the constructional backfill of the middle sanctuary retaining wall.

In addition, nearly 70 other fragments were retained from the excavations,[146] over 30 of which clearly belong to linear-style pyxides.[147] A number of these fragments (12), including four miniatures, were uncovered in largely undisturbed archaic levels[148] and only one, a fragment of a smaller-sized tripod pyxis, was found in an undisturbed archaic level (C13, 1, 4b). Nearly 60% of these uncatalogued fragments were found in the early Imperial backfill of the middle sanctuary retaining wall.

52   Pl. 10   Sb. 203–2   F11 2 1–2

Most of foot and part of adjoining body. Buff clay. Worn black glaze, crazed where thicker. Added red (purple). White inclusion in wall where clay has broken off. Encrusted.

MPH: 0.0478; MPW: 0.0635 (foot)

White, *Fourth Report*, 170, pl. 25, fig. 12.

High, straight foot. On the foot: siren with outspread wings to l. Added red on breast, central part of wings, and tail. Long hair and trace of incised fillet on siren.

This and the following three fragments (**53–55**) are related to Benson's *Gruppe der traurigen Sirene*, with **54** showing the closest relationship.

MC/LC, Related to *Gruppe der traurigen Sirene*

53   Pl. 10   Sb. 419–1a,b   F13/G13 1 2 and
                                F13/G13 2 2

Two fragments. Buff clay. Black glaze crazed where thick, brown where thin. Added red (purple) worn.

(a) MPH: 0.036; MPW: 0.0834; Est. D: 0.11

Over one-quarter of projecting rim, painted purple, with horizontal grooves on exterior, and part of body. Upper part of siren with outspread wings, head to l. Added red on neck and central section of wing. Trace of black band on interior of body. Mended from two joins: fragment with head of siren found in F13/G13, 1, 2.

---

140. See, for example, *Corinth* XIII, 121f., 141f., pl. 58 nos. 364–9, 366–14.

141. Only 5 other black-figure fragments were identified among the finds: 3 with lotus chains, 1 with a bird, and 1 with an avian.

142. For complete pieces, see, e.g., *CVA* France, fasc. 12 (Louvre, fasc. 8), pl. 23.10; *CVA* USA, fasc. 4 (Robinson Collection, fasc. 1), pl. 14, 15; *CVA* USA, fasc. 1 (Hoppin Collection), pl. 1, 3. Hopper, 215 dates this type to LC. See also *CorVP*, 455 n. 57.

143. As a result, we have dated them to MC/LC.

144. *GkV*, 55 no. 93. See also *CorVP*, 327 (Sad Siren Group),

455 n. 57.

145. *CorVP*, 257.

146. These include 18 rim, 16 rim-body, 15 body, 15 foot, and 5 smaller pyxis fragments. Six of the rims had horizontal grooves as in some of the catalogued examples. Notable among these fragments are 2 with poorly preserved figured decoration (D12/13, A, 4 West and F13/G13, 1, 2) and 3 with lotus chains, as in our catalogued examples and cited therein (see *infra* **59**).

147. Including 5 of smaller size.

148. Excluding the miniatures, whose find spots are mentioned in their relevant section, the 8 sherds were found in the following contexts: D12/13, B, 4 (1); D12/13, A, 3 (3); D12/13, A, 4 (1); and D12/E12, D, 3 (3).

(b) MPH: 0.042; MPW: 0.0755; MPW: 0.0634 (foot)

One foot, broken at top, and part of body. High, straight foot. On the foot: siren with outspread wings to l., red on central section of wings and neck. Incised rosette beneath wing.

For the type, see *CVA* Belgium, Brussels: *Musée Royaux du Cinquantenaire*, fasc. 1 (IIIc), pl. 1, no. 20 (*NC* 923, dated MC).

MC/LC, Related to *Gruppe der traurigen Sirene*

54   Pl. 10   Sb. 176   C15/D15   1   1,2

Part of foot and body. Light green clay. Glaze mostly gone, metallic and crazed in preserved patches. Added red (purple). Heavily encrusted.

MPH: 0.033; MPW: 0.0547 (foot)

Siren with outspread wings to r., most of head missing. Added purple on wing sections. The fragment is quite similar in style to pyxides that Benson has attributed to the *Gruppe der traurigen Sirene*.[149] For the type, see *Corinth* XV:3, pl. 39, no. 852 (KP 1930), dated to LC I and identified as the work of the Painter of the Disconsolate Siren; and *Mégara Hyblaea*, 66, pl. 54, 3, dated MC.

LC I, *Gruppe der traurigen Sirene*?

55   Pl. 10   Sb. 49–5   E11   3   3

Foot and part of body, preserving complete profile (base to rim). Light green clay. Fugitive black glaze. Fragment burnt and encrusted. Traces of black glaze on projecting and horizontally grooved rim.

MPH: 0.047; MPW: 0.0392

Straight, high foot and rather shallow body. On the foot: siren to r., wings outspread.

Only the shadow of the siren remains. Notably, this fragment was found in a largely undisturbed archaic level. Similar to **54**.

LC I, Related to *Gruppe der traurigen Sirene*

56   Pl. 10   Sb. 51–2   E11   4   2

Part of foot and body. Buff clay. Worn black metallic glaze. Added red, worn. Encrusted.

MPH: 0.0384; MPW: 0.0542

Straight, high foot and rather shallow body. On the foot: swan with closed wings to l., poorly preserved. An almost identical example has been found in the Potters' Quarter at Corinth (KP 1845),[150] dated to LC I, and a similar one was found in a grave in Athens.[151]

LC I

57   Pl. 11   Sb. 288–10   F13/G13   1   2

About one-third of pyxis, preserving about one-sixth of rim. Light greenish clay. Fugitive black glaze. Fugitive added red (purple). Encrusted.

MPH: 0.043; MPW: 0.0596; Est D: 0.09

Within a panel on the foot, a swan with folded wings to r.; f.o. of blobs. On the interior, trace of band around floor. Rather squat form with shallow body. Added red on the thickened, horizontally grooved rim.

LC I

58   Pl. 11   Sb. 288–7   F13/G13   1   2

Fragment, preserving about one-third of pyxis. Buff clay with pinkish core. Purplish black glaze, crazed where thick. Added red. Encrusted.

MPH: 0.0454; MPW: 0.061; Est D: 0.08

On the foot, a bird to r., head missing, set in a panel. F.o. of cross-shaped blobs and lines. Horizontal band at bottom of foot. On the interior, trace of a red band on floor. Low, slanted foot and very deep body, in contrast to our preceding examples, and thickened rim.

For an almost identical pyxis, but with the addition of spoked circle filling ornament, from the sanctuary of Demeter Malophoros, see *MonAnt* 32 (1927), pl. lxxxviii, no. 5. This pyxis has been attributed by Amyx to the Long Duck Painter.[152] A similar pyxis was found at Tocra, but the bird is rendered in silhouette (*Tocra* I, 31, no. 169, pl. 14), and others are known from Perachora (*Perachora* II, 187).

LC I, Long Duck Painter

59   Pl. 11   Sb. 133   D12/E12   D   4

Most of foot and part of adjoining body. Buff clay with pale orange core. Black glaze worn, brown where thin. Added red. Encrusted.

MPH: 0.0533; MPW: 0.0513

Very shallow body and a high, straight foot. Rim broken off. On the foot: chain of three alternately reversed lotuses with crosshatching on petals.[153] Added red on bases of lotus, delineated by incised horizontal lines. Thin band at bottom of foot.

A nearly identical pyxis occurs in *Corinth* XV:3, pl. 39, no. 861 (KP 1915), dated to LC I and attributed to the TP workshop.[154] Another pyxis from the Potters' Quarter at Corinth (*Corinth* XV:3, pl. 39, no. 858) is very similar, and Amyx has listed it as "related to the Severeanu Painter."[155] Other fragments of this type were found in E12, 1, 3; F13/G13, 1, 2; and F13/G13, Wall Test, but this is the only example to have been found in a largely undisturbed archaic level.

LC I, TP Workshop

60   Pl. 11   Sb. 419–3   F13/G13   2   2

Fragment, preserving complete profile, with small section of bowl. Light greenish clay. Black glaze worn and crazed. Added red, fugitive. Surface worn and chipped. Encrusted.

MPH: 0.056; MPW: 0.0594

Shallow body, projecting rim, square in section, with horizontal grooving on exterior. On the foot: chain of three alternately reversed lotuses, with crosshatching for the petals. Added red on bases of lotus, set off by horizontal incisions.

Same as preceding.

LC I, TP Workshop

61   Pl. 11   Sb. 288–11   F13/G13   1   2

Fragment, preserving less than one-third lower body. Buff clay. Resting surface of foot chipped. Black glaze, brown where thin. Added red (purple).

MPH: 0.0273; MPW: 0.0546

Low, outward slanted foot and very deep body. Exterior: black-and-red band; band of narrow rays with thin black band above and below; red band; dot band flanked by thin black band above and below; dot band between two narrow red bands. Interior: glazed bands on wall, trace of possible white band.

This fragment differs from our other linear-style pyxides by its more diversified decoration, more abundant use of added red, and slightly better quality.

Late MC or LC

---

149. *GKV*, 55, no. 93.

150. *Corinth* XV:3, pl. 39 no. 856, p. 164.

151. R. Young, "Sepulturae Intra Urbem," *Hesperia* 20 (1951), pl. 38, d, as also cited in *Corinth* XV:3, 164 n.1 (no. 856).

152. *CorVP*, 456 n. 58 and 257, where to no. 3 (Corinth KP 2411), add *Corinth* XV:3, no. 862, pl. 106

153. Cf. *NC*, 154, fig. 62f.

154. This type is also mentioned in *Perachora* II, 187 where the lotus chain is referred to as the late "scraggy" type. Amyx refers to these as late ("Severeanu") type in *CorVP*, 455 n. 53.

155. *CorVP*, 257 no. 1 (Corinth KP 1951).

62   Pl. 11   Sb. 80–3a,b   D12/13 A 3 East

White-style fragments, each preserving part of foot and body. Top of body and rim broken off. Buff clay. On fragment (a) glaze ranges from black to metallic blue to brown, with added red. On fragment (b) glaze ranges from black to brown to red.

(a) MPH: 0.0384; MPW: 0.0294

Exterior: vertical herringbone pattern on side, delimiting a reserved panel; at the base, a red band and dot band between two glazed bands; band along bottom edge of foot. Interior: floor of body glazed.

(b) MPH: 0.027; MPW: 0.023

Same decoration.

The bowl is relatively deep and the foot slants slightly outward.

A close analogy for our example occurs at the North Cemetery in Corinth (*Corinth* XIII, 116, no. 159–13, pl. 24), but here there are two separate vertical hatched bands on each side of the foot, framing the panel.[156] A similar pyxis was found in Tocra (*Tocra* I, 31, no. 173, pl. 14), but the framing decoration for the foot consists of a vertical zigzag between double lines.[157]

The two fragments were found in a largely undisturbed archaic level.

LC I

63   Pl. 12.   Sb. 342–1   D12/13 F 2, S scarp

Less than one-third pyxis, preserving complete profile. Light greenish clay. Black glaze, mostly gone, grayish where preserved. Encrusted.

MPH: 0.0415; MPW: 0.0332; Est D: 0.065–0.07

Small pyxis with outward slanting foot and very deep body. Groove on the top of flat surface of projecting rim. Exterior: banding on the rim, broad band below, three bands, band of vertical stripes, four bands. Interior: band below rim and band around edge of floor.

For the form and similar pattern decoration, see *Corinth* XIII, 208, pl. 32, no. 239–3 (larger size), from a grave dated to "probably third quarter sixth century." Also comparable to our example is an LC I pyxis in Stockholm (*CVA* I, 37–39, pl. 17, 6, fig. 77), which, however, is of substantially larger size and has added red decoration. The flat flanged lid (**94**), found in C13/D13, 1, 6, probably belongs with this pyxis.

LC I or LC II

64   Pl. 12   Sb. 297–3   F13/G13 1 2

Lower part of foot and part of bowl. Buff clay. Black glaze ranges to red, brown where thin, and worn.

MPH: 0.0287; MPW: 0.067

Outward slanting foot and deep body. Exterior: alternately reversed triangles, the smaller upright triangles with dotted centers, the larger pendant triangles with strokes in the center; three bands below.

The dotted triangle is not a common motif on pattern vases. Triangles with dotted centers, though not in the same decorative scheme as our example, also occur on the foot of a large tripod pyxis from the North Cemetery at Corinth (*Corinth* XIII, 320–321, pl. 88, X–133).[158] A closer parallel for our triangular motif occurs on a lid from Perachora (*Perachora* II, pl. 114, no. 2740), but the centers of the triangles are not dotted.[159]

LC

65   Pl. 12   Sb. 288–12   F13/G13 1 2

Fragment, preserving about one-third lower body. Light green clay. Glaze brown. Added red. Encrusted.

MPH: 0.0328; MPW: 0.0583

Low foot and deep body, common to the linear tripod pyxides. Exterior: alternating black and red bands; band of hook maeanders, bordered by band above and below; red band around base of foot.

For a hook maeander band on the lower body of a late pyxis, see *Délos* X, pl. 32, no. 508.

LC II/III

POWDER PYXIDES

In our catalog, there are 17 examples, including 12 lids and five bottom-halves, all belonging to powder pyxides in the linear style; presumably all are LC.[160] The powder pyxis is, in fact, not decorated in black-figure, though occasionally with silhouette friezes.[161] The lids have either a flat or a slightly convex top, and there is a projecting molding on the top edge, often horizontally grooved, at the juncture with the straight side wall. Both the deep (**66**) and shallow (**70, 71, 76**) lid types are represented. More lids, which range in size from large to small, than bottoms are preserved.

Interestingly, the powder pyxides from the Demeter Sanctuary do not, for the most part, correspond to the better-known published examples, such as those with vertical wavy lines either in groups[162] or in a continuous band.[163] Our fragments do, however, supplement the known decorative repertoire of this linear-style group. Particularly noteworthy are **66–68**, found in the backfill of the middle sanctuary retaining wall, with their elaborate and carefully rendered pattern motifs and concentric moldings. The tops of these three large lids all bear the same patterns, but arranged in different schemes: maeander band, dou-

---

156. Grave 159 is dated to about the middle of the first quarter of the sixth century (*Corinth* XIII, 185).

157. See also Paul Clement and Margaret MacVeagh Thorne, "From the West Cemetery at Isthmia," *Hesperia* 43 (1974), no. 7, 406, pl. 85.

158. For the same decoration at the rim of a concave-sided pyxis from the North Cemetery at Corinth, see *Corinth* XIII, 115, 190, pl. 27 no. 170–5, dated to the end of MC.

159. Akin to this triangular decorative scheme is the decoration on a broad-bottomed oinochoe from the Vrysoula Deposit at Corinth, dating to the second half of the fifth century B.C. (E. G. Pemberton, "The Vrysoula Deposit from Ancient Corinth," *Hesperia* 39 [1970], pl. 69, no. 24).

160. The shape also occurs in miniature (see section on miniatures).

161. For a discussion of powder pyxides, see Hopper, 217; *Perachora* II, 187 f.; and *CorVP*, 456.

162. For example, see *Tocra* I, pl. 15, 230; *CVA* Deutschland, Bd. 7 (Karlsruhe, Bd. 1), pl. 39, 2; Fairbanks, pl. 44, 441–442; *Corinth* XIII, pl. 23, 157–t, pl. 27, 168–9; *Corinth* XV:3, pl. 62, 1508.

163. For example, see *Corinth* XIII, pl. 24, 159–12, pl. 27, 168–8.

ble-dot band, alternating red and black tongues of varying thickness and with individual outlines, and a row of black dots on at least one of the moldings. These lids recall the decorative style of the LC II kothons which can be placed in Amyx's "Winchester Group."[164] We have also included two fragments (**73**, **74**) which, because of their unusual form, can only hesitatingly be identified as powder pyxis lids.

Although over half of the catalogued fragments were found in the backfill of the middle sanctuary retaining wall,[165] several of our catalogued pieces were found in largely undisturbed archaic levels: **77** and **78**, probably a match of lid and bottom, in D12/13, B, 4 West and **73** in E11, 3, 3. A bottom-half (**80**) was found in an undisturbed archaic (D16/17, 1, 4) level. Among our 55 uncatalogued powder pyxis sherds, which include 37 lid and 18 bottom-half fragments,[166] five were found in largely undisturbed archaic levels,[167] while one, a lid, was found in an undisturbed archaic level.[168] Where discernible, these uncatalogued sherds appear to be exclusively in the linear style.

66 Pl. 12   Sb. 419–11   F13/G13 2 2
Lid fragment, preserving part of top and vertical side wall. Mended from three joins. Buff clay. Fugitive black glaze, mostly shadows of decoration remain. Added red (purple). Heavily encrusted.
MPH: 0.07; MPW: 0.067; MPL: 0.048 (top of lid); Est D: 0.17

Very broad and relatively tall lid. Flat top, decorated with two half-round moldings about midway between center and edge, and a small single molding near the large, horizontally grooved molding at junction of top and side wall. Thickened rounded edge at bottom of lid.

On top of lid from center: edge of molding; band of two-row dicing; meander band; banding; traces of dots on interior half-round molding; band of tongues with individual outlines in dilute yellow; molding; added red on edge molding.

On side wall: three horizontal bands; wide band, bordered by black band above and red band below, consisting of groups of vertical wavy lines, an upright rectangle painted red, and an hourglass pattern[169] between two thin vertical lines.

The pattern decoration is neatly applied. The elaborate moldings, decoration, and use of added red or purple imply an LC date.[170] A similar design with hourglass, rectangles, and wavy lines appears on the side wall of an appreciably smaller powder pyxis lid from the North Cemetery at Corinth, dated to the first quarter of the fifth century, and found in an infant grave. However, the decoration on the top of the lid is much simpler on the Corinth pyxis.[171] There is no exact parallel for this fragment or the two that follow. Nonetheless, they have a strong connection with the kothons (**214–216**) which can be added to Amyx's Winchester Group.
LC II, Related to Winchester Group

67 Pl. 12   Sb. 288–22   F13/G13 1 2
Part of top of lid. Buff clay. Black glaze worn. Added purple worn.
MPL: 0.0512; MPW: 0.051

From center: band of rather wide, alternating black and red tongues with individual outlines; thin concentric black, red, purple, black, red lines; three half-round moldings (the first two painted black [?], the third painted red); double-dot band, bordered by thin black lines above and a red line below; maeander band flanked by thin black lines; purple band; two half-round moldings, black dots on the narrower molding, red on the other; black band.

The fragment belongs to a rather large lid (the entire radius is not preserved), perhaps 15 cm. in diameter. The decorative scheme here, and the use of half-round moldings show close similarity to the preceding fragment. This piece is unusual in the use of three adjoining concentric moldings on the top of the flat lid. Black dots occur on a raised band on the side wall of an LC powder pyxis from the Potters' Quarter at Corinth.[172]
LC II, Related to Winchester Group

68 Pl. 13   Sb. 420–1   F13/G13 2 2N
Lid fragment, preserving less than one-eighth of top. Side wall broken off. Deep buff clay. Black glaze worn and yellow where dilute. Added purple worn.
MPL: 0.0486; MPW: 0.0622

From center: double-dot band; red line; band of narrow alternating red and black tongues with individual outlines in dilute yellow, bordered by thin black lines above and below; purple band; two concentric quarter-round moldings, one with black dots, the other painted purple; maeander band in black-and-yellow dilute glaze between two thin black lines; slight molding painted purple; part of thickened rounded edge molding with horizontal grooves, painted purple.

Similar to the two preceding fragments.
LC II, Related to Winchester Group

69 Pl. 13   Sb. 288–13   F13/G13 1 2
Lid fragment, preserving part of top and side wall. Pinkish to pale yellow buff clay. Black glaze ranges to red, brown where thin. Added purple.
MPH: 0.024; MPW: 0.06; Est D: 0.09

Slightly domed lid and vertical side wall. On top of lid: purple line; band of purple tongues with individual outlines in dilute glaze and with short lines between outlines, bordered by a line above and below; purple on projecting edge molding, grooved only on top surface.

On side wall: alternating purple and black bands of varying thickness. For a band of outlined tongues on the top of a lid, see *Corinth* XV:3, pl. 65, no. 1646.
LC II

---

164. *CorVP*, 474.

165. The percentage of uncatalogued sherds of this shape from this area is smaller, only 36%.

166. Among these, 2 were burnt and 2 (also found in F13/G13, 2, 2), were very similar to **66**.

167. A lid in E11, 3, 3, a burnt bottom-half in E11/12, Pit Area, 3, and 3 lids in D12/13, F, 3.

168. D16/17, 1, 4. This lid does not go with the aforementioned catalogued bottom-half found in the same context.

169. For an hourglass pattern on a lid, tentatively dated to EC, see *Corinth* XV:3, 276, no. 1507, pl. 62. For the upright rectangle, see discussion under no. 1090, pl. 47, p. 203, an LC III powder pyxis.

170. Another such fragment was found in this area (F13/G13, 2, 2).

171. *Corinth* XIII, 144, pl. 41, 288–2, p. 226 (grave dated to first half fifth century); see also p. 144 where Palmer notes that "the decoration is derived directly from the sixth century group."

172. *Corinth* XV:3, no. 1646, pl. 65.

70   Pl. 13   Sb. 103–1   E11/12   Pit 2

Lid fragment, preserving part of top and side wall (complete profile). Buff clay. Firm black glaze, brown where thin. Added purple.

MPH: 0.0374; MPW: 0.067 (top of lid); MPL: 0.026; Est D: 0.11

Slightly domed, rather shallow lid.

On top of lid: alternating purple and black bands. Red on thickened edge molding; uneven ridge below. On side wall: red band, band of horizontal petals between two black bands; purple on slightly thickened bottom edge.

The petal, though generally vertically placed, is a common LC motif.[173]

LC II

71   Pl. 13   Sb. 528–3   F12/G12   Tunnel A

Lid fragment, preserving side wall (complete profile) and part of top of lid. Light-greenish buff clay. Dull black glaze, worn. Added red, worn. Surface chipped. Encrusted.

H: 0.0267; MPW: 0.0584; Est D: 0.09

Shallow lid with straight sides and flat top. Rounded molding at edge of top and at bottom edge. On top of lid: broad red and narrow black concentric bands; black on molding. On side wall: thin black band; broad red overpainted band, thin black band; and red on bottom molding.

LC II

72   Pl. 13   Sb. 516–9   F14/G14   1   2

Lid fragment (?), preserving part of side wall and top of lid. Deep buff to pinkish clay. Black glaze, brown where dilute. Added red, worn on molding. Surface slightly worn and encrusted.

MPH: 0.0424; MPW: 0.0528; Est D: 0.075

Flat top that rises slightly upward toward center, straight side wall, and molding at juncture of top and side. On top of lid: traces of concentric banding. Added red on molding. On side wall: horizontal banding (brown, narrow red, two thin brown, red, black, two thin brown).

LC

73   Pl. 13.   Sb. 49–4   E11   3   3

Lid fragment (?), preserving about one-eighth of side wall. Buff clay. Worn black glaze. Added red. Encrusted.

MPH: 0.04; MPW: 0.05; Est D: 0.12

Bottom edge unusual in the extent to which it broadens out, to a triangular form, below the second of the two half-round moldings on the side wall. On side wall exterior: red band; band of triple dicing with thin line above and below; black band above and on first molding; thin red band below molding; red on second molding and on bottom edge. On side wall interior: black glaze on the flat resting surface of the bottom edge and to a height of 0.034; remainder unglazed.

This very unusual fragment is tentatively assigned to a powder pyxis cover.[174] The form of the wall has no analogy, while the presence of the black glaze on the interior further calls into question the proposed identification. The fragment was found in a largely undisturbed archaic level.

LC

74   Pl. 14   Sb. 516–7   F14/G14   1   2

Lid fragment (?), preserving about one-fifth bottom edge and part of side wall. Buff clay. Black glaze, brown where thinly applied. Added red. Surface slightly worn and chipped.

MPH: 0.0346; MPW: 0.047; Est D: 0.095

Bottom with thickened double molding on exterior and ridging on resting surface. Slightly curved side wall. On side wall: tip of ray, two narrow bands, black band with traces of added purple overpainting; added red on bottom molding and resting surface, extending toward interior. Interior unglazed.

The fragment in all probability belongs to a powder pyxis cover. However, the features of the bottom molding are uncommon.

LC

75   Pl. 14   Sb. 103–2   E11/12   Pit 2

Lid fragment, preserving part of top and side wall. Pale orange clay with buff surface. Black glaze fired mostly red.

MPH: 0.0194; MPW: 0.0323; Est D: 0.09

Small, domed lid with finely grooved projecting molding and apparently straight side wall. On top: group of five vertical zigzags, glazed band, and painted molding. On side wall: reserved band between two glazed bands and remains of tongues.

Groups of vertical zigzags occur on lid tops.

LC

76   Pl. 14   Sb. 40–6   E11   1   2

Lid fragment, preserving part of top and complete side wall. Light green clay. Fugitive black glaze. Added purple. Soil-stained and encrusted.

H: 0.036; MPW: 0.0662; Est D: 0.13

Shallow lid with slightly convex top and quarter-round molding at edge and half-round molding at bottom. On top: trace of glazed band; groove inside molding filled with red. On side wall: red band below top molding; faint traces of some four painted bands; purple on molding at bottom edge.

LC

77   Pl. 14   Sb. 76–4   D12/13   B   4 West

Lid fragment, about one-third preserved, including part of top and side wall. Deep buff clay. Metallic black glaze, worn and ranges to red. Added red. Mended from two joins. Chipped. Soil-stained and slightly encrusted.

MPH: 0.016; MPW: 0.056; Est D: 0.065

Small cover with flat top and two circular concentric grooves in center; projecting, horizontally grooved molding; and straight side wall. On top from center: red in two circular grooves in center; glazed band and red bands; band of blobs; two thin bands around edge; edge molding glazed (ranges from black to red). On side wall: red band below molding; thin dilute band; broad black band. Small rings in center of lid top occur on a miniature pyxis from Corinth.[175] Possibly the lid for the following bottom-half fragment (**78**), both of which were found in a largely undisturbed archaic level.

LC

78   Pl. 14   Sb. 76–3   D12/13   B   4 West

Small bottom-half fragment, preserving about one-fifth base and part of side wall. Buff clay with slight pinkish tinge. Black glaze, fired red or added red. Soil-stained and encrusted.

MPH: 0.0244; MPW: 0.038; Est D: 0.08

Vertical side wall, small flange, and flat underside. On the side wall exterior, a band on the wall and on the edge

---

173. See, for example, *CVA* Heidelberg (Bd 1), pl. 16, no. 6 on an LC II kotyle; *Corinth* XIII, pl. 34, nos. 257–5, 258–1.

174. See *Perachora* II, 189, fig. 15b for moldings along the vertical wall, but attribution of this fragment as belonging to a pyxis lid is also questioned.

175. *Corinth* XV:3, pl. 68, no. 1780.

of the flange. On the side wall interior, painted and red (?) band in center of floor.
See preceding **77** for possible lid.
LC

79   Pl. 15   Sb. 506–11   F14/G14 1 Test 2
Bottom-half fragment, preserving about one-third base and part of side wall. Clay ranges from deep buff to orange to muddy dark yellow. Glaze gone. Encrusted.
MPH: 0.022; MPW: 0.104; Est D: 0.12
Projecting flange with a camber on the exterior for the lid. A groove around the flat horizontal portion of base.
LC (?)

80   Pl. 15   Sb. 140   D16/17 1 4
Bottom-half fragment, preserving about one-quarter base and part of side wall. Pinkish buff clay. Worn black glaze. Added red. Surface worn and encrusted.
MPH: 0.019; MPW: 0.0563; Est D: 0.085
Narrow flange for lid. Groove (0.01 from edge) around flattened horizontal part of base. Side wall curves inward slightly. On side wall: traces of two painted bands and red band above flange. It should be noted that this fragment was found in an undisturbed archaic level.
LC (?)

81   Pl. 15   Sb. 179   C15/D15 1–B 2
Bottom-half fragment. Deep buff clay. Worn black glaze ranges to red. Added red. Encrusted.
MPH: 0.029; MPW: 0.0785; Est D: 0.16
Slightly convex underside with narrow flange and vertical side wall. Black band with red line above at base of side wall. Black glaze on edge of flange.
LC (?)

82   Pl. 15   Sb. 115–2   E10 Balk Bldg between E Wall and Terrace E Wall
Bottom-half fragment from a shallow type, preserving about one-third base and complete side wall. Light greenish-yellow clay. Surface worn and encrusted.
H: 0.026; MPW: 0.0788; Est D: 0.09
Vertical side wall, flattened base with horizontal squared-off flange.
LC (?)

Lids (83–109)

The 27 fragments in our catalog, ranging in date from EC through LC II/III, include flat and domed lids as well as knobs. Our earliest examples are flat lids decorated in the black-polychrome technique (**83–85**). Although there are a number of MC fragments, most of the catalogued pieces are from the LC period. With four possible exceptions,[176] all the catalogued fragments belong to pyxis lids. Lids decorated in the linear style are clearly the most common, though there are several fragments of black-figure as well as one silhouette style and one red-ground piece among the flat lids. The majority of the examples come from the backfill of the middle sanctuary retaining wall. Only two pieces, both from flat lids, were found in largely undisturbed archaic levels: **89**, a black-figure fragment, and **94**, a linear-style fragment.

About 190 other lid fragments were retained from the excavations, exclusive of the powder pyxis lids discussed in the previous section. Where preserved, the decoration on most of the uncatalogued sherds is in the linear style. Fragments of identifiable flat, flanged lids outnumber those belonging to domed lids. The largest concentration of finds, as is the general pattern at the sanctuary, was in the backfill of the middle sanctuary retaining wall, where over 60% of the sherds were found.[177] A significant number of fragments (19) were found in largely undisturbed archaic levels,[178] while four were found in undisturbed archaic levels.[179]

FLAT, FLANGED LIDS

These lids generally have a flat, slightly convex, or conical upper surface, a short flange, and a knob that varies from a high-molded to a button (flat or rounded) or to an inverted cone-shaped form. They were designed to be covers for concave pyxides, convex pyxides without handles, and tripod pyxides. Two of our pieces (**91**, **99**), however, may in fact be lekanis lids. The flat lids are notable for the diversity of decorative techniques they exhibit and for their chronological range, which extends from EC to LC II.

Of the 17 examples in our catalog, those in the linear style are generally representative of most of the finds from the site. The 3 pieces (**83–85**) in the black-polychrome technique may be assigned to EC,[180] while a fourth, **86**, with a high-molded knob, may be MC. **83** and particularly **85**, with its more

---

176. **91**, **99**, **105**, **109**.

177. The breakdown by type will be noted below, with the exception of the unattributable fragments, which number less than 20.

178. E11, 3, 3 (black-polychrome fragment), D12/13, B, 4 (molded knob), D12/13, A, 3 (1 black-figure fragment, 1 truncated cone-shaped knob, 1 lid with part of knob), D12/13, A, 4 (black-figure fragment), E11/12, Pit Area, 3 (molded knob), D12/E12, D, 3 (flat flanged lid fragment), D12/13, F, 3 (knob), D12/13, F, 4 (linear-style flat lid fragment with double-dot band), D13/E13, 1, 4 (linear-style domed lid fragment, C13/D13, 1, 5 (burnt linear-style flat flanged lid fragment), C13/D13, 1, 6 (1 flat flanged lid fragment, 4 knobs), C13, 1, 4a (1 silhouette?-style flat flanged lid fragment and 1 flat button knob).

179. C13/D13, 1, 7 (1 knob, 1 lid fragment), E15, 1, 4 (molded knob, similar to our catalogued examples), and C13, 1, 4b (small flat flanged lid with glaze gone).

180. Four other such black polychrome fragments were found, 1 each in E11, 3, 3 (see *supra* n. 178); F11, 1, 3; D12, Balk, 2; and F13/G13, 2, 2. Professor Amyx has confirmed that **83–85** are EC.

elaborate and colorful decoration, deserve mention. Also noteworthy are the 3 black-figure fragments:[181] **87**, our only example with part of an animal frieze, dated to MC; and **88–89**, with their unusual horizontal lotus decoration, both probably LC. There is one MC/LC silhouette-style fragment, **90**, with a file of crude figures.[182] Quite unusual is the LC red-ground fragment (**95**). Among the linear-style pieces, **96** is interesting for its reserved leaf pattern and **98** for its neat workmanship and moldings, related to Amyx's Winchester Group.[183] The fragmentary linear-style lid (**94**) may belong with one of our catalogued tripod pyxides (**63**), representing our only possible match of lid and pyxis among the finds.[184]

Over 70 other fragments of this type of lid were retained from the excavations.[185] Seven were uncovered in largely undisturbed archaic levels[186] and one was uncovered in an undisturbed archaic level.[187]

83   Pl. 16   Sb. 288–1   F13/G13   1   2
Fragment, preserving less than half of flat lid with flange. Light grayish buff clay. Black glaze worn, crazed where thick. Added white. Rim and flange chipped. Knob broken off.
MPH: 0.0126; MPL: 0.0852; MPW: 0.0545; Est D: 0.10
From the center: black band around knob; reserved band; broad black band with double incised verticals, radiating from the center; vertical row of white dots in every third strip; two alternating reserved and black bands around edge.

Such lids are generally dated to EC. The rows of white dots seem further to indicate an EC date for this fragment. The same decoration of vertical double-incised lines with a row of white dots in every third panel occurs on a concave-sided pyxis from Perachora (see *Perachora* I, 101, pl. 33, no. 14) ascribed to EC on the basis of the white dots (see Hopper, 207, EC?). A concave-sided pyxis from the North Cemetery at Corinth (*Corinth* XIII, pl. 18, 128–g), with black polychrome decoration in double incised vertical stripes and a row of white dots down each black stripe, is also dated to EC.[188]

For a virtually identical lid, with a row of white dots in every third panel and banding around the edge, from Megara Hyblaea, see *NSc* (1954), 112, fig. 36,5.[189]

EC (EC - Amyx)

84   Pl. 16   Sb. 501–5   F14/G14   1   Test 1
                                              mixed with some St 2
Fragment, broken on all sides. Flange not preserved. Light-yellow buff clay. Black glaze almost entirely worn off. Added red ranges to purple.
MPL: 0.0325; MPW: 0.0537
Double-incised verticals with red overpaint in four adjacent panels (BBRRRR).[190] The lid is perhaps of the type illustrated in *Tocra* II, pl. 4, no. 1870, but the added red strips alternate. See also J. L. Caskey and P. Amandry, "Investigations at the Heraion of Argos, 1949," *Hesperia* 21 (1952), 191, 193, pl. 52, nos. 172 and 175, dated to EC.
EC (EC - Amyx)

85   Pl. 16   Sb. 288–19   F13/G13   1   2
Flat lid fragment, preserving less than one-quarter of rim, body, and flange. Pale buff clay. Worn black glaze, ranges to dark purple and brown. Added red (ranges to purple), worn. Added white worn. Mended from two joining fragments.
MPH: 0.015; MPL: 0.0823; MPW: 0.0433; Est D: 0.12
From the center: bands of red, brown, and purple; broad dark purple band consisting of double-incised verticals with applied white (W.WW.W) in the stripes, alternating with panels containing white dot rosettes; red band between two reserved bands; double-dot band with added red preserved on some of the dots, bordered by a black band above and below; black band along edge of rim.

The combination of double-dot band around the edge and incised vertical with overpainting in the stripes is a rather common feature on early lids.

This is one of the most unusual lids from the sanctuary. The white dot rosettes are indicative of an EC date for the fragment. A white dot rosette appears in a broad panel on the wall of a concave-sided pyxis, otherwise decorated with double-incised verticals, from Megara Hyblaea, which is dated to the Transitional period.[191]

EC (EC - Amyx)

86   Pl. 16   Sb. 420–4   F13/G13   2   2N
Fragment preserving complete high-molded knob (except for missing chip) and small section of adjacent lid. Light green clay. Black glaze gone except for a few tiny spots.
MPH: 0.036; MPL: 0.0352; MPW: 0.0375; H: 0.026 (knob)
Lid apparently had a slightly convex upper surface and a flange. Knob originally decorated with bands; only slight traces remain. On lid: double-incised verticals radiating

---

181. Only 3 other black-figure sherds were identified among the uncatalogued finds: 2 preserved part of a bird (one from D12/13, A, 4, West, the other from D12/13, A, 3, West, both largely undisturbed archaic levels) and 1 with a rosette (F13/G13, 1, 2).

182. Another fragment in the silhouette style was found in E12/13, E, 2. A sherd from C13, 1, 4a, a largely undisturbed archaic level, may also bear traces of silhouette figures.

183. *CorVP*, 474.

184. Except for **77** and **78**, probably matching powder pyxis lid and bottom half.

185. Uncatalogued are 74 fragments, including 4 with double-incised verticals (black-polychrome technique), 3 with black-figure decoration, and 1 or possibly 2 with silhouette decoration; the remainder (where decoration is preserved) appear to be in the linear style.

186. E11, 3, 3 (black-polychrome fragment), D12/13, A, 3 (black-figure fragment) D12/E12, D, 3 (1 fragment), D12/13, F, 4 (linear-style fragment with double-dot band), C13/D13, 1, 5 (burnt linear-style fragment), C13/D13, 1, 6 (1 fragment), C13, 1, 4a (silhouette?-style fragment).

187. A rather small lid, whose glazed decoration has disappeared, found in C13, 1, 4b (see also section on miniature lids).

188. See also *CVA* Heidelberg, Bd. 3, pl. 133, no. 14, dated to EC.

189. As also cited in *Corinth* XV:3, 275, no. 1504, but found in a grave containing Attic black-figured lekythoi of the early fifth century.

190. Three similar fragments, but lacking the red overpaint, were found in F11, 1, 3; D12, Balk, 2; and F13/G13, 2, 2.

191. See *Mégara Hyblaea*, 55, pl. 38,13.

from knob. This high knob has slightly convex sides with a thick disk, concave on top and with a protuberance in the center.[192] Such knobs are associated with lids for concave, kotyle, and convex pyxides without handles. For similar knobs, see *Tocra* I, pl. 15, nos. 206, 211; *CVA* Stockholm I, fig. 70, pl. 15, 2.[193] See also **108** (a similar knob).
MC?

87   Pl. 16   Sb. 516–4   F14/G14 1 2
Fragment, broken on all sides, with section of flange preserved. Buff clay with light yellowish cast. Black glaze, worn in frieze. Added red, appears as a muddy brown. Encrusted.
MPH: 0.021; MPW: 0.0643; MPL: 0.0415; Est D: 0.08 (flange)
Flat lid rises upward toward the knob. From the center: part of tongue rosette (around missing knob) with traces of red on tongues; thin black band; double-dot band, bordered by black bands above and below; black band; A.f: panther (head and forequarters preserved) to r. and rear of goat (?) to r. Added red on neck and shoulder muscle of panther and on rear body of goat between incised body details. Both animal torsos have numerous curved incisions for body markings and two short parallel arcs along the back. F.o. of incised rosettes.
A similar decorative scheme with tongue rosette, double-dot band, and frieze of panthers and goat occurs on a pyxis lid from Perachora, but the style of the animal frieze is very different.[194] A closer parallel comes from Old Smyrna where the lid fragment, dated late MC, preserves the same decorative scheme of rosette tongues, double-dot band, and animal frieze.[195]
MC

88   Pl. 16.   Sb. 90   F16 2 1
Fragment, preserving about one-eighth rim, flange, and part of body. Buff clay. Black glaze almost gone. Added red ranges to purple. Encrusted.
MPH: 0.014; MPW: 0.051; MPL: 0.086; Est D: 0.16
Flat lid rises slightly upward toward center. From the center: three concentric bands (BRB) with tips of tongues (?) extending over bands; frieze with part of a large horizontal lotus, tendrils (?), and bud (?) near rim; traces of added red on floral ornament; band around edge of rim.
The horizontal positioning of the lotus is most unusual as floral decoration on lids usually contains a vertical lotus as part of a chain.[196] The workmanship is quite sloppy.
LC ?

89   Pl. 17.   Sb. 49–3   E11 3 3
Small fragment, preserving part of rim and flange. Creamy buff clay. Black glaze worn, metallic where preserved. Added red. Encrusted.
MPH: 0.015; MPW: 0.0314; MPL: 0.035
Part of horizontal lotus, incised blob rosette, and part of a petal (?). Red band along edge of rim.
This fragment was found in a largely undisturbed archaic level, which also yielded a sherd in the black-polychrome technique, related to our catalogued examples.[197]
Similar to preceding, but neater.
LC ?

90   Pl. 17   Sb. 506–1   F14/G14 1 Test 2
Fragment, preserving about one-quarter of lid and flange. Light green clay. Black glaze, mostly gone, and crazed on one of the figures. Heavily encrusted.
MPW: 0.0386; MPL: 0.0744; Est D: 0.115
From the center: shadows of two bands; file of crude silhouette penguin-like figures to r., bordered by band above and below; band along edge of rim. No trace of f.o. preserved.
The figures in the frieze appear to be a much-debased version of female figures on two lids from Perachora.[198] A parallel for our fragment is a silhouette-style MC pyxis lid from Corinth with dancing women holding hands.[199]
This subject of a frieze of processional or dancing women, rendered in the silhouette style, is not common on pyxis lids.[200]
MC/LC

91   Pl. 17   Sb. 420–7   F13/G13 2 2N
Fragment, preserving part of top of lid, broken on all sides, and complete strap handle. Light yellowish buff clay. Fugitive black glaze. Slightly encrusted.
MPH: 0.029; MPL: 0.061; MPW: 0.0443
The linear decoration is virtually indiscernible—barely shadows remain. Traces of vertical bands on strap handle. On top of lid: traces of vertical stripes beneath handle; thin concentric bands around handle; band of zigzags(?).
The fragment may belong to a flat pyxis lid or a lekanis lid.[201] Pyxis lids with strap handles are uncommon.[202]
MC or LC

92   Pl. 17   Sb. 400   C12/D12 G 2
Fragment, preserving part of top of lid, complete knob, and flange. Light green to pale pinkish buff clay. Worn glaze, fired red. Added red. Encrusted. Mended from two fragments.
MPH: 0.029; MPL: 0.075; MPW: 0.07; Est D: 0.11
Top of lid rises toward the center. Flat wide knob with sharp edges. On knob: traces of three concentric bands on top and glaze on sides. On lid, from center: two bands; red band; band of zigzags, bordered by band above and below; two narrow red bands; thin red band along edge of rim.

---

192. Other such knobs were found in E11/12, Pit Area, St 3; F11, 1, 3; 2 in F13/G13, 1, 2; E15, 1, 4; F14/G14, 1, Test 2; D15/16, 1, 3.

193. For some other examples, see *Corinth* XIII, pl. 19, 141–6 (lid on a BF convex pyxis), pl. 24, 159–13 (lid on a tripod pyxis), pl. 23, 157–r and 157–q (kotyle pyxis), pl. 20, 156–10, pl. 18, 154–4; *CVA* Heidelberg (Bd. 1), pl. 17, no. 3 (MC BF convex pyxis); *CVA* France, fasc. 12, pl. 23, nos. 7–9; Caskey and Amandry, *Hesperia* 21 (1952), pl. 52, no. 256; see also Lo Porto, fig. 70b for lid type with incised verticals, but different high knob, and fig. 92b for similar knob (on lid for convex pyxis).

194. *Perachora* II, no. 1830, pl. 74, dated MC; see also *Perachora* I, pl. 27, no. 12 for tongue rosette around knob and double-dot band.

195. J. K. Anderson. "Old Smyrna: The Corinthian Pottery," *BSA* 53–54 (1958–1959), pl. 28, no. 133.

---

196. Cf. *Corinth* XV:3, pl. 39, nos. 859–860.

197. See **83**, **84**, **86**.

198. *Perachora* I, pl. 27, 10 (MC); *Perachora* II, pl. 77, no. 1899 (black-figure).

199. *Corinth* XV:3, pl. 111, 1303.

200. For a discussion of the fairly more common theme of processional or dancing women on convex pyxides without handles, rendered in black-figure, see *Perachora* II, 170 ff.

201. Cf. *Perachora* II, 185.

202. *Perachora* I, pl. 31, 5; *Perachora* II, pl. 114, 2740; cf. also *Tocra* I, pl. 14, 192, a domed lid with a loop handle; *CVA* Stockholm, pl. 15, no. 11, a domed lid with a loop handle.

For a similar lid, see *CVA* Heidelberg (Bd 1), pl. 18, no. 8, dated MC or LC I (590/50 B.C.).
MC or LC I

93 Pl. 17 Sb. 528–4 F12/G12 Tunnel A
Fragment, preserving less than one-quarter of lid along with flange. Light yellowish buff clay. Thinly applied brown paint. Added red. Encrusted.
MPH: 0.0158; MPL: 0.038; MPW: 0.055; Est D: 0.11
From the center: red band; broad purplish red band; brown band; double-dot band, bordered by band above and below; three bands; edge of rim reserved.
Double-dot bands are a frequent motif on MC and LC pyxis lids in the linear style. For a lid with similar decoration, see *CVA* Heidelberg (Bd 1), pl. 18, no. 7, dated MC or LC I.
MC or LC I

94 Pl. 17 Sb. 350–1 C13/D13 1 6
Almost complete lid, except for missing knob and section of adjoining body. Light green to gray clay. Glaze fugitive. Fragment apparently burnt (gray surface). Mended from three joining fragments. Chips on edge of rim and edge of flange.
MPH: 0.0162; D: 0.069 (lid); D: 0.048 (flange)
Top of rim has slightly conical surface, rising toward center. From center: traces of two broad bands; thin band; narrow band of vertical stripes, bordered by lines above and below; two narrow bands around edge.
For a similar lid, see *Mégara Hyblaea*, 68, pl. 56, 2, a tripod pyxis lid, dated to LC I.[203]
Although found in C13/D13, 1, 6, a largely undisturbed occupation level,[204] this lid appears to belong to a tripod pyxis (**63**) found in D12/13, F, 2, a fill associated with the earthquake and its cleanup in the Porch Building S14.[205] The clay is similar, even though the lid appears to have been burnt, and the same decorative motif, a band with vertical stripes, appears on both.
LC

95 Pl. 17 Sb. 421–7 F13/G13 2 2
Fragment, broken on all sides, preserving small section of top of lid and part of flange. Buff clay. Muddy pinkish orange slip. Worn black glaze. Added red. Surface worn and chipped.
MPH: 0.0158; MPL: 0.0436; MPW: 0.024
From the center: trace of black band; rather broad black band; two thin black bands; part of band of alternating black and red tongues with individual outlines, bordered by band above and below; traces of banding.
The presence of the red slip makes this a highly unusual fragment. The red-ground technique is generally found only on larger vases decorated with figured scenes.[206]
LC

96 Pl. 18 Sb. 288–5 F13/G13 1 2
Fragment, preserving about one-eighth of rim and flange. Buff clay. Glaze ranges from brown to red. Added red.
MPH: 0.016; MPL: 0.054; MPW: 0.035; Est D: 0.12
From center: black band; broad painted band with reserved alternate leaf pattern of broadly spaced leaves; red band; black band; black dots on edge of rim.
This leaf pattern is not common on Corinthian vases, though a very close analogy appears on the underside of a kothon from Délos, (*Délos* X, pl. 37, no. 528a), dated LC II by Payne.[207]
LC II

97 Pl. 18 Sb. 295–1 F13/G13 1 2
Fragment, preserving less than one-quarter of lid and part of flange. Dull black glaze, brown where thin. Added red (purple). Encrusted.
MPH: 0.016; MPL: 0.0373; MPW: 0.051
From the center: black and red bands; broad band of pendant cones (stepped triangles) and triangles with row of crosses in the spaces between; two narrow black bands; red band on edge of rim.
Although exact parallels for the decoration are lacking, stepped cone or triangle patterns are quite common on many LC II vases, such as plates,[208] lekanis lids,[209] kotylai,[210] and kothons[211]; they also occur on LC I and LC III vases. In contrast to our combination, generally, these stepped cones are alternately inverted (sometimes referred to as the Antiparos pattern).[212] Crosses, as on our example, appear on a powder pyxis from the North Cemetery at Corinth.[213]
LC II

98 Pl. 18 Sb. 419–13 F13/G13 2 2
Fragment, preserving over one-third lid with conical upper surface, including small portion of rather long flange. Buff clay. Fugitive black glaze. Added red fugitive. Surface worn.
MPH: 0.0255; MPL: 0.0954; MPW: 0.0324; Est D: 0.11
Top of lid rises toward the center, with molding midway and along edge. From the center: band of dot rosettes; grooved half-round molding painted red; band of alternating black and red tongues with individual outlines in dilute paint, bordered by band above and below; black glaze on rounded edge molding.
The two moldings, midway and around the edge, are quite unusual. The horizontally grooved molding recalls those on a few of our powder pyxis lids (**66, 68**); such a rounded edge molding is unparalleled on a flat flanged lid. Unfortunately, the paint has almost entirely disappeared from this fragment. Judging from what remains, however, the workmanship was very neat, particularly in the band of tongues.
For similar decorative motifs (rosettes and tongue pattern) on a lid, see the LC II tripod pyxis *NC*, fig. 176, no.

---

203. For a band of vertical stripes on a rather small lid, see also E. Brann, *Hesperia* 25 (1956), pl. 53, no. 50.

204. White, *Final Reports* I, 114

205. White, *Final Reports* I, 115

206. *NC*, 104; see also *Perachora* II, 284–286 on Corinthian imitations of Attic black-figure and note reference to two cup fragments in this technique (found by T. Burton-Brown at Cyrene).

207. *NC*, no. 1525. The pattern occasionally occurs on MC vases; see also *Corinth* XV:3, pl. 34, no. 741, but the leaves are not as broad.

208. For example, *Corinth* XV:3, pl. 66, nos. 1659, 1662.

209. For example, *Perachora* II, pl. 114 no. 2761; *Corinth* XIII, pl. 90, no. 291-3, from a grave dated to the mid-first half of the fifth century.

210. As in *NC*, 334 fig. 181a (LC II) *Perachora* II, pl. 114, no. 2678

211. *CVA* France (fasc. 12), pl. 27, no. 18, pl. 22 no. 8; *CVA* Karlsruhe (Bd 1), pl. 42, 13.

212. D. Amyx, "Dodwelliana," *CSCA* 4 (1971), 22 n. 2, who also notes MC occurrences of the pattern.

213. *Corinth* XIII, pl. 41, no. 292-1, from a grave dated to the early fifth century.

1508 (Athens, Empedocles Collection). The walls of this pyxis also have a series of moldings. See also *CVA* Heidelberg, Bd 1, pl. 18, 1–2, with a flat lid and dot rosettes in a red band. Amyx has included both these pyxides in his Winchester Group. Our lid fragment bears a relationship with this group.[214]

LC II, Related to Winchester Group

99   Pl. 18   Sb. 420–6   F13/G13 2 2N

Fragment, preserving top of lid, broken on all sides, and complete knob with small chip missing from its edge. Flange not preserved. Dull orange clay with buff surface. Black glaze worn on knob. Added red.

MPH: 0.028; MPL: 0.056; MPW: 0.0416

Upper surface slightly convex. Knob consists of a cylindrical base and a truncated conical top. Black glaze on top of knob and around edge of cone portion. From the center: broad red band; thin band of black dots; red band.

Both the form of the knob and the decorative scheme, particularly the broad added red band, are uncommon on lids. The fragment belongs either to a flat pyxis lid[215] or a lekanis lid. A somewhat similar knob, but with a shorter stem, occurs on a lekanis lid from the North Cemetery at Corinth, found in a deposit dated to the third quarter of the fifth century.[216] There appears to be no analogy for the decorative scheme on this lid.

LC

DOMED LIDS

Domed lids were generally used as covers for convex pyxides,[217] particularly for those with upright handles where the lid fit over the top of the rim.[218] Five of our catalogued pieces, all in the linear style with banded decoration, and all apparently LC, belong in this category. One is definitely of the late sixth century angular type (**104**),[219] and one may be of this type (**101**). **105**, whose identification is uncertain, is most unusual with its inordinately broad knob compared to the diameter of the top of the lid. The knobs on these domed lids include button types (**100**) and inverted truncated cone-shaped varieties (**101, 102**). Because the pattern decoration is either not well-preserved or repetitive, we have only catalogued these few examples of the approximately 40 other domed lid fragments retained from the excavations. Only one of the uncatalogued fragments came from a largely undisturbed archaic level.[220]

100   Pl. 18   Sb. 515–7   F14/G14 1 2

Fragment, preserving less than one-quarter of lid. Yellowish buff clay. Black glaze worn. Added red. Encrusted.

H: 0.0282; Est D: 0.075

Flattened button-type knob with traces of banded decoration. Sloping top. Sidewall slants slightly outward. On top of lid, from the center: concentric bands (thin black, dilute brown line, broad red band, black band); red on slightly thickened rim.

For the type, see *Tocra* I, pl. 14, no. 181.

LC

101   Pl. 18   Sb. 515–8   F14/G14 1 2

Fragment, broken on all sides. Complete knob. Light pinkish buff clay. Firm black glaze, yellowish where dilute. Added red. Encrusted on interior.

MPH: 0.02; MPL: 0.0726; MPW: 0.0436

The fragment belongs to either a flanged or an angular type domed lid, with top of lid rising toward the center. Inverted truncated cone-shaped knob with flat top.

Top of knob: black concentric bands. Black glaze on sides of knob. Top of lid: two black bands, red band (overpainted) with thin black band above and below; black band; and thin dilute line.

For the type (domed lid of angular type), see *Tocra* I, pl. 14, no. 195; for the flanged type, see *CVA* Stockholm, pls. 17, 6, fig. 77.

LC

102   Pl. 18   Sb. 420–5   F13/G13 2 2N

Fragment, preserving complete knob, top of lid to edge (side wall broken off). Buff clay. Firm black glaze, brown where dilute. Added red.

MPH: 0.025; MPL: 0.0645; MPW: 0.057

Inverted truncated cone-shaped knob with rounded top. Top of knob: two concentric black bands. Black glaze on sides of knob. Top of lid: brown band (at base of knob), broad red band, three thin brown bands, broad black band, thin brown and red band (bRbbbBbr).

For the type, see *Tocra* I, pl. 14, no. 182.

LC

103   Pl. 19   Sb. 139–4   D16/17 1 3 NW Corner

Fragment, preserving less than one-half of lid with complete knob and two sections of side wall, but with edge broken off. Creamy buff clay. Worn, fugitive black glaze. Heavily encrusted.

MPH: 0.036; MPL: 0.058; MPW: 0.0746

Sloping top and almost vertical side wall. Broad, echinus-shaped knob with a concavity in center of flat top. Top of knob: two concentric bands around a central dot. Black glaze around edge of knob. Top of lid: traces of five concentric bands.

The knob is rather large in proportion to the lid.

LC

104   Pl. 19   Sb. 421–10   F13/G13 2 2

Fragment, preserving less than one-half top of lid. Knob missing. Deep buff clay. Black glaze unevenly fired to red. Added red (purple).

MPH: 0.028; MPL: 0.063; MPW: 0.0235; Est D: 0.075

Slightly convex top projects beyond high, slightly flaring side wall. Top of lid: trace of red line; black line; broad black band; thin black line. On side wall: black band, thin brown band; and red band.

For the type, see *Tocra* I, pl. 14, no. 194, dated to the late sixth century (angular type); *Corinth* XV:3, pl. 46, no. 1052 (LC III).

LC II/III

---

214. *CorVP*, 474.

215. As, for example, *CVA* Heidelberg, pl. 18, 3, but the knob resembles **86**.

216. *Corinth* XIII, 144–146, 304–305, pl. 90, Deposit 17–b.

217. *Tocra* I, 31.

218. Hopper, 210, as in *Corinth* XIII, pl. 23, 157–p; Amyx, *CSCA* 4 (1971), pl. 11, 2, but cf. pl. 8, 3–4 with a flat lid.

219. Only one other such lid fragment was identified among the uncatalogued sherds.

220. D13/E13, 1, 4.

105 Pl. 19   Sb. 536–5   F12/G12 1 2
Fragmentary lid (?), with edges of rim chipped and broken, and edges of knob broken off. Light gray buff clay. Fugitive black glaze. Heavily encrusted.
MPH: 0.0298; D: 0.0592
High knob with tall shank and thin, flat horizontal top. Top of lid flat with grooves on sides, but length of overhang cannot be determined. On top of knob: traces of rosette in center surrounded by concentric bands. On top of lid: thin stripe around base of knob and traces of banding.
The top of the knob is unusually wide compared to the diameter of the the lid, which itself is relatively small. The lid appears to be of late angular type, but the identification of this piece is uncertain.[221]
Not analogous, but see *Corinth* XV:3, pl. 46, no. 1052 (LC III) for an angular domed lid with petals on the top of the rather broad knob.
LC

KNOBS

The examples in our catalog include a flat-button type knob with traces of a rather fine rosette (**106**),[222] a rounded button type knob with a whirligig (**107**), and a high-molded knob (**108**), a fairly common type on flat, flanged lids.[223] The fourth knob in our catalog (**109**) with its tall shaft may not belong to a pyxis lid.

While our catalog includes only four knobs, this is not representative of either the frequency or variety of these finds at the sanctuary. Over 50 other knob fragments were retained from the excavations,[224] which range from high-molded to flat or rounded button and to inverted cone shape. Quite a number were found in largely undisturbed archaic levels,[225] and two were uncovered in undisturbed archaic levels.[226]

106 Pl. 19   Sb. 120   E12/13 C Polygonal Wall
Fragmentary knob and adjoining top of lid. Light green clay. Fugitive black glaze. Added red fugitive. Surface chipped and piece missing from knob. Encrusted.
MPH: 0.0214; D: 0.0566
Broad button-type knob with slightly rounded top and small protuberance in center. Top of knob: eight-petaled rosette with individual outlines in black and presumably red centers (tiny patch of added red preserved in one of the petals); band around edge.
Though little remains visible, the drawing appears careful. Rosettes on knobs are not common. For a very similar rosette on the knob of a linear-style lid, see *CVA* Brussels I, III C, pl. 1, 5.[227] A knob with a rosette, but lacking the filled petals and individual outlines, occurs on a fragmentary flanged lid (MC or LC) from the Potters' Quarter at Corinth.[228]
MC

107 Pl. 19   Sb. 288–9   F13/G13 1 2
Complete knob and part of adjoining lid with broad ridge. Buff clay. Black glaze with some minor flaking. Added red.
MPH: 0.0295; MPL: 0.0383; MPW: 0.044; D: 0.034 (knob)
Button-type knob with rounded top. On top of knob: whirligig encircled by a black band on top. Black glaze on shank. On top of lid: alternating bands of red and black, varying in width. Whirligigs are not particularly common on the knobs of either flat or domed lids. For some examples, see *NC*, pl. 28, 5 (MC flat lid); Fairbanks, pl. 47 no. 482 (domed lid); *CVA* Stockholm, fig. 76, pl. 17, 5 (a flat lid), and *Greek Vase-Painting in Midwestern Collections*, No. 28, pl. 28 (flat lid).[229] The raised ridge around the base of the knob is also uncommon.[230]
MC or LC I

108 Pl. 19   Sb. 506–2   F14/G14 1 Test 2
Complete high-molded knob. Light green clay. Fugitive black glaze. Encrusted.
MPH: 0.0302; D: 0.0235 (knob)
The knob has convex sides, a thick disk with a central protuberance. Traces of bands around edge of top and on shank of knob. Black glaze on top of disk.
This type of knob is fairly common on flanged lids (**86**). This knob may possibly be associated with a lid fragment in the silhouette style (**90**).
MC or MC/LC

109 Pl. 19   Sb. 476–1   D15/16 1 2, possibly mixed with St 3
Complete knob from a pyxis (?) lid. Buff clay with pale orange core. Fugitive black glaze. Added red.
MPH: 0.0354; D: 0.0184 (knob)
Tall, narrow shank of uneven form surmounted by a thickened ring and rounded "button." Red band on top of the thickened ring. Black glaze on shank.
There is no precise analogy for the form on a pyxis lid or any other lid. A similarly tall shaft, however, is on a pyxis lid

---

221. A somewhat similar fragment was found in F13/G13, 2, 2N.

222. The only other similar example from among the uncatalogued finds is a rounded knob with a tongue pattern from F14/G14, 1, 2.

223. A total of 10 such knobs, 2 associated with flat lids, are among the uncatalogued finds. Two were found in largely undisturbed archaic levels (D12/13, B, 4 and E11/12, Pit Area, 3), and 1 was found in an undisturbed archaic level (E15, 1, 4).

224. In addition to the 55 uncatalogued stand-alone knobs, there were some 25 lid fragments that preserved knobs of various types.

225. D12/13, B, 4 (molded knob), D12/13, A, 3 (truncated cone-shaped knob), E11/12, Pit Area, 3 (molded knob), D12/13, F, 3 (1 fragment), C13/D13, 1, 6 (4 knobs), C13, 1, 4a (flat button knob).

226. C13/D13, 1, 7 and E15, 1, 4 (molded knob).

227. As also cited in *Corinth* XV:3, 274 n. 1 (under no. 1498, dated to EC).

228. *Corinth* XV:3, pl. 64, no. 1590.

229. See also *Corinth* VII:1, pl. 41, 328 on an MC black-figured lid, where the whirligig design is different.

230. Ridges or steps can be seen on the lids of late unglazed lekanides (see *Corinth* XIII, 146 f.).

from the Vrysoula Deposit at Corinth, dated to the first half of the fifth century.[231]
LC II/III

Kotylai (110–164)

Kotylai were, by far, the most numerous of all Corinthian vases at the Demeter sanctuary.[232] These cups were ubiquitous, occurring in almost every trench and stratum where Corinthian pottery was found.[233] To give an idea of the volume, it should be noted that some 1600 kotyle fragments[234] were retained from the excavations, including over 500 bases. Among them were 335 bases belonging mainly to standard-size but also to some large kotylai, and 182 bases belonging to small kotylai.[235] Given this massive number of sherds, only about half, however, could be assigned with certainty to particular types of kotylai; the state of preservation of the other half of these fragments precluded attributions.[236] These numbers are in vivid contrast to the other classes of shapes uncovered at the sanctuary: The pyxides form the second largest group, but as a class are numerically substantially below the kotylai.

The catalog contains 55 of the best-preserved examples of kotylai in the black-figure, silhouette, linear, conventionalizing, and black-glazed styles uncovered from the sanctuary. They range in date from MC to LC III. The black-figure and silhouette fragments constitute the MC to LC finds, while the linear, conventionalizing, and black-glazed pieces are exclusively LC. Based on the relative proportions of the fragments retained from the excavations, it would appear that linear-style kotylai were the most common, followed in descending order of frequency by black-glazed, black-figure, silhouette style, and conventionalizing kotylai.

In general, there is a correspondence with the much better preserved types found at Tocra,[237] and specific parallels are noted in the catalog. A notable exception, however, among the black-figure pieces is the absence of any fragments that could be attributed to the C–47 or the Patras Painter at Cyrene.

Although about 60% of our catalog entries are from the backfill of the middle sanctuary retaining wall, the concentration of the uncatalogued finds from this area is less—about 32%. In addition, almost 20% of the uncatalogued sherds were found in largely undisturbed archaic levels,[238] with the largest concentration in D12/13, B, 4 (about 45% of the total sherds from largely undisturbed archaic levels), followed by D12/13, A, 3 and D12/13, F, 3.[239] On the other hand, only some 20 sherds (about 1%) were found in archaic levels undisturbed by later intrusions, with about half from C13, 1, 4b.

The miniature kotylai are discussed in a separate section, with the exception of those decorated in the silhouette style, in keeping with the customary treatment of this style of vase decoration.

BLACK-FIGURE

The black-figure kotylai from the sanctuary are represented by 19 examples in the catalog. These pieces, belonging to standard and large size kotylai, date to the MC and LC periods. The other identifiable black-figured fragments retained from the excavations number 110. Of these, 80 were body fragments of different kotylai, and the rest were rims.[240] Clearly, black-figure kotylai constitute a relatively small group.

Our rather poorly preserved pieces, with a few exceptions, belong to kotylai of the standard Corinthian repertoire. At least 10 fragments are from large kotylai whose diameters are well over 20 cm. On these, the rim decoration varies from a lotus-palmette chain (**113, 114**) to a lotus-and-bud chain

---

231. E. G. Pemberton, "The Vrysoula Deposit," *Hesperia* 39 (1970), 288, pl. 70, 51.

232. This situation is paralleled at Tocra, see *Tocra* I, 24 f.

233. By also taking into account finds of miniature kotylai, the following are the only exceptions, and virtually all these contexts contained very little Corinthian: E11, 2, 3; E11/12, balk, 1; D11/E11, balk, 3 North half; D16/17, 1, 1; C17, 1, 1 SW Sondage; F11, 1, 1; F11, 1, 4; F11, 2, 4 (Foundation of S7 Sacred House); D16/E16, 1, 3; D15, 1, 1; C11, 2, 1; E12/F12, balk, 3; and C17, 2, 2.

234. Of these, only 15 showed evidence of having been burnt.

235. In addition, fragments of the standard to large-size kotyle included 262 rims, 145 rim-handles, 97 handles, and close to 500 body sherds. The small kotylai fragments also included 10 rims, 18 rim-handles, 30 handles, and 36 body sherds. 29% of the standard and large-size kotylai, but over 53% of the small kotylai bases were found in the backfill of the middle sanctuary retaining wall.

236. These included the following: 125 rims (27 with vertical stripes in the handle-zone, of which 12 belonged to large kotylai); 155 body fragments; 86 handles (4 belonging to large kotylai); 102 rim-handles (5 of which belonged to large kotylai); and almost 340 base and/or lower body fragments (14 of which belonged to large kotylai), including almost 80 with rays around the base.

237. *Tocra* I, pls. 23–27 and *Tocra* II, pls. 6–7

238. Many of these were unidentifiable; those that could be ascribed are noted in the sections below.

239. D. White *Final Reports* V, 50, 190.

240. It was virtually impossible to associate any of the bases retained from the excavations with black-figured kotylai.

(**119–121**) and to vertical wavy lines (**115, 122**). Where preserved, the animal friezes typically contain panthers. Notable among these large kotylai, are three MC(?) fragments (**111–113**), whose glaze has entirely worn off, which may all belong to one kotylai with an unusual double frieze, possibly even a kotyle-pyxis. There are also examples of MC/LC kotylai with broad-frieze decoration and no decorative band in the handle-zone (**123, 124**). Among the other fragments, one piece (**110**), in particular, is of better than average quality: with a siren in the upper of its two friezes, drawn in a fine, distinctive style.

Five of our catalogued examples were found in largely undisturbed archaic levels: three (**111, 112, 123**)[241] in D12/13, A, 3; one (**125**) in D12/13, A, 4; and one (**115**) in D12/E12, D3. Among the uncatalogued finds, there are at least 30 identifiable[242] black-figure kotyle fragments, mainly body sherds, that were found in largely undisturbed archaic levels.[243] Except for three, all of these were concentrated in the D12/D13 area. In contrast, only two black-figure kotylai fragments were found in undisturbed archaic levels: D16/17, 1, 4 and C13, 1, 4b each yielded one body fragment. Oddly, only a dozen black-figure fragments were from the backfill of the middle sanctuary retaining wall, the most prolific source of the sanctuary's pottery.

*Illustration 3 (**110**)*

110 Pl. 20; Ill. 3 Sb. 61–3a,b   E12 1 3
Two body fragments (a,b), no join. Light grayish buff clay. Black glaze worn. Added red. Encrusted.
  (a) MPH: 0.029; MPW: 0.0262; Th: 0.0044
Band above frieze: head of siren to r., with part of r. outspread wing and l. sickle-shaped wing. The siren has a fillet, incisions marking hair on top of head, double-incised eye, and rather carelessly rendered ear. Wavy incised line for hair.
(b) MPH: 0.062; MPW: 0.055; Th: 0.005
Contains portions of two friezes. Main frieze: part siren to r., with outspread wings. Rather thick f.o. of incised rosettes, blobs, and dots. Dividing band. Lower frieze: rosette with large center bordered by two incised lines and short petals. Added red preserved in patch on one of the petals.[244]

The (b) siren, missing its head, tail, most of the l. wing, and part of the r. wing, is svelte with a vertical posture. The long tresses, descending down the r. wing, are outlined with incised wavy lines. The head on (a) does not belong to the body of (b). The incision work is especially good on (b) and both the style and drawing are distinctive. The partially preserved rosette, with the very large center, is presumably part of a rather narrow rosette frieze.

The fragments belong to an unusual kotyle with a double frieze. Such double friezes, large main and narrow lower frieze, occasionally occur on EC kotylai or kotyle-pyxides. There appears to be no parallel for either the rendering of the siren or for the rosette in the lower frieze. The decoration above the band of (a) cannot be determined.

MC, Early (?)

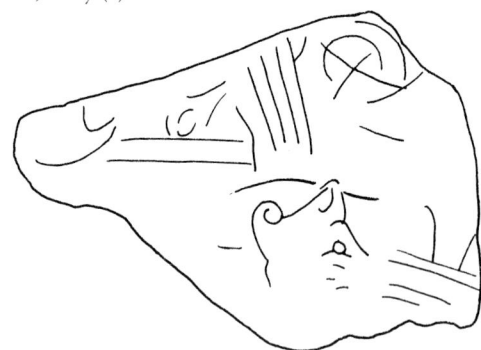

*Illustration 4 (**111**)*

111 Pl. 20; Ill. 4 Sb. 80–2   D12/13 A 3 East
Body fragment from a kotyle or kotyle-pyxis (?). Light green clay. Glaze gone. Surface very worn and slightly encrusted.
MPH: 0.032; MPW: 0.045; Th: 0.006
Fragment preserves sections of two friezes divided by a narrow band. Upper frieze: tail feathers of bird to l. (?); f.o. of incised crisscross rosette, and traces of dots. Lower frieze: head of siren to r.; part of floral complex, slightly tilted. Incised lines on siren indicate top of head, fillet, hair on forehead, ear, brow, eye, and profile of nose.[245]

---

241. As noted above, 2 of these may belong to 1 kotyle.

242. There are, in addition, a number of rim fragments, which may belong to black-figure kotylai.

243. D12/13, B, 4 (1 rim, 2 body fragments), D12/13, A, 3 (6 body fragments), D12/13, A, 4 (10 body fragments), E11/12, Pit Area (2 body fragments), D12/E12, D, 3 (body fragment), D12/13, F, 3, including burnt section (6 body fragments), D13/E13, 1, 4 (1 body fragment with a bird), and C13/D13, 1,

4 (rim fragment with a lotus-and-bud chain in the handle-zone).

244. Added red on an occasional petal of a double-centered rosette, but in the main frieze, occurs on an EC kotyle from Perachora (*Perachora* II, pl. 98, 2438).

245. Cf. *NC*, 102, fig. 35d, dated MC, for similar rendering of features.

Judging from the thickness of the fabric (0.006), the fragment belongs to a rather large kotyle, perhaps a kotyle-pyxis, which would offer a sufficient surface for having the decoration divided into two registers.[246] The kotyle pyxis is not only an early shape, but a relatively rare shape.[247] Moreover, two-zone animal frieze decoration is also uncommon on Corinthian kotylai.[248]

This fragment was found in a largely undisturbed archaic level (see below **112**, **113**).

MC (?)

112   Pl. 20; Ill. 5   Sb. 80–1   D12/13 A 3 East
Body fragment. Light green clay. Glaze gone. Surface very worn and slightly encrusted.
MPH: 0.061; MPW: 0.05; Th: 0.0058
A.f.: outspread wing of avian. Two sets of vertical incisions and two horizontal incisions at far l. below the wing. These are possibly tail markings, in which case the wing would appear to slightly overlap the tail, an uncommon rendering. F.o. of incised rosette to l. of wing.

This and the preceding fragment, both found in the same largely undisturbed archaic level, may belong to one kotyle.
MC (?)

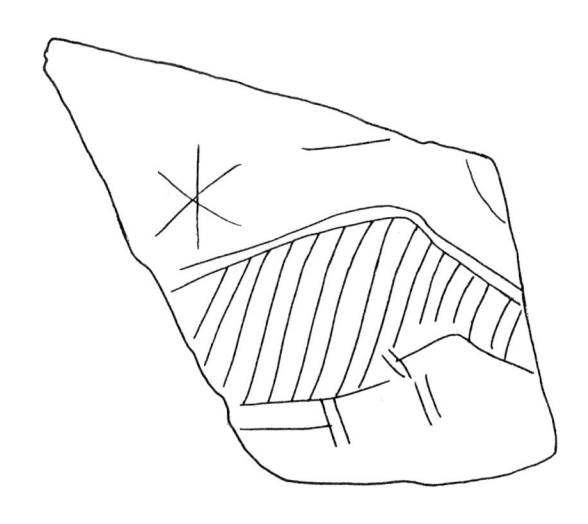

*Illustration 5 (**112**)*

113   Pl. 20; Ill. 6 Sb. 81–1   D12/13 A 2
Rim and body fragment. Light green clay. Glaze gone. Rim chipped. Surface very worn and slightly encrusted.
MPH: 0.089; MPW: 0.0753; Th: 0.007
Very slight trace of band at rim and just below it. Lotus-palmette chain, alternately reversed, with band below.
A.f.: grazing goat to l., with shoulder, rib, and haunch-markings as well as two short arcs at rear of back preserved. F.o. of incised rosettes and incised filler. Band below frieze. Another frieze is indicated by an incised curved line in the lower-right corner of the fragment.

The possibility cannot be excluded that this and the two preceding fragments come from the same large kotyle, given their find spots, fabric, and state of preservation. The closest parallel for our lotus-and-palmette chain appears on a MC kotyle from Perachora (*Perachora* II, no. 2481,b, pls. 102, 110).
MC (?)

*Illustration 6 (**113**)*

114   Pl. 20   Sb. 300–1   D13/E13 Balk 3
                                           South of Back Wall
Rim fragment. Light gray clay. Glaze gone except for a few tiny patches. Burnt and encrusted.
MPH: 0.032; MPW: 0.0366
Band (?) at rim. Chain of lotus and palmette, alternately reversed. On interior, flaking and worn black glaze. The florals are solid and compact. Although not an exact parallel, for the type, see the rim decoration on a MC kotyle in *Corinth* XV:3, pl. 29, no. 604.
MC

115   Pl. 20; Ill. 7 Sb. 130   D12/E12 D 3
Rim and upper body fragment. Light green clay. Glaze almost gone. Slightly chipped rim. Very heavily encrusted.
MPH: 0.0554; MPW: 0.085
Band of vertical wavy lines in handle-zone with two bands below. A.f.: panther to l., head, neck, upper body, and end of tail preserved. F.o. of incised rosettes, incised blobs, and dot. On the interior, unidentifiable bands at rim.

The face of the panther is rather well drawn, with incisions to indicate the facial whiskers. The shoulder and rib markings are also incised. The fragment belongs to a

---

246. For examples, see *Perachora* II, no. 2589 (dated EC), pl. 95, where a heraldic composition with floral ornament between also occurs in the lower frieze; *Corinth* XV:3, no. 370, pl. 19.

247. Hopper, 224; *Perachora* II, 268–269.

248. For EC examples, see *Perachora* I, pl. 27, 5 (by the Duel Painter), and *Corinth* XV:3, pl. 18, 345; for an MC kotylai with double frieze, see LoPorto, figs. 111c, 115.

*Illustration 7 (**115**)*

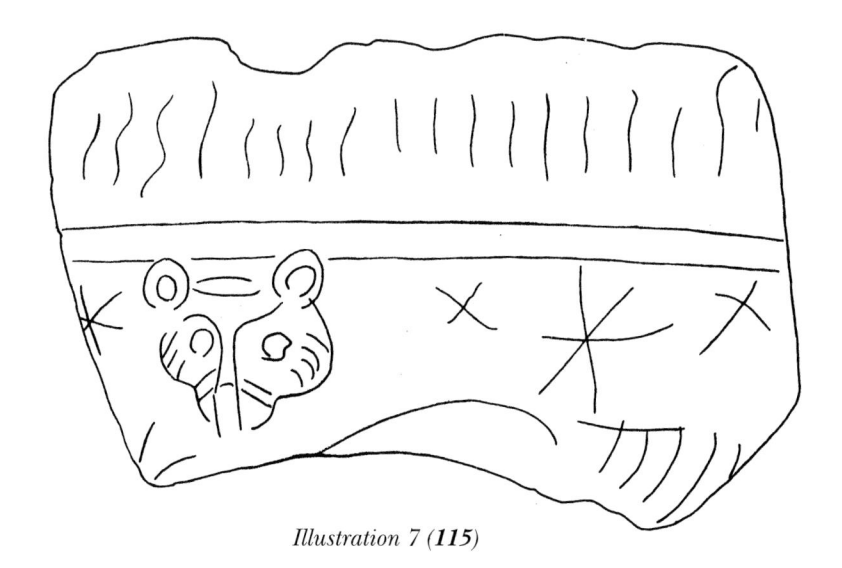

large kotyle of common type and style during the MC period,[249] which, however, is not well represented at the sanctuary. Only two other such fragments were identifiable with certainty as belonging to this type of black-figure kotyle,[250] although there were a significant number of rim fragments with vertical stripes in the handle-zone.

This fragment was found in a largely undisturbed archaic level.

MC

116   Pl. 20   Sb. 520–8   F14/G14 1 3
Body fragment. Chalky gray to light blue clay. Black glaze gone in a.f. and crazed in the dot band, where thickly applied. Burnt.
MPH: 0.0402; MPW: 0.043
Triple-dot band with band above and below. Band above frieze. A.f.: rear of goat to l., shadow of haunch and tail preserved. F.o. of double-centered incised rosette. On interior: thin black glaze.
Dot bands below the rim band are often found on EC and MC kotylai. More common, however, are double-dot bands, especially during the MC period,[251] rather than the triple-dot band on our example. In fact, most published examples with a triple-dot band are EC.[252] Exceptions include a MC kotyle-pyxis from Corinth (*Corinth* XV:3, no. 635, pl. 30) and a kotyle by the Giessen Painter (*CorVP*, pl. 71).
MC

117   Pl. 21   Sb. 210–6   E12/13 E 2
Body fragment. Creamy buff clay. Worn black glaze, fugitive on interior. Added purple. Soil-stained.

MPH: 0.05; MPW: 0.045
A.f.: Foreleg(s?) of unidentified creature to l., possibly a seated sphinx. F.o. of blob and large centered incised rosette. Red and traces of black band below frieze. Double-dot band with red and glazed band below. Tip of ray.
The rosette is unusually large and recalls, though its center is not double incised, the rosette of **110**.[253] Also, the preserved subsidiary decoration of double-dot band[254] and the apparently rather widely spaced rays suggest an MC date for this large kotyle.
MC ?

118   Pl. 21   Sb. 288–21   F13/G13 1 2
Body fragment. Buff clay. Firm black glaze, brown where dilute, but flaking on interior.
MPH: 0.044; MPW: 0.045
Part of double-dot band. Black band above frieze. A.f.: torso of quadruped (panther?) to l., shoulder and rib markings preserved. F.o. in a pattern of centered rosette alternating with two superimposed black dots.
The unusual symmetrical arrangement of the f.o. is in some way reminiscent of the MC rosette kotyle.[255]
MC ?

119   Pl. 21   Sb. 421–1   F13/G13 2 2
Rim fragment of a large kotyle. Buff clay. Black glaze, mostly worn. Added red. Surface worn and soil-stained. Mended from two joins.
MPH: 0.0536; MPW: 0.1155; Est D: 0.26
Band at rim. Lotus-and-bud chain in handle-zone.[256] Added red on buds and central leaf of lotus. Glazed and red

---

249. See the comment by Amyx in *Corinth* VII:2, 36, no. 111.

250. One was found in D12/E12, D Around the Polygonal Wall, the other in F13/G13, Wall Test.

251. For example, see *Perachora* II, nos. 2471–2472, pl. 100; *CVA* Heidelberg, 1, pl. 16, 1–3; *Corinth.* XV:3, no. 533, pl. 26, no. 586, pl. 28; *Corinth* VII:2, no. 104, pl. 17, no. 116, pl. 18, no. 127, pl. 19. For an LC example, see *Perachora* II, no. 2509, pl. 105.

252. As in *Corinth* VII:1, no. 189, pl. 27; *Corinth* XV:3, no. 342, pl. 18, no. 364, pl. 19; *Corinth* XIII, 159–5, pl. 83, p. 105 ("a survival of an Early Corinthian type").

253. For a similarly large rosette on an MC kotyle, see *Corinth*

XV:3, no. 552, pl. 27.

254. Cf. *Perachora* II, no. 2472, pl. 100; *Corinth* XV:3, no. 533, pl. 26 and no. 586, pl. 28.

255. See *Corinth* XV:3, pl. 26, nos. 526–528a, and *Perachora* II, no. 2495, pl. 100, where the rosettes are much more carefully incised.

256. A total of 21 similar fragments were found, two of which were found in largely undisturbed archaic levels (C13/D13, 1, 4; C13/D13, 1, 5): 3 in Area 1, 1, 3; 1 in E11, 2, 2; 1 in F16, 2, 2; 1 in D11/E11, balk, 2; 1 in C15/16, 1, 3, tank; 2 in C15/16, 1, 4, tank; 1 in C15/D15, 1–B, 4; 1 in F11, 2, 3; 3 in F13/G13, 1, 2; 3 in F13/G13, 2, 2; 1 in C13/D13, 1, 4; 1 in C13/D13, 1, 5; 1 in E16, 1, 3; and 1 in F14/G14, 1, Test 2.

band below. Double-dot band. Thin black-and-red band. A.f.: two incised rosettes and black dot. On interior: red band at rim, reserved line, red line, and remainder covered with black glaze.

For a similar example, see *Corinth* XV:3, no. 629, pl. 29, dated MC.[257]

MC

120   Pl. 21   Sb. 288–3a,b   F13/G13   1   2

Two rim fragments (a, b) from a large kotyle. Light gray clay with buff surface. Black glaze unevenly worn. Added red worn. Surface worn and soil-stained.

(a) MPH: 0.0476; MPW: 0.0484
(b) MPH: 0.0745; MPW: 0.07

(a) Preserves part of rim and loop handle. Same subsidiary decoration as (b).

(b) Band at rim. Lotus-and-bud chain in handle-zone. Added red on buds and central leaf of lotus. Black band. Double-dot band. Glaze worn off on band above frieze. A.f.: part of head of panther to r., part of unidentified winged creature to r. F.o. of dots (only shadows) and incised blobs. On interior: red band at rim, reserved line, bands of red, black, red, and remainder black.

Similar to preceding.

MC

121   Pl. 21   Sb. 198–2a,b   F12   2

Two rim fragments (a, b) of a large kotyle. Light greenish clay. Mostly fugitive black glaze on exterior, thin and flaking on interior. Added red preserved only on interior of (a) and (b). Surface worn and encrusted.

(a) MPH: 0.0712; MPW: 0.13; Est D: 0.25
(b) MPH: 0.0425; MPW: 0.034; Est D: 0.25

Mended from three joins, (a) preserves about one-eighth of rim. Originally, band at rim. Lotus-and-bud chain in handle-zone with band below. Double-dot band. Two bands. A.f.: part of elongated quadruped to l., upper part of back and tail preserved; panther to l., head, neck, and part of shoulder marking preserved. F.o. of incised rosette, incised blobs, and dots. Face of panther carelessly drawn and lopsided. On interior: red band below rim, reserved band, red overpainted (?) band, and thin black glaze.

Rim fragment (b) is severely worn and encrusted, with only small patches of black glaze preserved in the lotus-and-bud chain in the handle-zone. On interior: trace of red band at rim.

Similar to the preceding two examples.

MC

122   Pl. 21   Sb. 422–4   F13/G13   2   2

Fragment, preserving part of rim, root of loop handle, and part of body. Light gray clay with slight greenish tinge. Surface not carefully smoothed. Black glaze mostly worn. Fragment burnt. Mended from two joins.

MPH: 0.084; MPW: 0.073

Vertical stripes, bordered by black band above and below, in handle-zone. Band above frieze. A.f.: goat to r., head, horns, neck, part of shoulder and forelegs extant; head of panther to l., about half preserved. F.o. of incised rosette, incised filler (above neck of goat), and blobs. Band below frieze. Trace of rays. On interior: flaking black glaze. Rather sloppy workmanship.

Kotylai with routine animal friezes which included goats and panthers were particularly common in the MC period. Though from a larger kotyle, our fragment recalls *Perachora* II, no. 2514, pl. 101, dated LC.

MC/LC

123   Pl. 22   Sb. 83–1   D12/13   A   3 West

Fragment, preserving part of rim and body. Clay ranges from deep buff to light gray. Black glaze ranges from metallic to an olive-green, and worn off in top half of fragment. Added red. Mended from two joins. Soil-stained and encrusted.

MPH: 0.057; MPW: 0.091; Est D: 0.16

Red band just below rim. A.f.: siren with raised sickle-shaped wing to r.; avian to r., only wings preserved. F.o. of incised elongated fillers or "shaded" rosettes[258] and blobs. Added red on wing section of siren and on interior top section of wing of avian. On interior: flaking black glaze.

The siren's hair ends in an incised scalloped line and incisions mark the siren's fillet, hair, brow, and eye. The feathers of the siren's wings are not quite the norm in having an incised curved and contoured end.[259] The drawing of the avian's wings is rather unusual in not being symmetrical;[260] in the straight horizontal line of the l. wing, which, as a result, appears to overlap the r. wing; and in the straight verticality of the incisions marking the divisions of the l. wing. The fragment belongs to the group of somewhat less common kotylai with a large broad frieze and no decoration in the handle-zone, known in the EC,[261] MC,[262] and LC I periods,[263] but there seems to be no exact parallel for our fragment either in style or composition. A kotyle of the same type from Tocra is decorated with three sirens, but the style is very different.[264] The f.o. with its parallel incisions shows a resemblance to that on the kotylai by the Patras and C-47 Painter, though this type of "shaded" rosette or filler occurs on other MC vases, more often with diagonal incisions

This fragment was found in a largely undisturbed archaic level.

MC/LC

124   Pl. 22   Sb. 32–1   D13 (Area 2)   2   3

Fragment, preserving less than one-quarter of rim, part of body, and root of loop handle. Light yellow-green clay, grayish green in handle, which appears burnt. Black glaze

---

257. For the lotus-and-bud chain, see also *Mégara Hyblaea*, pl. 53, an MC kotyle.

258. This is a term used by Amyx; see *Corinth* VII:2, 36, no. 108, pl. 17.

259. This type of incision also appears on the wing of a sphinx on three EC kotylai (*Perachora* II, nos. 2436 and 2437a, pl. 98, no. 2445, pl. 100) and an MC kotyle (*Perachora* II, no. 2471, pl. 100); and on the wings of some of the avians on vases attributed to the Dodwell Painter, e.g., *Corinth* VII:2, pl. 29, 166a (sickle-shaped wing of siren), and *CSCA* 4 (1971), pl. 4, 1 (siren with raised wing on l.). For other examples painted by a yet unnamed artist, see the sphinxes with sickle-shaped wings on the shoulder on a broad-bottomed oinochoe (EC/MC) in *Greek Vase-Painting in Midwestern Collections*, no. 15 on p. 25, and also the siren on an MC kylix in *Corinth* XV:3, no. 648, pl. 30.

260. For a somewhat similar rendering, see the wings of the griffin on a kylix in *Corinth* XIII, pl. 30, 44–b, and those of a bird on a kylix, pl. 84, 157–c.

261. For some EC examples, see *Corinth* VII:2, pl. 102, An 129 and 102.

262. For some MC examples, see *Corinth* VII:2, An 66 (where it is stated that "this syntax is canonical for kotylai with large, 'monumental' animals"), pls. 66 and 90; *Corinth* XV:3, pl. 28, no. 593, and pl. 29, nos. 606, 607, 610 (all attributed to the Patras Painter).

263. See *Corinth* VII:2, pl. 39, 209.

264. *Tocra* I, no. 337, pl. 24, fig. 27.

worn and flaking, ranges to brown, and crazed where thick. Mended from two joins.
MPH: 0.03; MPW: 0.0666; Est D: 0.10
Band at rim. A.f.: swan to r., with folded wing. F.o. of palmette-like filler (top part preserved), blobs, and dots. Added red on wing section. On interior: glaze worn and gray. Double incised circle for the eye of the swan and two curved arcs on neck.
This fragment also belongs to the type of kotyle with no decoration in the handle-zone and a broad frieze on the body. A somewhat similar swan with dot f.o. in the space between the head and neck, though with only two dots, appears on a kotyle with handle-zone decoration from Perachora.[265]
MC/LC (?)

125 Pl. 22 Sb. 78bis–1 D12/13 A 4
Between rubble walls
Body fragment. Grayish buff clay. Black glaze fired mostly brown.
MPH: 0.037; MPW: 0.027
A.f.: feline to l., rear leg preserved; avian to r., part of tail preserved. F.o. of incised blob rosette. Two thin bands below frieze. Thin and closely set rays below. On interior: glaze worn and ranges from brown to a pale red.
This fragment was found in a largely undisturbed archaic level.
MC/LC

126 Pl. 22 Sb. 210–3 E12/13 E 2
Body fragment. Pale buff clay. Black glaze somewhat worn, brown where thick, and crazed where thick. Added red. Mended from two joins. Surface soil-stained.
MPH: 0.038; MPW: 0.0516
A.f.: bird to r., with head, neck, and part of wing preserved; feline (probably panther) to r., hindquarter preserved. F.o. of incised blobs and dots. Added red on wing. Traces of two bands below frieze. Rays not preserved.
For the type, but without f.o., see *Tocra* II, pl. 6, no. 1885.
Probably LC

127 Pl. 22 Sb. 210–2 E12/13 E 2
Body fragment. Grayish clay with deep buff surface. Dull black glaze worn. Added red. Apparently burnt.
MPH: 0.0315; MPW: 0.0313
A.f.: lower part of bird to l.; f.o. of dots and blob. Added red on wing sections. Band below frieze. On interior: flaking, grayish black glaze.
The bird appears to be "floating," since its feet are above the f.o. and the band. This strange positioning is occasionally seen on kotylai in the silhouette style.[266]
LC

128 Pl. 22 Sb. 520–7 F14/G14 1 3
Body fragment. Light grayish clay. Worn black glaze. Added red.
MPH: 0.076; MPW: 0.0338
A.f.: feline, probably panther to l., forelegs preserved. F.o. of dots and incised blob. Black and red banding below frieze (bbBRBRbb). Shadow of one ray. On interior: black to brown glaze.
The numerous painted bands between the frieze and rays seem to suggest a late date.[267]
LC

SILHOUETTE STYLE

Kotylai in the silhouette style were relatively uncommon at the sanctuary. In our catalog, there are 11 examples of kotylai with silhouette animals, which range in date from MC to the early LC I period. The fragments fall into two groups: relatively small kotylai, averaging about 7–8 cm. in height, and miniatures. The former group includes two MC pieces (**129**, **130**) with a frieze of well-formed "running dogs" and dot filling ornament; a body fragment (**131**), probably MC/LC, with a frieze between two red bands containing goats and a bird as well as "hailstorm" filling ornament; and another MC/LC body fragment (**132**) with the elongated body of a goat between two broad red bands and no filling ornament. **133** with its unusual foot may belong to either a silhouette or a black-figure kotyle.

Six of our examples are miniatures (**134–139**), datable to the MC or MC/LC period. This type is characterized by vertical stripes in the handle-zone, a frieze of "running dogs" with no filling ornament, two bounding lines above the frieze, a band below the frieze, and a glazed foot.[268] The most complete piece of this group, though its surface is encrusted, is **134**, which has the band of vertical stripes in the handle-zone, a rare patch of red on the haunch of the running dog, and a bounding line below the frieze.[269]

The uncatalogued silhouette-style fragments, almost exclusively body fragments, retained from the sanctuary totaled 36: three have hailstorm filling ornament and 24 are miniatures with "running dogs." Over 60% of all the retained finds, both catalogued and uncatalogued, in the silhouette style belong to miniatures decorated with "running dogs."[270]

With two exceptions,[271] our catalogued finds are from the backfill of the middle sanctuary retaining wall.[272] Among the uncatalogued finds, six fragments, four of them miniatures, were found in largely undisturbed levels.[273] Two fragments, one with hailstorm

---

265. *Perachora* II, no. 2474, pl. 101, dated MC or later.

266. E.g., see *Perachora* II, pl. 101, no. 2371, but without f.o. beneath the feet; *Corinth* XV:3, pl. 53, no. 1289.

267. Cf. *Corinth* XV:3, pl. 41, nos. 885a and b, LC II kotyle fragments with a number of red-and-black bands below frieze and widely spaced rays.

268. On the development, see *Tocra* I, 25.

269. Because of the encrustation, bounding line(s) above the frieze cannot be determined.

---

270. For a discussion of the silhouette style, see Hopper, 185–192; *Corinth* XIII, 100.

271. Both (**129**, **133**) were found in E10, balk, 2/3.

272. About half of the uncatalogued sherds were also found here.

273. The findspots are: D12/E12, D, 3 (fragment with hailstorm) and D12/13, F, 3; miniatures were found in E11, 3; E11/12, Pit Area, 3; D12/E12, D, 3; and C13, 1, 4a.

filling ornament, were also found in C13, 1, 4b, an archaic level undisturbed by later intrusions. These can all also be dated to MC/LC period.

Our finds are similar to those found at Tocra, where they are more complete.[274] No recognizable EC kotylai in this style, however, occur at the Demeter Sanctuary at Cyrene.

129 Pl. 22   Sb. 109–2   E10 Balk 2/3
Lower body fragment. Light green clay. Brownish black glaze, crazed where thick, brown where dilute, and gray in bands intersecting the rays. Glaze gone on rays. Added red. Chip on body. Encrusted.
MPH: 0.0427; MPW: 0.0332
A.f.: hindquarter of "running dog" to l.; f.o. of amorphous blob and dot. Red and glazed band below frieze. Thin, close-set rays at base intersected at top by two thin glazed lines. Interior: dull, flaking, and encrusted black glaze.
For a similar type, see *CVA* Louvre, fasc. 8, pl. 27, nos. 1 and 5, and *Corinth* VII:1, pl. 42, no. 341 (MC). From Tocra, see *Tocra* I, pl. 25, no. 356, where there are close-set vertical stripes rather than rays above the base. Our dog,[275] as far as preserved, is not so debased, however, as those in the preceding references.
MC

130 Pl. 22   Sb. 516–10   F14/G14 1 2
Body fragment. Light gray clay. Black glaze mostly gray. Encrusted.
MPH: 0.0307; MPW: 0.0234
Wider black band above frieze and narrower black band below. A.f.: hindquarter of running dog to r.; f.o. of dots. On interior: thin, grayish black glaze.
As in the preceding example, the preserved portion of the dog is rather well formed and recognizable. For a similar type, but with more debased dogs, see *Corinth* VII:1, pl. 42, nos. 339 (without f.o.), 341[276]; and *CVA* Louvre, fasc. 8, pl. 27, nos. 1 and 5.
MC

131 Pl. 23   Sb. 515–4   F14/G14 1 2
Body fragment. Buff clay. Black glaze ranges to dark brown and reddish brown. Added red. Soil-stained.
MPH: 0.0396; MPW: 0.0534
Tips of three vertical lines of handle-zone. Thin band of black and brown below. Broad red band above and below frieze. A.f.: part of goat to r., bird to l., and goat (?) to r. Thick dot or "hailstorm" f.o. with some of the dots extending into the bounding band above and below. Black band below. Tips of base rays extend through the black band and into the red band above. On interior: black glaze with some flaking.
For the type, see *Corinth* XV:3, pl. 53, no. 1286, which is somewhat neater than our example. Such kotylai with crude elongated goats and sometimes an occasional bird are rather common within the group of silhouette-style kotylai. For similar kotylai, also see *Corinth* XIII, pl. 25, nos. 163–1,2, both dated MC; *Tocra* I, pl. 26, nos. 370, 371, 392, dated early LC; and *NC*, fig. 150, no. 966. A parallel for our bird occurs on a pyxis lid from Tocra (*Tocra* II, pl. 4, no. 1869).
MC/LC

132 Pl. 23   Sb. 288–14   F13/G13 1 2
Body fragment. Deep buff clay with pinkish tinge. Black glaze, brown where dilute. Added red. Encrusted.
MPH: 0.047; MPW: 0.046
Broad red band above and broad black band below narrow frieze. A.f.: goat to r., head and neck missing. No f.o. Thin dilute band. On interior: flaking black glaze.
For the type with no f.o., see *Délos* XVII, pl. 58, no. 83,[277] and *Corinth* XV:3, pl. 54, 1316, dated LC I. Our goat, however, has a much heavier form than that on the Corinth kotyle.
MC/LC

133 Pl. 23   Sb. 109–1   E10 Balk 2/3
Fragment, preserving intact foot with beveled edge and part of lower body. Buff clay. Glaze fired from black to brown. Encrusted.
MPH: 0.032; MPW: 0.055; D: 0.045 (base)
Trace of silhouette (?) decoration, feet of either a bird or an animal to l. in the main frieze. Two thin glazed bands. Thin, close-set rays at base, whose tips intersect with the two bands above and extend into the frieze. Very thin black glaze on foot. Underside: very narrow resting surface reserved; inside of foot ring black; concentric black band around bottom; two small concentric rings in center. On interior: swirled glazed ranges from black to brown with minor peeling.
The fragment appears to belong to a kotyle in the silhouette style, but may also be from a black-figured kotyle—too little of the decoration in the frieze is preserved to be certain. There is no known parallel for the profile of the beveled foot with its angular top part and straight-sided bottom part as well as high inner edge.
MC/LC ?

134 Pl. 23; Fig. 1 Sb. 288–6   F13/G13 1 2
Fragment, preserving about one-third rim, wall, complete base, and part of one loop handle of a miniature kotyle. Buff clay. Glaze brown. Added red. Surface worn and encrusted.
H: 0.032; D: 0.0238 (base); Est D: 0.06 (rim)
Vertical lines in handle-zone. A.f.: runnings dogs to r., leg and head of one dog and most of body of second dog preserved. Patch of added red on dog's haunch. Black band below frieze. Brown paint on foot. On underside: small raised disk in center. On interior: unevenly applied glaze, ranging from black to brown.
For the type, see *Tocra* I, pl. 25, no. 352, dated MC?; *Corinth* XIII, pl. 28, nos. 182–1,2[278]; *Corinth* XV:3, pl. 53, no. 1290 (probably MC); *MA* 32, pl. 87, 9.[279] All these examples, however, have two double lines above the frieze. For an example with no bounding lines above the frieze, see Stucchi, *L'Agorà di Cirene*, 43, fig. 21d, pl. XII, 8. The surface of our fragment is too heavily worn and encrusted to show any indication of such bounding lines above the frieze. Our fragment is unusual in having the patch of red on the dog's haunch. There is generally no use of added red in this group of miniature running dog kotylai. The disk on the bottom also occurs on a slightly larger kotyle in *Corinth* XV:3, 232, pl. 53, no. 1278, dated MC, which, however, has rays around the base.
MC

---

274. *Tocra* I, 25, 29, pl. 25–26.

275. Cf. the running dog on an EC kotyle in *Perachora* II, pl. 99, no. 2459.

276. In the catalog, p. 78, no. 340 actually refers to no. 339 on pl. 42.

277. Dated MC by Hopper, 189.

278. From a grave dated to the late first or early second quarter of the sixth century (p. 195); see also p. 105.

279. Hopper, 186 dates the Selinous kotyle to MC.

135   Pl. 23   Sb. 418–5   F13/G13 2 2
Fragment, preserving complete base and part of lower body, from a miniature kotyle. Buff clay. Glaze fired brown and worn.
MPH: 0.019; MPW: 0.039; D: 0.024 (base)
Part of running dog to r. Traces of two bands below frieze and glaze on foot. Small raised disk in center of bottom. Glaze worn on interior.
Similar to preceding.
MC

136   Pl. 23   Sb. 501–3   F14/G14 1 Test, St 1 mixed with some St 2
Fragment from a miniature kotyle, preserving about one-half of base and part of lower body wall. Creamy buff clay. Black glaze ranges to a brown and dull gray. Glaze crazed where black and worn off on the two horizontal bands. Encrusted.
MPH: 0.0174; MPW: 0.0314; D: 0.025 (base)
Part of running dog to r. Traces of two horizontal bands below frieze. On interior: flaking black glaze.
Similar to preceding
MC

137   Pl. 23   Sb. 536–6   F12/G12 1 2
Fragment from a miniature kotyle, preserving less than one-half of base with foot ring and part of lower body wall. Deep buff clay. Dull crazed black glaze, brown where dilute. Slightly encrusted.
MPH: 0.0264; MPW: 0.0357; D: 0.0217 (base)
Parts of two running dogs to r. One thin band below frieze and another above foot. Black glaze on foot ring. Small raised disk in center of bottom. Glaze worn on interior.
This fragment differs from the preceding in having slightly flaring foot ring.
MC

138   Pl. 24   Sb. 528–8   F12/G12 Tunnel A
Fragment from a miniature kotyle, preserving less than one-half of base with foot ring and part of lower body wall. Pale buff clay. Crazed and flaking black glaze, brown where dilute. Surface not smoothed.
MPH: 0.0297; MPW: 0.0459; D: 0.0218 (base)
Parts of two running dogs to r. Band below frieze. Band above small spreading ring foot. On interior: flaking and thinly applied black glaze.
Similar to preceding except for lack of raised disk in center of bottom.
MC

139   Pl. 24   Sb. 421–6   F13/G13 2 2
Rim and body fragment from a miniature kotyle. Pale buff clay. Black glaze crazed on dog and worn on rim. Surface worn and encrusted.
MPH: 0.018; MPW: 0.033; Est D: 0.06 (rim)
Vertical stripes in handle zone. A.f: running dog to r., torso and part of haunch preserved. On interior: flaking dark bluish-gray glaze.
MC

CONVENTIONALIZING

Kotylai in the "conventionalizing" style are the least frequent of all the types of this shape. The four fragments in this section belong to a group with floral decoration, known as lotus kotylai.[280] The body frieze on these large kotylai (**140–143**) contains a lotus-and-bud chain or a bud chain, with no trace of incision in the florals.[281] Among the uncatalogued finds, only seven[282] other fragments could be attributed to this type of kotyle, one of which was found in a largely undisturbed archaic level (D12/13, F, 4).

140   Pl. 24   Sb. 520–6   F14/G14 1 3 and
                                F14/G14 1 Test 2
Rim fragment from a large kotyle. Buff clay. Flaking and worn black glaze. Added red worn. Mended from three joining fragments: one (l. fragment) found in F14/G14, 1, 3; the other two in F14/G14, 1, Test 2. Soil-stained and encrusted.
MPH: 0.0408; MPW: 0.1018; Est D: 0.19
Red band at lip. Black vertical wavy lines in handle-zone. Black band and traces of two red (?) bands below. In frieze: lotus-and-bud chain, only one black lotus and one bud visible, shadows of others. Traces of added red on bud. No evidence of incision preserved on the extant flower. On interior: red band at lip; remainder black.
This fragment belongs to a common LC type, known as lotus kotylai. For the type, see *Tocra* II, pl. 7, no. 1895.
LC II

141   Pl. 24   Sb. 536–4   F12/G12 1 2
Fragment from a large lotus kotyle, preserving about one-fifth of rim, part of upper body, and part of loop handle. Rim chipped. Dark buff clay. Glaze-fired black to red on exterior and black on interior with some flaking and brown where dilute. Added red. Encrusted.
MPH: 0.0555; MPW: 0.0868 Est D: 0.20
Red line just below rim. Vertical wavy lines in handle-zone. Alternating black, red, black lines. In frieze: lotus-and-bud chain. Added red on buds and in centers of lotus flowers. No trace of incision. On interior: red line at rim, reserved band, and traces of red band; rest uneven black glaze.
Similar to preceding.
LC II

142   Pl. 24   Sb. 520–9   F14/G14 1 3
Fragment from a large kotyle, preserving part of rim and complete loop handle. Buff clay. Flaking black glaze, brown where dilute. Added red. Encrusted.
MPH: 0.038; MPW: 0.073; Est D: 0.20
Red band at rim. Black glaze on handle to within 0.025 of root. Black band below handle-zone whose decoration is not preserved. Red band. In frieze: bud chain (tips of two buds preserved), apparently alternating red and black.

---

280. See *Corinth* XV:3, 172; *NC*, 334, no. 1516, fig. 180, LC II.

281. **144** with a net pattern may also, in fact, belong to a conventionalizing kotyle (see below).

282. One each was found in C15/16, 1, W-4, Area 4; D12/13, F, 4; D14/E14, 2, 2; F13/G13, 2, 2; and F14/G14, 1, 2; 2 were found in F13/G13, 1, 2.

Added red on one bud. On interior: reserved band at rim, red band, remainder thin and flaking black glaze.

This is another example of the group of lotus kotyle, bearing a variant of the floral decoration: a bud chain. For other examples, see *Perachora* II, pl. 114, nos. 2668–9; *Tocra* II, pl. 7, no. 1896.

LC II

143   Pl. 24   Sb. 516–25   F14/G14 1 2
Body fragment from a large kotyle. Buff clay. Black glaze, brown where dilute. Added red. Soil-stained.
MPH: 0.018; MPW: 0.051
In frieze: dilute interlacing stems connecting buds or lotus-and-buds. Red and black band below. On interior: flaked black glaze.
Similar to preceding examples.
LC II

LINEAR STYLE

In our catalog, there are 14 examples of linear-style kotylai, including those of large, standard, and small size. All the fragments date to the LC II period, and those of the small kotylai continue into the early part of the LC III period. The pieces, though predominantly fragmentary, nonetheless, represent the best-preserved examples of kotylai in this style from the sanctuary.

Presumably, the linear-style kotylai constituted the largest of the five different stylistic types of kotylai from the sanctuary; this cannot, however, be firmly substantiated on the basis of our finds because of their very poor state of preservation. Among the mass of uncatalogued finds from the sanctuary, the linear-style kotylai of standard size were difficult to identify with certainty, especially when the sherds preserved only the subsidiary decoration, e.g., vertical stripes in the handle-zone or rays above the base.[283] Undoubtedly, a significant portion of these unassignable kotyle sherds (about 800 fragments) belong to this group of linear-style kotylai; the number of clearly recognizable, attributable fragments, however, number less than 60.[284] Owing to a better state of preservation, the small linear-style kotylai, probably votive in character, were easier to identify. In addition to the examples in the catalog, some 275 fragments of small kotylai were retained from the excavations, 66% of which were bases.[285] The bottoms of the bases vary: some have small or large, often reserved, raised disks in the center, while others are flat and decorated with concentric rings.

The miniature votive kotylai are treated in a separate section. The distinction between some of the small kotylai and the miniatures is often difficult to make. Often it is an arbitrary decision,[286] based on height.[287] In our catalog, kotylai under 4 cm. are considered miniatures.

The catalog contains one large LC II rim fragment (**144**), which may belong to a conventionalizing kotyle, that has an unusual net pattern in the handle-zone. The five standard-size kotyle fragments (**145–149**) are also LC II. They are representative of a common type, which also occurs in a smaller size, with various patterns in the handle-zone and banding on the body. Two fragments (**145**, **146**) have a row of buds in the handle-zone, while two others (**148**, **149**) have alternately inverted cones in the handle-zone. Of particular interest is the base fragment (**147**) with alternately inverted stepped cones in a band above the base and elaborate decoration on the underside of the foot.

The eight small kotylai (**150–157**) are mostly LC II/III. With the exception of **150**, a body fragment reminiscent of the white style, they all also belong to the very common type with patterns, such as vertical stripes (**156**) or horizontal zigzags (**151**, **152**, **157**), in the handle-zone and banding on the body (broad red-and-black bands or broad black bands alternating with horizontal stripes).

The majority of our catalogued pieces come from the backfill of the middle sanctuary retaining wall. Notably, however, two of the small kotylai (**156**, **157**), one (**156**) of which is the best-preserved kotyle from the sanctuary, were found in an undisturbed archaic level (F14/G14, 1, 4). A similar fragment, though burnt, was found in F14/G14, 1, 5, also an undisturbed archaic level. Although fragments of kotylai in the largely undisturbed archaic levels were quite numerous, it was not possible to definitely assign these fragments to linear-style kotylai.

144   Pl. 24   Sb. 288–15   F13/G13 1 2
Rim fragment from a large kotyle. Buff clay. Black glaze, fired mostly red on interior. Added red (purple). Soil-stained.
MPH: 0.0392; MPW: 0.036
Red band at rim. In handle zone, net pattern formed by diagonal lines in dilute glaze with alternating large black and small red dots at intersections and small red dots in the small triangular spaces at the top and bottom of the band. Overpainted red band below. On interior: reserved line at rim, overpainted red band, remainder unevenly fired black glaze.
The net pattern is an uncommon and late motif in the handle-zone of kotylai.[288] For examples similar to ours, see

---

283. Such fragments could equally be assigned to black-figure kotylai.

284. Most of these (33) are body sherds; the rest are rim-body fragments and four bases.

285. See *supra* n.235 for a numerical breakdown.

286. See Benson's comments in *Corinth* XV:3, 309 and *Perachora* II, 290.

287. In *Corinth* XIII, for example, vases under 3 cm. in height are considered miniatures.

288. See *Perachora* II, 277 comment under no. 2682.

Perachora II, pl. 114, no. 2682; *Corinth* XV:3, pl. 41, nos. 886a and 903 (a lotus kotyle),[289] all of which, however, lack the additional red dot at the intersection of the diagonal lines.
LC II

145 Pl. 24   Sb. 516–5   F14/G14 1 2
Fragment from a standard-size kotyle, preserving over one-quarter of rim and complete loop handle. Buff clay with orange core. Worn and unevenly fired glaze ranges from black to red to reddish brown. Added red. Encrusted. Soil-stained.
MPH: 0.032; MPW: 0.068 (without handles); Est D: 0.095
Band at lip. Alternating glazed and red buds in handle-zone. Thin band below. Broad band. On interior: trace of band at rim and flaking black glaze, unevenly fired.
This fragment belongs to a common LC group of kotylai with buds in the handle-zone.[290] For this type, which often tends to be smaller in size than our example, see *CVA* Heidelberg I, pl. 16, 6; *Corinth* XIII, pl. 34, no. 257–5, but with black buds only and said to be unusually large (H: 0.08, D: 0.099); and *Corinth* XV:3, pl. 44, no. 999,[291] a smaller example.
LC II

146 Pl. 24   Sb. 85   F10 and F14 Along NW edge of Terrace 3/4 below line of railroad
Fragment from a smaller standard-size kotyle, preserving part of chipped rim and body. Buff clay. Black glaze adheres well, brown where dilute. Added red.
MPH: 0.045; MPW: 0.039
Band at rim. Band of black buds in handle-zone. Thin band below. Bands on body (BbrBrB). On interior: black glaze.
Similar to preceding, but smaller size and all black buds.[292]
LC II

147 Pl. 24; Fig. 1 Sb. 420–2   F13/G13 2 2N
Fragment from a standard-size kotyle, preserving part of lower body and base. Buff clay with gray core. Black glaze slightly worn on foot, firm on interior, and on exterior ranges from black to dark brown where dilute. Added red. Mended from three joining fragments of which the far l. was found in F13/G13, Wall Test.
MPH: 0.022; MPW: 0.072; D: 0.0566 (base)
On body: black and red bands; band of alternately inverted stepped cones. The tops of the some of the cones protrude into the red band above. Black glaze on spreading foot ring. Underside: black glaze on rounded resting surface and inside of foot; reserved band; circle of black dots between two concentric red lines; whirligig in center. On interior: firm black glaze.
The alternately inverted stepped cone, or "Antiparos pattern," is a favorite LC motif on linear-style vases. A kotyle from Corinth has such a pattern above the base.[293] Whirligigs on the bottom of kotylai are also known in the LC period.[294] A fragmentary LC kotyle base from Perachora (*Perachora* II, pl. 113, no. 2661) has a similar decorative scheme on the underside with a row of dots but with a rosette rather than a whirligig in the center.
LC II

148 Pl. 25   Sb. 536–3   F12/G12 1 2
Rim fragment. Pale buff clay. Black glaze with some flaking, brown where thin. Added red.
MPH: 0.0314; MPW: 0.0447; Est D: 0.085
Thin red band at lip, barely visible. Band of alternately inverted cones or triangles in handle-zone. Thin black line below. On body: broad black band, thin brown band, and part of a broad brown band. On interior: trace of red (?) band at lip, rest black.
This fragment belongs to a common LC II kotyle type,[295] which is well represented at the sanctuary, with various patterns, including vertical and horizontal zigzags, in the handle-zone and horizontal bands, often alternating red and black, on the body.[296] For the type, but a smaller version, see *Tocra* II, pl. 7, no. 1900; *Corinth* XV:3, pl. 44, no. 995, p. 187 n.1, where additional bibliography is cited. The kotyle in *Hesperia* 7 (1938), fig. 15, no. 123, while smaller than our kotyle, is perhaps the closest, together with *Délos* XVII, pl. 58, no. 85. A fragment of the same type was also found at Megara Hyblaea.[297]
LC II

149 Pl. 25   Sb. 520–13   F14/G14 1 3
Rim fragment from a small or standard-size kotyle. Buff clay. Glaze ranges from a bluish black to black to brown. Added red worn. Encrusted.
MPH: 0.033; MPW: 0.0343
Alternately inverted cones or triangles in handle-zone. Banding below: thin red, broad brown, broad red, reserved and thin brown. Black interior.
Similar to preceding.
LC II

150 Pl. 25   Sb. 516–17   F13/G13 2 2
Body fragment of a small kotyle, preserving side wall from tip of worn rim to near base. Buff clay. Glaze-fired black to reddish orange. Added red worn. Encrusted.
MPH: 0.0384; MPW: 0.032
Trace of band at lip and one below. Band of unidentified pattern, resembling row of musical notes, possibly sloppily applied vertical squiggles. Band of double-row dicing bounded by band above and below. Narrow red band and trace of another narrow band below. Apparently, large reserved area. Thin band near base. On interior: flaking, barely preserved glaze fired red.
This is a somewhat unusual piece, almost white style in quality. Though on a much smaller scale, it recalls the white-style kotyle in *Corinth* VII:1, pl. 44, no. 367, and *Corinth* VII:2, An 42, pl. 66, particularly in the checker or dou-

---

289. Benson, p. 173, refers to the pattern as a pomegranate net. The lines at the tips of our black dots do not resemble those of a pomegranate.

290. Another such fragment was found in D12/13, F, 2.

291. See additional references on p. 188 under no. 999.

292. Two other identifiable smaller kotyle fragments with this decoration were found in C15/D15, 1–B, 4 and F13/G13, 2, 2.

293. M. T. Campbell, "A Well of the Black-Figured Period at Corinth," *Hesperia* 7 (1938), 592 (where the text seems mistakenly to refer to 127 on fig. 20 as bearing the double row of cones above the base), fig. 20, no. 126.

294. Cf. *Corinth* XV:3, pl. 45, no. 1008, a ray kotyle, but with alternating red and black as well as incised whorls, dated LC III; Campbell, *Hesperia* 7 (1938), 589, fig. 20, also a ray kotyle. In both these examples the whorls are not as numerous as on our example.

295. Another example with cones in the handle-zone was found in F13/G13, 2, 2.

296. See *NC*, 334, fig. 181A; *Corinth* XIII, 105.

297. *Mégara Hyblaea*, pl. 58, 1.

ble-dicing pattern. This double-row dicing or checker pattern is not uncommon on linear-style kotylai. Quite a number of kotylai with this pattern, but more often with a double-dot band, were found in the North Cemetery at Corinth, beginning in EC[298] and continuing through MC[299] and LC.[300] In all of these, however, this pattern occurs between broad bands, with the exception of three kotylai from Grave 172 that are dated to late in the first quarter or perhaps early in the second quarter of the sixth century.[301] In the kotylai from Grave 172, the double-dot band is in the middle of the wall between narrower bands and there are rays at the base. No evidence of rays is preserved on our fragment.
LC II?

151   Pl. 25   Sb. 528–6   F12/G12   Tunnel A
Rim fragment from a small kotyle. Buff to pinkish clay. Glaze-fired red and ranges to a yellowish red in the handle-zone; on exterior body, it ranges from red to black. Added red.
MPH: 0.0387; MPW: 0.0366
Trace of band at lip. Horizontal zigzag in handle-zone with thin band below. On body: broad red band, narrow stripe, broad black band, and stripe. Interior glazed.
Our fragment resembles the kotyle in *Corinth* XIII, pl. 32, 231–1, from a grave that is probably of the third quarter of the sixth century B.C. The type, of course, is a very common one in LC II, occurring in both this small as well as miniature size, and continuing into the early part of the fifth century. The decorative scheme of our fragment is related to Type 4 of the Tocra classification of miniature kotylai, dated to the late sixth-early fifth century.[302] The horizontal zigzag of our example is neater and narrower and belongs to a somewhat larger kotyle.[303]
LC II

152   Pl. 25   Sb. 520–12   F14/G14   1   3
Fragment of a small kotyle, preserving part of rim, body, foot, and roots of loop handle. Pinkish buff clay. Glaze ranges from black to brown to red. Soil-stained.
H: 0.042; MPW: 0.0485; Est D: 0.06
Black band at rim. Horizontal zigzag in handle-zone with black stripe below. On body: two alternating broad and thin black bands. Spreading foot ring. On interior: sloppy black glaze.
Similar to preceding except that the broad bands on the body are both black[304] rather than red and black, the more common scheme.
LC II

153   Pl. 25   Sb. 516–13   F14/G14   1   2
Base fragment of a small kotyle, preserving about three-quarters of the splayed foot ring and part of the adjacent lower body. Pale buff clay. Sloppily applied thin black glaze. Added red. Chips on surface. Encrusted.
MPH: 0.0324; D: 0.0506 (base)
Banding on body: broad red and broad black band and two thin black stripes (RbBb). Red on outside of foot. On underside: red on resting surface of foot; three concentric circles around a central dot. On interior: thin, flaking black glaze.
LC II/III

154   Pl. 25   Sb. 165–2   C15/16   1   4 Tank
Base fragment of a small kotyle, preserving part of foot and adjacent lower body. Buff clay. Black glaze, light brown where dilute. Added red worn. Mended from two joins.
MPH: 0.031; MPW: 0.0527; D: 0.0507 (base)
Red and black horizontal banding on body (rrbBbb). Black on top edge of ring foot, bottom part reserved. On underside: thin concentric glazed band on resting surface of foot; red overpainted band; and large raised central disk with concentric black band.
LC II/III

155   Pl. 25   Sb. 418–6   F13/G13   2   2
Fragment of a small kotyle, preserving most of foot and part of body. Deep buff clay. Black glaze, brown where dilute. Added red worn. Encrusted.
MPH: 0.03; MPW: 0.0445; D: 0.0314 (base;) D: 0.017 (raised disk)
Two broad red and three narrow black bands (RbRbb) on body. On underside: concentric band with reserved raised disk in center.
LC II/III

156   Pl. 25; Fig. 1 Inv. No. 78–421 F14/G14   1   4
Complete small kotyle, few chips on rim. Creamy buff clay. Black glaze almost entirely worn off, only a few patches remain on exterior and around rim of interior. Added red. Soil-stained.
H: 0.04; D: 0.0596 (rim); D: 0.036 (base)
Vertical stripes in handle-zone (visible as a result of staining of reserved surface) with thin band below. Wide red band. Traces of two horizontal lines. Trace of broad black band. Turned foot with beveled bottom edge. Underside of foot slightly concave with central disk. On interior: black glaze mostly disappeared and trace of red overpainted band below rim.
Found in an undisturbed archaic level, this is the best-preserved kotyle from the sanctuary and representative of a very common group of LC II kotylai. For the type, see *NC*, 334, fig. 181B, no. 1517; and for similar examples, see *Délos* XVII, pl. 58, no. 106, as well as *Corinth* XIII, 225, pl. 40, 285–2, dated to the first half of the fifth century. Among the sanctuary finds, only two fragments were clearly of this type of kotyle with vertical stripes: one was found in E10/11 (Area 1), 1, 3, the other, which was burnt, in F14/G14, 1, 5, also an undisturbed archaic level.[305] The steep wall, wide base, and decorative scheme, with the exception of the vertical stripes in the handle-zone, connects it to Type 4 of the Tocra classification of miniature kotyle, dated to the late 6th to early 5th century.[306]
Undoubtedly a votive, the size of this kotyle might place it in the miniature class.
LC II/III

157   Pl. 26   Sb. 525–1   F14/G14   1   4
Fragmentary small kotyle, about one-third preserved. Buff clay. Black glaze almost entirely worn off. Added red. Mended. Soil-stained.
H: 0.04; Est D: 0.06 (rim); D: 0.033 (base)
Horizontal zigzag in handle-zone (visible because of staining of reserved surface) with trace of thin band below.

---

298. *Corinth* XIII, pl. 18, 135–1.

299. *Corinth* XIII, pl. 19, 142b; pl. 20, 156–3; pl. 24, Deposit 4 a–e.

300. *Corinth* XIII, pl. 25, 163a; pl. 33, 224–2.

301. *Corinth* XIII, 191, pl. 26, 172 c–e.

302. *Tocra* II, 9, 14, pl. 7 no. 1942, pl. 8, nos. 1941–1943.

303. At least 2 other such fragments were among the sanctuary finds: one from F13/G13, 2, 2, the other from F14/G14, 1, 3.

304. Another such fragment was found in E10/11 (Area 1), 1, 3.

305. Two other sherds, found in F14/G14, 1, 3, are related.

306. *Tocra* II, 9, pl. 7, 1942; pl. 8, 1941–1943.

Broad red band, black line, broad black band, black line. Low foot with raised central disk on underside.

This fragment, with the exception of the horizontal zigzag in the handle zone,[307] is almost identical to the preceding. Both were found in the same area and stratum, an undisturbed archaic level. Similar fragments were found in D12/13, A, 3 East, a largely undisturbed archaic level.

LC II/III

BLACK-GLAZED

The catalog contains seven examples of the black-glazed kotylai from the site, which range in date from LC I to LC III. The examples, consisting of two fragmentary vases, four bases, and one rim fragment, represent kotylai of Palmer's group ii (**159**) and iii (**160, 161**),[308] ray kotylai (**162**), and at least one semi-glazed skyphos (**164**). Also included are fragments, two of which were found in a largely undisturbed archaic level, of either an early LC black-glazed or a black-figure kotyle (**158**).

Over 250 black-glazed sherds were identified among the finds from the excavation, of which just over 50 were base and/or lower body fragments. Presumably, almost all of these are LC.[309] Because of their fragmentary nature and state of preservation, specific identifications of these uncatalogued sherds were difficult to make. On the whole, the black-glazed kotylai did not constitute a particularly numerous group.

The best preserved of the black-glazed kotylai is **161**, dated to LC II, which was found in a largely undisturbed archaic level (C15/16, 1, 4–2, Area 5). The large base fragment (**162**) with widely spaced rays belongs to a LCII/III ray kotyle. The burnt fragmentary semi-glazed skyphos (**164**) with heavy foot, dating to the second or third quarter of the fifth century, is of particular interest on two counts: (a) this type was almost never exported[310] and (b) it documents the longevity of Corinthian imports, though sparse, into the first half of the fifth century.[311]

Although two (**158, 161**) of our catalogued pieces were found in largely undisturbed archaic levels, nearly 50 other fragments also come from such deposits, with the largest concentration occurring in D12/13, B, 4.[312] Among these uncatalogued fragments, there were 10 lower body sherds with thin rays that apparently belong to Palmer's group ii or iii.[313] In addition, three fragments were found in archaic levels undisturbed by later intrusions: a lower body fragment with widely spaced rays, presumably from a LC II/III ray kotyle, found in C12/G12, G, 3; a base with thin rays, Palmer's group ii or iii, found in F14/G14, 1, 6; and a body fragment from C13, 1, 4b.

158   Pl. 26   Sb. 103–4   E11/12 Pit Area 2
and
E11/12 Pit Area 3

Base fragments (a, b) of a large kotyle. Light yellowish green clay. Glaze fired from a reddish brown to brown to orange, and mostly worn off. Added red. Encrusted.

(a) MPH: 0.0373; MPW: 0.0794; D: 0.073 (base)

Fragment (a), preserving part of foot and lower body, is mended from two joins: the larger found in E11/12, Pit Area, 2, the smaller in E11/12, Pit Area, 3, a largely undisturbed archaic level. Chips on edge of foot ring, most of floor missing. Rather widely spaced rays rise from a thin red band at edge of foot. Red on exterior of foot. On the underside: reserved band and concentric red band on the flat resting surface of the foot ring and trace of concentric band on bottom. Interior originally black.

(b) MPH: 0.0266; MPW: 0.029

Fragment (b) also found in E11/12, Pit Area, 3, preserves small part of foot ring and lower body with parts of two rays rising from a red line. Red on exterior and bottom of foot ring.

The profile and section of the spreading foot ring is close to Type VII in *Corinth* VII:2, fig. 2, datable to the beginning of LC.[314] The rays are rather carefully drawn, suggesting that the pieces may be from a MC-LC black-glazed kotyle.[315] On the other hand, the possibility cannot be excluded that they belong to a black-figured kotyle.

Early LC I

159   Pl. 26; Fig. 1 Sb. 418–7   F13/G13   2   2

Base fragment. Deep buff clay. Black glaze ranges from black to olive green. Added red.

MPH: 0.033; MPW: 0.0824; D: 0.055 (base)

Section of black-glazed body. Two thin red lines. Relatively narrow band with thin, closely set rays or stripes, rising from a black band. Red on outside of foot. On underside: black glaze on resting surface of foot; two concentric black bands with two small concentric circles in center of bottom. On interior: dark-olive green glaze.

To the extent to which it is preserved, our fragment seems to belong to Palmer's group ii of black-glazed skyphoi.[316] This is indicated by the two red bands above the narrow reserved band of thin rays and by the red on the

---

307. For some other examples, see *Corinth* XIII, pl. 35, 250–9, 253–1.

308. *Corinth* XIII, 106–108.

309. Of these, at least 16 had thin, close-set rays above the foot, which would place them in Palmer's group ii and early group iii; 3 had the broader, wide-spaced rays of the ray kotylai, and 12 had an Attic-type foot, indicative of a late date in the second quarter of the fifth century. In addition, there were almost 100 rim fragments, over 40 rim-handle fragments, and over 60 body fragments.

310. See **163** and *infra* n. 324.

311. **163** may possibly also belong to a semi-glazed skyphos.

312. 38 fragments, half of which are rims, come from this level. The findspots of the other fragments are: 3 in D12/13, A, 3; 1 in E11/12, Pit Area, 3; 3 in C15/16, 1, 4–2, Area 5; 2 in C13/D13, 1, 4.

313. Seven were found in D12/13, B, 4 and 3 were found in C15/16, 1, 4–2, Area 5.

314. See pp. 73–78 for a discussion of the criteria for dating kotylai, and pp. 75 and 78 in particular.

315. Cf. *Corinth* VII:1, no. 342, pl. 42.

316. Another such base fragment was also found in this area.

exterior of the foot. However, our fragment has black glaze on the underside rather than the more frequent red.[317] The profile most closely resembles that of the kotyle from Grave 164 in the North Cemetery at Corinth, which is dated to the second quarter of the sixth century.[318]
LC I

160   Pl. 26   Sb. 296–2   F13/G13   1   2

Fragment, preserving about one-eighth of rim of a large kotyle. Deep buff clay. Dull black glaze, slightly worn and unevenly fired at rim. Added red. Encrusted.

MPH: 0.059; MPW: 0.0782; EstD: 0.20 (rim)

Red band at rim. Two red bands (0.029) below rim. On interior: flaking black glaze with red band at rim and another red band below.

As preserved, the scheme of decoration, with red at rim, two red bands below the level of the handles, and red lines on the interior, places it in Palmer's Group iii of black-glazed skyphoi, which date mainly to the second half of the sixth century.[319] Our fragment appears to belong to a kotyle whose size is larger than those normally found in this group. However, large kotylai of this type have also been found at Tocra.[320]
LC II

161   Pl. 26; Fig. 1 Sb. 169   C15/16   1   4–2 Area 5

Fragmentary kotyle, preserving about one-third wall, with pieces missing, and large portion of spreading foot ring (edge of about one-third broken off). Thin-walled. Deep body. Flat bottom. Complete profile except for missing handle. Clay ranges from grayish green to pinkish buff. Glaze-fired mostly red (leaving orange surface), but ranges to reddish brown and black around handle roots. Discoloration on the interior of the lower body wall and floor where clay is gray. Added red. Mended from 14 pieces. Surface worn, mottled, and encrusted.

H: 0.082; MPW: 0.101; D: 0.069 (base); Est D: 0.105 (rim)

Band at rim. Two bands below handle. Reserved band (H: 0.021) with thin, closely set rays or stripes rising from a band above foot. Added red on outside of foot. On underside: thin band around edge of resting surface of foot ring; red on inside of foot; band around bottom; and three concentric rings in center of bottom. On interior: pattern of bands difficult to discern: band (?) at rim, band below and on wall, and trace(?) of another band above discoloration on lower body wall and on floor.

This kotyle appears to belong to Palmer's Group iii of black-glazed skyphoi, judging from the profile and the traces of interior red lines.[321] The group iii kotyle are dated to the third and fourth quarters of the sixth century. Our kotyle may be early in the series, because the band of rays is not wide. For the closest parallel, see *Corinth* XIII, 208, pl. 32, 240–2, from a grave dated to the middle or third quarter of the sixth century.[322]

This kotyle was found in a largely undisturbed archaic level, which also yielded three similar lower body fragments with thin rays.
LC II

162   Pl. 26   Sb. 15–4   E10/11 (Area 1)   1   3

Base fragment from a large kotyle. Buff clay with light gray core. Black glaze, flaking on interior. Added red. Encrusted.

MPH: 0.0315; MPW: 0.0847; D: 0.0765 (base)

Widely spaced rays rising from a black line at base of foot. Red on outside of spreading ring foot. On underside: rounded resting surface reserved; red on inside of foot; concentric black band near foot; and dilute ring with dot in center.

The fragment presumably belongs to a late black-glazed or ray kotyle, as it is also known.[323] For the type, see *NC*, 335, no. 1518, fig. 182 (LC II); *Hesperia* 7 (1938), 589 (nos. 101–114), fig. 15; *Corinth* VII:1, pl. 44, no. 368; *Délos* XVII, pl. 57, no. 75; *Corinth* XV:3, no. 1002, pl. 44, dated LC III.
LC II/III

163   Pl. 26; Fig. 1 Sb. 520–5   F14/G14   1   3

Base fragment, preserving intact Attic-type foot with beveled edge and tiny portion of adjacent lower body wall. Buff clay. Black glaze slightly worn. Added red. Encrusted.

MPH: 0.0246; D: 0.0704 (base)

Reserved area with no trace of rays preserved. Black band above foot. Red on upper part of foot, black on bottom part. On underside: reserved band on edge of resting surface; concentric red band on inside of foot; two concentric black bands around periphery of flat bottom; dilute yellowish-brown ring with dot in center of bottom. On interior: flaking black glaze and overpainted red band above floor.

Because the very small lower body section above the foot is encrusted, there are no visible traces of rays. This being the case, there are two possible identification of this base. Since the angular profile of the foot resembles that of a black-glazed kotyle of Palmer's group of "black-glazed skyphoi with rays and heavy foot" (*Corinth* XIII, 124, fig. 11, 296–1, pl. 41), dated to the first and second quarter of the fifth century and showing Attic influence, the base may belong to a kotyle of this group. If, however, this area was not decorated with rays, the fragment may perhaps belong to Palmer's group of "semi-glazed skyphoi with heavy foot," produced from the second quarter into the third quarter of the fifth century, with a limited distribution and "seldom exported."[324] If the latter identification is correct, then our piece and the following (**164**) represent yet two other examples,[325] in addition to one found at Olynthos, of the export of semi-glazed skyphoi with heavy foot.[326] There is also a somewhat similar kotyle from the Potters' Quarter (*Corinth* XV:3, pl. 43, no. 941, dated LC III), but the profile of the foot is rounded and not beveled as in our example.
LC III

164   Pl. 26; Fig. 1 Sb. 139–2   D16/17   1   3   NW Corner

Fragmentary semi-glazed skyphos, preserving a complete profile except for handles (broken off), with complete base, including torus foot. Most of wall missing. Three other fragments (one rim and two from the body) do not join. Buff to light gray clay. Worn black glaze. Added red. Burnt. Mended from three joins. Encrusted.

---

317. *Corinth* XIII, 108.

318. *Corinth* XIII, no. 164-2, p. 188, fig. 11, pl. 25.

319. *Corinth* XIII, 106–108. See also *Hesperia* 7 (1938), 589 (nos. 89–100), figs. 15 and 16.

320. *Tocra* I, 26, nos. 447–452. See no. 449, pl. 27, in particular.

321. *Corinth* XIII, 106, 108, fig. 11.

322. While there is no exact parallel for our profile among those of fig. 11, 249-2 has the closest resemblance.

323. For a discussion of ray kotylai, see *Corinth* XV:3, 188–189.

324. *Corinth* XIII, 124; and see pl. 62, 379-2, whose foot appears particularly close to our fragment. There is, however, no mention of the use of added red on these skyphoi.

325. Two other fragments of semi-glazed kotyle were found: one in E11, 4, 2, the other in D12/13, A, 2.

326. *Corinth* XIII, 124.

H: 0.074; D: 0.06 (base); Est D: 0.09 (rim)
Black glaze on approximately upper two-thirds of body wall. Trace of red band at juncture of glazed area (spills over the red) and the wide reserved area above the foot. Black line above foot. Edge of torus foot glazed. On underside: two red bands on inside of foot and traces of concentric bands on concave bottom. On interior: flaking black glaze.

This example seems to belong to Palmer's semi-glazed skyphoi with heavy foot (*Corinth* XIII, pl. 45, 328-1; pl. 58, 363-2; pl. 62, 379-2). The Attic foot here does not have the angularity of the previous example. See comment above (**163**) regarding export of this type of cup.

This kotyle was found in the fill from the southwest corner of the middle sanctuary.
LC III

Kylikes (165–176)

The kylix, also known as the "cup with offset rim," was among the less frequent of the vase types at the sanctuary. Our catalog contains 12 of the 60 fragments[327] retained from the excavation. The majority of the catalog entries belong to the disparaged LC "bird cups,"[328] discussed by Amyx.[329] These cups are characterized by black-figure friezes containing avians (**165**), birds, mostly with reverted heads, griffin-birds (**171**), sirens (**166, 167**), and swans (**173**).[330] On some, incision is finally dispensed with, and the figures are rendered as in silhouette (**174, 175**). The earliest of our cups (**165, 166**) are probably late MC. In general, our series is closely matched at Tocra,[331] with the exception of the unusual and unparalleled black-figure fragment with a feline paw (**176**). A few of the uncatalogued sherds may belong to black-glazed kylikes.

The distribution of kylikes provides a rather vivid contrast to the other vases found in the sanctuary, where the major concentrations occur in the backfill of the middle sanctuary retaining wall. Granted that this is a much smaller sampling of fragments, yet of all the sherds, only 10 were found there. A proportionally high number of fragments, however, were found in archaic contexts: four in undisturbed archaic levels;[332] and seven, including three in our catalogue (**165, 168** from D12/13, A, 3 and **166** from D12/13, A, 4), in largely undisturbed archaic levels.[333] Interestingly, the largest single concentration of kylix fragments comes from E11, 1, 2, where a total of 15 were found, including two in our catalog (**169, 175**).[334]

165   Pl. 27   Sb. 80–4   D12/13 A 3 East
Body fragment. Pale, yellowish buff clay. Black glaze crazed and slightly worn. Added red overpainted and added white. Soil-stained.
MPH: 0.0322; MPW: 0.0505
On exterior: avian (probably a siren) to r. and griffin-bird (?) to l. (tip of sickle-shaped wing preserved at right edge of fragment), with added red on neck and wing band. No f.o. On interior: crazed and flaking black glaze; red, white, and red bands.
For the type, see *Corinth* XIII, pl. 84, 156–5 (T1720), 157–c (T1589), both attributed by Amyx to the Painter of Corinth T-1589.[335] Though the size of our fragment precludes the possibility of any attribution, it is of sufficiently good quality to warrant an MC date. It was found in a largely undisturbed archaic level.
Late MC

166   Pl. 27   Sb. 78bis–2   D12/13 A 4
                                    Between Rubble Walls
Upper body fragment. Creamy buff clay. Black glaze severely worn and ranges from brown to red on interior. Added red overpainted. Encrusted.
MPH: 0.0255; MPW: 0.0366
Band at juncture of offset rim and bowl. On exterior: head of siren to r., and part of wing. On siren's head, an incised fillet and edge of hair incised in a scallop pattern. Added red on siren and wing. On interior: glaze and red band.
For an analogous siren, but head turned left, which is the more common pose, see two kylikes, attributed to the Painter of Corinth MP–6[336] (*Corinth* VII:2, no. 139, pl. 22; *Corinth* XIII, pl. 30, Deposit 44–c).
Late MC

167   Pl. 27   Sb. 109–3   E10 Balk 2/3
Body fragment. Creamy buff clay. Rather firm black glaze, crazed where thick and brown where thin. Glaze worn on siren's face. Added red overpainted. Soil-stained and slightly encrusted.
MPH: 0.035; MPW: 0.052
On exterior: part of bird (?) to r.; siren to l., with raised wing. Added red on face, part of neck, and wing of siren. Incised fillet on head and edge of hair incised in a scallop pattern. Band below frieze. No f.o. On interior: black glaze.

---

327. The 48 uncatalogued fragments consist of the following: 5 rims, 1 handle, 11 rim-upper body, 28 body, and 3 foot sherds.

328. About 55% (26 sherds) were black-figure, and of these at least 20 certainly can be attributed to the LC "bird cups," as can 4 fragments with silhouette figures; 1 fragment bears the head of a goat, possibly MC.

329. On the "bird" or "birdie cups," see Amyx, "The Medallion Painter," *AJA* 65 (1961), 12, and n. 40; for a fuller discussion, see *CorVP*, 251 ff. (Some Late Corinthian Kylikes).

330. See *CorVP*, 251–254.

331. *Tocra* I, nos. 276–291, pl. 19. See also, pp. 34 and 36 where the cups are classified into groups. In addition, see *CorVP*, 254 (Coda).

---

332. D16/17, 1, 4 (lower body), C13/D13, 1, 7 (2 "bird cup" fragments, one with part of an avian, the other with a black-figure or silhouette figure), and C12/D12, G, 3 (lower body).

333. D12/13, A, 3 (black-figure body), E12/13, C, 4 (foot fragment?), D12/E12, D, 3 (black-figure body with part of a bird). D12/E12, D, 3 also yielded a miniature kylix rim-body-handle fragment with traces of a silhouette figure.

334. This level yielded 3 rim-upper body fragments (2 black-figure of which one preserved a griffin-bird) and 10 body fragments.

335. *CorVP*, 196, pl. 78, 3a–b (T1589).

336. *Corinth* XIII, 310, 44–c (T3225) and *CorVP*, 202–203, nos. 1 and 2 (T3225); no. 2 should read D–44c, illustrated on pl. 30.

The siren is very oddly proportioned with an inordinately thick neck and abbreviated body. The incision work is sloppy. Althought there is no exact analogy for such a rendering of a siren, it recalls the sirens on aryballoi from Rhodes (*CVA*, Rodi 2, pl. 6, no. 3, and pl. 7, no. 4). For sirens with raised wing on kylikes, see *Corinth* XIII, pl. 30, Deposit 44–b; pl. 84, nos. 156-5 and 157-c (MC); Amyx, *AJA* 65 (1961), pl. 2b (MC); and *Perachora* II, no. 2548, pl. 108 (Beginning LC).
LC I

168 Pl. 27   Sb. 83–2   D12/13 A 3 West
Fragment, preserving part of offset rim, upper body, and one handle root. Buff clay. Black glaze, brown where dilute, and flaking on interior. Added red. Mended from two fragments. Encrusted.
MPH: 0.0466; MPW: 0.071
On exterior: thin black band below reserved rim; avian to l., top of sickle-shaped wing and tail preserved; tail of bird to r.; f.o. of dots. On interior: black glaze with four red bands overpainted (two at rim, one at top edge and one above offset; one midway up bowl; and one near bottom of bowl).
For the type, see *Tocra* I, 34 (Group I), nos. 276–284, pl. 19;[337] *Corinth* XV:3, no. 645, pl. 30, p. 129–130, n. 2 for additional bibliography.
This fragment was found in a largely undisturbed archaic level.
LC I

169 Pl. 27   Sb. 40–3   E11 1 2
Lower body fragment. Pale light green to pale orange clay with buff surface. Black glaze, fired metallic to red on interior. Added red worn. Soil-stained.
MPH: 0.026; MPW: 0.056
On exterior: part of tail and body of avian to l., band below (glaze gone); no f.o. On interior: black glaze and two red bands.
LC I

170 Pl. 27   Sb. 488–2   F15 1 2
Lower body fragment, broken off at foot juncture. Grayish buff clay. Black glaze, flaking and ranges to brown on interior, firm on exterior except where worn off in the thin bands. Added red. Soil-stained and slightly encrusted.
MPH: 0.06; MPW: 0.0434
On exterior: Tail and portion of sickle-shaped wing of avian to r.; concentric black bands below (one narrow, one broad, five narrow); no f.o. On interior: black glaze with red band near bottom of bowl and about one-third up bowl.
LC I

171 Pl. 27   Sb. 302–1   F13/G13 1 2
Fragment, preserving part of offset rim and upper body. Buff clay. Fugitive black glaze. Added red fugitive. Mended from two pieces. Soil-stained.
MPH: 0.032; MPW: 0.0654
On exterior: band below rim; griffin-bird to r. (head, neck, and end of sickle-shaped wing preserved), neck of bird with reverted head (?) facing griffin-bird. On interior: trace of red band overpainted on black glaze (small section preserved) on offset rim; glaze gone on upper body except for a small strip.
For the type, see *Tocra* I, nos. 276–277, 282, pl. 19; *CVA* Stockholm, pl. 20, nos. 5–8, dated LC II. A similar fragment was found in the E10 Building Foundation Trench.
LC I/II

172 Pl. 28   Sb. 462–1   C13 1 3b
Lower body fragment. Light green clay. Glaze-fired brown, light brown where dilute, flaking where thick. Encrusted on interior.
MPH: 0.0312; MPW: 0.056
On exterior: barely visible legs of bird (?) to r., part of avian to r., with incisions on tail; band below frieze; broad band and three narrow bands. On interior: flaking glaze.
Very sloppy work. The thick legs of the avian recall those of a sphinx on a LC kotyle from Perachora.[338] The poor "style" is reminiscent of the birds on an LC I cup from the Potters' Quarter at Corinth (*Corinth* XV:3, pl. 38, 837). A similar fragment was found in a largely undisturbed archaic level (D12/E12, D, 3).
LC I

173 Pl. 28   Sb. 418–8   F13/G13 2 2
Body fragment. Buff clay. Flaking black glaze. Added red (purple).
MPH: 0.041; MPW: 0.0513
On exterior: bird (swan?) with closed wing to l., part of another bird (?), probably with reverted head judging from small section of body preserved, to its left (?); f.o. of incised blob (behind neck of bird on r.). On interior: flaking black glaze, and a red and reserved band.
The incision on the heads of both birds as well as that on the neck of the bird on the right in the fragment is quite unusual. The style is poor, and there seems to be no exact parallel for the rendering of the bird/swan.
LC

174 Pl. 28   Sb. 515–3   F14/G14 1 2
Lower body fragment. Deep buff clay. Dull glaze ranges from black to brown where thinly applied. Added red.
MPH: 0.0514; MPW: 0.088
On exterior: tail of silhouette avian to l., part of silhouette bird (?) to r.; broad band below; two narrow bands; and band around foot. On interior: a number of black, reserved, and narrow red bands (Brrr.r.B.rr.B.B) above a reserved central medallion.
For the type, see *Tocra* I, 36 (Group II with no incision), no. 290, pl. 19.
LC I

175 Pl. 28; Fig. 1 Sb. 38   E11 1 2
Fragment, preserving part of lower body and over three-quarters of conical foot. Conical hollow underneath foot. Buff clay. Black glaze, brown where dilute. Soil-stained and encrusted.
MPH: 0.033; MPW: 0.086; D: 0.0585 (foot)
On exterior: part of body and leg of bird (?) to r., part of tail and leg of bird to r.; band below frieze, broad band, two thin bands, broad band. No trace of incision. Foot glazed on exterior with reserved edge. Underside of foot reserved. On interior: thin, peeling black glaze; two concentric circles in central medallion bounded by two bands.
LC I

176 Pl. 28   Sb. 506–6   F14/G14 1 Test 2
Lower body fragment. Buff clay. Glaze, firm on interior, slightly flaked on exterior, and brown where dilute. Encrusted.
MPH: 0.027; MPW: 0.064
On exterior: paw and part of head (?) of a fallen feline to r., large incised rosette; narrow bands and part of double-dot band. On interior: black glaze.
The position of the paw, with its large, rather crude drawing, suggests a fallen feline, an uncommon subject on kylikes. A double-dot band on a kylix appears on an exam-

---

337. See also Amyx, *Gnomon*, 41:7 (1969), 683, on the LC I dating of the Tocra cups; *CorVP*, 254.

338. *Perachora* II, no. 2523, pl. 105.

ple from Taranto.³³⁹ This subject is difficult to parallel on Corinthian vases.
LC?

Bowls and Related Open Shapes (177–190)

In this section, lekanides, lekanai, and bowls have been grouped together, since it is not possible in all cases to differentiate, given the fragmentary nature of some of our pieces. Moreover, there appears to be a rather loose application of the term "lekanis-lekane."³⁴⁰ Although the lekanis proper has an inset lip to hold the lid,³⁴¹ the term "lekanis" or "lekane" is also applied to vessels with reflex handles,³⁴² which lack this type of lip,³⁴³ including the stemmed variety.³⁴⁴

The 14 pieces in the catalog, half of them found in the backfill of the middle sanctuary retaining wall, represent a substantial portion of the lekanis and bowl³⁴⁵ fragments retained from the sanctuary. They consist mainly of linear style and black-glazed forms. Among the uncatalogued finds retained from the sanctuary, only seven other lekanis-type fragments³⁴⁶ and 12 bowl fragments were identified. With one exception, all the bowl fragments were black-glazed.³⁴⁷ Two of the black-glazed bowl rim fragments, similar to **183**, were found in largely undisturbed archaic levels.³⁴⁸

Our catalogued pieces range in date from about MC to the first half of the fourth century B.C., as represented by a black-glazed echinus bowl (**187**); this bowl is the latest Corinthian import found in the sanctuary. The examples tentatively assigned to the MC period include our only black-figured fragment (**177**), perhaps from a lekanoid bowl³⁴⁹ that preserves the head of a panther and two linear-style bases (**188**, **189**). The fine fabric of **189** is notable. The other fragments belong to the LC period.

Only two of the fragments, both LC, can certainly be identified as lekanides (**180**, **181**). The two LC linear-style rim fragments (**178**, **179**) may be part of a lekanis/lekane or bowl.

The nine bowl fragments range in size from large to small. Among these are five, mostly small, black-glazed examples. Two (**184**, **186**) are relatively well preserved, though mended. **186**, a LC II black-glazed bowl with a slightly everted rim, is the only catalogued piece uncovered in a largely undisturbed archaic level. The three linear-style bowls include two large examples (**188**, **189**) and one smaller example (**182**), presumably LC in date. **190** has only tentatively been identified as the foot of a stemmed bowl.

177   Pl. 29   Sb. 515–2   F14/G14   1   2
Fragment of black-figure lekanis or lekanoid bowl, preserving less than one-quarter of rim, part of wall, and one spur of reflex handle. Creamy buff clay. Black glaze worn and brown where dilute. Surface encrusted.
MPH: 0.0378; MPW: 0.108; Est D: 0.155
Black glaze on top of flat thickened vertical lip. Traces of black-glazed dots on edge of rim. Trace of black glaze on handle spur. A.f.: head and neck of panther to r., part of large double-centered incised rosette below handle.
The incision work is rather careless. The shape is not a common one, particularly in black-figure. For a related type, see *Corinth* VII:2, 44, no. 145, pl. 24.
MC?

178   Pl. 29   Sb. 31   D13 (Area 2)   2   1,2
Fragment of linear-style lekanis or bowl, preserving about one-fifth of rim, part of body wall, and one spur of reflex handle. Light green buff clay. Black glaze mostly worn off and flaking where preserved. Added red, overpainted on interior. Surface worn and slightly encrusted.
MPH: 0.032; MPW: 0.065; Est D: 0.12
Three thin concentric bands on top of flat everted rim. Added red on top of spur. Handle-zone: leaf or petal pattern in two rows with trace of horizontal band above and below. Shadows of banding below. On interior: added red overpainted band (worn) below rim and alternating red and black bands on wall.
The petal pattern is a late feature. Our example may have originally had a central stem connecting the petals, as in *Perachora* II, pl. 113, 2642 (upper).³⁵⁰
LC II

---

339. Lo Porto, 134, figs. 104b, 105–106.

340. See also Hopper's comments on lekanai, 229–230 and *Agora* XII, 164 n. 1, as well as Amyx's discussion of the inconsistency in terminology in *CorVP*, 465–466.

341. As in the fifth-century series from the North Cemetery at Corinth, see *Corinth* XIII, 144–146.

342. In this study we use the term "reflex handle" rather than "spurred-ribbon handle" or "recurved handle."

343. See *Tocra* I, 34, no. 270, fig. 17, and p. 24 n. 5, where the lekanai from Tocra are mostly compared to Payne's bowls with offset rim. Also, cf. Palmer's reference to Payne's pyxis with convex sides and horizontal handles in *Corinth* XIII, 117.

344. See *Tocra* I, 34, nos. 271–2, fig. 17.

345. The miniature black-glazed bowls are discussed in the section on miniatures.

346. One in D12/13, F, 2c; 4 in F13/G13, 2, 2; 1 in C14/D14, 2, 2; and 1 in F14/G14, 1, 2.

347. Three were base fragments, the others were rim or rim-and-body fragments; they were found in: F11, 1, 2 (rim with lug handle), E11, 1, 2 (rim fragment), D12/13, B, 4 (everted rim), D12/13, A, 3 (everted rim), E11/12, balk, 2/3 (linear style with incurving rim), F13/G13, 1, 2 (2 bases, 1 of which is high-footed), C12/13, 1, 2 (small black-glazed bowl), D14/E14, 1, 2 (base), D15/16, 1, 2 (flat everted rim), F14/G14, 1, 3 (rim with 2 loop handles), E11, 3, 2 (small black-glazed rim-body).

348. D12/13, B, 4 and D12/13, A, 3.

349. This term was used by Amyx and Lawrence in *Corinth* VII:2, 44 (No. 147), and, as noted by Amyx in *CorVP*, 466, to "sidestep the lekane/lekanis problem."

350. The upper fragment numbered 2642 on pl. 113 should probably be 2633 on p. 274.

179   Pl. 29   Sb. 516–6   F14/G14   1   2

Fragment of linear-style bowl or lekanis, preserving about one-fifth of rim, part of body wall, and one spur of reflex handle. Buff clay. Black glaze worn and flaking, especially on interior. Added red. Surface encrusted.

MPH: 0.0294; MPW: 0.0644; Est D: 0.135

Shadows of five concentric bands on top of flat everted rim.[351] Added red on edge of rim. In handle-zone: three black vertical stripes near handle, band of alternately reversed triangles. Black band below. Two thin red bands. Two broad black bands. On interior: thin red band at rim, flaking black glaze, brownish where dilute.

The pattern of alternately reversed triangles is a common one in the the LC II period, especially on kotylai,[352] as well as in the LC III period. For the pattern on other shapes, see *Corinth* XV:3, pl. 45, nos. 1024, 1030. For the pattern on a miniature bowl, see *Perachora* II, 301, no. 3065, pl. 121.

Shape similar to preceding.

LC II or LC III

180   Pl. 29   Sb. 15–5   E10/11 (Area 1)   1   3

Fragment of a lekanis, preserving about one-eighth of rim and small section of wall. Buff clay. Thinly applied black glaze on exterior. Interior unglazed.

MPH: 0.027; MPW: 0.062; Est D: 0.15

Black glaze on inset rim. Thickened, projecting, and upward curving flange decorated with black dots. There is no exact parallel for this form, the closest being a much smaller lekanis from Corinth (*Corinth* XV:3, pl. 49, no. 1189), dated to the LC III period. A band of dots, but not on a projecting flange, occurs on an earlier lekanis from Corinth (*Corinth* XIII, pl. 19, 142e).

LC

181   Pl. 29   Sb. 338–1   C12/13   1   Wall 2, Backfill from N of Wall 2

Fragment of a lekanis, preserving part of rim, body, and root of horizontal loop (?) handle. Deep buff clay. Metallic black glaze, worn. Addded red. Heavily encrusted.

MPH: 0.0313; MPW: 0.0338; Th: 0.0035

Added red on inset rim. Band of black tongues in handle-zone. Remains of black glaze on convex side wall. For a similar type, but with different pattern and a miniature, see Campbell, *Hesperia* 7 (1938), 594, no. 134, fig. 15.

LC II/III, probably LC III

182   Pl. 29   Sb. 51–1   E11   4   2

Fragment of a bowl, preserving section of rim and body. Creamy yellow buff clay. Worn and metallic black glaze. Added red.

MPH: 0.03; MPW: 0.047; Th: 0.0045

Elongated dots on top of flat, slightly thickened, and incurved rim. On interior: traces of narrow banding and a red band. On exterior: band below rim. For a related example, with similar rim decoration, see *Corinth* XV:3, 283, no. 1537, pl. 63, which Benson suggests as possibly MC.

Probably LC

183   Pl. 29   Sb. 528–9   F12/G12   Tunnel A

Fragment of a black-glazed bowl, preserving about one-eighth of rim, slightly chipped, and part of body wall. Light greenish buff clay. Severely worn black glaze. Encrusted.

MPH: 0.029; MPW: 0.059; Est D: 0.12

Everted rim with flat surface.[353] Black-glazed except for narrow reserved band on wall. For a similar type, but without the reserved band, see *Corinth* XV:3, pp. 305–306, no. 1668–1669, pl. 66. The rim of our example is closer to no. 1668, while the body is more rounded as no. 1669. The rim of **179** is also similar.

LC

184   Pl. 30; Fig. 1 Sb. 515–9   F14/G14   1   2

Fragmentary black-glazed bowl, preserving over one-half rim, most of body, and less than two-thirds flaring ring foot. Pale buff clay. Black glaze worn, dark brown where thinly applied, and fired orange around base. Lime inclusion in wall where surface layer has broken off. Mended from three joining fragments. Encrusted.

MPH: 0.033; D: 0.083 (rim); D: 0.047 (base)

Flat rim, very slightly thickened and everted. Shallow body with curved wall tapering to a flaring ring foot. Underside unglazed.

The rim and shape of our bowl bears a strong resemblance, with the exception of the foot, to a small black-glazed bowl found in an LC context in the Anaploga well in Corinth (*Corinth* VII:2, 101, An9, pl. 69). Except for the less projecting rim, our piece is also close to *Corinth* XV:3, 306, no. 1669, pl. 66, dated by Benson to the second or third quarters of the sixth century, in both proportion and profile. See also Campbell, *Hesperia*, 7 (1938), 587, no. 83, fig. 15.

LC

185   Pl. 30   Sb. 528–10   F12/G12   Tunnel A

Fragment of black-glazed bowl, preserving section of rim and body. Buff, light greenish clay. Black glaze ranges from black to reddish brown. Added red.

MPH: 0.0324; MPW: 0.022; Th: 0.0055

Flat thickened, sharp-edged, and outward projecting rim. Rim curves inward on interior. Rather thick-walled rounded body. Added red overpainted on top of rim. Added red band on edge of rim. Thin red band on interior of lip.

This type of rim is not so common on Corinthian black-glazed bowls. Although our rim does not project out as much, there is a resemblance in profile to that of a stemmed bowl from Tocra (*Tocra* I, 34, no. 269, fig. 17, pl. 18).

LC

186   Pl. 30   Inv. No. 71–721 D12/13   B   4

Fragmentary black-glazed bowl, missing over one-half body. Full profile preserved. Light greenish buff clay. Black glaze mostly worn off on interior and exterior. Mended from four joining pieces. Encrusted.

H: 0.04; Est D: 0.09 (rim); D: 0.038 (base)

Small bowl with rounded walls, flat narrow rim, slightly everted, and narrow ring foot.

For a related type with similar proportions, see *Corinth* XIII, 203, pl. 32, 218–3, found in a grave dated to the middle of the sixth century B.C. and *Corinth* XV:3, 306, no. 1669, pl. 66.

This bowl was found in a largely undisturbed archaic level.

LC II

---

351. The profile, as far as it is preserved, bears some resemblance to an MC bowl in *Corinth* XV:3, no. 774, pl. 116. The top of our rim is appreciably flatter. See also pl. 66, nos. 1668 and 1669, two black-glazed bowls, dated second and third quarter of the sixth century, which are smaller than our example but whose rims seem quite close.

352. See *supra* Kotylai, **148**, and references cited.

353. Three of the uncatalogued bowl finds from D12/13, B, 4; D12/13, A, 3; and D15/16, 1, 2, respectively, had a similar flat everted rim.

187   Pl. 30   Sb. 175   C15/16   1   W-4 Area 4

Fragment of an echinus bowl,[354] about one-half preserved. Chipped rim. Buff clay. Black glaze severely worn off. Encrusted.

H: 0.03; D: 0.087 (rim); D: 0.045 (foot); Th: 0.005

Black-glazed bowl with flaring walls, incurved rim, and ring foot. Judging from the diameter, our bowl appears to belong to G. Roger Edwards' "saucer group" of echinus bowls, dated to the first half of the fourth century.[355] There seems, however, to be no exact match for the profile of our bowl with those illustrated from the group on pl. 2. For other echinus bowls, see also *Corinth* XV:3, 225, nos. 1232, 1233, and 1235, pl. 51.

This bowl is particularly notable for being the latest of the Corinthian pottery finds from the sanctuary. Its find spot corresponds to the area west of Fountain House F2 that was used as dump for pottery and lamps in the Hellenistic period.[356]

First half of fourth century B.C.

188   Pl. 30; Fig. 1 Sb. 294–1   F13/G13   1   2

Fragment of a large bowl, preserving part of lower body and base with flaring foot ring. Light green clay. Dull black glaze, crazed in spots. Added red, ranges to purple, and added white. Slightly encrusted.

MPH: 0.029; MPW: 0.084; Th: 0.0056; D: 0.08 (foot)

Exterior: broad black band with three narrow overpainted bands (white, red, white); band of black tongues around base; purple on foot. Interior: black glaze and bands of red, overpainted purple, and white in center of floor. Underside of foot: resting surface reserved; black band around inside on foot; and black circle in center.

MC or LC

189   Pl. 30   Sb. 15–3   E10/11 (Area 1)   1   3

Fragment of a large bowl or lekane, preserving part of lower body and base with flaring ring foot. Fine, creamy yellow buff clay with orangey core. Black glaze, good and adheres well on interior, worn and fired from black to red on exterior. Added red, ranges to purple. Mended from three joins. A small non-joining fragment is not illustrated. Encrusted.

MPH: 0.028; Est D: 0.13 (foot); Th: 0.0036

Exterior: purple and black band; purple on outside of foot. Interior: black glaze. Underside of foot: two thin dilute lines on inner and outer edge of reserved resting surface; purple on inside of foot; two thin concentric lines around floor near inside of foot.

The quality of the clay is exceptionally fine, and the fabric is quite thin for a vessel of this size.

MC ?

190   Pl. 30   Sb. 506–8   F14/G14   1   Test 2

Foot fragment of a stemmed bowl (?), preserving about one-third foot and part of floor of bowl. Buff clay. Thin black glaze worn and ranges to a light brown. Added red. Encrusted.

MPH: 0.0312; Est D: 0.07 (foot)

Floor of bowl, originally glazed and now orange with only patches of black glaze. Fillet around short, broad stem with traces of red above. Top of Attic-type foot sloppily glazed. Edge of foot and resting surface reserved. Interior of foot, once glazed and now orange with traces of black and red. Reserved just below floor. There is no exact analogy for this piece.

MC or LC?

Plates (191–210)

Although plates are numerically only fairly well represented, they provide some of our most interesting examples of Corinthian pottery from the Demeter Sanctuary. The catalog, which contains 20 examples, is divided into three sections: Black-Figure, Silhouette Style, and Linear-Style plates. The 10 black-figure plates include a fragment that is broadly related to the Carrousel Painter and three fragments attributable to the Chimaera Group. The latter enhance our knowledge of the repertoire of this distinctive and significant MC group. The six plates in the silhouette style, however, are quite standard. The linear style is represented by two unique fragments, only tentatively assigned to the EC period, and by two mildly interesting LC fragments. With the exception of the Chimaera Group and the linear-style LC examples, there is a similarity to the types found at Tocra.

In addition to the catalog entries, a total of 46 other plate fragments have been retained from the excavations, including 34 rims,[357] 2 rims with double-roll foot, 1 rim with roll foot, 3 double-roll foot pieces, and 6 floor sherds.[358] Given their state of preservation, most cannot be identified with certainty. Among these, notably, are 2 fragments that were found in undisturbed archaic levels: a double-roll foot, presumably MC, from C13/D13, 1, 7; and a floor sherd, with silhouette animals and "hailstorm," of the late MC period from C13, 1, 4b. Three other fragments were uncovered in largely undisturbed archaic levels: a rim and a black-figure floor sherd (D12/E12, D, 3) as well as a rim with double-roll foot (C13, 1, 4a).[359] All these uncatalogued fragments seem to be MC or MC/LC, with the exception of one LC floor fragment. A large portion of all the finds (43%), both catalogued and uncatalogued, was uncovered in the backfill of the middle sanctuary retaining wall.

---

354. I wish to thank Elizabeth Pemberton for initially suggesting this identification.

355. *Corinth* VII:3, 29–30, 32, nos. 35–45, pls. 2 and 44.

356. White, *Final Reports* I, 92, 115.

357. One was burnt and five others had discernible decoration preserved: one with traces of rays on the interior, the other four with concentric bands, which may possibly belong to plates with silhouette animals.

358. Two belong to plates with silhouette animals and "hailstorm," 2 to black-figure plates, and 1 to a plate with traces of bud-chain, possibly LC; 1 bears traces of concentric bands.

359. One of the catalogued examples (**206**), consisting of 2 floor fragments of a plate with silhouette animals was also found in a largely undisturbed archaic level (D12/13, B, 4).

BLACK-FIGURE

The 10 catalogued pieces represent almost all the identifiable examples of black-figure plates from the sanctuary.[360] As noted above, **191** is related to the Carrousel Painter. The three plates of the Chimaera Group (**192–194**), represented by small fragments,[361] all have floral motifs, a lotus-palmette complex, on the interior and figured decoration on the exterior. This combination is atypical of the plates, particularly those with floral decoration, by painters of this group. The only analogy for this is a fragmentary plate from Perachora, attributed to the Painter of the Copenhagen Sphinxes. Since the floral complex on the Perachora plate is almost identical to **194**, our plate must surely be by the same painter. Moreover, two of the plates (**192**, **193**) bear a remarkable disk-rosette motif, unparalleled among the recognized works of painters of this group. Unfortunately, the three Chimaera Group plates are very poorly preserved, and the figured representations on the backs of the plates are problematic. **195**, with its fugitive glaze and uncertain decoration, may also be related to the Chimaera Group.

The other black-figure fragments belong to plates with more conventional animal frieze decoration, but their poor state of preservation precludes any attempts at attributions. The little that remains of the figured decoration of **196**, with its whirligig center, is quite puzzling. The other three fragments (**197–199**), with animal frieze decoration seem very close and are perhaps from the same workshop; they are characterized by a rather careless style, use of incised shaded fillers, and a similar foot form, which is preserved on two of the pieces.

191 Pl. 31 Sb. 536–1 F12/G12 1 2
Floor fragment. Buff clay. Worn glaze fired reddish brown. Added red fugitive.
MPL: 0.0816; MPW: 0.083; Th: 0.007
Interior a.f.: panther with frontal head to r., hindquarter and most of forelegs missing; goat to l., part of neck and head preserved. Added red on neck, shoulder, body, probably along underbelly (only patch preserved), and in a stripe along rear of neck of panther. Added red on neck of goat. F.o. of incised double-centered rosette, incised blob rosettes, amorphous fillers with incisions, and dots. One narrow black and two, possibly three, red concentric bands in center of plate. Exterior: traces of concentric bands.

The incision work is rather good, particularly that on the panther's face, which is quite neat and fairly distinctive. As such, it recalls the panther on a plate from the Potters' Quarter at Corinth (see *Corinth* XV:3, pl. 35, no. 767). The fragment, moreover, appears to belong to a plate that bears stylistic analogy with a few plates from Tocra (*Tocra* I, 37, pl. 20, no. 297 and pl. 21, nos. 298–299). Amyx has identified no. 297 as "descended from the Carousel (sic) Painter."[362] Our piece, then, certainly also bears some relation to the Carrousel Painter.[363]

MC, Related to the Carrousel Painter

192 Pl. 31; Fig. 2 Sb. 515–5   F14/G14 1 2
Fragment, preserving about one-sixth of floor, double-roll foot ring, and small portion of rim. Pale buff to pinkish buff clay. Dark purplish black glaze, crazed, and worn in spots, especially on back. Added red ranges to purple. Unexplained deliberate chisel marks (gouging) on upper-right edge along break and on adjacent top and underside surfaces, evidently made in ancient times after the fragment was broken. Soil-stained.
MPL: 0.117; MPW: 0.1206; Th: 0.0094
Reserved rim with red- and dark-glazed band at its base. Black, red, and purple lines around edge of floor. Interior floor: part of large lotus-palmette complex. Part of palmette with two tiers of alternating red and black petals: outer row with larger petals and inner row with narrow petals, both rows similar in height. Outer leaves of palmette extend into two intertwined tendrils and third tendril ends in a round compass-drawn disk. Perimeter of disk inscribed by two concentric compass-drawn incised lines. Centered within disk, carefully incised 17-petaled rosette with double center, set within another compass-drawn circle and surrounded by a circle of 23 purple dots. Part of one lotus sepal with double-incised outlines and with purple overpainted.

Exterior: part of lion, probably with head turned back, only mane with locks and part of shoulder remain. Added purple over black glaze on neck (badly crazed and peeled) and in one of shoulder muscles. F.o. of incised blob rosette (glaze worn off). Edge of underside surrounded by two concentric bands, now worn off, a thin orange band, and traces of red near the double-roll foot, where glaze is also worn off.

This is one of the most notable fragments from the sanctuary, characterized by its exceptionally fine, careful, and elaborate drawing and style. **193** is very similar and both must be from the same workshop, and possibly by the same hand.

There are a number of traits that place our fragment in the Chimaera Group and close to the Chimaera Painter: the bold and monumental style, the use of the tondo, the reserved rim, the use of polychromy, and the crazed black paint.[364] The Chimaera Painter, however, generally did not

---

360. Only 4 other sherds can with any certainty be attributed to black-figure plates: 1 rim with traces of rays and 3 floor sherds with very poorly preserved decoration, one of which was found in a largely undisturbed archaic level (D12/E12, D, 3).

361. These were all found in the backfill of the middle sanctuary retaining wall.

362. However, in *Gnomon* 41:7 (1969), 684, Amyx mentions that nos. 298 and 299 are closer to the Carrousel Painter; *CorVP*, 166 (Near the Carrousel Painter).

363. On the Carrousel Painter, see P. Lawrence, "Notes on the Chimaera Painter," *AJA* 66 (1962), 185–186, and *CorVP*, 166–167. I wish to extend my thanks to Patricia Lawrence for pointing out the generic rather than specific lineal relationship of our piece to the Carrousel Painter.

364. See P. Lawrence, "The Corinthian Chimaera Painter," *AJA* 63 (1959), 349–363, and *CorVP*, 167–170.

decorate the exterior of his plates with figured decoration.[365] In the few attributed examples of decoration on both sides of the plate, it is always figural. Until recently, the only example of a plate with a floral motif, a lotus-palmette cross, assigned to the Chimaera Painter by Lawrence, is one in Berkeley (UCMA 8/104)[366] where the palmette is completely unlike our example. It should be noted, however, that there are red dots on the tendrils of the palmettes on the Berkeley plate.[367] This unusual use of red dots as a decorative enrichment may be compared to the circle of red dots surrounding the rosette in the disc of our fragment.

On the other hand, plates by painters of the Chimaera Group do more frequently bear large floral motifs. Lawrence mentions six pieces connected to the Chimaera Painter, but not definitely attributable to him, including three plates (Athens NM 12941, Louvre A417, and BM 64.10–7.20), all with palmette cross.[368] The form of the subsidiary palmettes is similar to our palmette in being "fan-shaped," but the two tiers of petals are lacking. Yet, the elaborate interlocking tendrils (of which something remains on our example) points to a further relationship. There are also a few plates from the Potters' Quarter at Corinth with lotus-palmette complexes, which have been attributed to the Chimaera Group.[369] In contrast to our piece, none of the aforementioned plates has figured decoration on the underside.

The only published parallel for a floral motif on the interior of the plate and a figured representation on the exterior occurs on a fragmentary plate from Perachora (*Perachora* II, no. 1970, pls. 80, 82, p.198),[370] which Callipolitis-Feytmans has attributed to the Painter of the Copenhagen Sphinxes, one of the recognized painters of the Chimaera Group.[371]

There is, in fact, no exact analogy for our palmette with its two tiers of petals. The closest parallel appears on a plate fragment from Corinth with a two-tiered palmette, which according to Benson "seems to be related to the Chimaera Group."[372] Although the proportions of the leaves differ from our example, there is a definite kinship. Two-tiered palmettes also appear on some flat-bottomed aryballoi that Benson has attributed to the Otterlo Painter.[373] The workmanship, form, and proportions of the petals are totally unlike our piece, however.

Moreover, there appears to be no analogy in all Corinthian vase-painting for the two-tiered palmette whose tendril terminates in a large, carefully incised, compass-drawn disk rosette. A distant parallel for the disk is a hand-incised disk rosette, which forms the central core of a massive lotus cross on an alabastron in Taranto (NM 107.639), attributed by Benson to the Otterlo Painter.[374] The contrast in style is striking, for it lacks the delicacy, exacting workmanship, and attention to detail of our disk rosette. A similar scheme is found on an alabstron from Delos.[375] Somewhat related disk-like rosettes appear on an another alabastron, probably MC, also from Delos.[376] Here, in the large central floral complex, a double palmette surmounted by a lotus, each volute of the lower palmette encircles a large hand-incised 16-petaled rosette, producing a disk-like effect. In the upper palmette, smaller disk-like rosettes are superimposed on the volutes. In all these examples, however, the incised rosette is large, completely filling the area of the incised disk.

The exterior of the plate with a lion filling the entire tondo is indicative of Chimaera Painter's style. In the preserved portion of the lion, we also see the same rendering of the locks of the mane and the use of added red in one of the segments of the shoulder muscle markings, characteristic of the Chimaera Painter.[377] The pose of the lion in the tondo is problematic and difficult to reconstruct. It cannot be compared to that of the lioness in Louvre S 1679[378] or the lion on the interior of the lekanoid bowl (BM 95.10.27.1),[379] because the raised foreleg(s) would have to be present on our fragment. There is a possibility that the pose, but with a single lion (because there does not appear to be room for more than one), was more akin to that of the lions on the interior of a fragmentary plate from Mykonos, where the raised forelegs extend onto the rim of

---

365. For exceptions, see *Corinth* VII:2, 117, An95, which mentions an example from Perachora, no. 1960; a plate in Copenhagen (Inv. no. 3289) attributed to the Chimaera Painter by Johansen; and the fragment from the Anaploga well (An95), also attributed to the Chimaera Painter. See also *CorVP*, 168, (i) 10 (Copenhagen) and 11 (Corinth) and p. 169, (i) 1 (Perachora plate, possibly by the Chimaera Painter).

366. On the Berkeley plate, see *CVA*, University of California, fasc. 1 (USA fasc. 5), pl. 6, 4; Lawrence, *AJA* 63 (1959), 352, no.10; *CorVP*, pl. 65, 3a–b. On recent attributions, see Patricia Lawrence's forthcoming article, "The Chimaera Group at Corinth," *Hesperia* (in press) where she has added four other plates with florals to the Chimaera Painter. I wish to thank Dr. Lawrence for kindly sending me a draft of this article and for her permission to use it. Regrettably, the results of her study on the painters of the Chimaera Group and new attributions could not be incorporated in this publication.

367. Lawrence, *AJA* 63 (1959), 353.

368. *AJA* 63 (1959), 357. For additional plates, see also *CorVP*, 174 and Lawrence (in press) *supra* n. 366 (also new attributions).

369. *Corinth* XV:3, pl. 35, nos. 750 (KP 1773), 751 (KP 1775), 753 (KP 1945); Callipolitis-Feytmans, 154, no. 72 (KP 1945), and 155, no. 73 (KP 1775); *CorVP*, 174, nos. 4 (KP 1773), 10 (KP 1775) and 11 (KP 1945). For other plates with florals, see Callipolitis-Feytmans, 154, no. 66, and 155, no. 74 and for new attributions of the floral plates of the Chimaera Group, see Lawrence (in press), *supra* n. 366.

370. See also **194** below.

371. Callipolitis-Feytmans, 135, no. 65 on p. 154. See also *CorVP*, 170, no. 3. However, also see Lawrence (in press) *supra* n. 366 who merges the Painter of the Copenhagen Sphinxes into the Painter of Louvre E 574.

372. *Corinth* XV:3, 148–149, pl. 35, no. 756.

373. J. L. Benson, "A Floral Master of the Chimaera Group: The Otterlo Painter," *AK* 4 (1971), heft 1, 15 nos. 23, 24, 26, 27; pl. 3, nos. 3, 4, 7, 8, for example. The palmette on the aryballos on the London Market (No. 23, pl. 3, no. 4) is perhaps the closest of these examples. I wish to thank Professor Benson for calling my attention to the Otterlo Painter.

374. J. L. Benson, "A Floral Master of the Chimaera Group: The Otterlo Painter," *Antike Kunst* 14 (1971), heft 1, 18, no. 40, pl. 5, 4.

375. *Délos* X, pl. 30, no. 430; *NC*, no. 438, p. 285.

376. *Délos* X, pl. 31, no. 440; *NC*, no. 433, p. 285.

377. Lawrence, *AJA* 63 (1959), pl. 87, figs. 1–3; pl. 88, fig. 7; *Greek Vase-Painting in Midwestern Collections* (Art Institute of Chicago), no. 22, pl. 36, p. 37.

378. *CVA* Louvre, fasc. 6 (France, fasc. 9), pl. 8, fig. 1; Lawrence, *AJA* 63 (1959), pl. 87, fig. 3.

379. Lawrence, *AJA* 63 (1959), pl. 88 fig.7.

the plate,[380] though this would be extremely awkward on the exterior rim.

The sole filling ornament, an oddly incised rosette-like form, with two short curved and parallel horizontal incisions below which there are several slanting incisions, does not appear on any plates attributed to the Chimaera Painter or Group. A similar filling ornament, however, appears on a head-pyxis in the Hermitage, Leningrad (inv. no. 5551), attributed by Lawrence to the Chimaera Painter.[381]

There is no exact parallel for our incomplete profile, which lacks most of its rim, in Callipolitis-Feytmans.[382]

Based on the foregoing, our example is most assuredly the work of a member of the Chimaera Group. The fragmentary nature of our fragment and the unparalleled disk rosettes, however, preclude further attempts at attribution to a specific artist.

MC, Chimaera Group

193   Pl. 31   Sb. 528–1   F12/G12 Tunnel A

Part of floor and single roll of double-roll foot ring. Pale, slightly yellowish buff clay with pinkish core. Glaze unevenly fired (ranges from red to orange to black) and crazed on exterior surface. Added red ranges to purple. Soil-stained.

MPL: 0.092; MPW: 0.074; Th: 0.0077

Interior: part of large lotus(?)-palmette complex. Two petals of palmette (one with red overpainted), a leaf ending in an incised compass-drawn disk rosette, and two intersecting tendrils. Disk rosette contains incised 16-petaled rosette in the center, surrounded by a circle of 20 red dots, now barely visible. Top edge of leaf (?). Traces of two thin bands (red and purple) around edge of plate.

Exterior: part of an unidentified animal. Blotch of added red between two of the incised curved lines, forming the muscle markings. Three thin bands (red, black, red) around edge of plate. Glaze gone from foot.

The floral complex on the interior of the plate very closely resembles that of the preceding plate (**192**), and the disk rosette is almost a duplicate. The quality of this fragment, however, is not quite comparable.

The preserved figured decoration on the exterior is quite problematic. It appears to be the rump of a lion with hairs incised. If this is taken to be the correct identification, the incised lines toward the right edge of the fragment (as we have positioned the photograph) are inexplicable, as they do not correspond to any known animal body markings. Interestingly, incising hairs along the back of an animal does not appear as a trait among the known pieces by painters of the Chimaera Group. Nonetheless, the striking similarity to **192** indicates that the two plates may be by the same painter, who, in any case, is definitely an artist of the Chimaera Group.

MC, Chimaera Group

194   Pl. 32   Sb. 288–16 a,b   F13/G13   1   2

Two floor fragments. Light greenish clay. Black glaze severely worn and crazed where preserved. Finely finished surface. Added purple. Soil-stained and slightly encrusted.

(a) MPL: 0.0492; MPW: 0.0584; Th: 0.0076

Interior: part of large lotus-palmette complex. Sepal of lotus, inner outline incised, with purple overpainted (only patch preserved) on black, curves outward. Part of double palmette with alternating black and purple petals (where preserved). Outer leaves of upper palmette terminate in volutes. Outer leaves of lower palmette extend into tendrils. Added purple on the member connecting the palmettes. Exterior: Double-centered incised rosette.

(b) MPL: 0.044; MPW: 0.0336; Th: 0.0068

Interior: part of large lotus-palmette complex. Part of palmette with traces of added red on the petals. Part of lotus calyx with zigzag pattern between two horizontal incised lines. Added purple on calyx. Exterior: unidentifiable decoration (no photograph), possibly part of a human or winged figure.[383]

The extremely fine, steady, and precise incision is noteworthy. Though there is no explicit evidence, we have placed the floral decoration on the interior and the figured on the exterior, as in the two foregoing examples. This arrangement is further substantiated by a fragmentary plate from Perachora (*Perachora* II, 198 no. 1970, pls. 80, 82).[384] As noted above, Callipolitis-Feytmans has attributed the Perachora plate to the Painter of the Cophenhagen Sphinxes.[385] Our plate must be by the same hand as the Perachora plate, as indicated not only by the virtually identical floral design on the interior, but also in the rendering of the double palmette, and the very finely finished surface. The Perachora plate, furthermore, gives us an idea of the disposition of the floral complex in the tondo. In addition, the Perachora plate is the only other known plate by a painter of the Chimaera Group, aside from our examples, to have a floral complex on the interior and figured decoration on the exterior.

MC, Chimaera Group, Painter of the Copenhagen Sphinxes

195   Pl. 32   Sb. 210–4   E12/13 E 2

Floor fragment. Light gray clay. Glaze gone. Fragment burnt. Soil-stained and slightly encrusted.

MPL: 0.0435; MPW: 0.0487; Th: 0.0052

Interior: double-centered incised rosette and part of a winged creature(?). Exterior: traces of concentric bands.

The decoration appears to have filled the tondo of the plate, but is difficult to identify. What remains of the decoration bears some remote resemblance to part of a sickle wing with feathers incised. However, the incised drawing is not consistent with the standard renderings of feathers on a sickle wing: the incised arcs curve inward too much and incision below the arcs is lacking.

Probably MC, Related to the Chimaera Group?

196   Pl. 32   Sb. 16–1   E10/11 (Area 1)   1   3

Part of center of floor. Creamy buff clay with slight greenish tinge. Glaze, most worn off, where preserved fired red on interior and brownish black on exterior. Soil-stained.

MPL: 0.053; MPW: 0.0587; Th: 0.0086

---

380. Lawrence, *AJA* 63 (1959), 351, pl. 87, fig. 4.

381. Lawrence, *AJA* 63 (1959), 354, pl. 90, figs. 18 and 20a to the right of the panther; pl. 90, fig. 20d, behind the lion's haunch; pl. 91, figs. 21, 23b between the rear legs of the lion.

382. Callipolitis-Feytmans, though no. 62 on fig. 17 may be the closest.

383. Cf. Siren on a plate, related to the Chimaera Group by Benson, in *Corinth* XV:3, pl. 34, no. 744.

384. Where it is remarked that the drawing and incision resemble incised metalwork and the drawing is compared to the Chimaera Painter.

385. Callipolitis-Feytmans, 135, no. 65 on p. 154. See also *CorVP*, 170, A (i) 3. However, see also Lawrence (in press) *supra* n. 371 on merging of the Painter of Copenhagen Sphinxes into the Painter of Louvre E 574.

Interior: center with whirligig surrounded by double-dot band; part of frieze with unidentified decoration, including paw(?) to l.,[386] and incised filler (?). Exterior: two concentric bands.

Given the very small section of the preserved a.f., it is impossible to identify the decoration, particularly the rectilinear and angular incision work in the upper left. It certainly bears no resemblance to an animal figure. The double-dot band around the central medallion is quite frequently seen on plates of the MC period.[387] The whirligig, by contrast, is an uncommon central motif on Corinthian plates, and there are only a few published examples.[388]

Late MC?

197   Pl. 33   Sb. 98–2   E11/12   Balk 2

Small section of floor and base of rim, single roll foot with simple ring or moulding inside. Very pale orange clay with yellowish green core. Glaze-fired red and worn on floor, otherwise fired black to reddish brown.

MPL: 0.091; MPW: 0.025; MPH: 0.014; Th: 0.0077

Interior: band around edge and part of a.f., with panther to l., upper part of head preserved. F.o. of incised shaded fillers and dots. Exterior: banding on foot roll and on its resting surface; ring foot glazed; and band around edge of floor.

There is no close parallel for the foot with the outer roll and narrow inner ring in Callipolitis-Feytmans, although one of the latest plates in the Chimaera Group is similar in basic form,[389] as is, to a lesser extent, one of the plates attributed by Callipolitis-Feytmans to the LC I *style orientalisant*,[390] which has a rounded inner foot unlike our example. Given the apparent placement of the animals in the frieze, with feet toward the center, the plate should belong to Callipolitis-Feytmans' group of *les plats de style orientalisant*, dated to LC I.[391] Benson, however, does not agree with this dating, and places the plates of this group in MC.[392]

MC or LC I

198   Pl. 33   Sb. 188   F11   1   1

Part of floor and simple ring foot (exterior roll foot broken off). Pale pinkish buff clay. Glaze-fired red and almost entirely worn off. Soil-stained and encrusted.

MPL: 0.055; MPW: 0.0258; Th: 0.0074

A.f.: Quadruped (goat?) to r., leg and belly preserved. F.o. of incised shaded fillers and dots. Band around edge of floor. Glaze on preserved foot ring.

Rather sloppy work. The style is reminiscent of the preceding example and both have a similar double foot with a simple ring on the inside.

Late MC?

199   Pl. 33   Sb. 40–5   E11   1   2

Fragment, preserving part of rim, edge of floor, and foot with single roll and simple ring or moulding on inside. Light green clay. Glaze-fired red on interior, mostly gone, and black to reddish brown on exterior. Soil-stained and encrusted.

MPH: 0.028; MPW: 0.081; Th: 0.005 (floor)

On rim interior: broad rays, tangent at bottom. Thin band around edge of floor. A.f.: f.o. of part of an incised shaded filler and incised line.

Ray decoration on the rim is not infrequent on MC plates.[393]

There is some similarity in the foot to our two preceding examples, **197** and **198**, for which we could find no exact parallel, as well as in the f.o. These three plate fragments appear to be related, perhaps from the same workshop.

Late MC?

200   Pl. 33; Fig 2. Sb. 112–1   E10   Bldg 1/2   Along SE edge

Fragment, preserving about one-ninth of rim and one roll foot (other broken off?). Pale pinkish orange clay with light green core. Glaze fired red and worn. Piece missing from roll foot. Surface nicked, soil-stained and encrusted.

MPH: 0.028; MPW: 0.041; MPL: 0.094

Rim interior: band at slightly thickened and flat edge; rays, tangent at bottom, between two bands. Exterior: band at edge and below thickening of rim; glaze on roll foot.

There is no parallel for the form of the rim in Callipolitis-Feytmans. For the rim decoration, see preceding.

MC

SILHOUETTE STYLE

In our catalog, there are six examples of plates (**201–206**) decorated with friezes of silhouette animals, four of which have "hailstorm" filling ornament.[394] The plates belong to a group that Payne

---

386. If our tentative identification of the paw is correct, based on Callipolitis-Feytmans' study, the feet of animals were toward the center in EC (p. 124) and again in LC (see pp. 137, 158–159, nos. 21–24 with no. 22 [KP 1779] illustrated in *Corinth* XV:3, pl. 35, no. 754; and see discussion of no. 754, which is dated MC by Benson, on p. 148).

387. Callipolitis-Feytmans, 126, and *Corinth* XV:3, 151 no. 767.

388. A whirligig is mentioned by Callipolitis-Feytmans on an EC plate fragment from Perachora (p. 148, no. 3) and on an MC plate from Aegina with padded dancers, where it is also surrounded by a double-dot band (p. 151, no. 25). In the publication cited therein for the Aegina plate (D. Feytmans, "Assiettes Corinthiennes Inédites," in Studies Presented to David Moore Robinson, Vol. II (1953), 39, pl. 9b), it is stated that the Aegina plate seems to belong to the late MC period, although it is also remarked that whorls do not occur on plates before the middle of the sixth century. Cf. also Benson's comments in Corinth XV:3, 147, no. 748, a plate with a whirligig on the exterior, dated to MC. An LC I white-style plate from Delphi with a

whirligig in the center is also listed in Callipolitis-Feytmans' catalog (p. 157, no. 1) and in *Studies . . . Robinson*, Vol. II, 40 ff., with a remark on p. 42 that this type of central decoration continues to be rare as in the preceding period. For another LC example, see *Corinth* XV:3, no. 1662, pl. 66.

389. Callipolitis-Feytmans, 134, fig. 17, no. 68, with characteristics of LC I, according to Callipolitis-Feytmans.

390. Callipolitis-Feytmans, fig. 21, no. 20.

391. Callipolitis-Feytmans, 137–138.

392. See *supra* n. 386, discussion of nos. 754 and 767 in *Corinth* XV:3.

393. See *Corinth* VII:2, 47–48, nos. 154 and especially 155, with references, pl. 28; Callipolitis-Feytmans, 132.

394. Three of these (**201–203**) preserve blob(s) among the "hailstorm."

E10/11, 1, 3

F11, 1, 2

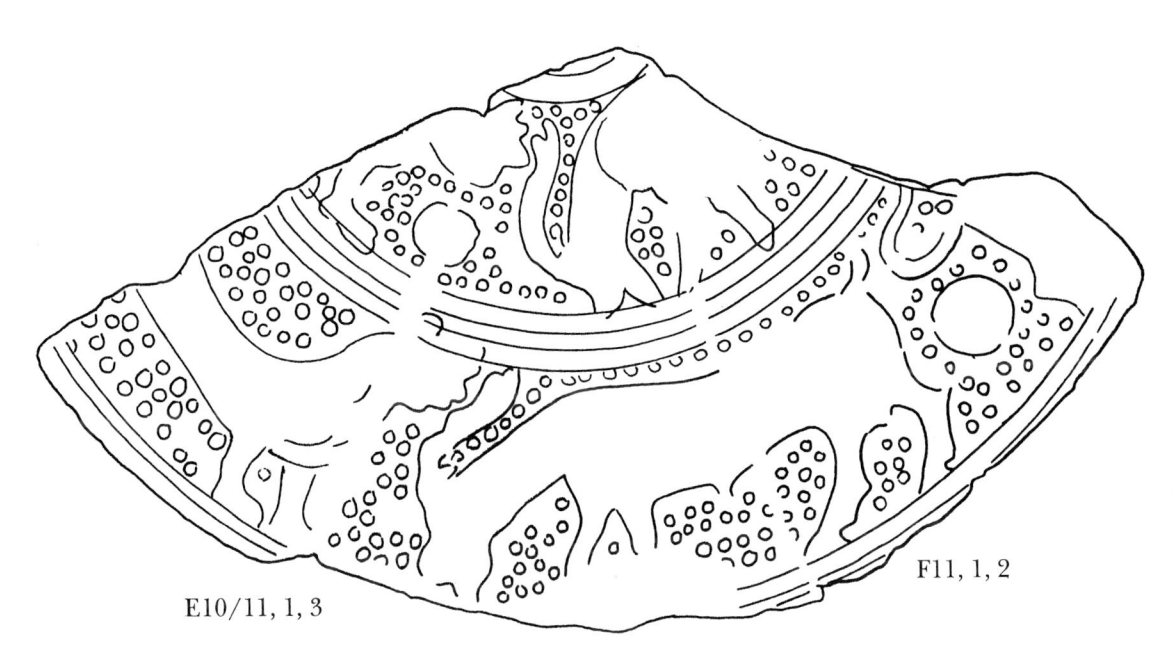

D12/E12 D (Balk), 2

*Illustration 8 (**201**)*

referred to as in the subgeometric technique,[395] and which Denise Callipolitis-Feytmans has termed *Atelier des plats de "technique subgéométrique*," active at the end of MC and the beginning of LCI.[396] This terminology has generally been replaced by silhouette style.[397] Among the uncatalogued finds, only two other fragments with "hailstorm" can definitely be attributed to this group,[398] although there are a number of rim fragments that may possibly belong to plates of this style.

These plates are characterized by two concentric animal friezes, separated by bands, around a central tondo of concentric rings. The animal friezes consist primarily of alternating panthers and goats rendered in silhouette. The filling ornament, when present, consists of dots, generally referred to as "hailstorm," sometimes interspersed with large blobs. The plates have a reserved rim with glazed bands at the base and along the outer edge, and a double-roll foot ring. Added red is used primarily for bands. The exterior is decorated with concentric bands. Our examples follow this syntax.

201   Pl. 33; Ill. 8   Sb. 127   E10/11 (Area 1) 1 3, D12/E12 D (Balk) 2, F11 1 2

Fragment, preserving about one-third of floor and single roll of double-roll foot ring. Rim broken off along with part of floor edge. Pale pink clay with buff surface. Glaze-fired red. Mended from four joining fragments.
  MPL: 0.0835; MPW: 0.165; Th: 0.0063; Est D: 0.20 (without rim)
  Interior: traces of two concentric circles of the center tondo and two animal friezes, separated by two concentric bands. Inner a.f.: panther to r., with head, neck, and foreleg preserved; goat to l., forepart preserved. Outer a.f.: panther to r. (hindquarter missing), goat to l., panther to r., tail and part of hindquarter preserved. Band around edge of floor. F.o. of "hailstorm" and large blobs. Exterior: bands of concentric circles.
  This piece is remarkable in that the joins were found in three different locations at the site (E10/11, 1, 3; D12/E12, D(balk), 2; and F11, 1, 2). The drawing (Ill. 8) indicates the find spot of each join.
  Analogies may be seen in *Tocra* I, pl. 22, no. 306; *Délos* X, pl. 6, no. 505; *MonAnt* 32 (1927), 312, fig. 129.
  Late MC

202   Pl. 34   Sb. 288–20   F13/G13 1 2
Part of floor and rim, and one roll of double-roll foot ring. Light greenish clay with buff surface. Black glaze somewhat worn and crazed. Added red. Mended from two fragments.
  MPL: 0.059; MPW: 0.079; MPDim: 0.0834
  Interior: part of two friezes separated by two red concentric bands. Inner a.f.: panther to r., f.o. of "hailstorm" and blob. Outer a.f.: panther to r., goat to l., with head bent toward ground, "hailstorm" f.o.; red band below and around edge of floor. Band on partially preserved section of rim.

---

395. Payne dates them MC; see *NC*, 313, nos. 1033–1039.

396. Callipolitis-Feytmans, 136–137, 156 (nos. 91–106), fig. 19.

397. See Hopper, 163, and *Perachora* II, 136.

398. One was found in an undisturbed archaic level (C13, 1, 4b).

Exterior: added red along inner edge of foot and concentric bands of black and added red.

See also *Tocra* I, pl. 22, no. 305; *Corinth* XV:3, pl. 54, 1309.

Late MC

203   Pl. 34   Sb. 422–5   F13/G13 2 2

Part of floor and one roll of double-roll foot ring. Deep buff clay with orange core. Black glaze worn in inner frieze, fired brown to red in outer frieze, brown where thin. Added red.

MPL: 0.0774; MPW: 0.0573; Th: 0.007

Interior: parts of two friezes separated by two concentric black bands. Inner a.f.: torso of animal to l., f.o of "hailstorm" and blobs. Outer a.f.: torso of goat to l., small section of tail of panther (?) to r., "hailstorm" f.o. Glazed and added red band around edge of floor. Exterior: concentric bands, fired red, and glaze on foot.

See also *Tocra* I, pl. 22, no. 306.

Late MC

204   Pl. 34; Fig 2. Sb. 203–1   F11 2 1–2

Part of rim, double-roll foot, and small section of floor. Clay with buff surface and orange core. Black glaze ranges from black to brown to red. Added red. Pitted and encrusted surface.

MPL: 0.0863; MPW: 0.053; MPH: 0.0237; MTh: 0.0065

Broad flaring rim with rolled overhang. Black band near base of rim. Band near groove at lip, and added red (?) and glazed bands on rolled lip. On floor: red band and glazed band around edge; a.f. with three legs of a quadruped, probably a panther, to r. and "hailstorm." Exterior: red on the underside of rolled overhang (or lip) and on double-roll foot ring.

The profile resembles Callipolitis-Feytmans, fig. 19, no. 103, in the silhouette style from the Heraion at Delos (see *Délos* X, pl. 6, no. 505, p. 147, fig. 5). There is also some similarity with *Tocra* I, fig. 18, no. 297, an MC black-figure plate. This is the only example from the sanctuary of a silhouette-style plate with "hailstorm" f.o. that preserves its entire rim.

Late MC

205   Pl. 34; Fig. 2 Sb. 96   E11/12 Balk 1

Part of rim, floor, and double-roll foot ring. Grayish green clay. Black glaze worn, where heavily only shadow of decoration remains, and brown where dilute. Added red. Rolled lip broken off from outward flaring rim. Interior foot roll smaller than exterior. Severely burnt, resulting in a gray and blackish surface. Mended from two joins. Soil-stained and encrusted.

MPL: 0.0952; MPW: 0.126; MPH: 0.0208; Th: 0.0085 (floor)

Interior: parts of two animal friezes, with no f.o., separated by two bands. Inner a.f.: trace of goat (?) to l., torso and legs preserved. Outer a.f.: part of unidentifiable animal, presumably panther to r., goat to l., and panther to r. (hindquarter preserved). Black band below frieze. Red band around edge of floor and thin red band at base of rim. Black band above base of rim and thin black lines near lip. One complete suspension hole and about one-third of another (distance of 0.042 from one to the other) preserved.

Exterior: glaze on foot rings worn; red band at edge of interior foot roll; two thin black bands and red band toward center of plate.

There is no exact parallel for the profile.[399] For the type, see *Tocra* I, pl. 22, no. 307, also with two suspension holes.

Late MC

206   Pl. 34   Sb. 76–2a,b   D12/13 B 4 West

Two floor fragments (a, b). Buff clay with grayish tinge. Black glaze heavily worn on (b). Added red overpainted. Each fragment preserves parts of two friezes, without f.o., separated by a black and red band.

(a) MPL: 0.068; MPW: 0.03

Inner a.f.: goat to l., part of hindquarter and two legs preserved. Outer a.f.: panther (head and forepart preserved) to r., goat to l., most of head preserved. Exterior: banding (rbrbbr).

(b) MPL: 0.041; MPW: 0.077

Mended from two fragments. Inner a.f.: trace of animal. Outer a.f.: part of head of panther to r.; goat to l.; panther to r., hindquarter preserved. Exterior: red and two black bands.

Same type as preceding. This is our only catalogued plate to have been found in a largely undisturbed archaic level.[400]

Late MC

LINEAR STYLE

The linear style is represented by only four fragments. The two examples ascribed to the EC period are quite unique: **207** shows some similarity with plates found at Tocra; **208** has no known parallel. Both were found in the constructional backfill of the middle sanctuary retaining wall and appear to have been burnt. There are also two fragments of the LC period: **209** is in the white style, and **210**, a rather small plate, is covered with patterns, characteristic of the LC II period. No other identifiable linear-style plate fragments were recognized among the uncatalogued finds.

207   Pl. 35; Fig. 2 Sb. 423–1   F13/G13 2 2

Fragment, preserving over one-quarter of rim, part of floor, and double-roll foot. Hard gray clay. Glaze ranges from brown to dark brown. Added red. Severely burnt as further indicated by traces of charcoal black on rim and floor. Hole (0.0046 D), presumably for suspension, unusually positioned near base of rim.[401] Large chip missing from rim and chips also missing from join. Raised ridge on rim also chipped. Mended from two joins. Soil-stained and encrusted.

MPH: 0.025; MPW: 0.0818; MPL: 0.1483; Th: 0.0093 (floor); Est D: 0.20

Rather short but thick outward curving rim with raised ridge 0.009 from edge. Squared-off edge on rim, rather than more common rolled overhang (or lip roll) of Corinthian plates (EC-LC). Small double-roll foot. Floor interior:

---

399. Callipolitis-Feytmans, fig. 19, no. 100, shows some similarity, but the rim forms a greater arc than our example.

400. As noted in the introduction, among the uncatalogued finds, a silhouette-style plate with "hailstorm" was also found in an undisturbed archaic level (C13, 1, 4b), and a black-figure floor sherd was found in a largely undisturbed archaic level

---

(D12/E12, D, 3).

401. Cf. Callipolitis-Feytmans, 123, who states that the hole is generally pierced below the rolled overhang. If it were a mend hole, however, it seems to be located too far from present break, and no evidence remains of the former presence of a metal rivet.

part of star pattern, with only one ray of star and circular band from which it emanates preserved; two narrow concentric bands around edge of floor. Rim interior: black and red lines at base, two very widely spaced rays; band on either side of raised ridge; and thin red band near reserved edge. Floor exterior: ray of star and two concentric black lines around edge. Inside of roll foot glazed. Resting surface of double-roll foot reserved. Rim exterior: narrow band at base; band of horizontal zigzags, alternating with groups of flat sigmas, between two bands.

There is no exact analogy for this unusual piece. Tocra has yielded three fragmentary plates with this type of star pattern on the floor in which the rays of the star rise from a circle.[402] However, the Tocra plates show some significant differences, e.g., a glazed rim, used of applied white, and a dissimilar form of the rim and foot, to cite a few. According to Hayes, these Tocra plates form a new EC group in which the star patterns and "the small simple feet are based on Protocorinthian and Transitional models," while the red and white lines place the plates in EC.[403]

The star pattern is known on a number of Protocorinthian plates, though its form differs from our example.[404] The widely spaced rays on the interior of the rim appear to be unique.[405] The decoration on the back of the rim, consisting of groups of sigmas alternating with a horizontal zigzag is also unparalleled among Corinthian plates. Furthermore, there is no exact parallel for the profile of our piece.

The fragment bears a number of apparent early traits: star pattern, the groups of sigmas, decoration on both sides of the plate[406] and a thick, arched rim with an unusual ridge. If we are to follow Callipolitis-Feytmans' criteria for the evolution of the Corinthian plate, however, the double-roll foot was introduced only in the MC period.[407] Although our double-roll foot is of small proportion (small size being an early trait), it is, nonetheless, a double-roll foot. This plate, then, presents a rather anomalous example.

EC?

208   Pl. 35; Fig. 2   Sb. 423–2   F13/G13 2 2

Fragment, preserving about one-ninth of rim, simple foot ring, and tiny portion of floor. Light green clay. Worn glaze, ranges from brown to olive green. Surface worn. Burnt, soil-stained, and encrusted.

MPH: 0.024; MPW: 0.044; MPL: 0.0672; Est D: 0.24

Rather short thick rim curved on interior and straight on exterior.[408] Thickening at edge of rim forms small flattened roll more pronounced on the exterior (predecessor of the lip roll?). Slight thickened ridge at juncture of foot and rim on exterior. Simple ring foot with flat resting surface.

Floor interior: traces of bands. Rim interior: fat vertical squiggles (six-bar sigmas); band above; band on edge of rim. Exterior: glaze on the rim and outside of foot; resting surface of foot appears to have been reserved.

The interior rim decoration is quite unusual, and seemingly an indication of an early date. Vertical squiggles or zigzags appear on a Protocorinthian plate from Perachora.[409] A Transitional plate from Megara Hyblaea is said to have thick zigzags on the rim.[410] Given the preserved decoration and profile, the fragment seems to be among the earliest pieces from the sanctuary, tentatively dated to the EC period, but it lacks parallels.

EC?

209   Pl. 35; Fig. 2   Sb. 102   D11/E11 Balk 3

Fragment, preserving about one-fifth of rim, part of floor and foot. Buff clay. Black glaze worn. Added red ranges to purple. Soil-stained and encrusted.

MPH: 0.022; MPW: 0.0879; MPL: 0.132; Th: 0.0074 (floor); Est D: 0.25

Arched, outward curving rim with single groove near rolled overhang. Two suspension holes (0.0394 apart) beneath the lip roll. Inside foot of the double-roll foot smaller and somewhat flatter. Interior: reserved rim with band (glaze now gone) along edge; thin dilute and thin purple band near groove at top edge of rim; thin black and broader purple band at base of rim; parts of two thin concentric purple bands on floor. Exterior: purple on lip roll; black glaze on outer roll foot and red on inner roll foot; purple circle toward center of floor.

Once again, there is no exact parallel for the profile in Callipolitis-Feytmans.[411] This is the only example of a white-style plate from the sanctuary. White-style plates seem, in general, not to have been common. Mme. Callipolitis-Feytmans lists only nine in her catalog, exclusive of two small plates.[412] With the exception of two from Delphi, all come from Corinth. Benson has dated four of the Corinth pieces to MC.[413] The rim fragments, published in *Corinth* VII:2, are dated to LC I, following Mme. Callipoltis-Feytman's dating.[414]

LC I (Possibly MC)

210   Pl. 35; Fig. 2   Sb. 422–1   F13/G13 2 2

Fragment, preserving about one-fifth rim, foot, and about one-third floor. Buff clay. Rather firm black glaze, brown where thin and fired red in places (on the exterior and edge of rim). Added red ranges to purple. Mended from three joins. Soil-stained and slightly encrusted.

MPH: 0.0163; MPW: 0.0914; MPL: 0.1073; Th: 0.009 (floor); Est D: 0.15

Small plate with horizontally everted, squared-off rim with two sets of grooves on top: two at outside and two at in-

---

402. *Tocra* I, nos. 294–296 on p. 37, pl. 20, nos. 294–295, fig. 18.

403. *Tocra* I, 24.

404. *Tocra* I, 24. To the references cited in n. 11 on p. 24, add *CVA* Stockholm, pl. 2, no. 11.

405. Interestingly, a Rhodian plate (late seventh century) with a star pattern on the inside and outside, found at Tocra, has rays on the interior of the rim, but they are closely set (*Tocra* II, pl. 31, no. 607).

406. Callipolitis-Feytmans, 124.

407. Callipolitis-Feytmans, 125.

408. In section, it bears some similarity to a Late Protocorinthian plate fragment from Megara Hyblaea; cf. Callipolitis-Feytmans, fig. 12.

409. *Perachora* II, pl. 34, no. 745.

410. Callipolitis-Feytmans, 148, no. 5, fig. 13.

411. Callipolitis-Feytmans, fig. 20, no. 3, is the closest, except for the double groove at the top of the rim.

412. Callipolitis-Feytmans, 157, nos. 1–9, fig. 20. To these should be added, no. 25 in her catalog of LC I plates on p. 159. (cf. *Corinth* VII:2, 57, no. 211 [CP-2451], pl. 39), making a total of ten.

413. See *Corinth* XV:3, no. 748 (= Callipolitis-Feytmans no. 2, KP 1157), no. 1608 (= Callipolitis-Feytmans no. 6, KP 315), no. 1609 (= Callipolitis-Feytmans no. 4, KP 2001), and KP 1437 (= Callipolitis-Feytmans no. 3), which is referred to under no. 1608 (see n. 1 under no. 1608, in particular).

414. See *Corinth* VII:2, no. 212 (= no. 9, CP-2453) and no. 211 (= no. 25, CP-2451).

side edge. Molding on underside of rim. Rather thick floor. Simple foot ring. Series of concentric raised ridges on underside of floor: two surround central boss and fourth midway to edge of floor.

Rim interior: black glaze on grooves; thin red band; double-dot band joined by diagonal lines; glazed band; black glaze on grooves; purple band on interior wall. Floor interior: black circle in center, surrounded by two concentric black bands; star-like pattern, formed by alternately inverted stepped cones, also known as the "Antiparos pattern,"[415] surrounded by three concentric black bands; band of tongues with individual outlines, surrounded by two black bands; band of alternately inverted stepped cones; and three concentric black bands.

Rim exterior: vertical stripes on flat vertical face of edge; black on molding; black and red band on horizontal underside. Floor exterior: reserved, except for black on three of the concentric moldings, and red on the fourth; two concentric bands around edge of the floor; black on foot. Black glaze on the exterior rim molding

There is no parallel for the profile in Callipolitis-Feytmans.

The fragment belongs to a series of late plates, characterized by linear motifs,[416] smaller dimensions, and angular rims, dating to the second half of the sixth century B.C.[417] The plate is neatly and extensively decorated. It probably dates early in the period, based on the presence of the concentric bands on the exterior, which were eventually dispensed with by the Corinthian potters, and the rather careful drawing. Concentric ridges on the underside also occur on an LC II plate from the Potters' Quarter at Corinth.[418]

LC II

Kothons (**211–227**)

Kothons or exaleiptra[419] were quite popular at the sanctuary.[420] Our catalog contains 17 of the more than 260 fragments retained from the excavation. The catalogued pieces range in date from MC through LC II, with most of them belonging to the LC period. There are three black-figure examples.[421]

A very small and burnt fragment (**211**), probably early MC, preserving part of a knucklebone handle with white dot rosettes, is most unusual as it appears to have traces of three friezes. The other two fragments (**212**, **213**) with animal friezes on the body, dated to MC, are in a rather careless style.[422]

The remaining examples, datable to LC, are in the linear style and include white-style pieces. They are generally representative of the LC linear-style fragments from the sanctuary, with shoulder decoration consisting of tongues, tongues with individual outlines, double-dot bands, and other patterns. Although the quality of the workmanship is, at best, quite average, **219**, a small rim-shoulder fragment, seems to be of a somewhat better style. There are examples of kothons that are both round and rectangular in section. The latter are generally rare and late,[423] but exhibit more careful drawing.[424] Although the inclusion of five such pieces (**214–219**) in our catalogue is disproportionate to the frequency of this type at the sanctuary,[425] they do stand out for their better workmanship. Three of them (**214–216**), in fact, can be associated with Amyx's Winchester Group.[426] Also to be noted is **225** with its unique decoration of linked and dotted ring rosettes. **227** is unusual for its simple loop handle. Most of the catalogued pieces were found in the backfill of the middle sanctuary retaining wall.

The overwhelming majority of the uncatalogued fragments, which number close to 250,[427] can be assigned to the linear style, and should be dated to the LC period. Owing to the poor preservation of our examples, it is often difficult to determine whether a linear-style piece is strictly speaking in the white style. Earlier in date, among the uncatalogued finds, are the knucklebone handles and the black-figure fragments, which could be MC. While 53% of the uncatalogued kothon fragments were from the backfill of

---

415. Amyx, *CSCA* 4 (1971), 22 n. 20; see also *NC*, 334, fig. 181, A.

416. For a similar alternately reversed stepped cone pattern on an LC II plate, but on the rim, see *Corinth* XV:3, pl. 66, no. 1659.

417. See Callipolitis-Feytmans, 138–140, fig. 22.

418. *Corinth* XV:3, pl. 120, no. 1665.

419. On the proper terminology (i.e., use of exaleiptron rather than kothon) and development of the shape, see *CorVP*, 470–474. We retain kothon, the more common, though improper, term.

420. The form also occurs in miniature, though much less commonly (discussed in the section on miniatures).

421. Only 7 other sherds with black-figure decoration were found. Black-figure kothons with animal friezes are also rare at

Tocra (see *Tocra* II, pl. 5, no. 1875, with frieze on the shoulder).

422. This is in keeping with Hopper's comment (p. 232): "Few of the examples with animal frieze are of good style."

423. Hopper, 232, no. 7; *NC*, 335, fig. 184.

424. The decoration and the use of moldings recall some of our powder pyxides; see **66–68**.

425. Only 8 other fragments of this type were found.

426. *CorVP*, 474.

427. The uncatalogued pieces include the following: 51 bases, 40 handles (including 15 knucklebone, 5 of which were pierced, and 10 reflex types), 19 rims, 20 body sherds (including 6 with black-figure decoration), and some 110 rim-shoulder, shoulder, or shoulder-body fragments, as well as the 8 rectangular section fragments mentioned above. Three of the fragments were burnt.

the middle sanctuary retaining wall, five pieces were found in undisturbed archaic levels[428] and 18 fragments were found in largely undisturbed archaic levels.[429]

211   Pl. 36   Sb. 297-2   F13/G13 1 2

Fragment, preserving part of an unpierced knucklebone handle[430] and adjoining body, round in section. Burnt[431] and slightly fire-cracked below handle. Chalky gray clay. Black-figure decoration blackened. Black glaze worn and crazed, brown where thin. Added red and white. Encrusted.

MPH: 0.035; MPW: 0.057

On shoulder: part of a floral (lotus?) chain with added red. On the body frieze: part of a rosette(?) to left of handle; part of wing (?) just below handle, may belong to a second body frieze. On black-glazed handle: a white dot cluster rosette on side and a row of dots (only three preserved) along the edge.

It is unfortunate that so little of this kothon is preserved, as it was, apparently, rather elaborately decorated with a floral frieze on the shoulder and possibly two friezes on the body.

According to Hopper, the knucklebone handle does not appear after the MC period.[432] Although there is no exact analogy for the white dot cluster rosette on the handle, a fragmentary kothon, also with two friezes, from Perachora has knucklebone handles covered with white dots.[433]

MC (Early ?)

212   Pl. 36   Sb. 443-1   F13/G13   Wall Test

Body fragment, round in section. Buff clay. Glaze ranges from black to dark brown to orange. Added red and possibly white. Exterior surface worn. Interior encrusted.

MPH: 0.035; MPW: 0.054

On shoulder: double-dot band, bordered by band above and below. Body frieze: foreparts of bird to r. and goat to l. Added red on breast and shoulder of bird and on neck of goat. F.o. of incised blobs. On lower body: alternating black and white (?) bands. On the interior, traces of black glaze.

For the type, see *CVA* Brussels, fasc. 1 (IIIC), pl. 7, 9a–b; *CVA* Louvre, fasc. 8, pl. 22, nos. 1–3, 5.

MC

213   Pl. 36   Sb. 288-26   F13/G13 1 2

Fragment, round in section, preserving part of shoulder and body. Buff clay. Black glaze worn and crazed, brown where thin. Added red. Encrusted.

MPH: 0.043; MPW: 0.095

On shoulder: double-dot band with band below. Body frieze: part of file of swans to r., added red on necks and wings. F.o. of dots. Black glaze on both exterior and interior lower body.

For the type, see *CVA* Louvre, fasc. 8, pl. 22, 4,6,9, which Amyx states as possibly still EC.[434] Swans were apparently a favorite frieze motif on kothons.[435]

MC

214   Pl. 36   Sb. 113   E10 Bldg., Not stratified

Shoulder fragment with part of side wall and hanging rim. Pale buff clay. Worn black glaze. Added red (purple) worn. Slightly encrusted.

MPH: 0.0092; MPW: 0.053; MPL: 0.043; Est D: 0.20

Rectangular in section, with horizontal shoulder, vertical side wall, and rounded moldings (two of unequal size at rim and one at juncture of shoulder and side wall).[436]

From the center: red on hanging rim that has a single groove below molding; short black vertical squiggles on broader interior molding; red on edge of molding; red on second molding; broad red band; thin black band; double-dot band, bordered by thin black band above and below; band of alternating black and red tongues with individual outlines, bordered by thin black bands above and below; black on edge molding.

For the type, see *NC*, 335, fig. 184 (1520, Winchester), and *Délos* X, pl. 37, 524 a–b. Amyx has assigned the Winchester and Delos vases to his Winchester Group,[437] to which our fragment with its neat workmanship may be added.

LC II, Winchester Group

215   Pl. 36   Sb. 520-4   F14/G14 1 3

Shoulder fragment, hanging rim and side wall broken off. Buff clay. Glaze almost entirely worn. Added red worn. Heavily encrusted.

MPL: 0.04; MPW: 0.043; Est D: 0.18

Rectangular in section, horizontal shoulder and moldings (two at rim and one at juncture of shoulder and side wall).

From the center: glaze on moldings gone; band; double-dot band, bordered by band above and below; band of alternating black and red tongues (RBRBBRB) with individual outlines, bordered by band above and below; band; trace of black glaze on edge molding. The red tongues are narrower than the black tongues.

Similar to preceding.

LC II, Winchester Group

216   Pl. 36   Sb. 520-3   F14/G14 1 3 and
                                      F13/G13 2 2

Fragment, preserving about one-fifth of shoulder and part of side wall. Buff clay. Firm black glaze. Surface orange where originally overpainted with red. Mended from three fragments: surface worn on the two joining fragments found in F13/G13, 2, 2.

---

428. E11, 2, 3 (2 shoulder-bodies, encrusted), C13/D13, 1, 7 (a base), C13, 1, 4b (body fragment, possibly from a black polychrome kothon, with black glaze and traces of purple), and F14/G14, 1, 4 (reflex handle).

429. E11, 3, 3 (knucklebone handle, 2 shoulder sherds, and a base), D12/13, B, 4 (shoulder, a handle, white-style body fragment with part of a reflex handle), D12/13, A, 3 (shoulder-body fragment with a double-dot band and traces of black-figure, a linear-style shoulder fragment, and a possible base), E11/12, Pit Area, 3 (rim overhang, knucklebone handle, and a base), D12/E12, D, 3 (a floor, a shoulder, and a shoulder-body fragment) and D12/13, F, 4 (2 white-style body-handle fragments).

430. Fifteen other knucklebone handle fragments were found, 7 of them pierced, but none had a white rosette.

431. Three other kothon fragments showed evidence of burning.

432. For the handle type, but without the white dot rosette, see *CVA* Louvre, fasc. 8, pl. 22, 1–6, 9; R. M. Burrows and P. N. Ure, "Kothons and Vases of Allied Types," *JHS* 31 (1911), fig. 2.

433. See *Perachora* II, 203 no. 2003 (not illustrated), dated perhaps EC.

434. *CorVP*, 472.

435. Cf. *Perachora* II, 203.

436. Four similar fragments were found during excavations in the following locations: E11, 1, 2; E11, 2, 2; E10, Balk South; and F11, 2, 2.

437. *CorVP*, 474.

MPH: 0.022; MPL: 0.17; MPW: 0.035; Est D: 0.20

Rectangular in section, horizontal shoulder, vertical side wall, and molding both at rim and at juncture of shoulder and side wall.

From the center: edge of molding; red band; double-dot band, bordered by black and red lines above and below; band of alternating reserved, black and red tongues (B.BRB.BRB.BRB.BRB.BRB.BRB.B) with individual outlines, bordered by thin black lines above and below; red line; black glaze on molding.

Similar to preceding.

LC II, Winchester Group

217   Pl. 36   Sb. 118–2   E10 Bldg. Balk 3 (Over and Under Fallen Blocks)

Body fragment, preserving edge of shoulder, part of vertical side wall, and handle attachment. Light green clay. Glaze fugitive. Added red (purple) worn. Encrusted.

MPH: 0.0382; MPW: 0.0397

Rectangular in section with molding at juncture of shoulder and side wall and at juncture of vertical side wall and inward sloping lower body. On shoulder: red and trace of black band near edge molding. On side wall: two thin red bands near lower molding and trace of black glaze on molding.

LC II

218   Pl. 36   Sb. 40–4   E11 1 2

Fragment, preserving less than one-quarter of vertical side wall and lower body. Side wall broken off at shoulder molding. Buff clay. Black glaze, peeling. Added red. Surface worn and encrusted.

MPH: 0.056; MPW: 0.151; Est D: 0.23

Rectangular in section with projecting half-round molding at juncture of side wall and lower body.

Exterior: band above molding; traces of black glaze on molding; black and red banding on lower body.

LC II

219   Pl. 36   Sb. 519–2   F14/G14 1 2

Fragment, preserving part of hanging rim and shoulder, round in section. Creamy buff to pinkish clay. Glaze-fired black to red, brown where dilute. Added red. Encrusted.

MPL: 0.031; MPW: 0.0474; Est D: 0.23

On hanging rim: added red and black bands. On shoulder: narrow red and black bands; maeander band with thin black band above and below; double-dot band with red band above and below.

The maeander band is not a common motif on kothons. For an example, see *Perachora* II, pl. 88, 2014, on a kothon of rectangular section.

LC II

220   Pl. 36   Sb. 420–8   F13/G13 2 2N

Fragment, preserving about one-quarter of hanging rim and part of shoulder. Round section. Buff clay. Metallic blue-black glaze ranges to brown. Added red ranges to purple. Surface worn and chipped.

MPH: 0.0254; MPW: 0.035; MPL: 0.088; Est D: 0.09 (interior)

On hanging rim: bands (three black and one red). On shoulder: glazed band around edge; reserved (?) band; band of black tongues with individual outlines alternating with panel containing dot-cluster rosette; red and glazed bands.

For a similar decorative scheme, with a dot rosette in a panel, but on a kothon with rectangular section, see *Délos* X, pl. 37, 524, and *NC*, fig. 184, attributed to the Winchester Group.[438]

LC II

221   Pl. 37   Sb. 520–1   F14/G14 1 3

Fragment, preserving about one-quarter hanging rim and part of shoulder. Round section. Creamy buff clay. Glaze ranges from brown to yellowish brown, somewhat worn. Added red. Mended from two joins.

MPW: 0.032; MPL: 0.108; Est D: 0.08 (interior)

On hanging rim: bands (worn). On shoulder: two bands; band of "hooks," bordered by dilute yellow bands above and below; thin glazed and red bands.

For a similar pattern on the shoulder, referred to as degenerate leaves, see Burrows and Ure, *JHS* 31 (1911), fig. 3 (BM A 1570).

LC

222   Pl. 37   Sb. 501–4   F14/G14 1 Test 1 mixed with some 2

Shoulder and body fragment along with tiny portion of hanging rim. Round section. Light grayish buff clay. Black glaze worn. Added red. Mended from two joins. Encrusted.

MPW: 0.067; MPL: 0.032

On shoulder: trace of band; band of alternating hooks, sloppily drawn and set at an angle, with thin red band above and below; black stripe and red band; slight traces of banding on side wall.

The alternating hook pattern on this white-style fragment is not a common motif on such vases, though the pattern is a common one in the LC period.[439]

LC

223   Pl. 37   Sb. 516–1a,b   F14/G14 1 2

Two fragments (a,b), round in section. White style? Deep buff clay. Black glaze ranges to dark brown, mostly worn. Added red.

(a) Two joining fragments (one found in F14/G14, 1, 2/3), preserving part of hanging rim and shoulder.

MPH: 0.024; MPW: 0.024; MPL: 0.087; Est D: 0.08 (interior)

On hanging rim: broad red band and worn black band. On the shoulder: black band; band of black tongues, carelessly drawn and of unequal size, bordered by two thin bands above and below; banding (four narrow black and one red).

(b) Shoulder fragment. Surface worn and chipped.

MPW: 0.023; MPL: 0.048

On the shoulder: band of black tongues, lower portion preserved; banding as in (a).

For a similar type, see *CVA* Stockholm, 51, pl. 23, no. 9, where the decoration in the shoulder band is referred to as "pendant dots," and attributed to Burrows' and Ure's Type A.II; as well as Campbell, *Hesperia* 7 (1938), fig. 18, 138 (lotus-bud pattern).

LC

224   Pl. 37   Sb. 422–2   F13/G13 2 2

Fragment, preserving about one-quarter of hanging rim and shoulder, round in section. Buff clay with orangey core. Black glaze ranges from brown to a deep red. Added red (purple).

MPH: 0.023; MPW: 0.037; MPL: 0.088

On hanging rim: red band between two glazed bands. On shoulder: two glazed and one red band; band of alter-

---

438. See **214**.

439. This hook pattern, for example, occurs on a number of miniature vases from Corinth. See *Corinth* XV:3, pl. 67, no. 1738, pl. 68, nos. 1788 and 1795, pl. 71, no. 1933, and pl. 74, no. 2092.

nating red and black buds; four alternating red and black lines.

For a similar example, see M. T. Campbell, *Hesperia* 7 (1938), 594, fig. 18, 135 (Burrows' and Ure's Type A.II).

LC

225 Pl. 37   Sb. 481-1   E10 Bldg. Clean-up under fallen N Wall

Body fragment, possibly from a stemmed kothon. Buff clay. Black glaze, mostly gone, and flaking on interior. Added red worn.

MPH: 0.0393; MPW: 0.0724; MPL: 0.0452

Part of side wall and lower body with rather angular profile. Half-round molding at juncture of side wall and steeply sloping lower body.

On side wall: linked rings with added red on dot in center of each ring. Lower body reserved. On interior: carelessly applied glaze and trace of red (?) band.

The motif of individual "dot-and-ring" occurs, alternating between lotuses, on an LC I kothon from the Potters' Quarter at Corinth (*Corinth* XV:3, 169, pl. 40, no. 884).[440] It also appears on EC and MC kothons where the motif alternates with zigzags.[441] Stylistically, it recalls the alternating loop pattern seen on kothons,[442] assigned by Amyx to the Serpentine Group.[443] There is no direct analogy for this pattern. The form of the body is also unusual, and an analogy is suggested by a stemmed kothon in Heidelberg (*CVA* Heidelberg, pl. 19, 8).

LC?

226 Pl. 37   Sb. 264   F13/G13 1 1

Fragment, preserving reflex handle and part of adjoining lower body. Buff clay with pale orange core. Worn black glaze. Slightly encrusted.

MPH: 0.03; MPW: 0.072

Traces of black glaze on top of handle. Thin black band below handle. Glazed band on interior, fired red.

Reflex handles were a common type in the LC period,[444] and are characteristic of Burrows' and Ure's Type A.II.[445] They occur on many white-style kothons.[446]

LC I/II

227 Pl. 37   Sb. 338-2   C12/13 1 Wall 2 Backfill from N of Wall

Fragment, preserving about one-quarter of kothon, round in section. Complete simple ring or loop handle.[447] Rim broken off and base missing. Light green clay. Fugitive black glaze. Encrusted. Mended from two joins.

MPH: 0.048; MPW: 0.133

Traces of banding on body and glaze on floor interior.

This type of handle is rare, if not unique, on kothons, except occasionally on miniatures. Generally, simple handles are of the ribbon variety.[448]

LC?

Oinochoai (228–251)

The catalog contains 24 fragments, representative of the identifiable oinochoai finds from the sanctuary: both standard and small broad-bottomed, trefoil, and conical types.[449] The entries, ranging in date from MC to LC II/III, include black-figure, black-glaze, and linear-style examples. For the most part, the types are conventional with an apparent predominance of oinochoai with double-incised verticals on the shoulder.[450] A large portion of our catalogued pieces comes from the backfill of the middle sanctuary retaining wall.[451]

Our series begins with three MC black-figured fragments, which are notable, though not exceptional. They are also, unfortunately, very poorly preserved—the glaze is fugitive and little remains of the animal frieze. **228**, from a broad-bottomed oinochoe, preserves double-incised tongues on the shoulder and part of a rather fine panther head. The other broad-bottomed oinochoe fragment (**230**) has a small section of the animal frieze with a winged creature and rays around the lower body. The third fragment (**229**), with incised shoulder tongues and part of a feline, may be from a globular oinochoe. **231**, an LC I/II fragment, perhaps from a globular oinochoe, has an unusual combination of incised verticals on the shoulder and a floral chain in the main frieze.

There are a number of black-glazed shoulder fragments with double-incised verticals and polychrome enhancements of only red or red and white (**232–234**) which may be from either black-glaze or black-figure oinochoai. Black-glaze types are also represented by conical oinochoai (**235, 236**) and a small broad-bottomed oinochoe (**248**). There are several

---

440. Benson refers to the motif as a ring rosette.

441. Cf. *Délos* X, pl. 36, no. 516; *Corinth* VII:1, pl. 37, nos. 296–297 (dated EC), where they are not yet actually ring rosettes, but "degenerating" from dot rosettes; *Mégara Hyblaea*, pl. 54, nos. 10–11 (dated MC).

442. *Délos*, X, pl. 37, 528; *CVA* Heidelberg, fasc. 1, pl. 19, 4–6.; *Corinth* XV:3, pl. 66, 1682.

443. *CorVP*, 473.

444. Hopper, 233. Also common in this period were simple band handles.

445. Burrows and Ure, *JHS* 31 (1911), figs. 3–4.

446. Examples are too numerous to cite. For profile drawing, see *CVA* Stockholm, figs. 112 and 113 (= pl. 23, 8 and 9, respec-

tively).

447. Two similar fragments were found in E11/12, balk, 2 and E10, balk south.

448. As, for example, *Délos* X, pl. 36, 512–514, 516; *Hesperia* 33 (1964), pl. 19 E23; and *Tocra* I, pl. 18, 257.

449. Fragments of globular oinochoe have been tentatively identified and are noted in the catalog.

450. This type of shoulder decoration is, of course, most easily recognizable. Even among the uncatalogued closed shape shoulder fragments, however, only 2 with black-figure friezes were identified and 1 with silhouette animals, see n. 484.

451. About 60% of the uncatalogued finds were also from this area.

neck fragments of which **242**, with its multiple moldings, is particularly interesting. The two trefoil oinochoe lids (**250, 251**) deserve mention.

The linear-style fragments belong to broad-bottomed oinochoai of both standard (**238, 239**) and small size. These small broad-bottomed or cylindrical oinochoai (**244–246, 249**), as they are also known, which are generally quite common in LC II and into LC III, are our latest examples. They are, however, not well represented at the sanctuary; besides our three catalogued examples, only two others were recognized among the uncatalogued finds. **244** preserves a loop pattern seen on the kothons of Amyx's Serpentine Group.[452] **245**, with a checker pattern, is the only fragment in our catalog to have been found in a largely undisturbed archaic level.[453] **246**, dating to LCII/III, is almost complete.

In general, oinochoai do not appear to have been numerous. In addition to our catalogued pieces, 55 other identifiable oinochoai fragments were retained from the excavations, 15 of which, for example, belong to full-size broad-bottomed oinochoai.[454] A significant portion, however, of the uncatalogued closed vase fragments, in all probability, also belong to oinochoai.[455] Of our uncatalogued finds, four were found in largely undisturbed archaic levels.[456]

228   Pl. 38   Sb. 61–1   E12   1   3
Fragment, preserving part of shoulder and belly frieze, probably from a broad-bottomed oinochoe. Pale buff clay with pinkish core. Glaze gone. Added red. Mended from two joins.
MPH: 0.0414; MPW: 0.062; Th: 0.004
Double-incised tongues on shoulder. Banding below gone except for one red stripe. A.f.: panther to l., part of head, neck, and shoulder markings preserved. F.o. of double-centered incised rosette and part of another rosette. The incision work for the ears, which are "doughnut-shaped," and the forehead is careful and distinctive.
MC

229   Pl. 38   Sb. 506–3   F14/G14   1   Test 2
Fragment, preserving part of shoulder and belly frieze, possibly from a globular oinochoe. Pale buff clay with pinkish core. Glaze almost gone. Added red. Slightly soil-stained.
MPH: 0.046; MPW: 0.068; Th: 0.0055
Double-incised tongues on shoulder. Fleck of added red preserved in third tongue from l. Banding below tongue zone has disappeared. A.f.: part of feline to r., faint shadow of form remains as well as incisions for shoulder, rib, and haunch markings. F.o. of incised centered rosettes and incised blobs or fillers.
MC

230   Pl. 38   Sb. 501–1   F14/G14   1   Test 1
mixed with some St 2
Lower body fragment from a broad-bottomed oinochoe. Light greenish clay. Black glaze almost gone. Added red. Soil-stained and encrusted.
MPH: 0.0625; MPW: 0.0667; Th: 0.005
A.f.: part of avian to l., tail and wing feathers preserved; foreleg of feline to l.; f.o. of blobs and dots. Band below frieze. Shadows of bands below and black and red band preserved. Shadows of rays, not tangent at base.
MC

231   Pl. 38   Sb. 516–2   F14/G14   1   2
Fragment, preserving part of shoulder and belly. Pale light green clay. Black glaze fugitive. Only shadows of decoration remain. Added red. Encrusted.
MPH: 0.0367; MPW: 0.059
Double-incised tongues on shoulder. Traces of banding. Frieze: lotus and bud chain with incision on lotus. Added red on buds.
The combination of incised tongues on the shoulder and a main floral frieze is rare, if not unique, on Corinthian oinochoai. I have found no parallel. Oinochoai, both globular and broad-bottomed, that bear this type of decoration on the shoulder are entirely covered with black-glaze or have black-figured decoration, or, occasionally, have silhouette figures in the main belly frieze.[457] The lotus-and-bud chain is a common floral motif, appearing often on pyxides of the LC period.[458] For a similar floral frieze on an oinochoe, but without incised verticals on the shoulder, see *Corinth* XIII, 109, pl. 33, 224–4, dated to about the middle of the sixth century.
LC I/II

232   Pl. 38   Sb. 288–23   F13/G13   1   2
Shoulder fragment. Pale buff clay. Worn black glaze. Added red worn. Added white fugitive (appears as discoloration on one of the tongues). Encrusted.
MPH: 0.061; MPW: 0.056; Th: 0.0056
Raised ridge or cordon at base of wide neck. Red band below. Black-glazed double-incised tongues on shoulder with color enhancements (.W?R..R). Polychrome bands, alternating red and black.
MC ?

233   Pl. 38   Sb. 528–5   F12/G12   Tunnel A
Shoulder fragment, broken on all sides. Buff to pinkish clay. Worn, rather lustrous black glaze. Added red ranges to purple.
MPH: 0.04; MPW: 0.0578; Th: 0.0043
Black-glazed incised double verticals, varying in width, and with added red enhancements (..RR.R.R). Narrow red band below tongues. Broad black band and red band below.
MC ?

---

452. *CorVP*, 473.

453. D12/13, B, 4 also yielded a broad-bottomed oinochoe base with horizontal bands.

454. The 55 uncatalogued fragments consist of: 11 handles (7 strap, 3 double-reeded, and 1 ribbon); 15 full-size broad-bottomed oinochoe bases, some with rays and some with bands; 2 small broad-bottomed oinochoe bases; 4 unidentified bases; 8 shoulder fragments (7 of which have double-incised tongues and 1 additionally has part of a severely worn black-figure frieze, and 1 has the root of a strap handle); 3 rims (1 from a conical and 1 from a trefoil-mouthed oinochoe); 7 neck fragments, 2 of which belong to narrow-necked broad-bottomed oinochoai; 3 trefoil lids; and 2 body sherds.

455. See introduction to closed shapes.

456. D12/13, B, 4 West (base of a broad-bottomed oinochoe with horizontal bands), D12/E12, D, 3 (strap handle and adjoining body with black-figured decoration), C13, 1, 4a (double-reeded handle and neck with horizontal zigzag).

457. See *Perachora* II, 204 ff.

458. Cf. *Délos* X, pl. XXXII, no. 506.

234   Pl. 38   Sb. 506–9   F14/G14 1 Test 2
Shoulder fragment, broken on all sides. Buff clay. Worn black glaze. Added red and white. Encrusted.
MPH: 0.039; MPW: 0.0463; Th: 0.0037
Rather broad double-incised verticals. Traces of red in center of two of the verticals. Polychrome banding (wRwBwrwr).
MC ?

235   Pl. 38   Sb. 419–4   F13/G13 2 2
Fragment of a black-glazed conical oinochoe, preserving about two-thirds of shoulder, part of body, and root of strap handle. Buff clay with pinkish core. Black glaze unevenly fired and applied, flaked off, but lustrous where preserved. Added red and white.
MPH: 0.072; MPW: 0.0726; Th: 0.005; D: 0.0365 (exterior mouth)
Double-incised verticals of varying width, with traces of added red in one and added white in another. Polychrome bands below (wrwwrw).
The glaze has flaked off in a curious fashion on the body, leaving the impression of traces of figured decoration, specifically the rear of a quadruped (haunch, rear leg and tail) and f.o. of blobs. It appears almost as if the artist had begun to decorate the oinochoe with a black-figured scene and later changed his mind and covered the body with black glaze.[459] The black polychrome conical oinochoe is a common type, particularly in the EC and MC periods.[460] The shape apparently continued into the early LC period, as illustrated by *Corinth* VII:2, pl. 63, An 53.[461]
MC

236   Pl. 38   Sb. 421–2   F13/G13 2 2
Neck fragment of large conical oinochoe. Buff clay. Black glaze flaking and unevenly fired (areas of reddish brown). Clay surface not carefully smoothed.
MPH: 0.1144; MPD: 0.0368
Tall cylindrical neck, somewhat misshapen in form. Rim missing and broken off at shoulder, only a tiny portion of which is preserved with traces of incised vertical lines. Interior is partially glazed. The fact that the neck is not carefully shaped may indicate a MC date.[462] It is possible that this neck belongs to the preceding fragment.
MC

237   Pl. 39   Sb. 111   E10 Balk, South 2/3
Fragment, preserving about one-quarter base and adjoining lower body of broad-bottomed oinochoe. Light yellowish green clay. Worn black glaze. Added red. Added white (?). Mended from two joins. Surface chipped and slightly pitted. Encrusted.
MPH: 0.0515; MPW: 0.1366; Est D: 0.165 (base)
Broad glazed band on body with trace of added white stripe (now mainly encrusted). Thin red stripe. Band of rays, not tangent at their bases. Red band and another red band on the upper part of the beveled foot. The form of the rays resemble those on an MC black-figure broad-bottomed oinochoe from the North Cemetery at Corinth (*Corinth* XIII, pl. 22, 155–b) and an MC linear-style broad-bottomed oinochoe from a grave at Examilia (*Hesperia* 33 [1964], 95, 100, pl. 19 E10).
MC ?

238   Pl. 39   Sb. 421–9   F13/G13 2 2
Fragment, preserving about one-third of base and part of adjoining lower body of a broad-bottomed oinochoe, probably decorated in the linear style. Buff clay. Black glaze, brown where dilute. Added red, flaking. Mended from two joins.
MPH: 0.022; MPW: 0.099; Est D: 0.10 (base)
On body, broad black band with thin red band below. Added red on slightly spreading foot. Groove around foot on underside.
For a similar type, see *Corinth* VII:1, pl. 44, 373, and *Corinth* XIII, pl. 24, 160–6 and pl. 29, 188–4.
MC or LC I

239   Sb. 516–19   F14/G14 1 2
Fragment, preserving over one-quarter base and part of adjoining lower body of a broad-bottomed oinochoe, possibly decorated in the linear style. Light grayish green clay. Glaze worn. Added red.
MPH: 0.0226; MPW: 0.0904; Est D: 0.105
Bands, two black and one red, on lower body. Added red on foot. Groove on underside of base where there is a trace of red.
Related to preceding, but less flaring foot.
MC or LC I

240   Pl. 39   Sb. 205   F11 2 1
Fragment, preserving about one-half of neck of a narrow-necked broad-bottomed oinochoe. Clay ranges from a light yellow-green to a pale pink. Black glaze fugitive. Added red.
MPH: 0.04; MPD: 0.0498 (with flange); MPD: 0.037 (without flange)
Relatively tall narrow neck with flange. Red band on interior at base of broken off rim. This type of neck occurs on black-glazed,[463] black-figured,[464] and linear-style broad-bottomed oinochoai.[465]
MC ?

241   Pl. 39   Sb. 506–10   F14/G14 1 Test 2
Fragment, preserving less than one-quarter of rather low, broad neck, and tiny portion of shoulder, from an oinochoe with a trefoil mouth. Buff clay with orangey core. Worn and flaking black glaze. Added red.
MPH: 0.0255; MPW: 0.0485; Est D: 0.06
Black glaze on neck with red band at base. Red on shoulder. On the interior, flaking black glaze.
Probably from a type such as *Corinth* XIII, pl. 20, 156–6, a MC black-glazed broad-bottomed trefoil oinochoe.
MC ?

242   Pl. 39   Sb. 506–7   F14/G14 1 Test 2
Fragment, preserving neck, root of handle, and tiny section of shoulder. Creamy buff clay, orange on interior. Black glaze worn. Added red. Encrusted.
MPH: 0.0364; MPW: 0.0513; D: 0.0334 (neck)

---

459. For an example of a conical oinochoe with incised verticals on the shoulder and black-figured frieze on the body, see *Perachora* II, pl. 73, no. 2133, p. 218, dated EC.

460. On the shape, see *Perachora* II, 218 ff. and 222 ff., in particular, for those with black polychrome decoration. For the type, see *Corinth* XV:3, no. 1513, pl. 62, a smaller version of our example, dated EC.

461. See discussion on pp. 82, 109 (An 53).

462. Cf. Benson's comment in *Corinth* XV:3, no. 1513, p. 277, and that of Amyx in *Corinth* VII:2, An53 on p. 109, dated to beginning of LC, because, among other traits, the neck is more sausage-shaped.

463. As in *Corinth* XIII, pl. 19, 141–4; *Corinth* XV:3, pl. 64, no. 1595 (MC); Fairbanks, pl. XLV, 472.

464. Cf. *Corinth* XIII, pl. 22, 155–a.

465. Lawrence, *Hesperia* 33 (1964), pl. 19, E10.

Five moldings on neck, originally painted red and black. Below moldings, black and red bands. Cordon at base of neck. Tops of painted tongues preserved on shoulder.

Such elaborate moldings are unparalleled on the necks of Corinthian oinochoai.

LC ?

243 Pl. 39   Sb. 139–1   D16/17 1 3 NW Corner

Fragment, preserving part of rim and neck, and tiny section of shoulder of a trefoil oinochoe. Buff clay. Peeling, flaking black glaze. Mended from two joins. Encrusted.

MPH: 0.033; MPW: 0.0736; D: 0.037 (neck)

Short, cylindrical, slightly convex neck. One of lobes broken off and part of another lobe missing from rim.

For a broad-bottomed type, but a miniature, see *Corinth* XIII, pl. 24, 160–8. Globular oinochoai also have similar mouths and necks (see *Corinth* XIII, pl. 25, 162–4).

MC or LC

244 Pl. 40   Sb. 40–2   E11 1 2

Fragment of a small broad-bottomed[466] or cylindrical[467] oinochoe, preserving part of body, shoulder, vertical handle, and edge of base as well as tiny portion of neck. Buff clay with pale orange core. Glaze-fired mostly red, and worn where black. Added red. Surface worn and encrusted.

MPH: 0.058 (with handle root); MPW: 0.036; Est D: 0.05 (base)

Red band at base of neck. Tongues on shoulder with red centers and black outlines. Six thin bands below, two of which are red and two black. Body frieze: alternating loop design of pear- or teardrop-shaped form with dots in center (originally overpainted in red) within each loop. Band at base.

For a a virtually identical pattern on a small broad-bottomed oinochoe, see *Perachora* II, pl. 112, no. 2610.[468] The same pattern occurs on LC kothons of Amyx's "Serpentine Group."[469]

LC II

245 Pl. 40   Inv. No. 71–375 D12/13 B 4

Fragment, preserving over two-thirds body and handle root of a small broad-bottomed oinochoe. Buff clay. Black glaze, brown where dilute. Added red. Mended from four joins. Encrusted.

MPH: 0.044 (with handle root); MPW: 0.0524; D: 0.055 (base)

Low body with vertical walls and flat rounded shoulder. Alternating cone or triangle pattern on shoulder with one red and two brown lines below. Two rows of elongated checkers, bounded by red lines above and below and separated by a reserved band. Black band on edge of foot. Underside concave with groove around edge.

There are numerous examples of similar oinochoai,[470] but none has such a broad reserved band separating the two rows of checkers[471] nor the same type of shoulder decoration.[472] Thus, our example represents yet another variant of this type.

LC II

246 Pl. 40   Inv. No. 74–240 D16/17 2 4

Almost complete small broad-bottomed oinochoe; only a small piece is missing from the bottom. Deep buff clay. Buff clay. Black glaze, brown where dilute. Added red. Traces of burning. Mended.

MPH: 0.1197 (with handle); MPD: 0.0755; D: 0.069 (base)

White, *Fourth Report*, 173, n. 28, Pl. 28, fig. 27.

Rather tall body, sloping shoulder, splayed foot, concave underside. Trace of black glaze on rim and high vertical handle. Red at base of neck, which forms slight elevation at juncture with shoulder. Alternating red and black tongues with outlines on shoulder, bounded below by four bands, alternating red and black. On body: row of black "leaves," or tongues, and row of small black dots below. Banding, including broad red band between two dilute bands. Red on foot.

For analogous decoration on the body, see *Délos* X, pl. 35, 484, whose shape is closer to our example, and *Perachora* II, pl. 112, no. 2608, dated fifth century?, a squatter and shorter vase.

LC II/III

247 Pl. 40   Sb. 528–11   F12/G12 Tunnel A

Fragment, preserving part of shoulder and body of small black-glazed broad-bottomed (?) oinochoe. Light greenish buff clay. Black glaze almost gone. Large white inclusion in wall.

MPH: 0.033; MPW: 0.039

Rounded, sloping shoulder and slightly convex wall. Double-incised vertical lines on wall.

The preserved section of the profile of this small closed shape appears to resemble that of a broad-bottomed oinochoe. However, the vertical incised stripes on the body are most unusual.

LC ?

248 Pl. 40   Sb. 488–3   F15 1 2

Fragment, preserving one-quarter of shoulder, part of body and vertical handle, and tiny section of neck, of small black-glazed broad-bottomed oinochoe. Buff clay. Flaking black glaze.

MPH: 0.039 (with handle section); MPW: 0.045

Cordon or ridge at juncture of neck and sloping shoulder. Vertical wall. Lower part of high vertical handle.

LC

249 Pl. 40   Sb. 290–2   F13/G13 1 2

Fragment, preserving incomplete rim and part of neck from a small cylindrical or broad-bottomed oinochoe.[473] Buff clay. Flaking black glaze. Added red. Encrusted.

MPH: 0.0254; MPW: 0.0325; D: 0.0162 (neck)

Black glaze on trefoil mouth, which has a piece missing. Red on neck overpainted with black, just below rim. Red band at base of neck.

LC II

---

466. Cf. *NC*, 336, nos. 1536–1541, figs. 189 and 190, where the shape is referred to as a small broad-bottomed oinochoe; and *Perachora* II, 272–3. Hazel Palmer in *Corinth* XIII, 109 includes an example (253-2, pl. 35) from the North Cemetery among the broad-bottomed oinochoai.

467. Benson in *Corinth* XV:3, refers to the shape as a cylindrical oinochoe (see entries under Oinochoe, Cylindrical on p. 419).

468. See also *Corinth* XV:3, 308, no. 1682 n.1, where an unpublished fragment in the University Museum, Philadelphia (L.224–56), is mentioned as well as references to similar loop patterns on kothons (cf. *CorVP*, 473).

---

469. *CorVP*, 473.

470. See *Corinth* XV:3, 302–3, no. 1652, pl. 65 (very close in shape to our example) for references.

471. For a narrow reserved band and similar shape, see *Corinth* XIII, pl. 35, 253–2.

472. Tongues appear to be more common.

473. For the type, see *NC*, figs. 189–190; *Perachora* II, pl. 112, no. 2604; *Corinth* XIII, pl. 35, 253–2, to cite a few examples.

250   Pl. 40   Sb. 313–1   D13 (Area 2) Ext.N 1

Lid fragment of trefoil oinochoe. Buff to light greenish clay. Black glaze, where preserved fired dark metallic blue to purplish brown and crazed, but mostly worn. Added red and white. Encrusted.

MPH: 0.062; MPW: 0.1022; D: 0.0485 (base)

Fragment preserves about one-third of lid, probably from a broad-neck trefoil mouth oinochoe. Molded knob (0.024 H) at center. Flat wire-drawn base. Black glaze originally on exterior and interior. Polychrome bands (wRw) above base on interior.

For the type, see the lid from the Argive Heraion in *Hesperia* 21 (1952), no. 168, pl. 52.

MC ?

251   Pl. 40   Sb. 422–7   F13/G13 2 2

Lid fragment of trefoil oinochoe.[474] Light grayish green clay. Black glaze fugitive. Burnt and encrusted.

MPH: 0.03; MPW: 0.033; MPL: 0.042

Fragment preserves less than one-third lid, probably from a narrow-necked broad-bottomed oinochoe. Molded knob in center.[475]

MC or LC ?

Amphoriskoi (**252–256**)

The amphoriskos was an infrequent vase shape at the sanctuary. There are five catalogued examples, all with black-figure animal frieze decoration on the shoulder and belly. Similar examples, but in a more complete state, have been found at Tocra and attributed to Benson's "*Gruppe der rückwärtsschauenden Vögel*," dated to the late MC period (ca. 580–575 B.C.).[476] Where preserved, our examples, with their rather thick filling ornament, do not exhibit the more common mixed animal friezes on the belly, but only files of birds (**252–254**). In fact, **252** actually preserves two birds with their heads turned back, as in the name of Benson's grouping. With the exception of **256**, the figured decoration is worn.

In addition to the fragments in our catalog, a total of 25 other fragments, dating to MC/LC, have been found, including 15 bases and/or lower body fragments,[477] two necks,[478] and eight body fragments with animal friezes. Over half of our amphoriskoi fragments were uncovered in the backfill of the middle sanctuary retaining wall. It should also be noted that two of the uncatalogued fragments (a base and a body sherd, possibly decorated in black-figure) were found in E11, 3, 3, a largely undisturbed archaic level. No examples with simple banded decoration were identified.

252   Pl. 41   Sb. 288–18a–c   F13/G13 1 2 and F13/G13 2 2a

Three fragments (a,b,c). Pinkish gray clay with buff surface. Worn black glaze. Added red.

(a) MPH: 0.057; MPW: 0.093; Th: 0.005

Fragment preserving shoulder (found in F13/G13, 1, 2), with roots of vertical loop handles, and belly (found in F13/G13, 2, 2). Surface worn, mostly fugitive black glaze. Added red. Mended from three joining pieces.

Shoulder a.f.: (A) panther to r., part of head and neck preserved; (B) long-necked bird (swan?) to r. Added red on neck of panther and on neck (?), breast, and wing of bird. Traces of four red dots on upper part of wing. F.o. of incised blobs, incised rosettes with and without centers, dots, and incised filler ornament below handle. Four narrow bands. Belly a.f.: part of file of long-necked birds to r., with heads turned back. Trace of added red on wing of one bird. F.o. of incised blobs, incised rosettes with and without centers, and dots. Two black bands below.

(b) MPH: 0.03; MPW: 0.038; Th: 0.0044

Belly frieze fragment. Traces of four bands above belly a.f. with long-necked bird to r., head turned back. Added red on neck, breast, and wing. Red dots on upper part of wing. F.o. of incised rosettes, blob, and dots.

(c) MPH: 0.055; MPW: 0.076; Th: 0.008

Lower body fragment, foot broken off. Black glaze severely worn.

Traces of two black bands. Rays rising from band above foot. Tips of rays in dilute glaze. Black glaze at base worn.

For the closest analogy, see *Délos* X, pl. 34, no. 473,[479] with a file of birds in the belly frieze. For a related type, see *Tocra* I, 22, 28, pl. 6, 14, with a mixed animal frieze, including a bird with head turned back on the belly.

Late MC

253   Pl. 41   Sb. 288–4   F13/G13 1 2

Large fragment, preserving part of shoulder with stump of vertical loop handle, belly, lower body, and foot (one-third broken off). Deep buff clay. Worn black glaze, ranges from brown to red. Added red. Surface very severely worn and encrusted. Mended from two joins.

MPH: 0.1306; MPW: 0.0864; D: 0.04 (foot)

Shoulder a.f: faint trace of animal and f.o. of incised rosette, incised blobs, and dots. Four narrow bands. Belly a.f: part of bird to r., red on wing; other figures not preserved. F.o. of incised rosette, incised blobs, and dots. Three bands below. On lower body: rays rise from a black band above foot. Black glaze on flaring foot.

Late MC

254   Pl. 41   Sb. 506–4   F14/G14 1 Test 2

Belly fragment. Creamy buff clay. Worn black glaze. Added red. Slightly encrusted.

MPH: 0.0434; MPW: 0.0623; Th: 0.005

Traces of three narrow bands above frieze. A.f.: Long-necked bird (swan?) to r., with added red on neck, breast, and rear of body, and row of dots (apparently originally red) on top of wing; wing of bird to r., with red blob on top of wing section. F.o. of incised rosettes, including one blob rosette, and dots. Traces of bands below.

See *Tocra* I, pl. 6, 14.

Late MC

---

474. Two other lid fragments were found in F13/G13, 2, 2 and 1 was found in F14/G14, 1, 2, which also appears to belong to a a narrow-necked broad-bottomed oinochoe.

475. Cf. *Tocra* II, no. 1829 = pl. 1, no. 1830, which has a spike rather than a molded knob in the center.

476. *Tocra* I, 22, 28 (nos. 13–19), pl. 6, but see Amyx's review of *Tocra* I in *Gnomon* 41:7 (1969), 683, in which use of this group is discouraged. On this group, see also *CorVP*, 292–293 (Appendix I).

477. Two are decorated with horizontal bands rather than the more common rays.

478. One belongs to a smaller amphoriskos.

479. *GkV*, 42, List 68, no. 4; cf. *CorVP*, 293 (no. 4).

255   Pl. 41   Sb. 422–3   F13/G13 2 2
Fragment, preserving over one-half of mouth (broken and chipped off edge), complete neck, one complete vertical loop handle, roots of other handle, and part of shoulder. Light greenish clay. Black glaze fugitive. Shadows of decoration remain. Added red preserved in two tiny patches.
MPH: 0.0413; MPW: 0.0656
Horizontal bands on rim. Horizontal zigzag on both sides of neck. Shoulder A.f.: (A) panther to l., with head, top edge of torso, and tail preserved; (B) swan or long-necked bird with raised wing to r. Small blotch of added red on wing section.
The decoration on the mouth and neck is typical of late MC and LC I amphoriskoi.
Late MC

256   Pl. 41   Sb. 98–1   E11/12 Balk 2
Fragment, preserving most of neck (mouth broken off), one vertical loop handle, and most of shoulder. Buff clay with pale orange core. Black glaze slightly worn and crazed. Soil-stained.
MPH: 0.033; MPW: 0.0523
Horizontal zigzag on each side of neck. Black-glaze stripe on handle. Shoulder A.f.: (A) Panther to r., most of head, neck, upper body, torso, and tail preserved. F.o. of incised blobs and dots. (B) Unidentified animal to r. (outline of head and short line of torso preserved). F.o of incised blobs, rosette, and dots.
Late MC

Closed Shapes (**257–279**)

The 23 fragments in this section belong to various closed vessels, most of which are only tentatively identified. Among the shapes, to which our fragments are ascribed with varying degrees of certainty, are oinochoai, olpai, amphorai, convex-sided pyxides, and a flat-bottomed aryballos. Two other vase shapes, a hydria and a lekythos, are also included here. Ranging in date from MC to LC III, the pieces include black-figure of the MC period (**257–265**), LC red-ground (**267–269**), LC conventionalizing floral types (**270–272**), and fragments with banded decoration (**275–278**). Our latest example (**279**) is an LC III lekythos rim fragment.

A number of the black-figure pieces exhibit traits that place them in the circle of the Dodwell Painter. There are two examples that can be attributed either to the Geladakis Painter or to an artist very close to him: **257** consists of 10 fragments of a large closed vase, presumably an olpe, with three animal friezes containing panthers, goats, birds, and an avian; the other, **258**, is a single body fragment that preserves the hindquarter of a quadruped. Two other fragments, one with part of a siren (**260**) and the other with part of a panther (**263**)[480] show a relationship, though a more questionable one, to the Geladakis Painter. They can, in any case, be assigned to painters in the circle of the Dodwell Painter as can **259**, **261**, and **262**. Interestingly, two fragmentary vases, one also an olpe, by an artist related to the Geladakis Painter have also been found at Tocra.[481]

The three LC I red-ground fragments, Corinthian imitations of Attic black-figure, deserve to be noted. The decoration on the fragment with the swan with outspread wings (**267**) has fared better than that on our other two fragments (**268**, **269**), which perhaps belong to small-panel amphorai. Although both are very poorly preserved, male heads are discernible in the panels. Their presence is significant from the perspective of Corinthian pottery exports.[482]

The LC conventionalizing types with florals, all body fragments, have either a bud chain (**270**) or lotus-and-bud chains (**271**, **272**). One (**272**) can be assigned to the LC II Arc-palmette Workshop.

Although the majority of our catalogued pieces are from the backfill of the middle sanctuary wall, three were found in largely undisturbed archaic levels: an LC red-ground fragment (**268**), a cylindrical-shaped oinochoe with banding on the body (**275**), and the base of a white-style closed vase (**277**).

Some 310 uncatalogued sherds, retained from the excavations, fall into the category of unidentified closed shapes. These include: over 190 body fragments from different vases, about 40 of which have black-figure decoration[483]; 90 fragmentary bases, some preserving rays or bands, but otherwise little or nothing of diagnostic value; three handles; five necks; 13 shoulders[484]; one rim; and six probable lekythos pieces, three of which had neck rings. While one fragment, an undistinguishable base, was found in an undisturbed archaic level,[485] 14 of these fragments, a number of poorly preserved black-figured sherds among them, come from largely undisturbed archaic levels.[486]

---

480. The similarity of **263** to the work of the Geladakis Painter was observed by Professor Amyx; see below under **263** and n. 503.

481. *Tocra* I, pl. 5, no. 6, an olpe (= Amyx, no. 10 on p. 35, By or Near the Geladakis Painter; and *CorVP*, 217, no. 9, Near the Geladakis Painter) and pl. 12, no. 137, a convex-sided pyxis (= Amyx, no. 7 on p. 36; *CorVP*, 217, no.5, Related to the Geladakis Painter).

482. A red-ground lid (**95**) has also been found.

483. The others include 20 with banded decoration, 2 with conventionalizing floral ornaments, 2 in black-glaze, 1 semi-glazed, and 1 with black polychrome decoration.

484. Two with black-figure, 1 with tongues, and 1 with silhouette animals.

485. E11, 2, 3.

486. E11, 3, 3 (shoulder fragment), D12/13, B, 4 (base, black-figure body fragment, and body fragment with bands), D12/13, A, 3 (black-figure sherd, lekythos neck-shoulder fragment with a necking ring, shoulder-body fragment with bands), E11/12, Pit Area, 3 (base with bands, black-figure body fragment), E12/13, C, 4 (black-figure body fragment), D12/E12, D, 3 (black-figure body fragment), C11, 2, 4 (base), and C13, 1, 4a (a black-figure body and an unidentified body fragment).

257   Pls. 42, 43   Sb. 210–1a–j   E12/13   E   2
      Ills. 9, 10

Fragments of a large closed vase, presumably an olpe. Pale light-green clay. Glaze worn, crazed, peeling where preserved, and ranges from brown to a maroon-brown to black. Added red worn. One large fragment (a) mended from 11 joins, with missing parts restored in plaster, and nine other fragments (b–j). Surface worn in varying degrees on all fragments.

(a) MPH: 0.165; MPW: 0.183; Th: 0.0048–0.0053

Preserves parts of three friezes, each separated by a band of red, brown, and red (rbr) stripes. Top frieze: part of avian to l., with added red on wing section; f.o. of three incised rosettes. Middle frieze (H: 0.068): part of neck, head, and horns of grazing goat to r.; panther to l., with long recurving tail, torso missing and restored in plaster; rear tail feathers of bird to r.; f.o. of incised rosettes, blobs, and dots along top edge of panther's body. Added red on neck of goat and also on neck and haunch of panther. Bottom frieze: grazing goat to r., forepart of body, neck, and horn preserved; panther to l., head, neck, shoulder, part of top of body, and long recurved tail preserved; rear of animal (?) to r.; f.o. of incised rosettes, blobs, and dots. Added red on neck of goat and panther.

(b) MPH: 0.0582; MPW: 0.068

Frieze: tail of panther to l. above head of recurved bird to r.[487]; panther to r., hindquarter and part of tail preserved; f.o. of incised rosettes, blobs, and dots. Added red dot on neck of bird.

(c) MPH: 0.0517; MPW: 0.034

Bird to l., with incised double-horizontal neck ring[488] and raised wing. F.o. of incised rosettes and dot. Added red on neck, outer wing section, and dot on neck.

(d) MPH: 0.0355; MPW: 0.0504

Part of winged creature(?) to r. F.o. of incised rosette. Red-and-black dividing band.

(e) MPH: 0.0444; MPW: 0.0417

Part of avian to r., with folded (?) wing and head turned back. Added red on neck and one of wing sections.

(f) MPH: 0.0526; MPW: 0.0376

Parts of two friezes. Upper frieze: paw of feline to r. Trace of dividing band. Lower frieze: part of shoulder and torso of goat to r.; f.o. of row of dots above top of body.

(g) MPH: 0.027; MPW: 0.0295

Part of avian to l., added red on wing. F.o. of incised rosette, incised petals of centered rosette, and dots.

(h) MPH: 0.0345; MPW: 0.0357

Part of upper frieze. Dividing band of red, black, and red. Lower frieze: incised ear of panther; f.o. of incised rosettes.

(i) MPH: 0.0375; MPW: 0.0352

Glaze gone. Dividing band. Frieze: feline (panther?) to l., part of torso with diagonal rib incisions and end of recurved tail preserved; f.o. of incised rosettes and traces of dots.

(j) MPH: 0.0262; MPW: 0.0363

Glaze gone. Frieze: double-centered incised rosette, trace of legs of bird to l., dividing band below.

The 10 pieces of this olpe with three animal friezes can certainly be attributed either to the Geladakis Painter or to a painter very close to him.[489] Although our fragments are poorly preserved, what survives exhibits most of the salient characteristics of this painter's style as described by Amyx.[490] The kidney-bean shape of the shoulder area can be seen in the panthers and goat of (a) and the goat of (f); however, rather than the more common two curved parallel lines beginning within the shoulder area, there is only one, a recognized variant rendering by the Geladakis Painter.[491] The belly-line is, unfortunately, not preserved on any of our fragments. The heavy, straight, parallel rib-markings, which most commonly slant downward toward the back, can be seen on fragments (f, i). The fringe of hair along the animal's hindquarter is visible on the panthers of (a) and (b). The faces of our panthers have disappeared, so it is difficult to judge whether they are broad-jowled (the shadows of the faces seem to indicate that our panthers did possess this

*Illustration 9 (**257i**)*

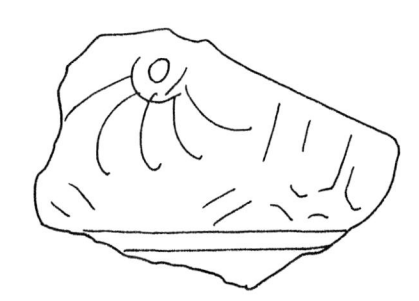

*Illustration 10 (**257j**)*

---

487. This example may be added to the list of recurved birds with double horizontal neck rings in S. Lukesh, "A New Corinthian Painter: The St. Raymond Painter," *AJA* 84:2 (1980), 185 n. 8.

488. See *supra* n. 487.

489. At least one fragmentary olpe from Catania has been attributed by Amyx to the Geladakis Painter (Amyx, 33, no. 40 = *CorVP*, 216, no. 47). Two others have been categorized by Amyx as "By or Near the Geladakis Painter": one (p. 35, no. 10) is an olpe from Tocra (*Tocra* I, pl. 5, no. 6, p. 27: Close to the Geladakis Painter, perhaps by him—Amyx); the other from Apollonia in Albania (p. 35, no. 9) has been identified by Amyx as "very near to the Painter." Most recently, however, Amyx

(*CorVP*, 216) has listed the Apollonia and Tocra olpai as "Near the Geladakis Painter" and certainly not by him.

490. See D. Amyx, "The Geladakis Painter," *Hesperia* 25 (1956), 73–77 (73–74 in particular), and Amyx, 29–40, especially p. 39 and pp. 29–36 for the list of attributions. On the Geladakis Painter, see also *CorVP*, 213–218, 321–322, 348–349.

491. As noted by Amyx in *Hesperia* 25 (1956), 76, this feature also appears on a pyxis in Reading and Munich. In addition, see the broad-bottomed oinochoe in *Corinth* XIII, no. 155–a (T1516), pls. A and 85 = Amyx, p. 32, no. 34 and *CorVP*, 215 (no. 40); the oinochoe in Syracuse = Amyx, no. 33, pl. 13, and *CorVP*, 215 (no. 38); and the globular oinochoe in London = Amyx, no. 36, pl. 14, 2, and *CorVP*, 215 (no. 42).

trait) and with lots of circular markings. The "whirling" rosette, however, is preserved on only one fragment (j). Finally, we can mention the presence of the "eagle" or "bird with head turned back" on fragments (b) and (e).[492] It should be remarked that the incision work is rather careful, perhaps more so than on some other pieces attributed to the Geladakis Painter. While these individual features indicate the work of the Geladakis Painter or that of a painter near to him, our fragments also reflect the overall Geladakian style.

MC, Geladakis Painter or Near the Geladakis Painter[493]

258   Pl. 43   Sb. 419–14   F13/G13   2   2

Body fragment, possibly from a convex-sided pyxis or an oinochoe. Buff clay with orange core. Black glaze somewhat worn. Added red.

MPH: 0.06; MPW: 0.0636

A.f.: quadruped to r., hindquarters and belly preserved. Added red on belly and originally where discoloration appears on the haunches. F.o. of incised blobs, a double-centered rosette, and blob. Edge of black dividing band. The quadruped's legs resemble those of a goat, while the haunch as well as the apparent length and arc of the tail are more consistent with the rendering of a panther.

This fragment may at least be attributed to an artist close to the Geladakis Painter, if not to the painter himself, based on the presence of the "whirling" double-centered rosette, the strong belly-line, and the straight, parallel rib-markings that slant downward toward the back.[494] In addition to having the same types of f.o., the sparse scattering of the f.o. recalls the effect seen on the Geladakis Painter's name-piece in New York, a stemmed pyxis (NY 06.1021.14). The markings on the haunches of the two panthers on the New York pyxis also show a very close similarity to our fragment.[495]

MC, Geladakis Painter or Near the Geladakis Painter

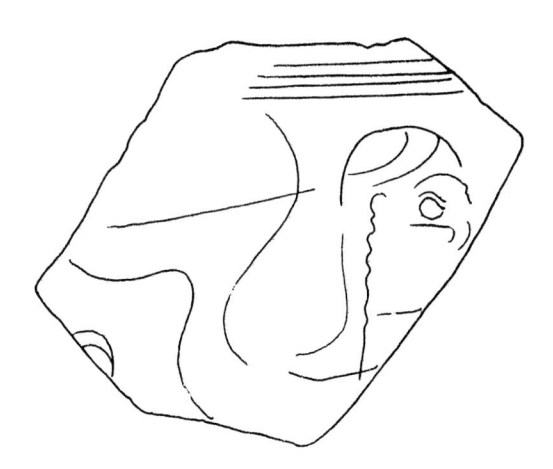

Illustration 11 (260)

259   Pl. 43   Sb. 98–3   E11/12   Balk   2

Body fragment, probably from an oinochoe. Pale yellowish buff clay. Worn black glaze, ranges from a dull black to a reddish brown. Added red.

MPH: 0.0413; MPW: 0.0484

Goat to r., forelegs, part of belly and neck preserved. Added red on belly. Heavy f.o. of double-centered incised rosette, incised rosettes, incised blobs, and dots. Band below frieze. Broad band.

The thick f.o. with its various, incised forms is reminiscent of the Elvehjem Painter, particularly the f.o. on his name-piece, a broad-bottomed oinochoe in the Elvehjem Museum of Art, University of Wisconsin-Madison.[496]

MC, Circle of the Dodwell Painter

260   Pl. 44; Ill. 11 Sb. 81–2   D12/13   A   2

Body fragment, possibly from a convex-sided pyxis. Light greenish clay. Glaze virtually gone. Only shadows of decoration remain. Traces of added red. Soil-stained.

MPH: 0.048; MPW: 0.0605

Trace of two red bands above frieze. In frieze: siren (head and part of wing preserved) to r., with raised wings.

As far as can be determined, a virtually identical rendering of the raised wing, with a straight horizontal incision demarcating the wings, occurs on two stemmed pyxides (London Market and New York), attributed to the Geladakis Painter.[497] In both, the sirens are on either side of two confronted, bearded male protomai. Although the drawing of the wings is distinctively similar, the size of the fragment precludes any compelling judgment on its relationship to the Geladakis Painter.

MC, Geladakian?

Illustration 12 (261)

261   Pl. 44; Ill. 12 Sb. 506–5   F14/G14   1   Test 2

Body fragment. Buff clay. Worn black glaze. Added red. Surface badly damaged and flaking. Heavily encrusted.

MPH: 0.0455; MPW: 0.051

Band of triple-dicing between two narrow bands. A.f.: part of unidentifiable figure or decoration and head of lion to l. F.o. of incised rosette. Added red on mane.

Ruff rendered by straight incisions, slanting slightly downward toward the face, and outlined by a wavy incised line at the face. Lion's ear drawn in an odd, forward slanting, almost horizontal position. The ear and the mane, except for the direction of the incised slanted lines of the ruff, are similar to those of a lion on a broad-bottomed

---

492. Amyx, 38.

493. My gratitude to Professor Amyx for confirming this Geladakian attribution.

494. Amyx, *Hesperia* 25 (1956), 73–74, and Amyx, 39. My thanks to Patricia Lawrence for confirming the close Geladakian connection and her comment that the fragment appears, in fact, to be by the Geladakis Painter.

495. Amyx, *Hesperia* 25 (1956), 73, pl. 28–c.

496. *Greek Vase-Painting in Midwestern Collections*, 28, no. 17. See also *CorVP*, 221–222 ("Follower of the Dodwell Painter"), pl. 92, 4.

497. London Market: Amyx, 32 (no. 29), pl. 12, 1–2; *CorVP*, 215 (no. 32). New York: *NC*, no. 908, pl. 29, 6 (NY 06.1021.14); Amyx, 31 (no. 25) and *CorVP*, 215 (no. 28).

oinochoe from Corinth, attributed to the Painter of Athens 931.[498] The convention of a solid mane and a ruff with straight, parallel incisions is seen on MC and LC lions, including those of of the Dodwell Painter and his circle. On these lions, however, the incisions slant downward away from the face. A ruff with horizontal incised lines is, however, seen on one of the lions on a convex-sided pyxis in Athens (N.M. 929) by the Dodwell Painter.[499]
MC, Circle of the Dodwell Painter

262   Pl. 44   Sb. 290–3   F13/G13   1   2
Body fragment, possibly from an oinochoe. Deep buff clay. Dull black glaze, somewhat flaking and brown where dilute. Added red and white.
MPH: 0.053; MPW: 0.039
On shoulder: broad black band with red and two narrow white bands overpainted. Red band above frieze. Frieze: siren to r., with outspread wings. Added red in strip along front of neck and in dots along inner edge of wings (three on l. wing and one on r. wing). F.o. of incised blobs. Red band below frieze.
The sloppy incision, crude facial features, and use of red dots deserve comment. A similar peak-like, angular incision marking a section of the siren's l. wing and row of red dots along the edge of the wing can be seen on a broad-bottomed oinochoe attributed to the Painter of Boston F 471.[500] Our siren is, however, more degenerate.
Late MC, Circle of the Dodwell Painter

263   Pl. 44   Sb. 419–2   F13/G13   2   2
Shoulder fragment, probably from an oinochoe. Broken at raised ridge at juncture between neck and shoulder. Buff clay. Firm black glaze. Added red fugitive.
MPL: 0.047; MPW: 0.049
Black glaze on ridge. A.f.: panther to l., head tilted and right foreleg raised. Indications of added red on chest and neck (now a discolored metallic bluish gray), in shoulder muscle, and in area of incised rib-markings. F.o. of incised double-centered rosette, blobs, and dots.
The panther's face, with its rather clumsy incision, is lopsided and the one preserved ear is spade-shaped. The pose with raised foreleg is not a common one. It occurs, for example, on a pyxis in St. Louis by the Dodwell Painter[501] and in the lower frieze of an MC column krater from Corinth.[502] Professor Amyx has noted some similarity to the Geladakis Painter.[503] Indeed, the fragment bears a resemblance, though somewhat more crudely rendered, in the shoulder muscle, and in the presence of the double-centered almost whirling rosette and the row of dots along the body. On the other hand, the incised arcs for the rib-markings are not consistent with the Geladakis Painter. The pose of the head has something of the quality of the panthers by the Dodwell Painter, the drawing of the panther's head recalls that seen on the panthers of the Painter of Athens 931,[504] and somewhat similar shoulder markings occur on the panthers of the Ampersand Painter.[505]
Late MC, Related to the Geladakis Painter

264   Pl. 44   Sb. 165–1   C15/16   1   4 Tank
Body fragment, possibly from a large flat-bottomed aryballos. Light green clay. Glaze fugitive. Mended from two joins. Encrusted.
MPH: 0.056; MPW: 0.053
Part of lotus-palmette cross. Rather careful incision, but the bases of the palmettes are not uniformly rendered. This is a common floral motif that appears on many different types of vessels from plates to oinochoe to alabastra. Unfortunately, the cross is incomplete with only one lotus, which is not even totally preserved. A rather close parallel is in the central motif on an MC flat-bottomed aryballos from Gela, except that the outer leaves flare out more than on our example, where the lotus is more compact.[506] For another comparable example, see also *Délos* XVII, pl. 56, no. 37 (Payne's Group B).
MC

265   Pl. 44   Sb. 516–11   F14/G14   1   2
Body fragment, from a small closed shape, possibly an alabastron. Creamy buff clay. Black glaze almost entirely worn off. Encrusted.
MPH: 0.033; MPW: 0.0442
Parts of two friezes separated by four narrow bands. Upper a.f.: belly and leg of feline to l.; f.o. of incised rosettes and dots. Lower a.f.: incised rosette and dots.[507] The four dividing lines between the friezes are not common.
MC (?)

266   Pl. 44   Sb. 443–4   F13/G13   Wall Test
Fragment. Buff clay. Good black glaze. Added red (worn) and white.
MPH: 0.031; MPW: 0.0186; Th: 0.004
Broad red tongue, vertical row of white dots between two incised lines, part of black tongue.
The fragment is difficult to identify. There is almost no curvature in the profile of the wall. It may possibly be a body fragment of a large alabastron with incised verticals.[508] However, I have found no parallel for the vertical row of white dots.
MC?

267   Pl. 45   Sb. 419–5   F13/G13   2   2
Red-ground fragment preserving part of neck and shoulder, possibly from an oinochoe or a neck amphora.[509] Buff clay. Pale orange slip. Black glaze, slightly flaking, and brown where dilute, particularly on wings. Added red.

---

498. Brann, *Hesperia* 25 (1956), pl. 52, 2= Amyx, 23 (no. 17); *CorVP*, 212 (no. 20), pl. 88, 3.

499. Amyx, 8 (no. 8), pl. 2,2.

500. *NC*, pl. 29, 4; Fairbanks, pl. 45, 471; *GkV*, no. 75,1; Amyx, 46–47 (no. 1) = *CorVP*, 221 (no. 1), pl. 91, 2.

501. *Greek Vase-Painting in Midwestern Collections*, 18–19, no. 12 = Amyx, 7 (no. 2); *CorVP*, 206 (no. 2), 346.

502. *Corinth* VII:1, pl. 38, no. 312 (center). Also on a flat-bottomed aryballos (Gela NM 9), attributed by Benson to the Otterlo Painter (J. L. Benson, "A Floral Master of the Chimaera Group," *AK* 14 (1971), pl. 4, 5). The pose is also mentioned by Amyx, *CSCA*, 17, as appearing on a convex-sided pyxis by the Dodwell Painter, his name-piece, in Munich (p. 7, no. 1).

503. My thanks to Professor Amyx for pointing this out to me during a visit in the fall of 1987. The piece's Geladakian appearance has also been noted by Patricia Lawrence.

504. Amyx, pl. 8, 4; *CorVP*, pl. 88, 2.

505. Moon, 34–35 = *CorVP*, pl. 90, 1a–b,d.

506. *NC*, 305, fig. 140 bis.

507. For a possible type, see *Délos* X, pl. 31, 459 and pl. 32, 455 (EC), neither of which, however, have the four dividing lines of our example.

508. Perhaps similar to *Délos* X, pl. 30, 428.

509. For the oinochoe, cf. Campbell, *Hesperia* 7 (1938), fig. 3, no. 22, and fig. 4, no. 20, dated ca. 530 B.C. For the amphora, cf. *NC*, pl. 40, 1–2, and *CorVP*, pl. 123, 1a–b.

MPH: 0.034; MPL: 0.0538; MPW: 0.0637; Th: 0.005

Black glaze on neck. Ridge at juncture of neck and shoulder with thin black line below. Shoulder: alternating black and red tongues with individual outlines in dilute glaze. Panel: part of swan to r., with outspread wings. Only incision is circle for the swan's eye. No f.o.

This piece appears to be without parallel.[510]

LC I/II

268   Pl. 45   Sb. 49–2   E11   3   3

Red-ground fragment, preserving part of neck and panel of a small amphora.[511] Buff clay with very slight pinkish tinge. Black glaze flaked and worn. Pale orange wash, worn around edges of fragment. Surface severely worn and encrusted.

MPH: 0.035; MPW: 0.0495; Th: 0.005–.008

Black tongues with individual outlines,[512] with band below. Indeterminable decoration in panel, but possibly a male head to l.

This fragment was found in a largely undisturbed archaic level.

LC I/II

269   Pl. 45   Sb. 15–2   E10/11 (Area 1)   1   3

Red-ground fragment, preserving part of neck and panel of an amphora or olpe. Deep buff or tan clay. Dull black glaze, peeling. Pale orange wash, worn. Surface severely worn and encrusted.

MPH: 0.089; MPW: 0.0766; Th: 0.0044–.008

Trace of tongues with individual outlines. Panel: head of bearded man to r. (faintly visible), top of head overlaps one of the tongues.

Similar to preceding.

LC I/II

270   Pl. 45   Sb. 419–15   F13/G13   2   2

Two body fragments (a, b), probably from a convex-sided pyxis. Buff clay with orange core. Unevenly fired. Glaze ranges from black to red. Added red.

(a) MPH: 0.048; MPW: 0.038; Th: 0.004
(b) MPH: 0.0703; MPW: 0.0526; Th: 0.004

Main frieze: bud chain. Added red on buds and on horizontal stripe below bud.[513] Red band below frieze. Banding (BRB).

For the type, see *CVA* Heidelberg, pl. 17, nos. 12–13.

LC I/II

271   Pl. 45   Sb. 516–18   F14/G14   1   2

Two body fragments (a, b), either from a convex-sided pyxis[514] or small broad-bottomed oinochoe.[515] Buff clay. Dull black glaze, worn on (b). Added red. Glaze ranges from black to red. Added red.

(a) MPH: 0.0485; MPW: 0.0273
(b) MPH: 0.046; MPW: 0.05

Frieze: alternating palmette-and-lotus chain. Added red on tendrils. Red band below frieze. Debased palmette in silhouette.

For a similar pattern, see *Corinth* XV:3, no. 912, pl. 42; and for an almost identical palmette, but as part of a palmette-and-bud chain, see *Mégara Hyblaea*, 2, pl. 57, 4 and 5, from a broad-bottomed oinochoe.

LC II

272   Pl. 45   Sb. 419–8   F13/G13   2   2

Body fragment. Buff clay. Black glaze ranges to red, brown where dilute. Added red.

MPH: 0.0474; MPW: 0.03

Frieze: lotus-and-palmette chain. Added red on lotus and in center of palmette. Incisions on lotus and palmette.

For a similar rendering of this type of floral chain with incisions (however, the volutes of the palmette are not incised in the same manner nor is the palmette of the same form as our example), see *Corinth* XV:3, no. 910 b, pl. 42, dated LC II and attributed to the Arc-palmette Workshop.

LC II, Arc-palmette Workshop

273   Pl. 46   Sb. 516–23   F14/G14   1   2

Body fragment. Buff clay. Worn black glaze. Added red.

MPH: 0.0378; MPW: 0.0328

Frieze of red blobs or pendant buds, with thin red lines alternating between a black and a red band (rBrR) below.

LC II/III

274   Pl. 46   Sb. 419–10   F13/G13   2   2

Fragment, preserving part of neck and shoulder and complete handle of a hydria.[516] Buff clay. Black glaze, generally firm, but with some flaking. Added red and white. Slightly encrusted.

MPH: 0.053; MPW: 0.062

Partially preserved (for a length of 0.044) everted and flaring rim with thickened edge. Short, broad neck with ridge at base. Ribbon strap handle. Flat unglazed shoulder.

Exterior: polychrome lines (rrbrwb) on rim; black glaze on neck and three evenly spaced white dot-cluster rosettes[517]; band of red at base of neck, ridge, and extends onto shoulder; black glaze on handle (ends at 0.016 from root). Interior: black glaze with white dot-cluster rosette on top of rim near edge; two groups of polychrome lines (wrwrw and rw(?)r).

There appears to be no parallel for this unusual semiglazed hydria fragment.

MC or LC

275   Pl. 46   Sb. 80–5   D12/13   A   3 East

Shoulder and body fragment. Deep buff clay. Black glaze, slightly worn. Added red.

MPH: 0.112; MPW: 0.059

Steep sloping shoulder. Angular juncture of shoulder and body. Banding on body (BBrBr).

The fragment seems to belong to a rather tall and slender oinochoe with an almost cylindrical body that narrows toward the base. A parallel for the shape may be an oinochoe, which was, however, originally covered with black glaze, from the Potters' Quarter at Corinth.[518]

---

510. Amyx (*CorVP*, 389) mentions that panel decoration on the LC I early red-ground vases included a swan or a flying bird.

511. Or possibly an olpe.

512. For a tongue pattern on a panel amphora, see D. Amyx, "The Honolulu Painter and the 'Delicate Style,'" *AK* 5 (1962), 4, pl. 2, 3–4. Also, *Perachora* II, pl. 115, nos. 2778–2780, all from small amphorai, in imitation of Attic black-figure, dated to late sixth century.

513. For an analogy, see *Corinth* XV:3, pl. 42, no. 921, on a plate rim, dated LC II.

514. Cf. Lo Porto, 218–219, fig. 195a, dated LC I; and *Corinth* XV:3, no. 912, pl. 42.

515. Cf. *Délos* X, pl. 35, 483; *Perachora* II, pl. 112, no. 2607; and *Corinth* XV:3, pl. 46, no. 1059, dated LC III.

516. For an inexact type, see *Délos* XVII, pl. 60, 131.

517. For white dot-cluster rosettes on the neck of a hydria, see *Délos* XVII, pl. 61, 139; *CVA*, U. of California, fasc. 1, pl. VI, 2.

518. *Corinth* XV:3, no. 1027, pl. 45, dated to LC III. Our example is taller.

This fragment was found in a largely undisturbed archaic level.
LC

276   Pl. 46   Sb. 422–6   F13/G13 2 2
Fragment, preserving complete foot ring and part of lower body wall. Buff clay. Black glaze worn and flaking. Added red worn. Mended from four joining pieces.
MPH: 0.077; MPW: 0.112; D: 0.072 (base)
The preserved portion of the ovoid body is decorated with three bands (BRB). Added red on the spreading foot ring is worn. Underside unglazed.
LC

277   Pl. 46   Sb. 76–1   D12/13 B 4 West
Fragment, preserving about one-half lower body and base. Buff clay. Black glaze somewhat worn. Encrusted.
MPH: 0.0525; MPD: 0.089; D: 0.059 (base)
Three thin black bands on lower body. Black glaze on low spreading foot with beveled edge. Ovoid body.
This white-style piece was found in a largely undisturbed archaic level.
LC

278   Pl. 46   Sb. 421–8   F13/G13 2 2
Fragment, preserving part of shoulder and body. Deep buff clay. Black glaze somewhat worn.
MPH: 0.036; MPW: 0.036
Horizontal black bands on sloping shoulder. Band with groups of short horizontal strips. Narrow black bands below. Perhaps from a small ovoid oinochoe.[519]
LC

279   Pl. 46   Sb. 516–20   F14/G14 1 2
Fragment, preserving complete mouth, part of neck, and root handle attached at neck. Light buff clay. Fugitive black glaze. Heavily encusted.
MPH: 0.0215; D: 0.027 (rim)
Small, shallow, rounded mouth appears to belong to a "black-glazed lekythos of archaic type," while the absence of a neck ring places it late in the series.[520]
For an approximate parallel, see *Corinth* XIII, pl. 37, 277–5, and fig. 15 (p. 141).
LC III, First half fifth century B.C.

Kraters (280–291)

Kraters were among the rarest vases in the sanctuary, with the dozen examples listed in our catalogue representative of virtually all the finds.[521] The pieces belong mostly to conventional black-figure column-kraters and possibly to two black-glazed kraters. This section also includes an unusual rim fragment (**291**), which may, in fact, belong to a a large bowl.[522]

The black-figure examples are MC. With the exception of one handle-plate (**285**) decorated with a bird, all are body fragments with frieze decoration. Unfortunately, the painted decoration is almost entirely worn off on our fragments.[523] A battle scene appears in the main frieze of two of our kraters (**280, 281**), and probably in a third (**282**), where all that now remains is the lower leg of a warrior. **280** and **281** show a convincing relationship to two painters, the Painter of Munich 237 and the Painter of Louvre E 627[524] whose work is close in theme, composition, and certain details that may be more generalized than diagnostic. **280** has part of a combat scene and a mounted horseman. The other krater (**281**) preserves only parts of two warriors from the battle scene, along with two other body fragments. There is also a strong likelihood that **282**, found in an undisturbed archaic level, with a small section of the main frieze and part of the animal frieze, may be related to **281**. The fragment with part of a mounted hoplite (**283**) belongs to another krater that may be attributed to the circle of the Detroit Painter. **284**, another body fragment, with part of a siren, apparently comes from below the arch of the handle. The fragmentary nature and state of preservation, particularly the fugitive glaze and soil encrustation, of our black-figure fragments prevents certain attribution.

287 is tentatively identified as a krater because of the filling ornament in the animal friezes. The rim fragment with a stepped zigzag (**286**), our only catalogued example to have been found in the backfill of the middle sanctuary retaining wall, belongs to an MC or LC I black-figure krater.

Our one definite black-glazed krater fragment is **290**. In addition, **288** and **289** are probably also from a black-glazed krater.[525]

The findspots of our fragments are of some note: seven were uncovered in the E10 and E11 Area, and three of these were from the area of the E10 Building;[526] two were found in the fill near Sacred House

---

519. I wish to thank Elizabeth Pemberton for suggesting this possible identification.

520. *Corinth* XIII, 140.

521. Of the finds retained from the excavations, only one other krater fragment could be identified with certainty. This was a base fragment with added red on the exterior of the foot and rays around the base, which was found in F13/G13, 1, 2. A black-figure body fragment with traces of a panther head found in E11/12, Pit Area, 2 may also belong to a krater, but the glaze is gone and the surface is encrusted.

522. It was found in the fill south of Sacred House S6 (see White, *Final Reports* I, 115).

523. **287** is the exception, since the glaze is not fugitive, but the three fragments are very small.

524. Benson, "The Three Maidens Group," *AJA* 73 (1969), 116–117, 121 (E–1a, E–2a) ascribed two kraters (E–1a=Louvre E 627 and E–2a=Naples MN 80997) to the Manner of the Painter of Munich 237. Amyx, however, in *CorVP*, 157, attributes both of these kraters to the Painter of Louvre E 627, who is "Close to the Painter of Munich 237.")

525. Both these fragments, with flaking glaze, may be from the same krater, and both were found in the E10 Bldg area.

526. **281** (E10/11, 1, 3), **282** (E11, 2, 3), **283** (E11, 1, 2), **285** (E10, Balk 3), **288** (E10 Bldg., 1/2, Along S Edge), **289** (E10 Bldg. Foundation Trench), and **287** (E12/13, E, 2). It should be noted that the E10 Building is now referred to in White, *Final Reports* V as the S7 Sacred House.

Illustration 13 (280)

S6 (**290, 291**); and two were from the C11 and C12 Area (**280, 284**).

Kraters are also rare at Tocra, where just three have been found. The one black-figure example, with a banquet scene in the main frieze, is unlike our examples.[527]

280   Pl. 47; Ill. 13 Sb. 341-1   C12/13 1 4, W of Wall 3

Fragment, preserving part of neck and upper body of a column-krater. Light greenish clay. Black glaze nearly fugitive. Mended from five joined fragments. Surface badly worn and soil-stained. Only shadows of original decoration preserved.

MPH: 0.087; MPW: 0.207; Th: 0.0075

On neck: black glaze (flaking and worn on exterior, fugitive on interior). Band of black tongues with individual outlines below neck. Main frieze: part of battle scene. From left to right: overlapping shield (approximately upper-right quadrant preserved) and part of spear (blade and part of shaft) held by a hoplite to r., who is not preserved; hoplite wearing crested helmet, which extends into the tongue zone, and corselet, to l., holding a shield bearing gorgoneion blazon and a spear in his raised hand; an eagle flying to the l. above shield with gorgoneion device; youthful horseman to r., with head turned back, holding a spear and reins; head, neck, upper body, and mane of horse preserved. No f.o.

Combat scenes were a rather frequent subject on MC kraters.[528] The central combatants on a krater in the Louvre (E 627),[529] and the combatants on a krater in Naples (Museo Nazionale 80997),[530] both attributed by Benson to the Manner of the Painter of Munich 237, a member of his "Three Maidens Group,"[531] and more recently attributed by Amyx to the Painter of Louvre E 627,[532] provide a complete depiction of the partially preserved duel on our fragment. Both the Louvre and Naples kraters also have flying birds, though differently placed than on our fragment.[533] On the Louvre krater, the birds appear on the sides of the frieze panel and as a shield device. On the Naples krater, the bird is placed beneath the shields of the two combatants on the left. Not surprisingly, moreover, the similarity in the combat scene extends to those on two kraters that are attributed to the Painter of Munich 237: Berkeley 8/361 and Aachen, Ludwig.[534] On the Berkeley krater, there is, once again, an eagle flying to the left between the heads of the two combatants on the right.[535] This bird, too, is not dissimilar to the birds (eagles) on the Louvre and Naples kraters. The kinship of our fragment with the painter of the Aachen krater[536] is further reinforced by the rider with his head turned back toward the two central combatants in the frieze. This is the only analogy for a rider looking back on a krater frieze where the composition is that of a battle scene.

---

527. *Tocra* I, 23–24, no. 233, pl. 16. The other two are black-glazed.

528. *Corinth* VII:2, 53 (no. 182).

529. Benson, "Some Notes on Corinthian Vase-Painters," *AJA* 60 (1956), p. 228, pl. 77, fig. 40 ("Battle Scene Painter").

530. Benson, *AJA* 73 (1969), 121 (E–2a), pl. 41, figs. 30–31.

531. Benson, *AJA* 73 (1969), 116, 121 (E–1a, E–2a). For a discussion of the validity of the "Three Maidens Group," see *CorVP*, 294.

532. *CorVP*, 157.

533. Benson, *AJA* 73 (1969), 116, discussed the virtually identical rendering of the eagles on both kraters. The surface of our fragment is too poorly preserved to make a comparison.

534. *CorVP*, 156 (nos. 5 and 6).

535. *CorVP*, pl. 60, 1.

536. *CorVP*, pl. 60, 2, identified as Basel, Antikenmuseum (Ludwig L–13), but cf. p. 156, no. 6, identified as Aachen, Ludwig. See correction, p. 313.

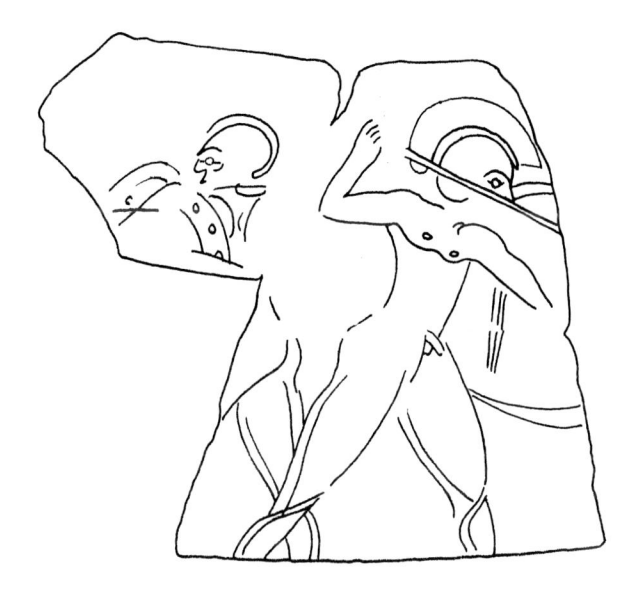

*Illustration 14 (**281a**)* *Illustration 15 (**281b**)*

Our rider, however, holds a spear. In addition, the mane of our rider's horse, with incised and slightly wavy lines, is rendered differently than on the Aachen krater.[537]

In our example, the battle scene was either flanked by horsemen, as on a krater by the Memnon Painter from Corinth,[538] or, with perhaps greater probability, the battle scene may have been flanked by one rider and a sphinx or some other creature as on the Aachen krater.

The gorgoneion shield device, while not as common as a whirligig on the shields of hoplites on MC kraters, occurs, for example, on a krater in New York (MMNY 12.2299), attributed by Benson to the Cavalcade Painter, one of the inner circle of his "Three Maidens Group,"[539] and on another krater in New York (MMNY 27.116),[540] attributed to the Detroit Painter. It also appears on a hoplite's shield on a krater in Basle, attributed by Benson to the Athana Painter.[541]

Our fragment shows a strong relationship with the Painter of Munich 237 and the Painter of Louvre E 627, in both style and frieze composition. Amyx has characterized the Painter of Louvre E 627 as "close to the Painter of Munich 237."[542] However, the kraters of the Painter of Munich 237 and the two kraters attributed to the Painter of Louvre E 627 (or Benson's "Manner of the Painter of Munich 237") do not have the band of tongues above the frieze of our fragment. Furthermore, the helmets of the warriors are different from that of our warrior with its raised crest.

Unfortunately, not only is little of this krater preserved, but what remains is in very poor condition. It would most certainly add to our knowledge of Corinthian krater painters.

MC, Related to the Painter of Munich 237 or the Painter of Louvre E 627

281 Pl. 47; Sb. 16–2a,b,c E10/11 (Area 1) 1 3
Ills. 14-16

Three krater fragments, two from upper body (a, b) and one from lower body frieze (c). Pale buff clay. Fugitive black glaze, only small, isolated patches preserved. Surface worn and encrusted.

White, *Second Report*, 193 n. 107, pl. 89e.

(a) MPH: 0.101; MPW: 0.108; Th: 0.009–0.01

Three joining fragments of main frieze and small portion of base of neck. Hoplite to l., wearing helmet and corselet, and holding shield with dots around border. Buttocks and

---

537. For this type of rendering, see *Perachora* II, no. 2246, pl. 78, which is very close to our horse's mane.

538. *Corinth* VII:2, no. 172, pls. 31, c and 32, b. See also no. 182 (particularly examples cited), pl. 35.

539. Benson, *AJA* 73 (1969), 119 (A5), pl. 34, fig. 3; see also *CorVP*, 198 (no. 6).

540. *CorVP* 196 (no. 5), pl. 79, 1a–c.

541. J. L. Benson, "Ein Korinthischer Krater der Dreimädchengruppe im Basler Antikenmuseum," *AK* 11 (1968), 82–85, pls. 23 and 24. See also Benson, *AJA* 73 (1969), 115–116, 120 (C2), pl. 36, fig. 14; *CorVP*, 235, pl. 104, 1a–b.

542. *CorVP*, 157.

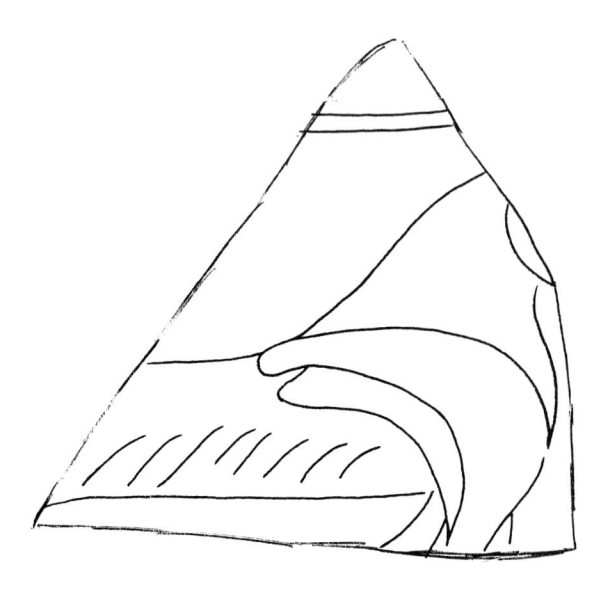

Illustration 16 (281c)

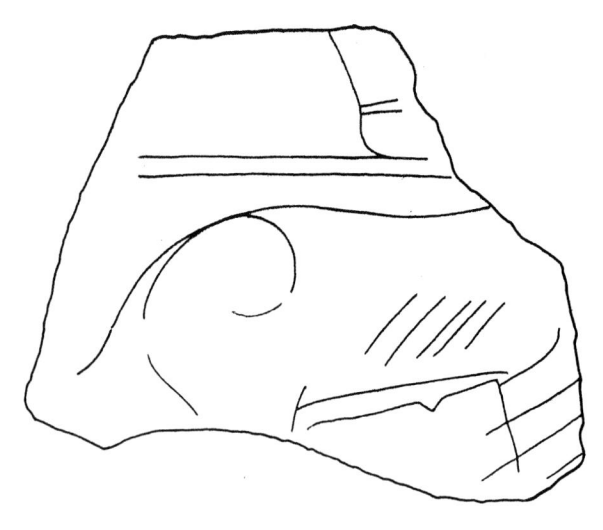

Illustration 17 (282)

most of right leg preserved, and faint trace of raised right arm. Helmeted nude warrior to r., wearing greaves, raised right hand holding a spear, and left holding a shield.[543] No f.o.

(b) MPH: 0.073; MPW: 0.067; Th. 0.008

Fragment, probably from below handle plate,[544] with part of winged creature, probably a siren with outspread wings to r. Part of lower left wing section, small portion of body and right wing (double-incised line dividing wing cap from feathers), and arched double incision indicating marking above right leg. Shadow of band near bottom of fragment.

(c) MPH: 0.061; MPW: 0.074; Th. 0.007

Fragment from lower animal frieze: panther to r., with edge of face, neck, and torso, with rib and shoulder muscle markings, preserved. Band above frieze. The shoulder marking is quite distinctive.

A very similar scene with two sets of battling hoplites appears on a krater in the Naples Museo Nazionale (80997), which Benson has attributed to the Manner of the Painter of Munich 237[545] and which Amyx has attributed to the Painter of Louvre E 627.[546] However, a comparison of the rendering of the panthers,[547] particularly the form of the shoulder muscle and the rib markings, in the lower animal frieze shows a weaker kinship.

A krater in Berkeley (8/361), attributed to the Painter of Munich 237,[548] also has two duels, and the two figures whose legs overlap in the center of the main frieze are comparable to the extant combatants on our fragment (a). The anatomical markings on the animals, however, do not show a close similarity to what remains of our panther.

As in the preceding fragment (**280**), there is a relationship with both the Painter of Munich 237 and the Painter of Louvre E 627, and, in keeping with the recognized kraters of these painters, there is also no tongue ornament in the frieze.

MC, Related to Painter of Munich 237 and Painter of Louvre E 627

282   Pl. 47; Ill. 17 Sb. 44   E11   2 'Pit'   3

Body fragment, preserving parts of two friezes. Buff clay. Fugitive black glaze. Added red fugitive. Surface worn and heavily encrusted.

MPH: 0.071; MPW: 0.085; Th. 0.008

Upper main frieze: lower leg, possibly with greave, and foot of male to r. Dividing band, originally overpainted with red. Lower frieze: grazing goat to l., part of neck, torso, and part of haunch preserved. Incised shoulder, rib, and haunch markings. Spot of added red on body.

The upper frieze, no doubt, had a scene of battling hoplites, of which only the lower leg of one of the hoplites remains. The incision on the goat, specific only for the shoulder muscle, is paralleled on the Berkeley krater (8/361), attributed to the Painter of Munich 237.[549] It is also paralleled on the ram of the Louvre krater (E 627)[550] and the goat of the Naples krater (MN 80997)[551] both attributed to the Painter of Louvre E 627. However, this type of incised curved line for the shoulder is not restricted to these painters.

This piece was found in an undisturbed archaic level.

MC, Related to Painter of Munich 237 and Painter of Louvre E 627

283   Pl. 47   Sb. 40-8   E11   1   2

Body fragment. Buff clay. Black glaze worn off except for two small patches. Surface worn and heavily encrusted.

---

543. For the warrior, cf. *Corinth* VII:1, pl. 40, 314.

544. As on the krater, attributed to the Detroit Painter with a siren, see Benson, *AJA* 73 (1969), pl. 40, fig. 25, or with a griffin, pl. 35, figs. 5–6. On decoration of this area of the krater, see *CorVP*, 508–509.

545. J. L. Benson, "The Three Maidens Group," *AJA* 73 (1969), 121 (E–2a), pl. 41, figs. 30–31.

546. *CorVP*, 157.

547. *AJA* 73 (1969), pl. 42, figs. 33 and 35.

548. *CorVP*, 156 (no. 5); Benson, *AJA* 73 (1969), 121 (E–4).

549. *CorVP*, pl. 59, 2a–b.

550. Benson, *AJA* 73 (1969), pl. 41, fig. 28.

551. Benson, *AJA* 73 (1969), pl. 42, fig. 23.

MPH: 0.066; MPW: 0.0735; Th: 0.007

From the upper frieze: hoplite mounted on horse to l. Part of shield with whirligig blazon and dots around edge, and rider's l. leg with greave preserved. Belly and l. foreleg of horse preserved. Presumably the incised line at the left edge of the fragment indicates the horse's r. foreleg. The r. foreleg is almost at a 45–degree angle to the l. foreleg, resembling almost a prancing position. Generally, the forelegs of horses in such rider friezes are set closer together. The placement of the r. foreleg can be compared to the position of the horse's l. foreleg on a globular oinochoe in Boston (MFA 01.8050).[552] The stance of the forelegs also has some resemblance to that of the horses, particularly the center horse, on a krater attributed to the Athana Painter.[553]

Amyx has commented that "the frieze of mounted hoplites is a stock subject on MC kraters," particularly among the painters in the sphere of Benson's "Three Maidens Group," such as the Detroit Painter.[554] The Detriot Painter's mounted hoplites also carry shields with whirligig blazons.

MC, Circle of the Detroit Painter ?

284   Pl. 47   Sb. 375–2   C11   1   3, N of Wall

Body fragment, from below arch of handle. Light green clay. Fugitive black glaze. Surface worn and encrusted.

MPH: 0.0602; MPW: 0.043; Th: 0.0068

Part of siren with spread wing to r., head turned back. Part of hair, chest contour, l. wing bow, divided into three sections, and wing feathers preserved.

See Benson, *AJA* 73 (1969), pl. 40, fig. 25 and pl. 36, 15, where the triple division of the siren's wing can also be seen.[555]

MC

285   Pl. 48   Sb. 119   E10   Bldg Balk   3

Handle-plate of column-krater.[556] Broken where originally attached to rim. Piece missing from right side. Top of handle adheres to underside. Creamy buff clay. Glaze worn, appears to be of good quality, peeling on edges, and brown where dilute. Surface chipped and encrusted.

MPL: 0.067; MPW: 0.06

White, *Third Report*, 38, pl. 5, fig. 9.

Bird to r., head turned back. Legs worn off. No f.o.

For the type, see *Corinth* VII:1, pl. 40, figs. 317, 319; *Corinth* VII:2, pl. 37, figs. 196–197; and *Mégara Hyblaea*, pl. 50, nos. 1–2, all dated MC.

MC

286   Pl. 48   Sb. 419–7a,b   F13/G13   2   2

Two column-krater rim fragments (a, b). Buff clay. Worn black glaze, except on interior of neck where rather thin and flaking, fired black to olive green where preserved. Added red. Surface soil-stained.

(a) MPH: 0.052 MPW: 0.0708

Preserves part of top of rim with diagonal stepped zigzags, edge broken off, and part of neck. Black glaze on neck and two red horizontal bands.

(b) MPH: 0.022; MPW: 0.0984

Preserves part of top of rim with diagonal stepped zigzags and part of outer edge.

Krater rims were decorated with stepped zigzags in both the MC and LC I periods,[557] when they become more common.[558] For MC examples, see *Corinth* VII:2, pl. 33, no. 173 and pl. 38, no. 202. For LC I examples, see *Corinth* XIII, 321, pl. 89, X–134; *Mégara Hyblaea*, pl. 55, 2; and Boardman, *BSA* 61 (1967), pl. 31, 3.

MC or LC I

287   Pl. 48   Sb. 210–5a–c   E12/13   E   2

Three body fragments (a, b, c) from a relatively narrow-walled krater (?). Black glaze worn, crazed, and ranges to a dark maroon brown. Added red. Soil-stained.

(a) MPH: 0.0244; MPW: 0.03; Th: 0.0041

Shadow of band. A.f.: part of unidentified figure or decoration. Mending hole (0.0053 D) on r. side of fragment. On interior: traces of black glaze.

(b) MPH: 0.035; MPW: 0.027; Th: 0.004

Animal to l., part of head, neck, shadow of foreleg, and shoulder with muscle incision preserved. Edge of head rendered by a circular incised line with two short curved incisions, indicating whiskers (?). F.o. of incised filler beneath leg and dot or blob near head. Added red on neck. On interior: worn maroon-brown glaze. Mending hole (D: 0.0036) in bottom right of fragment.

(c) MPH: 0.0453; MPW: 0.067; Th: 0.0043

Lower part of upper frieze with no trace of decoration preserved. Two bands. A.f.: goat to l., part of horn and body preserved. Added purple or maroon glaze on body. F.o. of two incised rosettes and dot. On interior: worn maroon-brown glaze. Mended from two joins.

Judging from the two mending holes, this vase must have had considerable value. Unlike our other black-figure kraters, these fragments represent our only example of a krater with animal friezes and f.o.[559]

For the fragment with part of a goat, see *Mégara Hyblaea*, pl. 50, no. 3, identified as an MC krater fragment, and where the f.o. is particularly similar to that of our piece.

MC?

288   Pl. 48   Sb. 112–2   E10   Bldg 1/2   Along SE Edge

Rim fragment, preserving less than one-eighth of rim and part of adjacent neck. Chipped edges, pieces missing from bottom of outside edge, and broken off at juncture of handle plate. Pale creamy buff clay. Black glaze worn, crazed, and peeling. Rather heavily encrusted.

MPH: 0.041; MPW: 0.029; MPL: 0.0782; Est D: 0.24

Preserved section of top of rim appears reserved. Black glaze along edge and on neck. On interior: a reserved (?) band at rim, remainder black.

The flat rim projects downward somewhat and the neck is straight. This type of rim would suggest an earlier date than neck fragment **290**. Possibly from a black-glazed krater and may belong with **289**.

MC or LC

---

552. Benson, *AJA* 73 (1969), 112, pl. 35, fig. 10; see also Amyx, *AJA* 65 (1961), 11 n. 35; *CorVP*, 319, B.B-1 (Near the Cavalcade Painter).

553. Benson, *AK*, 11 (1968), pl. 25, 1; *CorVP*, pl. 104, 1a.

554. *Corinth* VII:2, no. 181, pl. 35, but cf. Amyx's commentary on the "Three Maidens Group" in *CorVP*, 294. For the Detroit Painter's name-piece, see also Warren Moon, *Greek Vase-Painting in Midwestern Collections* (Chicago, 1979), 26–27 and bibliography cited.

555. For a discussion of subjects placed beneath the arch of krater handles, see *CorVP*, 508–509.

556. On the decoration of handle-plates, see *CorVP*, 507–508.

557. On this decoration, see *CorVP*, 506.

558. *NC*, 301.

559. See *Perachora* II, 230–231, for kraters with animal friezes and f.o.

289 Pl. 48; Fig. 2 Sb. 115–1 E10 Bldg Foundation Trench

Three fragments (a, b, c). Creamy buff clay. Black glaze, peeled, flaking, and slightly crazed where well preserved. Encrusted.

(a) MPH: 0.0424; MPW: 0.1208; Th: 0.006; D: 0.1346 (foot)

Preserves about half of foot ring, most of floor, and part of lower body. Mended from two joins. Chips on foot ring. Black glaze on exterior of foot. Underside unglazed. Black band at base of lower body with reserved area above (no trace of rays). Flaking black glaze on interior.

(b) MPH: 0.041; MPW: 0.0887
(c) MPH: 0.0447; MPW: 0.0382

Fragments b and c, which do not join, are both body fragments (not illustrated). The black glaze is flaking or fugitive on both exterior and interior of the two fragments.

The form of the echinoid foot resembles that of most black-figured and black-glazed column kraters. This and the preceding fragment (**288**) may belong to the same krater.

MC or LC

290 Pl. 48 Sb. 470–1 D14/E14 1 2

Krater rim fragment. Light greenish to yellow buff clay. Dull dark brown glaze worn. Traces of added red. Surface worn and encrusted.

MPH: 0.0744; MPW: 0.1138; Th: 0.0066; Est D: 0.28

Fragment preserves about one-eighth of rim and neck, presumably from a black-glazed column krater. Traces of two red bands on edge of rim, and possibly on interior of neck. The neck appears to be proportionately rather high and the "flat rim does not project downward."[560] Both these features suggest an LC date.

The fragment was found in the demolition fill between Sacred Houses S5 and S6.[561]

LC (?)

291 Pl. 48 Sb. 477–1 D15/16 1 3

Fragment from a krater or large bowl, preserving about one-tenth of rim and part of adjacent neck. Light green to buff clay. Worn black glaze. Surface worn.

MPH: 0.0334; MPW: 0.0744; Est D: 0.27

Narrow close-set rays on top of flat, thickened rim. Widely spaced double-centered incised rosettes below rim. Slight curvature of area below rim. On interior, crazed and flaking black glaze.

This fragment is difficult to parallel among kraters or large bowls. The rim, certainly, is unlike that of any conventional Corinthian krater, with or without handles.[562] Rays occur on the rims of EC kraters, but are usually not found on those of the sixth century.[563] Double-centered incised rosettes occur frequently on both EC and MC vases.[564]

MC (?)

Ring Vase (**292**)

This poorly preserved fragment is the only example of a ring vase identified among the finds retained from the Demeter Sanctuary.

292 Pl. 48 Sb. 40–1 E11 1 2

Fragment, preserving complete rim, neck, strap handle, and part of upper body. Buff clay. Black glaze almost entirely worn off. Surface worn.

MPH: 0.042; MPW: 0.0266; Th: 0.0036; Est H: 0.07–0.075

Traces of band (?) on top of rim and dots around edge of rim. Patches of black glaze on handle. Short tongues on shoulder. Incisions, possibly interior body markings of an animal, and patches of black glaze on body.

The ring vase is not a common shape in the Corinthian repertoire.[565] The surface of our example is, unfortunately, severely worn and its black-figured decoration is now unrecognizable. For the type, see *CVA* Louvre 8, pl. 20, nos. 28 and 31, and pl. 21; *CVA* Rodi 2, pl. 5, no. 5, and pl. 6, no. 5.

MC

Miniature Vases (293–391)

Miniature vases are plentiful, forming one-third of all the Corinthian pottery uncovered in the sanctuary. Because of their size, the miniature vessels tend to be more completely preserved than the full-size vases. The miniatures occur in a wide variety of shapes which, with a few exceptions, replicate the sanctuary's full-size vases. Most ubiquitous are the miniature kotylai decorated with linear patterns, with well over 800 individual vases identified.[566] Examples of this large and common votive class are found in nearly every area and stratum of the excavated portions of the sanctuary. In terms of popularity as a dedication, the kotylai are followed by the miniature black-glazed hydriai, which number over 200. These hydriai consititute the best-preserved series of vases uncovered from the excavations.

In contrast to the kotylai and even the hydriai, the other types of miniatures vases are decidedly far less numerous—together only totaling over 100 pieces from among the retained finds. Miniature pyxides,

---

560. Cf. *Hesperia* VII (1938), 583, nos. 59–62, fig. 12; *Corinth* VII:1, 63, no. 233, where Weinberg mentions that black-glazed kraters of taller form and with taller necks were common in Corinth during the sixth and fifth centuries.

561. White, *Final Reports* I, 115.

562. For the development of the plain krater without handles whose rim evolves from hardly more than an everted lip to a wide, level projecting rim, see *Corinth* VII:2, 81.

563. *NC*, 301; *CorVP*, 506.

564. For a similar disposition of double-centered rosettes below the rim on an MC kotyle, see *Corinth* XV:3, nos. 527, 528a, pl. 26.

565. See *Corinth* XV:3, p. 159, no. 815, and bibliography cited therein.

566. Standard- and small-size kotylai are also the most numerous of all the vase types recovered and retained from the excavations. See section on kotylai.

lids, and kothons, decorated with linear patterns, occur in small numbers as do black-glazed bowls.[567] Kylikes decorated with silhouette figures are even less frequent, while other miniature vases, such as phialai mesomphaloi, kana, oinochoai, and kraters or kratercups, are each represented by barely a few pieces.[568] There is also one relatively complete miniature black-glazed olpe.

Most of our miniature vases can be only broadly dated from the second half of the sixth century to the early part of the fifth century B.C., that is, to the LC II and early LC III periods. Some vases are fifth century in date. A few of the miniature black-glazed hydriai date to the latter part of the fifth century and possibly even to the fourth century B.C.

A considerable number of our miniatures were found in largely undisturbed archaic levels, with D12/13, B, 4, which may represent a votive deposit,[569] yielding the most fragments.[570] Far less frequent, totaling a score, were finds of miniatures in undisturbed archaic levels, though four vases in our catalog were found in such contexts: a lid (**303**) from C13, 1, 4b; a black-glazed oinochoe (**332**) from C11, 2, 5; and two black-glazed hydriai (**370, 371**) from F14/G14, 1, 5.[571]

Almost one hundred miniature vases are included in our catalog; more than half are miniature black-glazed hydriai. The painted decoration on our miniatures consists of linear patterns on pyxides, lids, kotylai, kana, and kothons; black-glaze on aryballoi (enhanced with double-incised verticals), kotylai, bowls, one kothon, oinochoai, an olpe, and hydriai; and silhouette figures on kylikes. About one-third of the catalogued vases were found in the backfill of the middle sanctuary T10 retaining wall.[572]

ARYBALLOI

Aside from the three catalogued aryballoi, no other miniatures of this shape were identified among the finds retained from the sanctuary. Two are flat-bottomed and decorated with double-incised vertical lines: **295**, in addition, has short tongues on the shoulder; **294** was found in a largely undisturbed archaic level. The third aryballos (**293**) does not preserve decoration on the body.

293   Pl. 49   Inv. No. 77–599 F13/G13 2 2
Fragmentary round aryballos. About one-third of rim broken off. Chip on shoulder. Grayish buff clay. Glaze fugitive.
H: 0.04; D: 0.042
Traces of concentric rings on top and edge of rim. No decoration preserved on body.
LC

294   Pl. 49   Inv. No. 73–737 D12/E12 D 3
Complete flat-bottomed aryballos. Pale greenish buff clay. Black glaze worn. Nicks on base. Heavily encrusted.
H: 0.0405; D: 0.038
On body: pairs of vertically incised lines. No other decoration clearly visible, though there may be a trace of a band on the shoulder.
Found in a largely undisturbed archaic level, it is a not too distant miniature version of *Tocra* I, no. 36, pl. 8.[573]
LC II

295   Pl. 49   Inv. No. 74–87 D16/17 2 3
Complete flat-bottomed aryballos except for small missing section of rim. Chipped on shoulder and base. Creamy buff clay. Black glaze worn and, apparently, thinly applied. Lightly encrusted.
H: 0.0394; D: 0.0388
Two black bands on top of rim and band around edge of rim. Small tongues on shoulder. Broad black band on body with widely spaced groups of two incised vertical lines, except in area below handle. Underside concave with two incised concentric circles in center.
Type related to preceding.
LC II

PYXIDES

Our catalog contains six of the 27 examples of miniature pyxides retained from the excavation of the sanctuary. The same pyxis types (concave, convex, tripod, and powder) occur as in the full-size and in the same order of frequency, but in much smaller numbers. Aside from the convex pyxides, each type is represented by one example in our catalog. All are decorated with linear patterns, except for the unusual fragment **296**, which appears to have been covered with black glaze and is only tentatively identified as a pyxis.

296   Pl. 49; Fig. 2 Inv. No. 77–411 D14/E14 1 2
Pyxis (?) fragment, about one-quarter preserved. Pinkish clay with traces of burning. Black glaze almost entirely worn off on exterior and interior.

---

567. There are 27 pyxis, 19 kothon, 19 bowls, and 15 lid fragments.

568. Isolated examples of other shapes include a miniature amphoriskos base, a plate? fragment, and some fragments of unidentified open and closed vases.

569. White, *Second Report*, 181–182; White, *Final Reports* V, 30, 53.

570. There were over 70 pieces, including 3 pyxides, 3 lids, 2 kothons, 54 kotylai, 3 bowls, and 8 hydriai. Eleven of these miniatures, including 6 hydriai, have been catalogued (**297, 304, 310, 311, 325, 335–339, 376**). The finds of miniatures in other largely undisturbed levels are noted in their respective sections.

571. The other uncatalogued pieces (a lid, about a dozen miniature kotylai, and 3 miniature black-glazed hydriai fragments) are noted in the text below.

572. Over 43% of the uncatalogued miniature-vase fragments (mostly kotylai, followed by hydriai) were also found here.

573. See also Ure, *AFR*, 24.

H: 0.024; Est D: 0.055

Flaring rim, concave side wall, flaring foot ring. Unusually thick fabric for the size of the vessel. Presumably, originally covered with black glaze. On underside of foot, three incised concentric circles.

The fragment has been included with the miniature pyxides, but the shape has no known parallel among published miniature vases.

LC II/III

CONCAVE PYXIDES

As with the concave-sided pyxides of full size, the miniatures of this shape are rare. Only one other miniature concave-sided pyxis fragment was identified among the finds retained from the excavations.[574] The linear surface decoration on our catalogued piece, which was found in a largely undisturbed archaic level, is poorly preserved.

297   Pl. 49; Fig. 2   Sb. 67   D12/13   B   4

Fragmentary pyxis, about one-half preserved, with three lug handles. Pale buff clay. Worn black glaze. Added red. Encrusted. Mended from two joins.

H: 0.034; D: 0.048 (rim); D: 0.0515 (base)

On exterior: red band at rim; vertical stripes in handle zone; alternating red and black bands on body; black band around base. On interior: black band below rim and black circle in center of floor. Bands are sloppily applied.

LC

CONVEX PYXIDES

In addition to our two catalogued entries from the backfill of the middle sanctuary retaining wall, ten other convex pyxis fragments were found: two of these belong to the type with flat rim and no handles (cf. **299**); seven others are from pyxides with short vertical rims and cylindrical handles. Three of these miniature fragments were found in largely undisturbed archaic levels,[575] and six were found in the backfill of the middle sanctuary retaining wall. **298** belongs to the type with a vertical rim, while **299**, notable for being virtually intact, has a flat rim.

298   Pl. 50   Sb. 519–3   F14/G14   1   2

Fragment preserving part of rim, shoulder, and body. Buff clay with traces of burning (gray on interior, neck, and shoulder). Black glaze mostly worn, brown where thin. Added red. Surface worn and encrusted.

MPH: 0.034; MPW: 0.042

Black glaze on vertical rim. On shoulder: band of tongues with red band above. Traces of banding on body (brown and red).

For a similar type, see the miniature white-style pyxis from Tocra (*Tocra* I, pl. 13, no. 157).

LC II

299   Pl. 50; Fig. 2 Inv. No. 77–654   F13/G13   2   2

Intact convex-sided pyxis, except for chips missing from edge of rim. Buff clay. Worn dull black glaze. Surface worn and slightly encrusted.

H: 0.0557; D: 0.0856 (max); D: 0.069 (rim); D: 0.053 (base)

Wide, flat rim, globular body, and ring foot. No handles.[576] Traces of black glaze on rim. Below shoulder, broad band with traces of groups of vertical stripes. Black horizontal bands on body. Trace of black glaze around exterior of foot. Black glaze on resting surface of foot. On underside of foot, two concentric black bands around a large central dot.

The pyxis is rather well made. Similar in shape (though our example is more rotund) and size, but with a different decorative scheme, are two convex pyxides from a grave at Examilia, dated to MC (*Hesperia* 33 [1964], 95, 100, pl. 19, E7 and E8).[577] For a somewhat smaller version of the shape, see *Perachora* II, pl. 122, no. 3184.

LC II

TRIPOD PYXIDES

Besides our one catalogued piece, eight other fragments of miniature tripod pyxides were among the finds from the sanctuary. Of these, four were found in largely undisturbed archaic levels.[578] All the fragments are decorated with linear patterns. The painting on our catalogued fragment (**300**) appears to have been relatively neat, especially for a vase of this size.

300   Pl. 50   Sb. 297–1   F13/G13   1   2

Tripod pyxis, about one-third preserved. Light green clay. Glaze brown and worn. Added red worn. Chipped and encrusted.

MPH: 0.0246; MPW: 0.025; Est D: 0.05

The pyxis has a projecting rim, deep body, and low foot. Exterior: red on top of rim, broad band, brown band, band of slanting lines with bands above and below, two bands at base of foot. Interior: band below rim and around edge of floor, ring around dot in center of floor.

LC II

---

574. The fragment, a base, was found in E11/12, Pit 2.

575. D12/13, B, 4 Middle (shoulder fragment with triangles); D12/E12, D, 3 (flat rim and shoulder fragment); and D12/13, F, 4 (burnt vertical rim-shoulder fragment with sigmas).

576. Corresponds to Dunbabin's Group 7 (miniature convex-sided pyxides without handles), for which see *Perachora* II, 305.

577. P. Lawrence notes on p. 100 that LC pyxides "have higher proportions and a more globular body" and that the Examilia pyxides "are not fully developed white style." Lawrence, however, does not classify these pyxides, which are 6 cm and 5.5 cm, respectively, in height, as miniatures.

578. D12/13, B,4 (1); D12/E12, D, 3 (2 foot fragments); and C15/16, 1, 4–2, Area 5 (1); the others were found in E12/13, C, 4 (1 foot); F13/G13, 2, 2 (1 fragment); and F14/G14, 1, 2 (2 fragments).

POWDER PYXIDES

Only two other miniature powder pyxis fragments were retained from the excavation,[579] aside from our one catalogued example, which is rather carefully decorated with linear patterns.

301   Pl. 50   Sb. 118–1   E10 Bldg Balk 3
Lid fragment, preserving about one-quarter top and part of side wall. Pale yellow buff clay with slight greenish tinge. Worn black glaze, ranges from black to brown. Added red. Encrusted.
MPH: 0.0152; MPW: 0.0345; Est D: 0.05
Projecting molding at juncture of horizontal top and vertical side wall. On top from center: black circle in center surrounded by a red band; band of sloppy triangles with dots between tips bordered by thin band above and below; band near edge; red on projecting edge molding. On side wall: black band and red band below.
LC II

LIDS

The catalog contains two miniature pyxis lids decorated with linear patterns, which belong to the flat type with flange. **302** may, in fact, not be a miniature (see below). About a dozen other miniature pyxis lids were retained from the excavations, half of which apparently belonged to lids of the domed type.[580] Four of the uncatalogued fragments were found in largely undisturbed archaic levels: three in D12/13, B, 4 and one, a knob, in D12/13, F, 4. In addition, a miniature flat, flanged lid was found in an undisturbed archaic level (C13/D13, 1, 7). **303**, rather neatly decorated, was also found in an undisturbed archaic level that yielded another small, almost complete, flat lid whose surface decoration was not preserved.

302   Pl. 50   Sb. 32–2   D13 (Area 2)   2   3
Fragment, preserving over one-half of lid, complete knob (chip missing from edge) and flange. Light greenish clay. Worn black glaze. Soil-stained.
MPH: 0.02; D: 0.061 (lid); D: 0.029 (flange)
Black band around top of the low, rounded knob. Upper surface of lid is almost flat, rising slightly toward the center. Top of lid decorated with black bands of varying width. The flange is curiously close to the center. Although the diameter of the lid might place it among lids of standard size, the small diameter of the flange seems to suggest that it was to fit a small or miniature pyxis.[581]
For similar banded decoration, see *CVA* Heidelberg (Bd 1), pl. 18, 6.
LC II

303   Pl. 50   Sb. 463–1   C13   1   4b
Almost complete lid, except for pieces missing from rim. Buff clay. Black glaze worn. Added red.
MPH: 0.02; D: 0.0497 (lid); D: 0.0306 (flange)
Three concentric rings (black, red, black) on top of low, rounded button-type knob. Top of lid: three thin black bands; a band of rather widely spaced vertical stripes between two black bands; thin red band; black band around the edge.
A related decorative scheme with a band of stripes, though not as widely spaced as in our example, appears on a larger LC lid from the Potters' Quarter at Corinth (*Corinth* XV:3, pl. 65, no. 1633).
LC

KOTYLAI

Kotylai are by far the most common of all the miniatures vases. From the over 1400 uncatalogued fragments retained from the excavations, over 820 individual kotylai were identified with certainty, but the number probably exceeds 1000.[582] Although the finds of miniature kotylai are extensively distributed throughout the excavated areas of the sanctuary, most of the pieces were poorly preserved and encrusted. As a result, only 18 miniature kotylai are included in the catalog.

The catalogued miniature kotylai range in height from 1.5 cm. to 3.9 cm. With the exception of one black-glazed miniature,[583] all are of the conventional type with linear decoration, and representative of the types found at the sanctuary. There are examples of kotylai with vertical stripes (**304–313**) and horizontal zigzags (**314–317**) in the handle-zone. The former are more common.[584] There is one example (**318**) with a band of dots in the handle-zone. All have horizontal bands, occasionally alternating red and black, and horizontal stripes on the body. The somewhat larger examples (**304, 314**) have a spreading ring foot. The underside of the foot varies: a flat reserved surface, often with a black dot or ring in the center

---

579. One was found in F11, 1, 3, the other in E12/13, E, 2.

580. The other fragments included 2 sherds from flat flanged lids, 2 knobs, and 2 unidentifiable fragments.

581. See *Corinth* XV:3, pl. 62, no. 1503, where there is a similar disproportion of the flange to the lid, but the lid is not considered to be miniature.

582. Of these, 773 were bases and 54 were rim-to-base fragments. To this number could be added 256 rim-handle fragments that preserve much of the body. The rims numbered 70, the handles 228, and the body fragments 47. Obviously, because of the small size of these vessels, body fragments were low in number.

583. The uncatalogued black-glazed sherds number only 19, 7 of which are bases.

584. This is corroborated by the uncatalogued finds for the recognizable handle-zone patterns showed 73 with vertical stripes and 45 with horizontal zigzags.

(**304**, **316**, **317**);[585] a raised central disk,[586] varying in diameter (**306**, **315**, **318–321**); a small button-like projection in the center (**313**);[587] and flat base with wire marks (**307**, **308**, **310**, **311**),[588] most prevalent on the smallest kotylai.

Well over half of the kotylai in our catalog were found in the backfill of the middle sanctuary retaining wall;[589] four were uncovered in largely undisturbed archaic levels: three (**304**, **310**, **311**) in D12/13, B, 4 and one (**314**) in C13, 1, 4a. The uncatalogued kotylai fragments have a fairly good distribution among the largely undisturbed archaic levels. Over 190 fragments, among which, minimally, 85 individual kotylai were identified,[590] were found in 18 of these archaic contexts. Over half of these fragments were concentrated in the D12/13, A and B areas.[591] In addition, over a dozen fragments, including 7 bases, were found in four archaic levels undisturbed by later intrusions.[592]

The miniature kotylai appear to date mainly to the second half of the sixth century and the early part of the fifth century.[593] There is a general correspondence, not only in terms of popularity as a votive but also in the range of types, with the miniature kotylai found at Tocra. Only some of our kotylai, however, could be assigned to Hayes's typology.

304 Pl. 51; Fig. 2 Sb. 75   D12/13 B 4 Middle
Fragment, preserving about one-third body from rim to base and complete spreading foot ring. Deep buff clay. Black glaze ranges to brown where thin. Added red. Surface worn and slightly encrusted.
H: 0.039; MPW: 0.049; D: 0.033 (base); Est D: 0.06 (rim)

Vertical wavy lines in handle-zone bounded by thin black line. Broad red band. Two thin black lines. Broad black band. Black on foot. On underside: black glaze on foot ring and small black ring in center of bottom. Black glaze on interior.

This is a very common variety of miniature kotyle of the latter part of the sixth century.[594] The type is illustrated in *NC*, fig. 181B. Our fragment exhibits a number of features indicative of Hayes's Type 1, dated second to third quarter of the sixth century:[595] size, turned base, and linear decorative scheme of vertical stripes in the handle-zone, as well as two bands and lines on the wall. Our fragment, however, is broader-based than the illustrated Tocra kotylai of Type 1. It resembles a miniature kotyle found in one of the infant graves in the North Cemetery at Corinth (*Corinth* XIII, pl. 40, 285–2), dated to the first half of the fifth century. For a similar type included among the linear-style kotylai, see **156**.

LC II

305 Pl. 51; Fig. 2 Sb. 288–25   F13/G13 1 2
Fragment, preserving part of body from rim to base and a complete slight foot. The wall rises in a continuous curve from the broad foot to the rim. Light gray clay. Black glaze somewhat worn on exterior and flaking on interior. Encrusted.
H: 0.03; MPW: 0.053; D: 0.035 (base); Est D: 0.06–0.07 (rim)

Vertical stripes in handle-zone with thin black line above and below. Thin black line. Broad black band. Two thin black bands. Black on slight foot. On underside: two concentric black rings. Flaking black glaze on interior.

The profile, as preserved, is rather unusual for this type of kotyle, and seemingly without parallel. In general, miniature kotylai with only one broad horizontal band and horizontal lines on the body have a narrower foot.[596] There are, of course, exceptions, such as *Corinth* XV:3, pl. 67, nos. 1685–1686.

LC

---

585. Only 12 such bases were recognized. They appear to be associated with the somewhat larger shapes.

586. Almost 240 such bases were found.

587. Some 180 bases of this type were identified.

588. Over 180 bases of this type were found.

589. Almost 42% of the uncatalogued sherds and 46% of the bases also come from this area.

590. There were 81 bases and 4 rim-to-base fragments. In addition, close to 60 of the sherds were rim and rim-handle fragments, which appeared to belong to different kotylai.

591. D12/13, A, 3 (34 fragments: 10 bases, 9 rim-handle fragments, 4 rims, 6 handles, 5 body sherds); D12/13, A, 4 (18 fragments: 9 bases, 1 rim-handle fragment, 8 handles); D12/13, B, 4 (51 fragments: 14 bases, 9 rim-handle fragments, 1 rim-body fragment, 12 rims, 14 handles, 1 black-glazed miniature). The other largely undisturbed archaic levels yielded: E11/12, Pit Area, 3 (2 bases), E12/13, C, 4 (2 bases and 4 rims), D12/E12, D, 3 (13 bases, 6 rim-handles, 2 body sherds), D12/E12, D, 4 (1 base, 3 rims, 1 body sherd), C15/16, 1, 4–2, Area 5 (7 bases, 3 rim-handles, 1 black glazed sherd), D12/13, F, 3 (6 bases, 3 rim-handles, 1 rim, 2 handles), D12/13, F, 4 (2 bases), D13/E13, 1, 4 (1 rim-body, 1 body, 1 handle), C13/D13, 1, 4 (4 bases), C13/D13, 1, 5 (2 bases, 5 handles), C13/D13, 1, 6 (4 bases, 1 rim-body), E15, 1, 4 (1 handle), E15, 2, 4 (1 base, 1 rim-handle), C11, 2, 4 (1 body), C13, 1, 4a (4 bases, 2 rim-handles, 1 rim-body, 1 rim).

592. D16/17, 1, 4 (1 base and 1 rim-handle), C13/D13, 1, 7 (3 bases, 1 rim with vertical stripes, 3 handles), C12/D12, G, 3 (2 bases, 1 handle), C13, 1, 4b (1 base, 1 rim-handle).

593. See discussion of miniatures in *Perachora* II, 290–1 and *Tocra* II, 9 and 14 in particular for classification of types.

594. Some 70 other fragments of this type were also found at the sanctuary: 1 in D13 (Area 2), 1,2; 1 in E11, 1, 2; 1 in D12/13, B, 2,3; 4 in D12/13, B, 4 West; 2 in D12/13, B, 4 Middle; 1 in E11/12, Pit Area, 2; 2 in D12/E12, D, 4; 1 in C15/D15, 1, 1 2; 1 in C15/D15, 1,1a; 3 in F12, 2; 1 fragmentary kotyle in D14, 1, 2; 1 in D16/17, 2, 3; 1 in D10/11, C, 5; 1 in D12/13, F, 3; 19 in F13/G13, 1, 2; 2 in Area 2, Ext N, 1; 1 in C12/13, 1, 3; 1 in C12/13, 1, 4; 1 in C13/D13, 1, 7; 1 in C13/D13, 2, 2; 1 in D11/12, 1, 4, S scarp clean-up; 12 in F13/G13, 2, 2; 1 in E14/15, 2, 1; 8 in F14/G14, 1, 2; 2 in F14/G14, 1, 3.

595. *Tocra* II, 14, nos. 1911–1919, pl. 7.

596. As in *Tocra* II, pl. 8, nos. 1922–1925 (Type 2), and *Perachora* II, pl. 119, no. 2954.

306   Pl. 51; Fig. 2 Sb. 418–1   F13/G13   2   2
Fragment, preserving part of body from rim to base and a complete foot. Buff clay. Black glaze worn. Encrusted.
MPH: 0.032; D: 0.055 (rim); D: 0.025 (base)
Vertical stripes in handle-zone with black line below. Broad black band between black lines above and below. Black on foot. On underside: concentric narrow black band around edge of foot and small disk in center of bottom.
This fragmentary kotyle appears to belong to Hayes's Type 2 of miniature kotyle, dated to the second and third quarter of the sixth century (*Tocra* II, 9, nos. 1922–1938, pl. 8).
LC I/II

307   Pl. 51   Inv. No. 78–355 F14/G14   1   3
Fragmentary kotyle, with complete profile. Pieces missing from wall. Handles dissimilar in size, section, and level at which attached. Flat base with wire marks. Creamy buff clay. Black glaze worn and fired mostly brownish black. Mended. Encrusted.
H: 0.0196; D: 0.038 (rim); D: 0.0212 (base)
Comparatively large vertical stripes in handle-zone with black band below. Broader black band on lower body. Black on exterior of foot. On underside: black glaze with reserved circle in center. On interior: streaky and worn black glaze.
This piece is representative of the very small and shallow miniature kotyle, a particularly common type.
For the type, see *Mégara Hyblaea*, pl. 57, nos. 6–7; and *Délos* X, pl. 36, nos. 495–496. Our example and some of those that follow are cruder, with fewer lines on the body than those kotylai of Hayes's Type 2, dated to the second and third quarter of the sixth century.[597] Yet, they are not quite as careless and abbreviated as those of Hayes's Type 3, with their few widely spaced stripes in the handle-zone.[598]
LC II

308   Pl. 51   Inv. No. 77–472 F13/G13   2   2
Fragment, preserving about one-third wall and complete flat base. Creamy buff clay. Black glaze worn.
H: 0.022; D: 0.024 (base)
Vertical stripes in handle-zone with thin black band below. Broad black band with thin band below. Black on foot. On underside: black glaze and slight, reserved, rounded protuberance in center. Flaking black glaze on interior. Similar to preceding.
LC II

309   Pl. 51   Inv. No. 78–414 F14/G14   1   2
Almost complete kotyle, one of horizontal loop handles and part of rim missing. Flat base with wire marks on underside. Creamy buff clay. Black glaze worn and crazed where preserved. Surface heavily encrusted.
H: 0.024; D: 0.0443 (rim); D: 0.0192 (base)
Barely visible vertical stripes in handle-zone with thin black band below. Broad black band on lower body wall. Black on exterior of foot. Black on underside of foot. Glaze almost entirely worn off on interior.
Similar to preceding and with a resemblance to the examples of Type 2 from Tocra.[599]
LC II

310   Pl. 51; Fig. 2 Inv. No. 71–377 D12/13   B   4
Fragmentary kotyle, mended from two joins, and missing piece of rim. Light yellowish buff clay. Black glaze almost gone. Flat base with wire marks. Surface worn, soil-stained, and encrusted.
H: 0.024; D: 0.0487 (rim); D: 0.0205 (base)
White, *Second Report*, 182 n. 49.
Traces of black vertical stripes in handle-zone. Dark brown bands on body.
This miniature cup also resembles the Type 2 kotylai from Tocra (*Tocra* II, pl. 8, no. 1925), somewhat more than the preceding examples, which are all quite similar. It was found in a largely undisturbed archaic level.
LC II

311   Pl. 52; Fig. 2 Inv. No. 71–369 D12/13   B   4
Almost intact, except for mended section of rim. Light buff clay with slight grayish tinge. Black glaze worn. Flat base with wire marks. Soil-stained and encrusted.
H: 0.02; D: 0.0394 (rim); D: 0.0206 (base)
White, *Second Report*, 182 n. 49, pl. LXXXVII, b.
Vertical stripes in handle-zone with horizontal stripe below. Trace of another band on body wall. Traces of black glaze on interior.
Similar to preceding, though slightly smaller. Found in a largely undisturbed archaic level.
LC II

312   Pl. 52   Sb. 516–21   F14/G14   1   2
Fragment, preserving about one-quarter rim, part of body, and one handle. Light grayish green clay. Black glaze, gray where thin. Encrusted.
MPH: 0.015; MPW: 0.0385
Vertical stripes at rim. Three horizontal bands on body. On interior: flaking black glaze.
For the type, see *Corinth* XV:3, pl. 67, 1711. The smallest of our miniature kotyle, it is similar to the preceding examples.
LC II

313   Pl. 52; Fig. 3 Sb. 418–4   F13/G13   2   2
Fragment, preserving part of body from rim to base and complete foot. Deep buff clay. Black glaze worn, brown where thin, and flaking on interior. Encrusted.
H: 0.035; MPW: 0.049; D: 0.0244 (base)
Vertical stripes in handle-zone. Bands on body poorly preserved. On underside: a small round disk ("button") in center of bottom.
LC II/III

314   Pl. 52; Fig. 3 Inv. No. 77–1277   C13   1   4a
Almost complete kotyle, except for chips missing from rim. Buff clay. Black glaze severely worn. Mended handle. Broad base with foot ring. Soil-stained and encrusted.
H: 0.0342; D: 0.055 (rim); D: 0.033 (base)
Faint traces of horizontal zigzag in handle-zone. Broad black band and traces of another band or bands on body wall. Ring foot with a large disk on the underside. On interior, black glaze peeling where partially preserved.
Miniature kotylai with horizontal zigzags are also common,[600] and as a group are somewhat later than those with

---

597. Cf. *Tocra* II, 9, 14, nos. 1922–1938, pl. 8, nos. 1922–1925.

598. *Tocra* II, 9 n. 13, 15, nos. 1939–1940.

599. Cf. *Tocra* II, 9, 14, nos. 1922–1938, pl. 8, nos. 1922–1925.

600. Some 45 other examples of this type from the sanctuary were found: 1 in Area 2, 1, 2; 4 in D12/13, B, 4 Middle; 1 in D12/13, A, 3 West; 1 in F16, 2, 1; 1 in F15, 3, 2; 1 in E10, balk south, 2/3; 1 in D16/17, 1, 3; 1 in C15/16, 1, 4 tank; 1 in C15/16, 4–2, Area 4; 1 in D16/17, 2, 3; 2 in D16/17, 2, 4; 8 in F13/G13, 1, 2; 1 in E15, 2, 3 4; 1 in D11/12, 1, 4, S Scarp cleanup; 5 in F13/G13, 2, 2; 1 in C14/D14, 2, 2; 4 in F14/G14, 1, 2; 10 in F14/G14, 1, 3.

vertical stripes at the rim.⁶⁰¹ The shape occurs in a broad-based variety,⁶⁰² as our kotyle, and in a more slender version,⁶⁰³ which is also represented by several examples in the catalog. The body is generally decorated with a horizontal red-and-black band. Our kotyle seems to have had only black bands. Nonetheless, it can be assigned to Hayes's Type 4. For an example with glazed bands only, as on our kotyle, see *Corinth* XIII, 225, pl. 41, no. 286–2, dated to the first quarter of the fifth century.

For other examples of this type, see *Corinth* XIII, pl. 35, 250–9 and 253–1 in particular, dated to the fourth quarter of the sixth century, and pls. 40, 285–1, and 287–1, dated to the first half of the fifth century.⁶⁰⁴ For a very close parallel for the shape of our kotyle, see *Corinth* XV:3, pl. 67, 1717, and *CVA* Heidelberg, pl. 16, 7.⁶⁰⁵

This kotyle was found in a largely undisturbed archaic level.
LC II/III

315   Pl. 52   Inv. No. 73–661 C15/16   1   4
Fragment, preserving about one half of body and most of the foot. Small ring foot. Buff clay. Black glaze worn in places and carelessly applied on interior. Added red. Soil-stained and slightly encrusted.
H: 0.0255; D: 0.036 (rim); D: 0.019 (base)
Horizontal zigzag in handle-zone. Broad red band, a black line, and traces of a broad black band above the foot. Black on exterior of foot. On underside: black on inside of foot and a small raised disk in center of bottom. Glaze heavily worn on interior.

This is another example of a common late type of miniature kotyle, particularly prevalent in the late sixth and early part of the fifth century. It is characterized by a horizontal zigzag at the rim, often with a black line below,⁶⁰⁶ and two broad bands, one red and one black band, which are generally separated by a thin black stripe, on the body.⁶⁰⁷ For the type, see *Perachora* II, 296, no. 2949, pl. 119; *Corinth* XV:3, 310, pl. 67, no. 1689; and *Tocra* II, 14 (Type 4), pl. 7, no. 1942, and pl. 8, nos. 1941, 1943. Our kotyle with its more slender proportions is closer to the kotyle from the Potters' Quarter at Corinth than to the Tocra examples, which are dated to the late sixth and early fifth centuries.⁶⁰⁸
LC II/III

316   Pl. 52   Sb. 516–16   F14/G14   1   2
Fragment, preserving about one-sixth of body, almost complete ring foot, and root of loop handle. Orangey buff clay. Firm black glaze, brown where thin. Added red.
H: 0.032; D: 0.026 (base)
Black stripe at rim. Horizontal zigzag in handle-zone with thin brown line below. Broad red and broad black band, separated by a thin black line. Black on exterior of foot. On underside: black on inside of ring foot and bottom reserved with black dot in the center.

Similar to preceding, except for underside of foot.
LC II/III

317   Pl. 52; Fig. 3 Sb. 516–14   F14/G14   1   2
Fragment, preserving about one-half of body, complete base, and one loop handle. Tooled base, but no ring foot. Pale light green clay. Black glaze, mostly worn. Added red. Slightly misshapen.
H: 0.0275; MPW: 0.039; D: 0.0189 (base)
Part of horizontal zigzag in handle-zone with black line below. Very broad red and broad black band, separated by a brown line. Black on handle. Thickened, tooled base, with some undercutting to create a foot. On underside: concentric black band on bottom periphery. Interior only partially glazed.

Decorative scheme similar to preceding.
LC II/III

318   Pl. 53; Fig. 3 Sb. 418–2   F13/G13   2   2
Fragment, preserving less than half of body and complete base. Deep buff clay. Glaze-fired brown and slightly worn. Added red worn.
H: 0.034; MPW: 0.042; D: 0.0244 (base)
Narrow band at rim. Band of dots or short petals in handle-zone with band below.⁶⁰⁹ On body: narrow band, broad band, and two narrow bands below. Glaze on exterior of foot. On underside: small raised disk in center of bottom. On interior: flaking glaze and worn added red bands.

For the type, see *Perachora* II, 296, pl. 119, no. 2953 with additional references cited. A related type has larger petals in the handle-zone, such as *Corinth* XIII, pl. 49, 334–2, and *Corinth* XV:3, pl. 67, no. 1718.
LC II/III

319   Pl. 53   Sb. 501–6   F14/G14   1   Test 1
                                                 mixed with some St 2
Lower body fragment. Pale pinkish clay. Black glaze, thinly applied, ranges to gray and brown. Encrusted.
MPH: 0.021; MPW: 0.042; D: 0.019 (base)
On body: broad black band and stripe above base. Black on exterior of foot. On underside: patch of black glaze around the base and small raised disk in center. On interior: thin black glaze.
LC II/III

320   Pl. 53; Fig. 3 Sb. 418–3   F13/G13   2   2
Fragment, preserving most of body with complete foot ring, rim broken off. Light green clay. Glaze gone. Slightly encrusted.
MPH: 0.03; MPD: 0.0542; D: 0.0284 (base)
Surface not smoothed. Small raised disk in center of bottom.
LC II/III

---

601. See comments in *Corinth* XIII, 123, and *Tocra* II, 9, 14 (Type 4), dated to the late sixth and early fifth centuries.

602. Cf. *Tocra* II, 14 (Type 4), pl. 7, no. 1942; pl. 8, nos. 1941, 1943, all dated to the late sixth and early fifth centuries.

603. See *Corinth* XV:3, 310.

604. The fifth-century kotylai, however, have both red and black bands on the body.

605. Both of these have the more conventional red and black bands on the body.

606. Our examples does not preserve bounding line below the horizontal zigzag.

607. Cf. *Mégara Hyblaea*, pl. 57, nos. 8–9, dated LC II; *CVA*, Heidelberg, pl. 16, nos. 7–8, 10–11, dated LC II; *Délos* XVII, pl. 58, nos. 99–105.

608. See Hayes's comments in *Tocra* II, 9 and *Tocra* I, 26 n. 3, for additional references, including the discussion in *Corinth* XIII, as cited in n. 3. The kotylai from the North Cemetery at Corinth, which are analogous to our kotyle, with the exception of pl. 49, 334–1 (a miniature), are taller vases (e.g., pl. 40, 285–1, 287–1; pl. 41, 291–2; pl. 50, 333–1). They range in date from the first quarter to the middle of the fifth century.

609. Two other fragments with this decoration were found: one in C15/D15, 1–B, 3 and the other in C13, 1, 4a (a largely undisturbed archaic level).

321   Pl. 53   Inv. No. 78–449 F14/G14 1 3

Intact, except for missing loop handle. Creamy buff clay. Dull black glaze, unevenly applied and fired, producing a mottled black-and-brown surface on both exterior and interior. Some flaking of glaze.

H: 0.0206; D: 0.0393 (rim); D: 0.0193 (base)

Rather wide body tapers to a relatively narrow base. On underside: raised disk in center of bottom.

Miniature black-glazed kotylai were far less common than those with linear decoration.[610] For the type and shape, see *Perachora* II, pl. 119, no. 2962. The miniature black-glazed kotylai from the North Cemetery at Corinth, dated mainly to the second half of the fifth century, have steeper walls and are not as wide-bodied as our kotyle.[611]

LC II

KYLIKES

Kylikes are rare in the Corinthian repertoire of miniatures.[612] At the Cyrene sanctuary, in addition to this one catalogued example in the silhouette style, seven other fragments of miniature kylikes were identified among the finds retained from the excavations.[613] Three of them also preserved traces of silhouette figures. One, in particular, is a smaller version of our catalogued kylix. Another, a rim-body-handle fragment, was found in a largely undisturbed archaic level (D12/E12, D, 3).

322   Pl. 53   Sb. 290–1   F13/G13 1 2

Fragment, preserving less than one–half rim (chipped), most of bowl, and foot with chips missing. Handles broken off. Light green clay. Worn black glaze. Added red worn. Mended from two fragments. Encrusted.

H: 0.0354; MPD: 0.0715; D: 0.037 (foot)

On exterior: thin band at top of offset rim; thin band below rim; decoration in frieze almost totally indiscernible, but appears to be crude rendering of bird or birds in silhouette; band below frieze; glazed conical foot. On interior: traces on two red bands on rim; red band on bowl; three concentric bands around two concentric circles in center.

LC II

PHIALAI MESOMPHALOI

Only one other phiale mesomphalos fragment, found in F13/G13, 2, 2, was identified among the finds retained from the sanctuary. Our catalogued example seems to have been black-glazed.

323   Pl. 53; Fig. 3 Inv. No. 73–1203   C15/D15 1–B 4

Complete flat-bottomed phiale mesomphalos. Creamy buff clay with slight yellowish tinge. Black glaze preserved in patches on exterior and interior. Mended from two joining fragments. Soil-stained and encrusted.

H: 0.015; D: 0.049 (rim); D: 0.028 (base)

This presumably black-glazed phiale has a low boss, rounded walls, and a flat wire-drawn base.

For the type, see *Perachora* II, 298, nos. 2980–3005, pl. 120 and for the shape, *Corinth* XV:3, 335, nos. 2018, 2023, 2025, pl. 73.

LC II/III

BOWLS

Miniature black-glazed bowls were not a frequent dedication at the sanctuary. The two catalogued examples consist of an unusual angular form with bevelled rim (**324**) and a more common (**325**) type with a molded-like rim, datable to the late sixth and early part of the fifth century B.C. In addition to these, three bases and 14 black-glazed bowl rim or rim-body fragments were retained from the excavations.[614] Among these were two everted rims, six inverted rims, one beveled (cf. **324**), and one thickened rim. Our one intact black-glazed miniature bowl (**325**) was found in a largely undisturbed archaic level. Three of the uncatalogued fragments are also from largely undisturbed archaic levels.[615]

324   Pl. 54; Fig. 3 Inv. No. 73–1121   C15/16 1 4

Fragmentary black-glazed bowl, missing about one-third rim and body. Buff clay. Worn and flaking black glaze.

H: 0.016; D: 0.047 (rim); D: 0.025 (base)

Beveled rim, concave walls, and flat wire-drawn base. This is an unusual shape for a bowl. For a close parallel, see Campbell, *Hesperia* 7 (1938), 587, no. 81, fig. 15. A somewhat similar beveled rim occurs on a miniature bowl, but on a high conical foot, in *Corinth* XV:3, pl. 71, no. 1939. The bowl was found in Well 1, where the latest finds date to the end of the sixth century B.C.[616]

LC II/III

325   Pl. 54   Inv. No. 71–671 D12/13 B 4

Intact black-glazed bowl. Deep buff clay. Dull, flaking black glaze on interior and exterior. Encrusted.

H: 0.017; D: 0.043 (rim); D: 0.022 (base)

---

610. As noted above, only 19 other pieces, including 7 bases, were found at the sanctuary.

611. *Corinth* XIII, 127. The black-glazed miniatures, dated to the second quarter of the sixth century, are taller and more carefully made (see p. 108, pl. 29, nos. 187–1, 188–2,3).

612. For example, there are none from Perachora, Tocra, or the North Cemetery or Potters' Quarter at Corinth.

613. A total of 5 fragments, including **322**, were found in the backfill of the middle sanctuary retaining wall.

614. Two were found in D12/13, B, 4; 1 in D12/13, A, 3 (between rubble walls); 1 in E10, bldg.; 1 in D14, 1, 3; 1 base in D16/17, 2, 4; 1 rim in D12/13, F, 2b; 3 in F13/G13, 1, 2; 1 in C11, 1, 3c; 1 in D12, Balk, 5e; 1 base on C11, 2, 3; 1 base in F14/G14, 1, Test 2; and 3 rims in F14/G14, 1, 2.

615. Two, including a fragment with an everted rim, were found in D12/13, B, 4; 1 a thickened rim, in D12/13, A, 3 (between rubble walls).

616. *Corinth* XV:3, 7.

Shallow, misshapen bowl with slightly thickened flat rim and flat wire-drawn base.

The shape is a quite common one among black-glazed miniature bowls. For the type, see Campbell, *Hesperia* 7 (1938), no. 82, fig. 15; *Corinth* XV:3, pl. 71, nos. 1948–1949, 1951–1952.

LC II/III

KANA

The two relatively well-preserved miniature kana in our catalog appear to be the only examples of this shape identified among the finds retained from the excavation.[617] Our first vase, **326**, was found in a largely undisturbed archaic level.

326   Pl. 54   Inv. No. 76–1025   D12/13   F   3

Intact kanoun except for one missing handle. Deep buff clay with pinkish tinge. Glaze fugitive, only slight traces of reddish orange paint. Slightly encrusted.

H: 0.0168; D: 0.052 (rim); D: 0.049 (base)

Vertical wall with thickened ridge at top. Two of original three cleft lug handles preserved, one of them chipped. Grooving on floor and flat underside. Tooling marks on surface.

The original painted decoration cannot be determined. For a similar shape and three lug handles, see *Corinth* XV:3, pl. 70, no. 1896, found in the deposit in Trench J, which is dated to the second half of the sixth century B.C.[618] Our example is more sloppily finished.

LC II/III

327   Pl. 54   Sb. 421–4   F13/G13   2   2

Intact kanoun except for chipped rim and handles. Buff clay. Black glaze somewhat worn. Added red. Slightly encrusted.

H: 0.021; D: 0.043 (rim); D: 0.042 (base)

Vertical, slightly concave wall. Flat base. Irregular rim with groups of short vertical grooves about every centimeter. Part of one lug handle preserved. Black glaze at rim with thin band below. Red band. Black band around base. The same decoration appears on a miniature kanoun from the Potters' Quarter at Corinth (*Corinth* XV:3, pl. 70, no. 1903); however, the shape, with more flaring walls, is different. The form of the rim is most unusual.

LC II/III

KOTHONS

The sanctuary has yielded 15 miniature kothon fragments, in addition to the four examples in our catalog: three (**328–330**), decorated in the white style, are representative of the uncatalogued finds; the fourth (**331**) is black-glazed.[619] Two of the uncatalogued pieces, one of which is decorated with a pattern of alternating triangles on the shoulder, were found in a largely undisturbed archaic level (D12/13, B, 4).

328   Pl. 54   Sb. 139–3   D16/17   1   3

Fragment, round in section, preserving about one-quarter of shoulder, part of hanging rim, and a complete reflex handle. Light greenish yellow clay. Metallic black glaze, worn. Added red. Encrusted.

MPH: 0.021; MPL: 0.056; MPW: 0.03 (with handle)

On hanging rim: black glaze and two red lines near edge of shoulder. On shoulder: band of carelessly drawn black tongues, bordered by band above and below. Black glaze partially applied to handle. Glazed line below handle.

For the type, see *Corinth* XV:3, pl. 73, nos. 2039, 2048; *Tocra* I, pl. 18, no. 260; *Tocra* II, pl. 5, no. 1877, where the decoration is almost identical.

LC

329   Pl. 54   Sb. 86   E15   3   3

Fragment, preserving about one-third of kothon, round in section, with reflex handle (almost entirely broken off). Rim broken off. Preserved portion of ring foot chipped. Light green clay. Fugitive black glaze. Added red. Encrusted.

MPH: 0.031; MPW: 0.068

On shoulder: two thin bands; double-dot band; bands (rbbr). Black band on body below handle. Traces of black glaze on top of handle roots. Interior of floor glazed. Underside of foot banded.[620]

For miniature kothons with dotted-band decoration on the shoulder, see *Corinth* XV:3, pl. 73, 2039; Lawrence, *Hesperia* 33 (1964), E 23, pl. 19.

LC

330   Pl. 55   Inv. No. 71–727   D12/13   B   2

Fragment, preserving about two-thirds of kothon, round in section, with roots of reflex handle. Most of hanging rim and portion of shoulder broken off. Part of missing floor restored. Creamy clay. Black glaze, mostly worn off. Added red. Mended from several pieces with restoration. Encrusted.

MPH: 0.029; MPD: 0.079; D: 0.06 (base)

On shoulder: double-dot band, bordered by line above and below; two concentric red lines. Patch of red on hanging rim. Trace of band below handle. Traces of black glaze on interior of floor. Trace of band on resting surface of ring foot.

Similar to preceding.

LC

331   Pl. 55; Fig. 3   Inv No. 73–756   C15/16   1   4

Intact one-handled black-glazed kothon. Buff clay. Black glaze severely worn off. Soil-stained and encrusted.

H: 0.018; D: 0.045 (shoulder); D: 0.024 (base)

Relatively wide opening, slightly inward sloping rim, small flat base, and reflex handle. For the shape, see *Perachora* II, pl. 121, no. 3135; *Corinth* XV:3, pl. 73, no. 2042.

LC III

---

617. For a discussion of miniature kana, see *Corinth* XV:3, 325–6. On the kanoun, see also Callipolitis-Feytmans, 118–119.

618. *Corinth* XV:3, 8–9; cf. also no. 1903, pl. 70, with cleft lug handles but without the straight walls of our example.

619. For a discussion of miniature kothons, see *Perachora* II, 303–304 and *Corinth* XV:3, 336–337.

620. Fragment of another miniature with double-dot band was found in F14/G14, 1, 2.

OINOCHOAI

Miniature oinochoai are rare. Our catalogued miniature black-glazed oinochoe is notable for its workmanship and for its find spot, an undisturbed archaic level (C11, 2, 5).[621] The few other finds of this shape include a miniature broad-bottomed oinochoe base; a neck-shoulder-handle fragment, which may be from a black-glazed oinochoe; a neck fragment of a conical oinochoe; and a shoulder fragment decorated with tongues, possibly from an oinochoe.

332   Pl. 55   Inv. No. 76–827 C11 2 5
Fragmentary trefoil-mouth oinochoe, with pieces missing from neck and body. Pinkish buff clay. Glaze-fired mostly red and worn. Mended. Slightly encrusted.
H: 0.047; H: 0.056 (with handle); D: 0.035 (max;) D: 0.027 (base)
Rather tall wide neck with trefoil mouth. High, vertical strap handle. Rounded shoulder and high belly. Slightly conical flat wire-drawn base.
Our piece is well made for a miniature. There is, however, no exact parallel for the shape among the finds from Perachora[622] or the Potters' Quarter at Corinth. In general, the form of the body recalls that of the late archaic miniature black-glazed hydriai.
LC II/III

OLPE

This fragmentary olpe is our only example of this miniature shape identified among the finds from the sanctuary.

333   Pl. 55   Inv. 76–1083   D13/E13 Balk 2
Fragmentary black-glazed olpe, with pieces missing from neck and body. Deep buff clay with pinkish tinge. Matt black glaze unevenly fired to reddish brown. Mended from numerous fragments.
H: 0.077; H: 0.097 (with handle); D: 0.053 (max); D: 0.035 (base)
Round mouth with flaring, everted rim. Tall, vertical looped strap handle. Flaring neck and steeply sloping shoulder. Flat base. A very close parallel comes from the North Cemetery at Corinth (*Corinth* XIII, 112, 213–14, pl. 34, no. 257-7), from a grave dated to the end of the sixth century B.C.
LC II/III

HYDRIAI

The miniature black-glazed hydriai, as a group, are the best-preserved vases from the sanctuary. A large number (54) have been catalogued here, primarily for this reason. These examples represent a generally neglected though not unimportant series, which demonstrates the variations in shape and workmanship of this miniature class. Our miniatures can be dated mainly to the latter part of the sixth and the early fifth centuries (LCII/III), with a smaller number of examples belonging well into the fifth and perhaps even the fourth century B.C.[623]

Among all the miniature dedications uncovered in the sanctuary, the hydriai are second only to the miniature kotylai in terms of frequency. A total of 160 other pieces, including 82 bases and 23 fragmentary hydriai were found.[624] Coupled with the fortunate preservation of many of the vases, the popularity of the hydria among the miniature dedications befits the sanctuary of Demeter and Persephone.[625] By contrast, only one full-size hydria, a semi-glazed one (**274**), was identified among the surviving pieces from the site.

The finds are not so very widely dispersed throughout the excavated areas of the sanctuary. There are two major areas of concentration. As might be expected, the middle sanctuary retaining wall (T10) backfill areas of F13/G13 and F14/G14 yielded the largest concentration, a total of 109 examples, or over 51% of the finds.[626] The other area, D16/17, yielded 29 pieces, including the 13 in the catalogue.[627] In addition, 10 hydriai were found in largely undisturbed archaic levels: D12/13, B, 4, which may represent a votive deposit,[628] yielded six catalogued examples (**335–339**, **376**) and two bases; C13/D13, 1, 5 and D12/13, F, 3 each yielded one catalogued

---

621. White, *Final Reports* I, 114.

622. *Perachora* II, pl. 117, no. 2828 has a similar body with a high belly, but our neck is taller.

623. For a discussion on dating, see *Perachora* II, 290–291, and *Tocra* II, 10, 14, 92; see also *Corinth* XV:3, 324 (nos. 1871–1890).

624. The other fragments consisted of 3 rims, 13 shoulders with either neck, handle, or belly attached, 31 bodies, some with horizontal handles attached, and 8 necks, some with vertical handles.

625. See *Tocra* I, 15 on the association of the hydria with the Demeter cult.

626. From F13/G13 there were 35 pieces in addition to the 7 catalogued examples; while from F14/G14 there were 59 pieces in addition to the 8 catalogued hydriai.

627. D16/17 (Tr. 1 and 2, St. 3), fill from the southwest corner of the middle sanctuary, yielded 9 catalogued hydriai and 5 other fragments; D16/17, 2, 4 yielded 4 of the catalogued hydriai and 5 bases. D16/17, 1, 2 yielded 2 fragmentary hydriai, one of which was burnt; D16/17, 2, 1/2 yielded 4 fragments, one of which had a globular body.

628. See *supra* n. 569.

example (**357**, **383**, respectively). Of particular interest are five hydriai found in archaic levels undisturbed by later intrusions: two of the catalogued hydriai (**370**, **371**) and two other fragments (a base and a number of sherds belonging to one hydria) from F14/G14, 1, 5,[629] as well as a base from D12 Balk, St. 5. The remainder of our finds occur in one or two examples in just over 30 contexts.

To some extent, many of our black-glazed hydriai are very small-scale versions of standard-sized hydria of the Corinthian period, which are characterized by ovoid bodies and decorated with figured and linear-style decoration.[630]

Our miniatures range in height from a minimum of 2.7 cm. to almost 5 cm., with a significant number being about 4 cm. tall. The hydriai of the classical period generally tend to be smaller than those of the archaic period. Their clay is mainly buff (varying from dark to creamy to pink to deep yellow), and only a few examples have the characteristic light greenish clay. The black glaze is most often worn and, occasionally, unevenly fired. Many of the miniatures are not carefully made, some, in fact, are quite sloppy, but a few are distinguished by their finer workmanship (e.g., **344**, **363**, **371**, **380**).

Our series bears some comparison with the miniature black-glazed hydriai from Tocra for which a typology was formulated.[631] For a majority of our hydriai, there is a general correspondence with the late archaic types at Tocra (Types 1 and 2),[632] which are characterized by a broad belly, wide neck, thin flaring rim, and base molding. Our hydriai have not been categorized according to the Tocra typology, however, though analogies with the Tocra types are noted in the catalog entries. Although a typology for the Cyrene series will not be attempted here, the following basic types can be differentiated:

LATE ARCHAIC TYPES

1. Flaring rim; tall, wide, often vertical neck; pronounced shoulder, occasionally slightly angular; ovoid body with broad, high belly:

335, **340**, **349**, **351** (Fig. 3), **352**, **354**, **371** (Fig. 3), **373**.

2. Flaring rim; wide but shorter and concave neck; pronounced shoulder; ovoid body with high belly:

336, **337**, **343**, **350**, **365**, **372**.

3. Flaring rim; tall and wide neck; slightly rounded, narrower shoulder, generally forming a more continuous curve with the high-bellied ovoid body:

334, **338** (Fig. 3), **357**, **360** (Fig. 3), **362**, **370**.

4. Flaring rim; short, concave, wide neck; sloping shoulder, often steeply; globular ovoid body with lower belly:

341, **345**, **348**, **353**, **361**, **363** (Fig. 3), **364**, **366**, **367**, **369**.

5. Flaring rim; rather tall, wide, and vertical neck; pronounced shoulder; rounded body:

342, **344** (Fig. 3), **346**, **355** (Fig. 3), **358**, **368**.

CLASSICAL TYPES

6. Flaring rim; short, rather wide, concave neck; flat shoulder, broad ovoid body with high belly, high base-molding:

376 (Fig. 3), **383**–**385**, **387**, **388**.

7. Flaring rim; rather slender neck; rounded, squat body:

374, **377**, **378**, **381**, **386**.

Within each of these groups, however, our hydriai exhibit variations in the rim, neck, shoulder, body, and base, which are noted in the text. In addition, there are hydriai that cannot be placed into any of the preceding types, e.g., **339**, **347**, **356**, **380**, **382**.

The catalog is arranged in two parts: late archaic (latter part of the sixth and early fifth centuries B.C.)[633] and classical periods (fifth-fourth centuries B.C.).[634] Within each section, the miniature hydriai are listed sequentially by inventory number. The major portion (over 70%) of our catalogued miniature hydriai belong to the late archaic period. Some of

---

629. See White, *Final Reports* I, 114. Final discussion of this important context will be included in the final volume on the site's architecture.

630. See Hopper, 245ff. and *Tocra* II, 10.

631. See *Tocra* II, 10, 14 (late archaic, types 1 through 3), 94 (fourth century B.C., types 4–5).

632. Type 2 is said to be a more slender version of Type 1 (*Tocra* II, 14).

633. See *Tocra* II, 14, Type 1: nos. 1953–1958, pl. 8; Type 2: nos. 1959–1962, pl. 8; Type 3 (vertical rim): no. 1963, pl. 8.

634. See *Tocra* II, 92, 94, Type 4: nos. 2369–2376, pl. 42; Type 5: nos. 2377–2378, pl. 42. Types 4 and 5 are thought to be of fourth-century date.

the hydriai are only tentatively assigned to the classical period.

LATE ARCHAIC

334 Pl. 55 Inv. No. 69–226 D13 (Area 2) 2 2
Fragmentary, missing part of neck and vertical handle. Buff clay. Black glaze worn and ranges to purplish brown. Soil-stained and rather heavily encrusted.
H: 0.045; D: 0.0415 (max. without handles); D: 0.023 (base)
Wide, flaring rim, rather tall and wide, almost straight neck. Narrow, sloping shoulder and tall, narrow ovoid body. Two horizontal handles, set high and bent upward. Unarticulated wire-drawn base. Somewhat similar to **370**, except for base.
LC II/III

335 Pl. 55 Inv. No. 71–370 D12/13 B 4
Incomplete, missing both horizontal handles and almost entire vertical handle. Buff clay with slight greenish tinge. Black glaze worn off. Surface chipped, soil-stained, and encrusted.
H: 0.0466; D: 0.037 (max); D: 0.03 (rim); D: 0.0208 (base)
Flaring rim, slightly thickened. Rather tall and wide, almost straight neck articulated with sloping shoulder. Ovoid body with broad and high belly. Juncture of vertical strap handle, which rises above the rim, preserved. Low and slightly flaring wire-drawn base. Rather well-made. Pronounced articulation between neck and shoulder. See *Tocra* II, pl. 8, no. 1960 (Type 2).
LC II/III

336 Pl. 55 Inv. No. 71–373 D12/13 B 4
Intact, except for missing vertical handle. Yellowish buff clay. Black glaze slightly worn. Slight surface chipping. Soil-stained and encrusted.
H: 0.0434; D: 0.037 (max); D: 0.0296 (rim); D: 0.0205 (base)
Flaring rim and wide, fairly short, concave neck curves into sloping shoulder. Slightly misshapen ovoid body with broad and high belly. Low and flaring wire-drawn base. Two horizontal handles bent upward.
Almost identical to **337**, both found in largely undisturbed archaic level.
LC II/III

337 Pl. 55 Inv. 71–376 D12/13 B 4
Intact, except for missing vertical handle. Buff clay. Black glaze worn. Slight surface chipping. Soil-stained and encrusted.
H: 0.0445; D: 0.0366 (max. without handle root); D: 0.0294 (rim); D: 0.0193 (base)
Flaring rim and wide, fairly short, concave neck curves into shoulder. Ovoid body with broad and high belly. Low and slightly flaring wire-drawn base. Two horizontal handles bent upward. Almost identical to preceding (**336**).
LC II/III

338 Pl. 56; Fig. 3 Inv. No. 71–478 D12/13 B 4
Fragmentary, with a few chips missing. Restoration in plaster on body and base. Light pinkish buff clay. Glaze fired from a dark brown to a reddish brown and slightly worn. Mended from several fragments.
H: 0.0475; D: 0.0373 (max. without handles); D: 0.031 (rim); D: 0.0196 (base)
Flaring rim with slight thickened edge and rather tall, wide neck. Articulation between neck and rounded, sloping shoulder. Ovoid body and broad, high belly. Two horizontal handles set high and bent upward. Vertical strap handle almost level with rim. Base damaged.
LC II/III

339 Pl. 56; Fig. 3 Inv. No. 71–479 D12/13 B 4
Fragmentary, missing piece of rim, one horizontal handle, and part of neck and body. Restoration in plaster for part of neck and body. Slightly yellow buff clay. Dull black to brown glaze worn. Mended from several pieces.
H: 0.0446; D: 0.0394 (max. without handles); D: 0.0315 (rim); D: 0.0204 (base)
Flaring, outcurved rim. Short concave, wide neck curves into shoulder. Globular body with broad belly. Horizontal handle bent upward. Rather tall and straight base.
LC II/III

340 Pl. 56 Inv. No. 71–673 D12/13 A 2
Fragmentary. Missing rim, part of neck, vertical handle, and most of one horizontal handle. Dark buff clay. Dull black glaze worn, crazed, and thinly applied on lower body.
MPH: 0.0404; D: 0.0365 (max); D: 0.0195 (base)
Outward flaring rim. Wide, concave neck and flat, pronounced shoulder. Ovoid body with broad, high belly. One preserved horizontal handle adheres closely to the body, forming a triangular projection. Relatively tall and straight base.
LC II/III

341 Pl. 56 Inv. No. 73–291 SW Sondage 1B 4a
Fragmentary, missing most of neck and vertical handle. Buff clay. Flaking and worn black glaze. Encrusted.
H: 0.035; D: 0.034; D: 0.021 (base)
Flaring rim. Rather short, wide, concave neck and sloping shoulder. Broad ovoid body. Two horizontal handles, one of which bent slightly upward. Low, slightly flaring wire-drawn base.
LC II/III

342 Pl. 56 Inv. No. 73–751 D16/17 1 3
Fragmentary. Pieces missing from neck, rim, and vertical handle. Buff clay. Black glaze almost entirely worn off. Mended. Soil-stained.
H: 0.047; D: 0.0416 (max); D: 0.0324 (rim); D: 0.0227 (base)
Flaring rim. Wide, almost cylindrical, neck and sloping shoulder. Rounded ovoid body. Horizontal handles pressed into body, forming triangular projections. Relatively high wire-drawn base with minimal flare. See *Tocra* II, pl. 8, no. 1953 (Type 1).
LC II/III

343 Pl. 56 Inv. No. 73–933 C15/16 1 4
Fragmentary, with pieces missing from neck, chips on base, and vertical handle broken off. Deep buff clay. Black glaze worn. Neck, rim, and one horizontal handle mended. Soil-stained and encrusted.
H: 0.0496; D: 0.0437 (max. without handles); D: 0.034 (rim); D: 0.0242 (base)
Flaring rim and short, wide neck curves into narrow, sloping shoulder. Ovoid body with high and broad belly. Horizontal handles set high and bent upward. Slightly flaring wire-drawn base. This is the tallest of our miniature hydriai. Similar to **337**, though the curve of the neck is not as concave.
LC II/III

344 Pl. 56; Fig. 3 Inv. No. 73–1068 D16/17 1 3
Intact, except for chips on rim. Deep buff clay. Dull flaking black glaze.
H: 0.0418; D: 0.0417 (max. without handles); D: 0.032 (rim); D: 0.0242 (base)

Outward flaring rim with flat vertical edge. Wide neck and pronounced shoulder. Globular body. Lug-like horizontal handles adhere closely to body, forming triangular projections. Wide, flaring base. This hydria is notable for having a rim with a vertical edge, unlike most miniature hydriai,[635] and for being among the most carefully made of our series.
LC II/III

345   Pl. 56   Inv. No. 73–1153   D16/17   1   3
Intact, except for missing vertical handle and chips on surface of one horizontal handle. Deep buff clay. Glaze, worn in spots and flaking, ranges from black to reddish brown and red.
H: 0.0398; D: 0.0359 (max. without handles); D: 0.0272 (rim); D: 0.021 (Base)
Wide, flaring rim. Short, wide, concave neck curves into steeply sloping shoulder. Globular ovoid body with low belly. Two horizontal handles bent upward. Low, unarticulated, flaring wire-drawn base. Cf. *Perachora* II, pl. 123, no. 3260, of similar shape, but slightly smaller size.
LC II/III

346   Pl. 56   Inv. No. 74–82   D16/17   2   3
Almost complete, part of rim and neck broken off. Chips on surface. Creamy buff clay. Glaze severely worn off, where preserved fired mostly red with small patches of reddish brown and black. Neck mended.
H: 0.042; D: 0.0424 (max. without handles); D: 0.0274 (rim); D: 0.0252 (base)
Slightly flaring rim with straight, rather short, wide neck. Pronounced sloping shoulder and squat globular body. Two horizontal handles on broad belly bent upward. Vertical strap handle rises above rim. Broad, flaring wire-drawn base. Rather well-made, despite the exaggerated belly.
LC II/III

347   Pl. 57   Inv. No. 74–83   D16/17   2   3
Fragmentary, with badly chipped rim and both vertical and one horizontal handle broken off. Creamy buff clay. Black glaze mostly worn off. Slight traces of burning on body. Lightly encrusted.
H: 0.0349; D: 0.037 (max. without handles); MPD: 0.024 (rim); D: 0.0217 (base)
Flaring rim with very short, concave, wide neck. Pronounced sloping shoulder and rounded body. Horizontal handle set almost perpendicular to body; does not rise upward as in previous examples. Broad, flaring wire-drawn base. For the type, see *Perachora* II, pl. 123, no. 3258.
LC II/III

348   Pl. 57   Inv. No. 74–84   E12/13   E   2
Fragmentary, with chipped rim and missing about half of neck and vertical handle. Creamy buff clay. Black glaze unevenly applied and fired.
H: 0.036; D: 0.0355 (max. without handles); MPD: 0.0258 (rim); D: 0.0208 (base)
Flaring rim with wide, concave neck curving into steeply sloping shoulder. Squat ovoid body. Two horizontal handles bent upward. Rather wide, flaring wire-drawn base. Smaller version of **345**, but rim does not flare outward. It also resembles *Perachora* II, pl. 123, no. 3262.
LC II/III

349   Pl. 57   Inv. No. 74–85   D16/17   2   3
Almost complete. Chipped rim, some chipping on surface, and part of neck broken off. Creamy buff clay. Black glaze almost entirely worn off. Encrusted.
H: 0.0454; D: 0.0418 (max. without handles); MPD: 0.032 (rim); D: 0.0195 (base)
Flaring rim with tall, wide, and slightly concave neck. Pronounced shoulder and ovoid body with high, broad belly. Two horizontal lug-like handles. Vertical strap handle rises just above the rim. Narrow and articulated wire-drawn base. It shows similarity with *Tocra* II, pl. 8, no. 1960 (Type 2), in the rim and neck, but our example has a broader and higher belly.
LC II/III

350   Pl. 57   Inv. No. 74–103   D16/17   2   3
Fragmentary, with part of rim and neck broken off. Light greenish buff clay. Negligible traces of black glaze. Mended at neck. Encrusted.
H: 0.039; D: 0.0336 (max. without handles); D: 0.0192 (base)
Flaring rim with relatively wide, concave neck. Pronounced shoulder and rounded ovoid body. Two horizontal handles vertically set at shoulder level. Vertical strap handle rises slightly above the rim. Slightly flaring wire-drawn base. It resembles *Perachora* II, pl. 123, no. 3260. The vertically set horizontal handle is unusual, however.
LC II/III

351   Pl. 57; Fig. 3   Inv. No. 74–125   D16/17   2   3
Intact, except for chips on rim. Creamy buff clay. Black glaze almost entirely worn off.
H: 0.0418; D: 0.036 (max. without handles); D: 0.0303 (rim); D: 0.0198 (base)
Flaring rim with very tall, very wide, slightly concave neck. Pronounced shoulder and ovoid body with high belly. Two lug-like horizontal handles diagonally set. Vertical strap handle rises just above the rim. Narrow, flaring, articulated wire-drawn base. The disproportionately tall and wide neck has no parallel. For a comparison in general terms, see *Tocra* II, pl. 8, no. 1960 (Type 2).
LC II/III

352   Pl. 57   Inv. No. 74–126   D16/17   2   4
Fragmentary, with most of rim broken off and chips on surface. Creamy buff clay. Black glaze worn and unevenly fired, ranging from red to brown to black where preserved.
H: 0.0445; D: 0.0358 (max. without handles); D: 0.0203 (base)
Flaring rim with wide, slightly concave neck. Pronounced narrow shoulder and ovoid body with high belly. Two lug-like horizontal handles adhere to body. Vertical strap handle rises just above the rim. Flaring wire-drawn base. For the type, see *Tocra* II, pl. 8, no. 1960 (Type 2).
LC II/III

353   Pl. 57   Inv. No. 74–213   D16/17   2   4
Fragmentary. Large portion of rim and neck missing and base chipped. Vertical handle and one horizontal handle broken off. Greenish buff clay. Black glaze almost entirely worn off. Soil-stained and encrusted.
H: 0.0343; D: 0.0356 (max. without handles); D: 0.0182 (base)
Flaring rim with wide, slightly concave neck. Pronounced shoulder and globular body with broad belly. One lug-like horizontal handle, adhering to body, preserved. Wire-drawn base.
LC II/III

354   Pl. 57   Inv. No. 74–214   D10/11   C   5
Fragmentary, missing rim, part of neck and body. Vertical handle broken off. Creamy buff clay. Black glaze worn. Mended.

---

635. A miniature hydria, decorated with linear patterns, from the North Cemetery at Corinth, found in a grave of the first quarter of the sixth century B.C., appears to have a similar flat vertical edge (see *Corinth* XIII, 186–187, no. 160–9, pl. 24).

H: 0.036; D: 0.0328 (max. without handles); D: 0.0166 (base)

Tall, straight, wide neck. Pronounced sloping shoulder and ovoid body with high, broad belly. Two lug-like horizontal handles form triangular projections, set almost perpendicular to body. Body tapers to relatively narrow and slightly flaring wire-drawn base.

LC II/III

355   Pl. 58; Fig. 3 Inv. No. 74–227   D16/17   2   4

Complete, except for one missing horizontal handle. Buff clay. Black glaze somewhat worn and flaking. Slightly encrusted.

H: 0.0414; D: 0.0373 (max. without handles); D: 0.0283 (rim); D: 0.02 (base)

Flaring rim with wide, straight neck. Pronounced shoulder and rounded body with broad belly. Horizontal handle set almost perpendicular to body. Vertical strap handle rises slightly above rim. Straight, slightly articulated wire-drawn base. Rather well-made. Cf. *Tocra* II, pl. 8, no. 1955 (Type I).

LC II/III

356   Pl. 58; Fig. 3 Inv. No. 76–49   C12/D12   G   2

Complete, except for one missing horizontal handle and chips on base. Creamy buff clay. Black glaze worn. Lightly soil-stained.

H: 0.046; D: 0.0346 (max. without handles); D: 0.0243 (rim); D: 0.025 (base)

Almost vertical rim with slightly concave neck. Steeply sloping shoulder with slight articulation at juncture with low belly. Horizontal handle bent upward. Vertical strap handle rises above rim. Rather tall and broad slightly flaring wire-drawn base. Sloppily made. The shape is unlike any miniature hydria. Cf. *Tocra* II, pl. 8, no. 1963 (Type III), for a type with vertical rim, but no resemblance in shape of body. The shape is reminiscent of an olpe.

LC II/III

357   Pl. 58   Inv. No. 76–325   C13/D13   1   5

Fragmentary, missing part of neck and vertical strap handle. Gray buff clay. Worn and unevenly applied dull black glaze.

H: 0.0468; D: 0.0366 (max. without handles); D: 0.0282 (rim); D: 0.0206 (base)

Flaring rim with tall, straight wide neck. Narrow, rounded shoulder. Ovoid body with high, broad belly. Two horizontal handles set high and bent upward. Flaring wire-drawn base. Similar in type to **338**. Cf. *Tocra* II, pl. 8, no. 1953 (Type I).

LC II/III

358   Pl. 58   Inv. No. 76–538   F13/G13   1   2

Intact, except for chips on rim and small hole in body. Buff clay. Black glaze almost entirely worn off. Slightly encrusted.

H: 0.037; D: 0.037 (max. without handles); D: 0.025 (rim); D: 0.0243 (base)

Flaring, unevenly formed rim with wide, almost straight, neck. Pronounced shoulder and squat rounded body. Two lug-like horizontal handles, carelessly formed, set almost perpendicular to broad body. Vertical strap handle rises relatively high above rim. Sloppy, broad flaring wire-drawn base. Carelessly made. Similar in type to **346**, which is, however, a much neater example.

LC II/III

359   Pl. 58   Inv. No. 76–789   F13/G13   1   2

Fragmentary, missing part of neck and vertical strap handle. Creamy buff clay. Black glaze severely worn. Slightly encrusted.

H: 0.0358; D: 0.0382 (max. without handles); D: 0.023 (base)

Low, wide neck and very slightly flaring rim. Sloping shoulder and heavy, globular body. Small horizontal handles rise upward. Almost straight wire-drawn base. For a somewhat similar shape, especially the wide, short neck, see **347** and *Perachora* II, pl. 123, 3258.

LC II/III

360   Pl. 58; Fig. 3 Inv. No. 77–152   F13/G13   2   2

Intact, except for chip on rim. Pinkish buff clay. Dull black glaze somewhat worn.

H: 0.039; D: 0.032 (max. without handles); D: 0.0264 (rim); D: 0.0192 (base)

Flaring rim with wide neck, curving into narrow, sloping shoulder. High-bellied ovoid body. Two horizontal handles, one bent upward, the other set perpendicular to body. Vertical strap handle rises slightly above rim. Slightly flaring wire-drawn base. Similar to **357**, but a smaller version and with handles not set so high. Rather well made.

LC II/III

361   Pl. 58   Inv. No. 77–182   F13/G13   2   2

Fragmentary, missing most of neck. Buff clay, fired a light pinkish orange in spots, with slight traces of mica and tiny white lime inclusions. Glaze fired from red to black, and mostly worn off.

H: 0.0414; D: 0.037 (max. without handles); D: 0.023 (base)

Short, wide neck, slightly sloping shoulder, and globular body. Horizontal handles bent slightly upward. Vertical strap handle rises above rim. Almost vertical wire-drawn base. Body resembles *Tocra* I, pl. 8, 1955 (Type 1).

LC II/III

362   Pl. 59   Inv. No. 77–641   F13/G13   2   2

Fragmentary, missing most of neck. Buff clay. Unevenly fired black glaze, with some flaking. Glaze on interior of mouth.

MPH: 0.04; D: 0.0346 (max. without handles); D: 0.0193 (base)

Wide neck and narrow shoulder. Ovoid body. Two horizontal handles bent upward. Vertical strap handle rises slightly above rim. Almost vertical wire-drawn base. The body resembles *Perachora* II, pl. 123, no. 3261.

LC II/III

363   Pl. 59; Fig. 3 Inv. No. 77–725   D15/16   1   3

Intact, except for broken off horizontal handle. Yellowish buff clay, fired to orange on one side of body. Black glaze almost entirely worn off, best preserved on interior of mouth. Slightly encrusted.

MPH: 0.0475; D: 0.0438 (max. without handles); D: 0.0367 (rim); D: 0.0268 (base)

Broad flaring rim and straight wide neck. Pronounced sloping shoulder and stout ovoid body with broad, lower belly. Two horizontal handles bent upward. Vertical strap handle rises just above rim. Articulated flaring wire-drawn base. Similar to *Tocra* II, pl. 8, no. 1954 (Type 1).

LC II/III

364   Pl. 59   Inv. No. 77–1026   C13   1   3a

Intact, except for broken off horizontal handle and chips on rim. Buff clay with light greenish tinge. Black glaze almost entirely worn off. Lightly encrusted.

H: 0.049; D: 0.043 (max. without handles); D: 0.029 (rim); D: 0.019 (base)

Flaring rim and wide, slightly concave neck. Rounded sloping shoulder and rounded ovoid body. One horizontal handle pressed into body. Vertical strap handle rises above rim. Articulated flaring wire-drawn base. Same type as **363**, but with a narrower lower body. For the type, see *Tocra* II, pl. 8, no. 1954 (Type 1).

LC II/III

365   Pl. 59   Inv. No. 77–1145   D15/E15   1   3
Complete, except for broken off horizontal handle. Buff clay. Dull black glaze worn. Mended. Lightly encrusted.
H: 0.039; D: 0.0345 (max. without handles); D: 0.0274 (rim); D: 0.0198 (base)
Thickened, flaring rim and wide, slightly concave neck. Sloping shoulder and ovoid body. One horizontal handle pressed into body. Vertical strap handle rises above rim. Articulated flaring wire-drawn base.
LC II/III

366   Pl. 59   Inv. No. 78–262   F14/G14   1   2
Fragmentary, missing two-thirds neck, part of shoulder, and vertical strap handle. Deep yellowish buff clay. Worn glaze, fired mostly red, black only around base. Small hole in center of base. Encrusted.
MPH: 0.038; D: 0.0363 (max. without handles); D: 0.024 (base)
Very slightly flaring rim. Wide, concave neck and sloping shoulder. Heavy globular body. Relatively wide, flaring wire-drawn base. Two horizontal handles rise slightly upward. Somewhat similar to **353**.
LC II/III

367   Pl. 59   Inv. No. 78–447   F14/G14   1   3(?)
Fragmentary, missing two-thirds neck. Creamy buff clay. Dull black glaze almost entirely worn off. Encrusted
H: 0.043; D: 0.0384 (max. without handles); D: 0.021 (base)
Flaring rim and wide neck. Sloping shoulder and globular body. Two horizontal handles pressed into body at different heights: one set higher and bent upward, the other set perpendicular to belly. Vertical strap handle rises high above rim. Tall and narrow, articulated, and slightly flaring wire-drawn base.
LC II/III

368   Pl. 59   Inv. No. 78–448   F14/G14   1   3
Fragmentary, missing most of neck and vertical strap handle. Chip on base. Yellowish buff clay. Worn dull glaze fired black to reddish brown. Traces of burning on one of horizontal handles and adjacent shoulder. Encrusted.
MPH: 0.038; D: 0.042 (max. without handles); D: 0.021 (base)
Wide neck and sloping shoulder. High and broad belly. Lower body misshapen. Two horizontal handles, set high, and bent upward. Flaring wire-drawn base. Crudely made.
LC II/III

369   Pl. 60   Inv. No. 78–513   F14/G14   1   2
Intact, except for few chips on rim. Buff clay with slight grayish cast. Matte black glaze mostly worn off. Encrusted.
H: 0.037; D: 0.035 (max. without handles); D: 0.03 (rim); D: 0.023 (base)
Flaring rim and wide, slightly concave neck. Sloping shoulder and squat ovoid body. Two horizontal handles pressed into body at diagonal and set at different heights. Vertical strap handle rises just above rim. Flaring wire-drawn base. Sloppily made. Similar to **348**.
LC II/III

370   Pl. 60   Inv. No. 78–565   F14/G14   1   5
Incomplete, missing vertical handle and piece from rim. One horizontal handle and base chipped. Light gray clay. Matte black glaze, mostly worn off. Very slightly encrusted.
H: 0.0494; D: 0.0394 (max. without handles); D: 0.0375 (rim); D: 0.023 (base)
Broad and thickened flaring rim and tall, wide, slightly concave neck. Narrow sloping shoulder and tall, narrow ovoid body. Two horizontal handles, set high and bent upward. Low, flaring wire-drawn base. Rather well-made and among the tallest of the miniature hydriai. Similar to **338** except for broader rim.
LC II/III

371   Pl. 60; Fig. 3   Inv. No. 78–566   F14/G14   1   5
Intact, except for chips missing from rim, base, and one horizontal handle. Buff to light gray clay, probably result of burning. Black glaze almost entirely worn off.
H: 0.0472; D: 0.042 (max. without handles); D: 0.038 (rim); D: 0.0248 (base)
Wide, flaring rim and wide, almost straight neck. Pronounced sloping shoulder and ovoid body with high, broad belly. Two horizontal handles, one larger than the other, set high and bent upward. Vertical handle rises above rim. Low, flaring wire-drawn base. Among the best made of our hydriai. Closely resembles *Tocra* II, pl. 8, no. 1954 (Type 1).
LC II/III

372   Pl. 60   Sb. 288–17   F13/G13   1   2
Complete, except for missing portion of rim and upper portion of neck. Buff clay. Flaking black glaze.
H: 0.0403; D: 0.0404 (max. without handles); D: 0.0246 (base)
Wide, flaring rim and short, concave neck. Pronounced shoulder and ovoid body with high, broad belly. Horizontal loop handles pressed into shoulder and rise slightly upward. Rather broad, wire-drawn flaring base.
LC II/III

373   Pl. 60   Sb. 516–22   F14/G14   1   2
Fragmentary, missing lower body and handles. Light gray clay. Flaking black glaze. Burnt. Mended from two joining fragments.
H: 0.036; D: 0.0385 (max. without handles); D: 0.0302 (rim)
Flaring rim, chipped on edges. Wide, vertical neck and sloping shoulder. High, broad belly.
LC II/III

CLASSICAL

374   Pl. 60   Inv. No. 71–176   E16   2   2
Fragmentary, part of neck and vertical handle broken off. Buff clay. Glaze fugitive. Heavily encrusted.
MPH: 0.032; D: 0.0346 (max. without handles); D: 0.0246 (base)
Rather slender neck and squat, globular body. Horizontal handles pressed into body, forming triangular projections. Low and slightly flaring wire-drawn base. The body resembles *Tocra* II, pl. 42, no. 2369.
Late fifth-fourth century B.C. ?

375   Pl. 60   Inv. No. 71–350   E12   1   3
Incomplete, missing piece from rim and one horizontal handle. Yellowish buff clay. Black glaze severely worn. Encrusted.
H: 0.035; D: 0.03 (max. without handles); D: 0.023 (rim); D: 0.02 (base)
White, *Second Report*, 182 n. 50, pl. 87c.
Wide, flaring rim with slender concave neck. Rather broad, steeply sloping shoulder and squat body with broad belly. One horizontal handle bent upward. Vertical strap handle level with rim. Uneven, flaring base. Carelessly made. Somewhat similar to *Corinth* XV:3, pl. 70, 1874, from the Circular South Shrine, dated to the third quarter of the fifth century.
Fifth century B.C.

376 Fig. 3   Inv. No. 71–682 D12/13 B 4

Intact, except for one missing horizontal handle and chips on belly and base. Dark buff clay. Dull black to brown glaze, slightly worn and flaking.

MPH: 0.0474; D: 0.0438 (max. with one handle); D: 0.031 (rim); D: 0.0262 (base)

Flaring rim. Wide, concave neck and flat shoulder. Broad, ovoid body with high belly. One preserved horizontal handle bent upward. Tall flaring base. Thicker fabric than most hydriai and more angular profile.

For the closest parallels, see *Perachora* II, pl. 123, no. 3257 (our shoulder is somewhat flatter), and *Corinth* XV:3, pl. 70, no. 1876 (our example is taller), found in the Shrine of the Double Stele, dated to the fourth century B.C.[636] The Perachora miniatures are broadly dated to the second half of the sixth and the early fifth century B.C.[637] Most of the fourth-century miniature hydriai, whose shape more closely resembles our hydria, tend to be smaller vases, as the Corinth example.[638] However, size may not necessarily be a dating criterion in this case.

Probably fifth century B.C.

377 Pl. 60   Inv. No. 73–606 D16/17 1? 3

Fragmentary, broken at neck. Juncture of vertical handle preserved. Yellowish buff clay. Glaze severely worn and fired red. Encrusted.

MPH: 0.0195; D: 0.036 (max. without handles); D: 0.023 (base)

Broad belly and very squat body. Wire-drawn base with hole in bottom. Handles adhere to the body. Resembles *Tocra* II, pl. 42, 2371.

Late fifth-fourth century B.C. ?

378 Pl. 61   Inv. No. 73–619 C15/16 1 4

Complete except for missing vertical strap handle, whose juncture at rim is preserved, but no evidence for its attachment to the body. Orange to buff clay. Flaking black glaze unevenly fired red (where clay orange) and black where clay buff. Encrusted.

H: 0.033; D: 0.0296 (max. without handles); D: 0.023 (rim); D: 0.024 (base)

Small lopsided, squat shape with flaring rim and rather slender neck. Sloping shoulder and broad belly. Two horizontal handles adhere to body. Wide, slightly flaring wire-drawn base. Carelessly made. The body recalls *Corinth* XV:3, 324, pl. 70, no. 1874, found in the Circular South Shrine, which is dated to the third quarter of the fifth century.

Late fifth-fourth century B.C.

379 Pl. 61   Inv. No. 73–652 C15/16 1 4

Fragmentary, missing rim, part of neck, and vertical strap handle. Buff clay. Crazed and flaking black glaze.

MPH: 0.0369; D: 0.0346 (max. without handles); D: 0.0209 (base)

Rather wide neck and sloping shoulder. Squat ovoid body. Two horizontal handles pressed into body. Low, flaring wire-drawn base.

Fifth century B.C. ?

380 Pl. 61; Fig. 3 Inv. No. 74–212 D16/17 2 4

Complete except for missing horizontal handles. Dark buff clay. Flaking glaze fired mostly red. Mended from several fragments. Slightly encrusted

H: 0.041; D: 0.037 (max. without handles); D: 0.032 (rim); D: 0.023 (base)

Flat, everted rim with rather short and slender neck. Sloping shoulder and globular body. Vertical strap handle rises above rim. Slightly flaring wire-drawn base. See *Corinth* XV:3, 324, pl. 70, no. 1871, dated to the first half of the fifth century, but our body is globular rather than ovoid.

Fifth century B.C.

381 Pl. 61   Inv. No. 74–1112 E13/14 1 1

Fragmentary, missing neck and vertical strap handle. Creamy buff clay. Black glaze fugitive. Slightly encrusted.

MPH: 0.0223; D: 0.0325 (max. without handles); D: 0.0206 (base)

Base of narrow neck preserved. Low, squat form with an almost bi-conical body. Thick horizontal handles adhere to body. Rather tall, flaring wire-drawn base. Similar to *Corinth* XV:3, 324, pl. 70, no. 1874, found in the Circular South Shrine, which is dated to the third quarter of the fifth century.

Fifth century B.C.

382 Pl. 61   Inv. No. 76–1020 E15 2 2

Intact, except for chips on rim, horizontal handle, and base. Buff clay. Black glaze worn and flaking. Slightly encrusted.

H: 0.0266; D: 0.028 (max. without handles); D: 0.016 (rim); D: 0.0165 (base)

Slightly flaring, almost vertical rim with short slender neck. Steeply sloping shoulder and sagging body with almost bi-conical form and low belly. Two horizontal handles rise upward. Vertical strap handle rises above rim. Rather tall flaring, wire-drawn base. Somewhat similar to *Corinth* XV:3, 212, 324, pl. 70, 1875, from Deposit 8 in the Terracotta Factory.

Fifth century B.C.

383 Pl. 61   Inv. No. 76–1021 D12/13 F 3

Complete, except for chips on rim and one missing horizontal handle. Buff clay. Black glaze mostly worn off. Slightly encrusted.

H: 0.039; D: 0.0418 (max. without handles); D: 0.0263 (rim); D: 0.0235 (base)

Flaring rim and rather wide, concave neck. Flat shoulder, slightly pushed in. Ovoid body with high, broad belly. Horizontal handle rises upward. Double-reeded vertical handle rises above rim. Tall, flaring, and articulated wire-drawn base. Except for the rim, our example resembles *Tocra* II, pl. 42, no. 2377. It is a slightly smaller version of **376**. The double-reeded handle is most unusual.

Fifth century B.C.?

384 Pl. 61   Inv. No. 77–906 F 1 3 / G 1 3   W a l l Sondage 1

Incomplete, missing part of neck and one horizontal handle. Chips on rim. Light greenish buff clay. Black glaze worn and fired mostly reddish brown. Slightly encrusted.

H: 0.0413; D: 0.0375 (max. without handles); D: 0.0216 (base)

Wide, flaring rim and short, concave, slender neck. Pronounced, rather broad sloping shoulder and ovoid body with high belly. Horizontal handle bent upward. Vertical strap handle rises above rim. Flaring and articulated wire-drawn base. The body is similar to *Tocra* II, pl. 42, no. 2377, except our example has a sloping shoulder.

Fifth century B.C.?

385 Pl. 61   Inv. No. 78-141 F16 2 1

Intact, except for large chip on rim and tiny chips on base. Creamy buff clay. Dull black glaze mostly worn off. Slightly encrusted.

---

636. *Corinth* XV:3, 214.

637. *Perachora* II, 290.

638. Cf. also the fourth-century B.C. series from Tocra (*Tocra* II, 94, Types 4 and 5, nos. 2369–2378, pl. 42).

H: 0.0314; D: 0.03 (max. without handles); D: 0.02 (rim); D: 0.0168 (base)

Everted rim and rather wide neck. Flat shoulder and squat ovoid body with broad belly. Two horizontal handles set at different heights, but both perpendicular to body. Vertical strap handle rises just above rim. Vertical wire-drawn base. The body is similar to *Perachora* II, pl. 123, no. 3269.

Fifth century B.C.?

386   Pl. 62   Inv. No. 78-142 F14/G14 Cubic Meter Test 2

Fragmentary, missing vertical strap handle, one horizontal handle, large piece from belly, and about one-half of rim. Base slightly chipped. Light grayish green clay. Glaze almost entirely worn off, bluish black where preserved in patch on base and around horizontal handle. Slightly encrusted.

H: 0.038; D: 0.039 (max. without handles); D: 0.0312 (rim); D: 0.0216 (base)

Flaring rim and rather tall, wide neck. Sloping shoulder and squat body with broad belly. Horizontal handle bent upward. Tall, flaring wire-drawn base. Carelessly made, resulting in lopsided body. Neck is disproportionate to body.

Fifth century B.C.?

387   Pl. 62   Inv. No. 78-411 F14/G14 1 2

Fragmentary, missing vertical strap handle and about two-thirds of neck. Few chips missing from body and base. Buff clay. Thinly applied matte black glaze worn. Soil-stained.

MPH: 0.0375; D: 0.0374 (max. without handles); Est D: 0.03 (rim); D: 0.02 (base)

Flaring rim and wide neck. Flat shoulder and ovoid body with broad, high belly. Two horizontal handles pressed into shoulder. Articulated and flaring wire-drawn base. Similar in type to **383**.

Fifth century B.C. ?

388   Pl. 62   Inv. No. 78-762 F13/14 1 1

Complete, except for missing horizontal handle. Surface chipped and worn. Deep buff clay. Glaze worn and ranges from metallic blue to reddish brown. Traces of burning resulting in gray areas. Slightly encrusted.

H: 0.0328; D: 0.0324 (max. without handles); D: 0.0244 (rim); D: 0.0213 (base)

Flaring rim and fairly wide, flaring neck. Flat shoulder and plump ovoid body with broad, high belly. Two horizontal handles pressed into shoulder. Wide, slightly flaring wire-drawn base. Similar in type to **383**.

Fifth century B.C.?

KRATERS AND KRATER-CUPS

The three examples included here represent virtually all the identifiable finds of miniature krater or krater-cups from the sanctuary.[639] **389**, with its more articulated shape, may be the earliest of the three.

The other two miniatures almost certainly belong to the fifth century.[640]

389   Pl. 62; Fig. 3 Sb. 519-1   F14/G14 1 2

Black-glazed krater, missing one-third rim and body as well as one handle. Buff clay. Flaking black glaze, unevenly applied. Mended.

H: 0.024; D: 0.042 (rim); D: 0.019 (base)

Flaring everted rim. Angular body tapers to a low conical base. Misshapen applied handle, pinched to join rim. Rounded projection in center of floor. Underside of base covered with glaze. For the type, see *Tocra* II, nos. 1966 (pl. 8 and fig. 5) and 1967 (pl. 8) as well as *Perachora* II, p. 309, pl. 119, no. 3223.

LC II/III

390   Pl. 62   Sb. 516-8   F14/G14 1 2

Fragmentary black-glazed krater or krater-cup, preserving about one-quarter rim, most of lower body and complete base. Muddy buff clay. Dull glaze, with some flaking, fired black to reddish brown.

H: 0.0238; D: 0.021 (base)

Slightly flaring rim. Applied handle roll. Flat wire-drawn base covered with black glaze.

Similar to preceding in its angular body, but the foot is straighter and broader. It bears some resemblance to the miniature krater from the Aphrodite Deposit in *Corinth* XV:3, pl. 68, no. 1758.

LC III (Early fifth century B.C.)

391   Pl. 62   Inv. No. 77-180 G12 1 Stray

Intact, miniature black-glazed krater or krater-cup.[641] Creamy buff clay. Dull worn black glaze unevenly fired, ranges to reddish brown and red.

H: 0.0166; D: 0.0314 (rim); D: 0.018 (base)

Slightly everted rim. Loop handles pressed into the rim. Flat base with wire marks. For the type, see *Perachora* II, pl. 119, no. 3220; Pemberton, *Hesperia* 39 (1970), pl. 74, no. 120, and *Corinth* XV:3, pl. 68, nos. 1761 and 1764.

LC III (fifth century B.C.)

Plastic Vases (**392–394**)

As illustrated by the three examples in our catalogue, Corinthian figured or plastic vases were unquestionably rare at the sanctuary.[642] These fragments were all found in the backfill area of the middle sanctuary retaining wall.

Our MC lion vase fragment with its panther head (**392**), though poorly preserved, has analogies with other vessels of this type, and may be attributed to Ducat's "Groupe de Mégara Hyblaea." The head fragment of possibly a hare vase (**393**) has no close parallel. The body fragment of a winged creature (**394**), with incision to indicate feathers, is most unusual

---

639. A black-glazed miniature lower base and body fragment, found in F12/G12, 1, 1, may belong to either a miniature krater or a krater cup.

640. For a discussion of miniature kraters, see *Corinth* XV:3, 314; *Perachora* II, 308 ff.

641. See Benson's discussion of miniature kraters in *Corinth* XV:3, 314, and cups on p. 312. Cf. also *Perachora* II, 297, where it is noted that among the miniature cups, black-glazed krater-like cups, dating to the fifth century, are common.

642. One other possible piece of a plastic vase was found in E10 Building Balk 3.

and would be quite a rarity for a Corinthian plastic vase.

392 Pl. 62   Inv. No. 77–219 F13/G13 2 2

Lion vase fragment, broken at shoulder and one ear missing. Buff clay. Black glaze fugitive. Surface very heavily worn and slightly encrusted.

MPH: 0.0316; MPW: 0.0406; Th: 0.0245

Face resembles that of panther. Oval-shaped vertical hole (D: 0.008) through head and two horizontal suspension holes through mane at different levels on either side of head.

The fragment apparently belongs to Ducat's "Groupe de Mégara Hyblaea," dated to late MC.[643] The lion vases listed under this group also have panther heads, but lion bodies. For the type, see Ducat, *BCH* lxxxvii (1963), figs. 18–19; and *CVA* Brussels IIIc, pl. 8, no. 11a, b.[644]

Late MC

393 Pl. 62   Sb. 289–1   F13/G13 1 2

Head fragment, with most of snout broken off. Light green clay. Black glaze worn. Surface worn and slightly encrusted.

MPH: 0.021; MPW: 0.018; MPL: 0.0273

Head of a bird(?) or a hare with vertical hole (D: 0.007) through head. Stippling on head. Two thin black concentric lines around hole. Both eyes preserved, rendered as large black circle surrounded by two concentric circles. Oval circle on forehead.

The identification of this fragment as part of a bird's head seems a possibility, despite the shape of the head, as preserved, which does not appear to extend at the proper angle to form a beak (cf. Ducat, *BCH* lxxxvii (1963), fig. 24, and *Tocra* I, pl. 102, no, 75). However, a similar rendering of the eye, surrounded by rings, appears on two bird vases from Tocra (*Tocra* I, 155, pl. 102, nos. 75–76), attributed to Ducat's "Groupe de visage attentif." Neither of these bird vases has the extensive stippling on the head of our example. In fact, such stippling is more often seen on the heads of hare vases (cf. *BCH* lxxxvii [1963], figs. 5, 10, 26 and LoPorto, fig. 45d).

MC

394 Pl. 62   Sb. 515–6   F14/G14 1 2

Body fragment of a winged creature, broken on all sides. Light grayish green clay. Black glaze fugitive, except for a few tiny patches. Traces of burning. Mold-made. Encrusted.

MPH: 0.0458; MPL: 0.0422; MPW: 0.0138

Part of shoulder and body. Parallel, horizontal incised lines and scalloped vertical incision to mark ends of feathers.

This unique fragment is unlike any of the known plastic vases of Corinthian manufacture.

MC ?

---

643. J. Ducat, "Les Vases Plastiques Corinthiens," *BCH* lxxxvii (1963), 447, 450, 458.

644. On lion plastic vases and this group, see *CorVP*, 526–527.

Conclusions

The Corinthian pottery from the Sanctuary of Demeter and Persephone, though considerably ill-preserved, provides a broad cross-section of products, ranging from good and mediocre figured vases to a variety of plainer and less expensive wares. Aside from the intrinsic interest of our material for Corinthian pottery studies, it is considered critical to dating the foundation of the extramural sanctuary.

Based on the currently available evidence of Greek pottery, the sanctuary appears to have been established a generation after the settlement of Cyrene,[645] traditionally dated to ca. 630 B.C. The oldest identifiable pieces of Corinthian pottery so far unearthed, a relatively small number of vase fragments datable to the Early Corinthian period, also suggest that the sanctuary at Cyrene may have been founded about 600 B.C. Regrettably, our Early Corinthian fragments form too small a percentage of the finds, and are too incomplete, to provide any proof that the sanctuary could have been founded much before the end of the seventh century or the beginning of the sixth century B.C. This date is essentially substantiated by the Attic as well as the Laconian and East Greek pottery, all of which begins by the early sixth century B.C. Even for the first decade of the sixth century, we encounter a similar situation, with only a few of our finds capable of being attributed to the early Middle Corinthian period. In fact, with the exception of the glyptic objects, specifically the Island Gems that date to the late seventh century B.C.,[646] as well as some figurines and tridacna shells, the sanctuary has not yielded material that can be confidently dated prior to the beginning of the sixth century B.C. Into the first quarter of the sixth century (Middle Corinthian period), there is a substantial increase in both the number and range of Corinthian pottery finds, an indication that the sanctuary was quite well established by this time. Further excavation in the sanctuary may, of course, alter this view and provide evidence of earlier and more substantial amounts of Corinthian wares datable to the last decades of the seventh century.[647]

Although Middle Corinthian pottery is fairly well represented at the Demeter Sanctuary, it appears that our main series begins in the second quarter of the sixth century (Late Corinthian I) when Corinth's pre-eminent position in the pottery export market as a producer of fine, figured vases begins its wane; this is not to say, however, that Corinthian pottery did not remain popular in overseas sites after the first quarter of the sixth century nor that high-quality vases were not painted along with the mass-produced variety.[648] Moreover, it is interesting to observe in the Corinthian pottery from the sanctuary that cheaper wares, mainly linear-style vases, continued to be imported in volume during the second half of the sixth century B.C. (Late Corinthian II). This demonstrates that although black-figure vase production had come to an end, Corinthian pottery trade could continue with less ambitious and less expensive wares still finding an overseas market. In the second half of the sixth century, at Cyrene, as elsewhere in the Greek world, Attic pottery imports fulfilled the taste and demand for fine, painted vases. However, concurrent with the Attic figured vases, the plainer, less costly wares of Corinth must also have satisfied a need, perhaps among the less affluent citizens of Cyrene.

Moreover, by the middle of the sixth century, in addition to the import of full-sized vases, there was a

---

645. White, *Final Reports* I, 23–24, 117. Schaus, *Final Reports* II, 93 ff. The earliest Attic black-figure studied by Mary Moore begins "in the very early sixth century B.C. . . . ." (*Final Reports* III, 1). White, *Final Reports* V, 5ff.

646. S. Lowenstam, *Final Reports* III, 10–13. Aside from these Island Gems, there is an amulet seal (no. 28) that dates to the first half of the seventh century B.C.

647. At Tocra (ancient Taucheira), for example, said to be a daughter colony of Cyrene, the earliest Corinthian pottery is Transitional, datable to the 620s, with the exception of one MPC conical oinochoe (see *Tocra* I, 13, 21, and *Tocra* II, 7).

648. See *Corinth* VII:2, 11, and *CorVP*, 394.

very strong demand for miniature vessels that continued throughout the late archaic period, as the mass of such miniatures, especially kotylai, attests. The popularity of these votives persisted, albeit far less intensively, into the fifth century and perhaps even into the fourth century B.C.

Given both the amount and quality of Corinthian black-figure, it appears that the finest products of Corinthian workshops were somewhat sporadically imported into Cyrene. In general, the Corinthian pottery assemblage gives the impression that a large amount of the more routine and less valuable or costly wares reached Cyrene, though with some particularly notable exceptions. Furthermore, the finds seem to indicate that the pottery was imported in batches from certain workshops. This is seen, for example, in repetitive types among the linear-style vases, the plates of the Chimaera Group, the closed vases that can be placed in the Circle of the Dodwell Painter, the number of black-figure tripod pyxides that can be associated with Benson's Sad Siren Group, the warrior aryballoi, "running dog" kotylai, the silhouette plates, and the miniatures, and to these may be added other groupings. To date, the products of many known Corinthian workshops are noticeably absent at the sanctuary.

On a historical note, the Corinthian pottery also confirms the conclusions drawn by studies of the East Greek, Island, and Laconian pottery that Cyrene escaped from Persian attack ca. 515 B.C.[649] This is further substantiated by the Attic black-figure and black-glazed pottery.[650] Corinthian pottery imports are quite numerous in the Late Corinthian II period and continue well into the fifth century B.C.

The question of ritual dining or feasting at the Demeter Sanctuary has been discussed by Gerald Schaus[651] and Donald White.[652] The represented shapes along with their quantity can be regarded as a potential index of the use of these vases at the sanctuary. Although the Corinthian pottery cannot provide supportive evidence either for or against ritual feasting, a few observations on these imports may offer some insight into this as yet unresolved issue.

Exclusive of the miniatures vessels, our vases divide into two large and broad classes: those associated with personal use (various scent or perfumed-oil containers and small boxes) and those associated with wine and its preparation, serving, and drinking (kraters, oinochoai, and cups). Vessels that can be associated with dining, such as plates, bowls, and lekanides, as a group are proportionally far less numerous.[653] Certainly, a considerable portion, about one-third,[654] of the full-size Corinthian imports (aryballoi, alabastra, amphoriskoi, kothons,[655] and the various pyxides)—i.e., vases in the category of personal use—were, possibly along with their contents, dedications to Demeter and Persephone. There is also no doubt as to the votive character of the miniatures, which constitute one-third of all the finds retained from the sanctuary. Among these, there is a preponderance of kotylai, forming 82% of the miniatures, followed by black-glazed hydriai, with their cultic association with the goddess,[656] forming over 12% of the miniatures. In other words, over half of all the Corinthian pottery imports certainly served primarily as gifts to the goddesses.

The vases related to the consumption of wine, on the other hand, could have served a dual purpose—utilitarian and dedicatory. The extraordinarily large number of kotylai, nearly half of our full-sized pottery finds,[657] may bespeak ritual drinking, particularly in association with the number of vases for mixing and pouring wine,[658] not only among the Corinthian imports, but also among the Attic[659] and Laconian wares.[660] Keeping in mind the rather high quality of many of these larger vessels, especially the black-glazed kraters of Laconian manufacture and the black-figure kraters that are painted in styles of recognized painters, as well as of some of the drinking cups, this dual purpose of ritual drinking and dedication does not seem unlikely. Indeed, among the Corinthian pottery, there are fragments of some very fine kraters, closed vessels attributable to painters in the Circle of the Dodwell Painter, and some interesting, though very fragmentary, large kotylai. In fact, there is nothing to preclude the possibility that, after the

---

649. Schaus, *Final Reports* II, 106.

650. Moore, *Final Reports* III, 1.

651. *Final Reports* II, 94–95. See also P. Crabtree, "The Faunal Skeletal Remains," in Warden et al. *Final Reports* IV, 117–118.

652. *Final Reports* III, xi. White, *Final Reports* V, 119.

653. They constitute less than 3% of all the Corinthian full-size vases retained from the excavation of the sanctuary. These may, of course, have been supplemented by imports from other Greek centers, e.g., East Greek fruitstands and dishes (see Schaus, *Final Reports*, II, 59–69) or by local wares.

654. Or just over 20% of the total number of vases.

655. *Agora* XII:1, 180 mentions that kothons with scented water

were used in religious ceremonies.

656. *Tocra* I, 15.

657. There are correspondingly large quantities of various types of drinking cups imported from other Greek centers: see Schaus, *Final Reports* II, 16–18, 29–45 (Laconian), 58–59 (East Greek), and 79–83 (Chian); for Attic cups, see Moore, *Final Reports* III, 32–38, 43.

658. We have excluded the amphorai here since they may have contained oil or grain and not necessarily wine.

659. Moore, *Final Reports* III, kraters (pp. 20–23 where 26 are catalogued), oinochoai and olpai (pp. 27–28).

660. Schaus, *Final Reports* II, oinochoai (pp. 20–22,) and kraters (pp. 24–28 where 40 are catalogued).

ritual feast, the cups and related vases were left as dedications, despite the lack of conclusive evidence to prove that ritual drinking did actually take place at the sanctuary.

Similarly, our plates and bowls may have been brought to the sanctuary with food offerings and then left as dedications. Although the bowls and related shapes are generally uninspired, some of our plate fragments represent the finest examples of Corinthian vase-painting from the sanctuary. Although few of the plate fragments preserve suspension holes, it may be assumed that some plates at least were displayed on the walls of sanctuary buildings.

Comparison with Tocra

There is a remarkable similarity between the Corinthian pottery assemblages at the Demeter Sanctuary and the deposits at Tocra (ancient Taucheira) in Cyrenaica which are to be associated with a sanctuary, presumably dedicated to Demeter and Kore.[661] The Tocra material, with more complete vases having survived, is far better preserved than our Corinthian pottery. There are analogies not only in the range and types, as reflected in the rather extensive comparanda from Tocra cited in our catalog entries, but also in the quality of the Corinthian imports. In fact, the introductory comments to the Corinthian pottery at Tocra are aptly descriptive of our material; specifically, "the low proportion of pieces of high quality" and the "range of Corinthian products—good, bad, and indifferent."[662]

At Tocra, Corinthian pottery also formed the largest portion of the imported Greek pottery (about 30% of the catalogued pottery).[663] In addition, the observation is made that "products of certain workshops occur in groups, while those of other contemporary ones are totally absent."[664] For this reason, the Corinthian material at Tocra is believed to have been imported in "large batches." As mentioned above, this seems to be the case for our material as well.

Products of particular Corinthian workshops found at our sanctuary, however, do not occur at Tocra. Among these, for example, are the Middle Corinthian plates of the Chimaera Group, the Late Corinthian I black-figure tripod pyxides of Benson's Sad Siren Group, and the Late Corinthian II powder pyxides related to Amyx's Winchester Group. On the other hand, types are found at Tocra that are so far unknown at Cyrene, such as the kotylai by the Patras Painter, the globular pyxides related to the Ampersand Painter, and the Early Corinthian pyxis lids by the Mykonos Painter. In all these cases, however, the pieces are relatively few in number.

In view of the marked parallels in the shapes and types, even to the same shape decorated by the same painter (e.g., an olpe by an artist near the Geladakis Painter),[665] the question of trade routes from Greece needs to be briefly considered. At the time of publication of the first Tocra volume, John Boardman, lacking sufficient comparative material from Cyrene, stated that Cyrene's port of Apollonia was not necessarily on the route of ships sailing from Greece to Tocra.[666] This question of trade routes was further discussed by Schaus in his publication of the East Greek, Island, and Laconian pottery from the Demeter sanctuary.[667] According to Schaus, to reach Cyrenaica, Greek merchant ships may have sailed across the Mediterranean from Greece or they may have traveled along the coast from Naukratis in Egypt, located to the east. Schaus has posited, given the Greek inclination to sail along the coast, that many merchant ships from Naukratis would have stopped at Cyrene's port of Apollonia and not continued the added distance of some 140 kilometers westward to Tocra, particularly in view of Cyrene's "greater size and wealth." His study of the East Greek and Laconian pottery at Cyrene as compared to the products of these schools uncovered at Tocra supports this view.

This view, however, cannot fully account for the Corinthian pottery assemblages at both sites, on whose striking similarity we have already remarked. Greek ships carrying Corinthian wares may have occasionally come from Naukratis to Cyrenaica in the west, and in all likelihood Apollonia was not the final destination on their course. Although Corinthian pottery of the late seventh to the early sixth centuries is found at Naukratis, and continues to be imported

---

661. *Tocra* I, 15.

662. *Tocra* I, 21.

663. *Tocra* I, 21.

664. *Tocra* I, 21. As at Tocra, aryballoi are far more common than alabastra.

665. **257**; cf. *Tocra* I, no. 6, pl. 5.

666. *Tocra* I, 14.

667. Schaus, *Final Reports* II, 107.

until about the middle of the sixth century, it does not occur in quantity.[668] By contrast, Corinthian imports at both Cyrene and Tocra form the largest percentage of the identified Greek imports during the archaic period. East Greek fabrics, for obvious reasons, as well as Laconian and Athenian are the dominant wares to be found at Naukratis.

Consequently, other explanations, which need not be mutually exclusive, for the resemblances in the types, quality, and range of the Corinthian imports at both Cyrene and Tocra should be sought. For instance, assuming a continuous route for Greek ships along the coast of Cyrenaica, merchants who put in at Naukratis may have "reserved" Corinthian pottery for both Cyrene and for the further westward site of Tocra in anticipation of a more certain market for these goods. Alternately, when the route of Greek merchants was across the open Mediterranean, ships may have stopped at either Apollonia or Tocra and then journeyed to the other site which lies at some distance. Finally, the possibility cannot be excluded that either Tocra or Apollonia was the final terminus on the passage for ships coming from the north or from the east, and that the similarities in the Corinthian wares were the result of local trade between these two Greek sites on the Cyrenaican coast.

---

668. Boardman, *The Greeks Overseas*, 125.

Appendix I
Find Spot Index

AREA	TRENCH	STRATUM	CAT.	SHAPE	DATE
C11	1	3 (N. of wall)	**12**	Alabastron	EC?
			284	Krater	MC
C11**	2	5	**332**	Oinochoe**M**	LC II/III
C12/D12	G	2	**92**	Lid Flat	MC or LC I
			356	Hydria**M**	LC II/III
C12/13	1 Wall	2 (backfill from N. of wall)	**227**	Kothon	LC?
			181	Lekanis	LC II/III
C12/13	1	4 (W. of wall 3)	**280**	Krater	MC
C13	1	3a	**364**	Hydria**M**	LC II/III
C13	1	3b	**172**	Kylix	LC I
C13*	1	4a	**32**	Aryballos	LC I
			314	Kotyle**M**	LC II/III
C13**	1	4b	**303**	Lid**M**	LC
C13/D13*	1	5	**357**	Hydria**M**	LC II/III
C13/D13*	1	6	**94**	Lid Flat	LC
C15/D15	1	1,2	**54**	Tripod Pyxis	LC I
C15/D15	1-B	2	**81**	Powder Pyxis	LC (?)
C15/D15	1-B	4	**323**	Phiale**M**	LC II/III
C15/16	1	4	**315**	Kotyle**M**	LC II/III

```
KEY

M       Miniature
*       Largely undisturbed archaic level
**      Undisturbed archaic level

***     Fragments of vase found in more than one context:          158  E11/12 Pit Area 2 and E11/12 Pit Area 3
    21  F14/15, 1, 1 and F15, 1, 2                                 201  E10/11 (Area 1) 1, 3; D12/E12 D (Balk) 2; F11, 1,
    45  F13/G13, 1, 2 and F13/G13, 2, 2                                 2
    53  F13/G13, 1, 2 and F13/G13, 2, 2                            216  F14/G14, 1, 3 and F13/G13, 2, 2
   140  F14/G14, 1, 3 and F14/G14, 1, Test 2                       252  F13/G13, 1, 2 and F13/G13, 2, 2a
```

AREA	TRENCH	STRATUM	CAT.	SHAPE	DATE
C15/16	1	4	**324**	Bowl**M**	LC II/III
			343	Hydria**M**	LC II/III
			331	Kothon**M**	LC III
			379	Hydria**M**	5th c.?
			378	Hydria**M**	late 5th-4th c.
C15/16	1	4 (tank)	**264**	Closed Vase	MC
			154	Kotyle	LC II/III
C15/16	1 W-4	Area 4	**187**	Bowl	First half 4th c.
C15/16*	1 4-2	Area 5	**161**	Kotyle	LC II
D10/11	C	5	**354**	Hydria**M**	LC II/III
D11/E11	Balk	3 (North half)	**209**	Plate	LC I (MC?)
D12/E12*	D	3	**115**	Kotyle	MC
			294	Aryballos**M**	LC II
D12/E12*	D	4	**59**	Tripod Pyxis	LC I
D12/13	A	2	**260**	Closed Vase	MC
			113	Kotyle	MC (?)
			340	Hydria**M**	LC II/III
D12/13*	A	3 (east)	**111**	Kotyle	MC (?)
			112	Kotyle	MC (?)
			165	Kylix	MC Late
		(west)	**123**	Kotyle	MC/LC
		(east)	**62**	Tripod Pyxis	LC I
		(west)	**168**	Kylix	LC I
		(east)	**275**	Closed Vase	LC
			36	Aryballos	LC?
D12/13*	A4	(between rubble walls)	**166**	Kylix	MC Late
			125	Kotyle	MC/LC
D12/13	B	2	**330**	Kothon**M**	LC
D12/13*	B	4	**206**	Plate	MC Late
		(west)	**77**	Powder Pyxis	LC
		(west)	**78**	Powder Pyxis	LC
		(west)	**277**	Closed Vase	LC
			297	Concave Pyxis**M**	LC
			186	Bowl	LC II
			245	Oinochoe	LC II
			304	Kotyle**M**	LC II
			310	Kotyle**M**	LC II
			311	Kotyle**M**	LC II
			325	Bowl**M**	LC II/III
			335	Hydria**M**	LC II/III
			336	Hydria**M**	LC II/III
			337	Hydria**M**	LC II/III
			338	Hydria**M**	LC II/III
			339	Hydria**M**	LC II/III

APPENDIX I

AREA	TRENCH	STRATUM	CAT.	SHAPE	DATE
D12/13*	B	4	**376**	Hydria**M**	5th c. probably
D12/13	F	2, S. scarp	**63**	Tripod Pyxis	LC I or LC II
D12/13*	F	3	**326**	Kanoun**M**	LC II/III
			383	Hydria**M**	5th c.?
D13 (Area 2)	2	1,2	**178**	Lekanis/Bowl	LC II
D13 (Area 2)	2	2	**334**	Hydria**M**	LC II/III
D13 (Area 2)	2	3	**124**	Kotyle	MC/LC?
			302	Lid**M**	LC II
D13 (Area 2)	Ext.N	1	**250**	Oinochoe Lid	MC ?
D13/E13	Balk	2	**333**	Olpe**M**	LC II/III
D13/E13	Balk	3	**114**	Kotyle	MC
D14/E14	1	2	**290**	Krater	LC?
			296	Pyxis?**M**	LC II/III
D15/E15	1	3	**365**	Hydria**M**	LC II/III
D15/16	1	2, mixed with 3?	**109**	Knob	LC II/III
D15/16	1	3	**291**	Krater/Bowl	MC?
			363	Hydria**M**	LC II/III
D16/17	1	1	**23**	Aryballos	MC
D16/17	1	3	**243**	Oinochoe	MC or LC
			103	Lid Domed	LC
			328	Kothon**M**	LC
			342	Hydria**M**	LC II/III
			344	Hydria**M**	LC II/III
			345	Hydria**M**	LC II/III
			164	Skyphos	LC III
D16/17	1 (?)	3	**377**	Hydria**M**	late 5th-4th c.?
D16/17**	1	4	**80**	Powder Pyxis	LC (?)
D16/17	2	3	**295**	Aryballos**M**	LC II
			346	Hydria**M**	LC II/III
			347	Hydria**M**	LC II/III
			349	Hydria**M**	LC II/III
			350	Hydria**M**	LC II/III
			351	Hydria**M**	LC II/III
D16/17	2	4	**246**	Oinochoe	LC II/III
			352	Hydria**M**	LC II/III
			353	Hydria**M**	LC II/III
			355	Hydria**M**	LC II/III
			380	Hydria**M**	5th c.

AREA	TRENCH	STRATUM	CAT.	SHAPE	DATE
E10 Balk Bldg	(between E wall and Terrace E wall)		82	Powder Pyxis	LC (?)
E10 Balk		2/3	129	Kotyle	MC
			133	Kotyle	MC/LC?
			167	Kylix	LC I
E10 Balk, S.		2/3	237	Oinochoe	MC?
E10 Balk Bldg	Foundation Trench		289	Krater	MC or LC
E10 Bldg	1/2 (along S. edge)		200	Plate	MC
			288	Krater	MC or LC
E10 Bldg	Clean-up (under fallen N. wall)		225	Kothon	LC?
E10 Bldg	Unstratified		214	Kothon	LC II
E10 Bldg	1	2	13	Alabastron	MC probably
E10 Bldg	Balk	3	285	Krater	MC
			217	Kothon	LC II
			301	Powder Pyxis	LC II
E10/11 (Area 1) 1		3	281	Krater	MC
			***201	Plate	MC Late
			196	Plate	MC Late?
			189	Lekane/Bowl	MC?
			44	Convex Pyxis	LC
			180	Lekanis	LC
			269	Closed Vase	LC I/II
			162	Kotyle	LC II/III
E11	1	2	292	Ring Vase	MC
			283	Krater	MC
			199	Plate	MC Late?
			76	Powder Pyxis	LC
			11	Alabastron	LC I
			169	Kylix	LC I
			175	Kylix	LC I
			218	Kothon	LC II
			244	Oinochoe	LC II
E11**	2 Pit	3	282	Krater	MC
E11	3	2	10	Alabastron	LC I
E11*	3	3	55	Tripod Pyxis	LC I
			268	Closed Vase	LC I/II
			73	Powder Pyxis?	LC
			89	Lid Flat	LC?
			51	Convex Pyxis	LC III
E11	4	2	56	Tripod Pyxis	LC I
			182	Bowl	LC probably

APPENDIX I

AREA	TRENCH	STRATUM	CAT.	SHAPE	DATE
E11/12	Pit	2	28	Aryballos	LC
			75	Powder Pyxis	LC
			70	Powder Pyxis	LC II
E11/12	Pit Area	2	41	Concave Pyxis	LC?
E11/12	Balk	1	205	Plate	MC Late
E11/12	Balk	2	259	Closed Vase	MC
			256	Amphoriskos	MC Late
			197	Plate	MC or LC I
E11/12*	Pit	2,3*	***158	Kotyle	LC I Early
E12	1	3	3	Alabastron	EC
			110	Kotyle	MC (Early?)
			228	Oinochoe	MC
			18	Aryballos	MC?
			375	Hydria**M**	5th c.
E12/13	C	Polygonal Wall	106	Knob	MC
E12/13	E	2	257	Olpe?	MC
			195	Plate	MC probably
			117	Kotyle	MC?
			287	Krater?	MC?
			127	Kotyle	LC
			348	Hydria**M**	LC II/III
			126	Kotyle	LC probably
E13/14	1	1	381	Hydria**M**	5th c.
E15	2	2	382	Hydria**M**	5th c.
E15	3	3	329	Kothon**M**	LC
E16	2	2	374	Hydria**M**	late 5th-4th c.?
F10 and F14	Along NW Edge of Terrace 3/4		146	Kotyle	LC II
F11	1	1	198	Plate	MC Late?
F11	2	1	240	Oinochoe	MC?
F11	2	1-2	204	Plate	MC Late
			52	Tripod Pyxis	MC/LC
F11	2	3B	19	Aryballos	MC?
			39	Aryballos	MC?
F12		2	121	Kotyle	MC
F12/G12	Tunnel A		138	Kotyle	MC
			193	Plate	MC
			93	Lid Flat	MC or LC I
			43	Convex Pyxis	MC/LC

AREA	TRENCH	STRATUM	CAT.	SHAPE	DATE
F12/G12	Tunnel A		233	Oinochoe	MC?
			183	Bowl	LC
			185	Bowl	LC
			9	Alabastron	LC I
			71	Powder Pyxis	LC II
			151	Kotyle	LC II
			247	Oinochoe	LC?
F12/G12	1	2	2	Alabastron	EC
			137	Kotyle	MC
			191	Plate	MC
			105	Lid Domed?	LC
			141	Kotyle	LC II
			148	Kotyle	LC II
F13/14	1	1	388	Hydria**M**	5th c.?
F13/G13	Wall Test		1	Alabastron	EC
			212	Kothon	MC
			266	Closed Vase	MC?
			22	Aryballos	LC
F13/G13	1	1	226	Kothon	LC I/II
F13/G13	1	2	83	Lid Flat	EC
			85	Lid Flat	EC
			15	Aryballos	EC?
			211	Kothon	MC (Early?)
			16	Aryballos	MC
			42	Convex Pyxis	MC
			120	Kotyle	MC
			134	Kotyle	MC
			194	Plate	MC
			213	Kothon	MC
			393	Bird?	MC
			202	Plate	MC Late
		***252	Amphoriskos	MC Late
			253	Amphoriskos	MC Late
			262	Closed Vase	MC Late
			61	Triped Pyxis	MC Late or LC
			27	Aryballos	MC or LC
			188	Bowl	MC or LC
			107	Knob	MC or LC I
			132	Kotyle	MC/LC
		***53	Tripod Pyxis	MC/LC
			17	Aryballos	MC?
			20	Aryballos	MC?
			118	Kotyle	MC?
			232	Oinochoe	MC?
		***45	Convex Pyxis	LC
			48	Convex Pyxis	LC
			49	Convex Pyxis	LC
			64	Triped Pyxis	LC
			305	Kotyle**M**	LC
			57	Tripod Pyxis	LC I
			58	Tripod Pyxis	LC I

APPENDIX I

AREA	TRENCH	STRATUM	CAT.	SHAPE	DATE
F13/G13	1	2	171	Kylix	LC I/II
			67	Powder Pyxis	LC II
			69	Powder Pyxis	LC II
			96	Lid Flat	LC II
			97	Lid Flat	LC II
			144	Kotyle	LC II
			160	Kotyle	LC II
			249	Oinochoe	LC II
			300	Tripod PyxisM	LC II
			322	KylixM	LC II
			65	Tripod PyxisM	LC II/III
			358	HydriaM	LC II/III
			359	HydriaM	LC II/III
			372	HydriaM	LC II/III
F13/G13	1	Wall Surface	14	Alabastron	MC?
F13/G13	2	2	207	Plate	EC?
			208	Plate	EC?
			30	Aryballos	MC
			119	Kotyle	MC
			135	Kotyle	MC
			139	Kotyle	MC
			235	Oinochoe	MC
			236	Oinochoe	MC
			258	Closed Vase	MC
			203	Plate	MC Late
			255	Amphoriskos	MC Late
			263	Closed Vase	MC Late
			392	Lion	MC Late
			8	Alabastron	MC Late or LC I
			274	Hydria	MC or LC
			251	Oinochoe Lid	MC or LC ?
			238	Oinochoe	MC or LC I
			286	Krater	MC or LC I
			122	Kotyle	MC/LC
			40	Concave Pyxis	MC/LC?
			31	Aryballos	LC
			95	Lid Flat	LC
			173	Kylix	LC
			224	Kothon	LC
			276	Closed Vase	LC
			278	Closed Vase	LC
			293	AryballosM	LC
			60	Tripod Pyxis	LC I
			159	Kotyle	LC I
			267	Closed Vase	LC I/II
			270	Closed Vase	LC I/II
			306	KotyleM	LC I/II
			66	Powder Pyxis	LC II
			98	Lid Flat	LC II
			210	Plate	LC II
			272	Closed Vase	LC II
			299	Convex PyxisM	LC II
			308	KotyleM	LC II
			150	Kotyle	LC II?

AREA	TRENCH	STRATUM	CAT.	SHAPE	DATE
F13/G13	2	2	50	Convex Pyxis	LC II/III
			104	Lid Domed	LC II/III
			155	Kotyle	LC II/III
			313	KotyleM	LC II/III
			318	KotyleM	LC II/III
			320	KotyleM	LC II/III
			327	KanounM	LC II/III
			360	HydriaM	LC II/III
			361	HydriaM	LC II/III
			362	HydriaM	LC II/III
F13/G13	2	2N	37	Aryballos	MC
			91	Lid Flat	MC or LC
			86	Lid Flat	MC?
			99	Lid Flat?	LC
			102	Lid Domed	LC
			68	Powder Pyxis	LC II
			147	Kotyle	LC II
			220	Kothon	LC II
F13/G13	Wall Sondage	1	384	HydriaM	5th c.?
F14/G14	1	2	4	Alabastron	EC/MC
			29	Aryballos	MC
			87	Lid Flat	MC
			130	Kotyle	MC
			192	Plate	MC
			239	Oinochoe	MC or LC I
			131	Kotyle	MC/LC
			5	Alabastron	MC?
			177	Lekanis?	MC?
			265	Closed Vase	MC?
			394	Avian	MC?
			25	Aryballos	LC
			33	Aryballos	LC
			46	Convex Pyxis	LC
			72	Powder Pyxis	LC
			74	Powder Pyxis	LC
			100	Lid Domed	LC
			101	Lid Domed	LC
			184	Bowl	LC
			223	Kothon	LC
			174	Kylix	LC I
			231	Oinochoe	LC I/II
			143	Kotyle	LC II
			145	Kotyle	LC II
			219	Kothon	LC II
			271	Closed Vase	LC II
			298	Convex PyxisM	LC II
			309	KotyleM	LC II
			312	KotyleM	LC II
			153	Kotyle	LC II/III
			273	Closed Vase	LC II/III
			316	KotyleM	LC II/III
			317	KotyleM	LC II/III
			366	HydriaM	LC II/III

AREA	TRENCH	STRATUM	CAT.	SHAPE	DATE
F14/G14	1	2	369	Hydria**M**	LC II/III
			373	Hydria**M**	LC II/III
			389	Krater**M**	LC II/III
			179	Lekanis/Bowl	LC II or LC III
			279	Lekythos	LC III
			390	Krater/Krater Cup**M**	LC III
			387	Hydria**M**	5th c.?
F14/G14	1	3	116	Kotyle	MC
			38	Aryballos	MC or LC
			26	Aryballos	LC
			35	Aryballos	LC
			47	Convex Pyxis	LC
			128	Kotyle	LC
			221	Kothon	LC
			***140	Kotyle	LC II
			142	Kotyle	LC II
			149	Kotyle	LC II
			152	Kotyle	LC II
			215	Kothon	LC II
			***216	Kothon	LC II
			307	Kotyle**M**	LC II
			321	Kotyle**M**	LC II
			368	Hydria**M**	LC II/III
		3?	367	Hydria**M**	LC II/III
			163	Kotyle	LC III
F14/G14	1 Test	1-2	84	Lid Flat	EC
			136	Kotyle	MC
			230	Oinochoe	MC
			7	Alabastron	MC?
			222	Kothon	LC
			319	Kotyle**M**	LC II/III
F14/G14	1 Test	2	229	Oinochoe	MC
			261	Closed Vase	MC
			254	Amphoriskos	MC Late
			190	Stemmed Bowl?	MC or LC?
			108	Knob	MC or MC/LC
			90	Lid Flat	MC/LC
			234	Oinochoe	MC?
			241	Oinochoe	MC?
			79	Powder Pyxis	LC (?)
			176	Kylix	LC ?
			242	Oinochoe	LC?
F14/G14	Cubic Meter Test	2	386	Hydria**M**	5th c.?
F14/G14**	1	4	156	Kotyle	LC II/III
			157	Kotyle	LC II/III
F14/G14**	1	5	370	Hydria**M**	LC II/III
			371	Hydria**M**	LC II/III
F14/15	1	1	***21	Aryballos	LC?

AREA	TRENCH	STRATUM	CAT.	SHAPE	DATE
F15	1	2	**170**	Kylix	LC I
			34	Aryballos	LC
			248	Oinochoe	LC
F16	1	2	**24**	Aryballos	MC/LC I
F16	2	1	**88**	Lid Flat	LC?
			385	Hydria**M**	5th c.?
G12	1	2	**6**	Alabastron	MC probably
G12	1	Stray	**391**	Krater/Krater Cup**M**	LC III
SW Sondage	1B	4a	**341**	Hydria**M**	LC II/III

Appendix II
Painters and Workshops

PAINTER/WORKSHOP	CATALOG NO.
MC	
Related to the Carrousel Painter	**191**
Chimaera Group	**192, 193, 195**(?)
Painter of the Copenhagen Sphinxes	**194**
Circle of the Detroit Painter (?)	**283**
Circle of the Dodwell Painter	**259, 261, 262**
Geladakis Painter or Close to the Geladakis Painter	**43, 257, 258**
Related to the Geladakis Painter	**260, 263**
Related to the Painter of Munich 237 and Louvre E 627	**280, 281, 282**
Groupe de Mégara Hyblaea	**392**
LC	
Arc-Palmette Workshop	**272**
Dot-Cluster Workshop	**51**
Late Warrior Frieze Group	**11**
Long Duck Painter	**58**
Related to the Sad Siren Group (*Gruppe der traurigen Sirene*)	**52, 53, 54, 55**
TP Workshop	**59, 60**
Winchester Group	**214, 215, 216**
Related to the Winchester Group	**66, 67, 68, 98**

وفي ضوء الأمثلة المقارنة الواضحة في الأشكال والأنماط فإن مسألة طرق التجارة من اليونان تحتاج إلى النظر فيها بشكل موجز . ولكي يصل المرء إلى منطقة برقة فلا بد أن السفن التجارية الإغريقية ربما أبحرت عبر البحر المتوسط من اليونان أو لعلها سارت بمحاذاة الساحل من نقراطيس في مصر . وافترض شاوس ، إذا أخذنا في الإعتبار ميل الإغريق للإبحار بمحاذاة الساحل ، أن العديد من السفن التجارية من نقراطيس كانت قد توقفت في ابولونيا ميناء قوريني ولم تستمر لقطع المسافة الإضافية وهي تقرب من ١٤٠كم غربا حتى توكره . خاصة وفي ضوء مساحة وثراء قوريني الكبيرين .

ومهما يكن فإن هذا الرأي لا يفسر التشابه المذهل لمجموعات الفخار الكورينثي في كلا الموقعين . وبالتالي فلا بد من البحث عن تفسيرات أخرى والتي ليس بالضرورة أن تكون مقصورة على الموقعين . ومن المحتمل أن السفن الإغريقية المحملة بالأواني الكورينثية جاءت من نقراطيس إلى برقة في الغرب في بعض الأحيان ، وعلى الأرجح لم تكن أبوللونيا المكان المقصود النهائي في سفرها . فمثلا ولنفترض طريق مستمر للسفن الإغريقية بمحاذاة ساحل برقة فإن التجار الذين يعملون في نقراطيس ربما " حجزوا " فخارا كورينثيا لكل من قوريني ولموقع توكره الغربي الأبعد توقعا لوجود سوق لهذه البضائع . بالتناوب عندما كان طريق التجار الإغريق عبر البحر المتوسط المفتوح ، ربما توقفت السفن إما في أبوللونيا أو توكره ثم توجهت إلى الموقع التالي . وأخيرا لا يمكن إستثناء هذه الإمكانية في كل من توكره وأبوللونيا لإنهما كانا الجهة النهائية لطريق السفن القادمة من الشمال أو من الشرق ، وإن التشابه في الأواني الكورينثية كان نتيجة للتجارة الداخلية بين مدينتين إغريقيتين على ساحل برقة .

ويتراوح تاريخ هذه القطع من طراز الفخار الكورينثي المتوسط إلى طراز الفخار الكورينثي المتأخر الثاني والثانية هي منطقة رديم ترتبط بزالزال عام ٢٦٢ ميلادية . وهنا أيضا يؤرخ الفخار من طراز الكورينثي المتوسط إلى الكورينثي المتأخر الثاني .

بخصوص كمية ونوعية الفخار الكورينثي الأسود يبدو أن أجود منتجات ورش الصناعة الكورينثية كانت قد إستوردتها قوريني بصورة متقطعة تقريبا عموما تعطي مجموعة الفخار الكورينثي الإنطباع أن كمية كبيرة من الفخار – العادي أو الأقل قيمة أو كلفة قد وصلت إلى قوريني ، وذلك مع بعض الإستثناءات التي يمكن ملاحظتها بصورة خاصة – بالإضافة إلى ذلك يبدو أن المعثورات تشير إلى أن الفخار كان قد جرى إستيراده ضمن مجموعات من ورش صناعة معينة .

يوجد تشابه ملحوظ بين مجموعات الفخار الكورينثي في حرم ديمتر المقدس وأماكن الرديم في توكره (تاوخيره القديمة) في منطقة برقة والتي ترتبط بحرم مقدس يعتقد أنه كرس لديميتر وكوري.

والمادة الأثرية من توكره بقيت في حالة أحسن بكثير من فخارنا الكورينثي وتوجد أوجه تشابه ليس في نطاق إنتشاره أو أنماطه فقط كما إنعكس في المقارنة مع توكره التي ورد ذكرها في مداخل كتالوجنا، ولكن في نوعية الفخار الكورينثي المستورد أيضا . وفي الواقع ، أن فخارنا من الطراز الأسود ليس غير متشابه مع مدى إنتشار الفخار الكورينثي في توكره ، بل يتميز بكونه " جيد ، رديء ، ووسط " وعلى أية حال فإن منتجات بعض ورش الصناعة الكورينثية الهامة التي وجدت في حرمنا المقدس لا نراها في توكره .

دراسات فخار شرق اليونان والجزر والفخار اللاكوني حيث أن قوريني نجت من الغزو الفارسي حوالي ٥١٥ ق.م. والفخار الكورينثي المستورد يوجد بكثرة في العصر الكورينثي المتأخر الثاني ويستمر في الإنتشار في القرن الخامس ق.م.

تتوزع معثورات الفخار الكورينثي بصورة جيدة عموما عبر المناطق التي جرى التنقيب فيها في الحرم المقدس . واكبر مصدر لمعثوراتنا ، وإنسجام مع تركيز أكثر الأواني المستوردة الأخرى هو الرديم الواقع خلف الجدار المساند لمنتصف الحرم المقدس والذي يعود إلى العصر الإمبراطوري المبكر (النصف الأول من القرن الأول الميلادي) . ويأتي نصف المادة التي وردت في الكتالوج من هذه المنطقة وأكثر من ٤٠٪ من الفخار الذي لم يدخل الكتالوج . وأن التوزيع الزمني لفخارنا من هذه المنطقة هو الفخار الكورينثي حتى الفخار الكورينثي المتأخر الثاني – الثالث ، كما وجدت معظم كسر الفخار الكورينثي المبكر في هذه المنطقة . وقدم مستوى طبقي لم يعبث به من العصر القديم ثاني أكبر كمية مركزة من المعثورات نسبة كبيرة من معثورات هذا المستوى الطبقي هي أواني صغيرة ونذرية من الفخار الكورينثي المتأخر الثاني – الثالث وأواني نسبيا في حالة محفوظة جيدا . وتعود أقدم كسرة إلى طبق زين بأسلوب التخطيط من طراز الفخار الكورينثي المتأخر الثاني . في حين أن غالبية الفخار من هذا العصر الكورينثي المتأخر الثاني . وفي منطقة مجاورة ، وهي أيضا مستوى طبقي لم يعبث به من العصر القديم ، وكانت نسبيا غنية بالفخار الكورينثي . وهنا تضمنت المعثورات طرز فخار كورينثي متوسط ومتأخر . وتوجد منطقتان أخريان فقط حيث يمكن وصفهما بمنطقتي تركيز أو كثافة . وكل منهما منطقة رديم . الأولى هي منطقة رديم من العصر الإمبراطوري تؤرخ قبل زلزال القرن الثالث الميلادي .

تأسس حوالي ٦٠٠ ق.م. ومما يؤسف له أن كسر العصر الكورينثي المذكورة تشكل نسبة مئوية صغيرة جدا من المعثورات وهي غير كاملة كي تزودنا بأي دليل يفيد بأن الحرم المقدس ربما كان قد تأسس أقدم بكثير من نهاية القرن السابع أو بداية القرن السادس ق.م . وفي الربع الأول من السادس ق.م. (العصر الكورينثي المتوسط) ، توجد زيادة ملحوظة في كل من عدد وإتساع نطاق معثورات الفخار الكورينثي ، وهي إشارة على أن الحرم المقدس كان قد تأسس منذ وقت في هذا العصر .

بالرغم من أن الفخار الكورينثي المتوسط يمثل بصورة جيدة في حرم ديميتر المقدس يبدو ان مجموعاتنا الرئيسية تبدأ في الربع الثاني من القرن السادس (الفخار الكورينثي المتأخر الأول) عندما بدأ يتضاءل مركز كورينث المتفوق في مجال سوق تصدير الفخار كمنتج للأواني الملونة الممتازة . بالإضافة إلى ذلك من الجدير بالملاحظة أن أواني أرخص ، بصورة خاصة طراز الأواني التخطيطية ، إستمر إستيرادها بكميات كبيرة خلال النصف الثاني من القرن السادس ق.م. (العصر الكورينثي المتأخر الثاني) . ويدل هذا على أن تجارة الفخار الكورينثي يمكن أن تستمر ولكن من خلال أوان أقل طموحا وثمنا والتي لا تزال توجد لها أسواقا خارج بلاد اليونان .

فضلا عن ذلك وفي منتصف القرن السادس ، وإلى جانب إستيراد الأواني ذات الأحجام الكبيرة ، كان هناك طلب كبير للأواني الفخارية الصغيرة الحجم التي استمرت طوال العصر القديم المتأخر . ودامت شعبية هذه التقدمات ، وإن يكن بكثافة قليلة جدا ، طوال القرن الخامس وربما حتى في القرن الرابع ق.م. ومن الناحية التاريخية يؤكد الفخار الكورينثي النتائج التي تم التوصل إليها من

الحزينة ، ورشة بنسون ت ب ، أواني شريط المحارب المتأخر أميكس ، مجموعة ليبجهاوس ، ورشة دوت كلستر وطراز الفخار الكورينثي الثاني من العصر القديم الذي يصور سعف النخيل ، مجموعة أميكس وينشستر " ومجموعة دوكات في ميجارا هيبلايا" .

ومع نهاية العصر القديم ، حين حدثت تغييرات في صناعة الفخار الكورينثي ، يوجد نقص في كل من إختلاف تقنية الزخارف وفي أحجام الأواني الفخارية .

وفي حرم قوريني المقدس تغطي صناعة الأواني الكورينثية حوالي قرنين من الزمان : تبدأ بحوالي ٦٠٠ ق.م . وتزداد في الكمية طوال القرن السادس ، وتستمر بصورة متقطعة ليس في القرن الخامس فقط بل حتى في الجزء الأول من القرن الرابع ق.م. وإن المعثورات الفخارية في كل نهاية لهذه الحقبة الزمنية الطويلة ليست عديدة . ومع ذلك فإنها تدعم النتائج التي تم التوصل إليها من خلال دراسة الفخار الأتيكي وشرق اليونان واللاكوني ، والتي تفيد بأن إستيراد الفخار يبدأ في مطلع القرن السادس . والفخار الكورينثي لا يملك الدليل بخصوص حل مسألة تأريخ تأسيس الحرم المقدس لسبب رئيسي واحد وهو الحالة الرديئة عامة لنماذج الفخار المتبقية .

بناء على الدليل الموجود حاليا من الفخار الإغريقي يبدو أن الحرم المقدس تأسس بعد جيل من إنشاء مستوطنة قوريني التي تؤرخ عادة حوالي ٦٣٠ ق.م. وأقدم القطع الفخارية الكورينثية التي أمكن التعرف عليها حتى الآن هي عدد صغير نسبيا من كسر الأواني الفخارية تؤرخ إلى العصر الكورينثي المبكر (٦٢٠-٦١٥ - ٥٩٥-٥٩٠ ق.م.) ، وتشير أيضا أن الحرم المقدس في قوريني ربما

خلاصة

يشكل الفخار الكورينثي قسما كبيرا من الأواني الفخارية الإغريقية من العصر القديم والتي اكتشفت في حرم ديمتير وابنتها المقدس خارج أسوار مدينة قوريني. ويضم كتالوج هذه الدراسة حوالي أربعماية قطعة من ضمن ما يزيد عن خمسة آلاف وماية كسرة جمعت من الحفريات. في حين أن هذه تمثل أقل من ٨٪ من الفخار الكورينثي الذي كان متوفر للدراسة من سبعة مواسم تنقيب في الحرم المقدس، إلا أنها تمثل أجود أنواع الفخار الكورينثي المتبقي في الموقع. ويظهر في الكتالوج كل شكل ونمط زخرفي تم التعرف عليه من بين المعثورات في الحرم المقدس. وتزودنا مادة الصناعة، بأنماطها وجودتها الواضحة والمتعددة، بالتبصر في كل من التاريخ المبكر للحرم المقدس وطبيعة أواني التصدير من هذا المركز الشهير للفخار الإغريقي.

ومجموعتنا هذه، التي تتكون من الأواني ذات الأحجام الكاملة والصغيرة، فهي متنوعة وتختلف من حيث الجودة والكمية وتحتوي على أواني مزخرفة بالطراز الأسود، والطراز التخطيطي والمظلل والأسود متعدد الألوان والأسود المزجج والرسم ذو القواعد المقررة وتقنيات الأرضية الحمراء. عدد قليل من الفخار الكورينثي يمكن نسبته إلى ملونين معروفين أو ورش صناعة. ومن فخار الطراز الأسود توجد المجموعات التالية: مجموعة كيميرا، ملون المخلوقات نصف الإنسان ونصف الحيوان في كوبنهاجن، ملون كاروسيل، ملون جيلاداكس، ملون دائرة دوديل، ملون ميونيخ ٢٣٧، ملون اللوفر ي٦٢٧، ودائرة ملون ديترويت. وأما المجموعات الأخرى فهي أميكس لونج داك، مجموعة سايرين

Figures

Figure 1

Kotylai

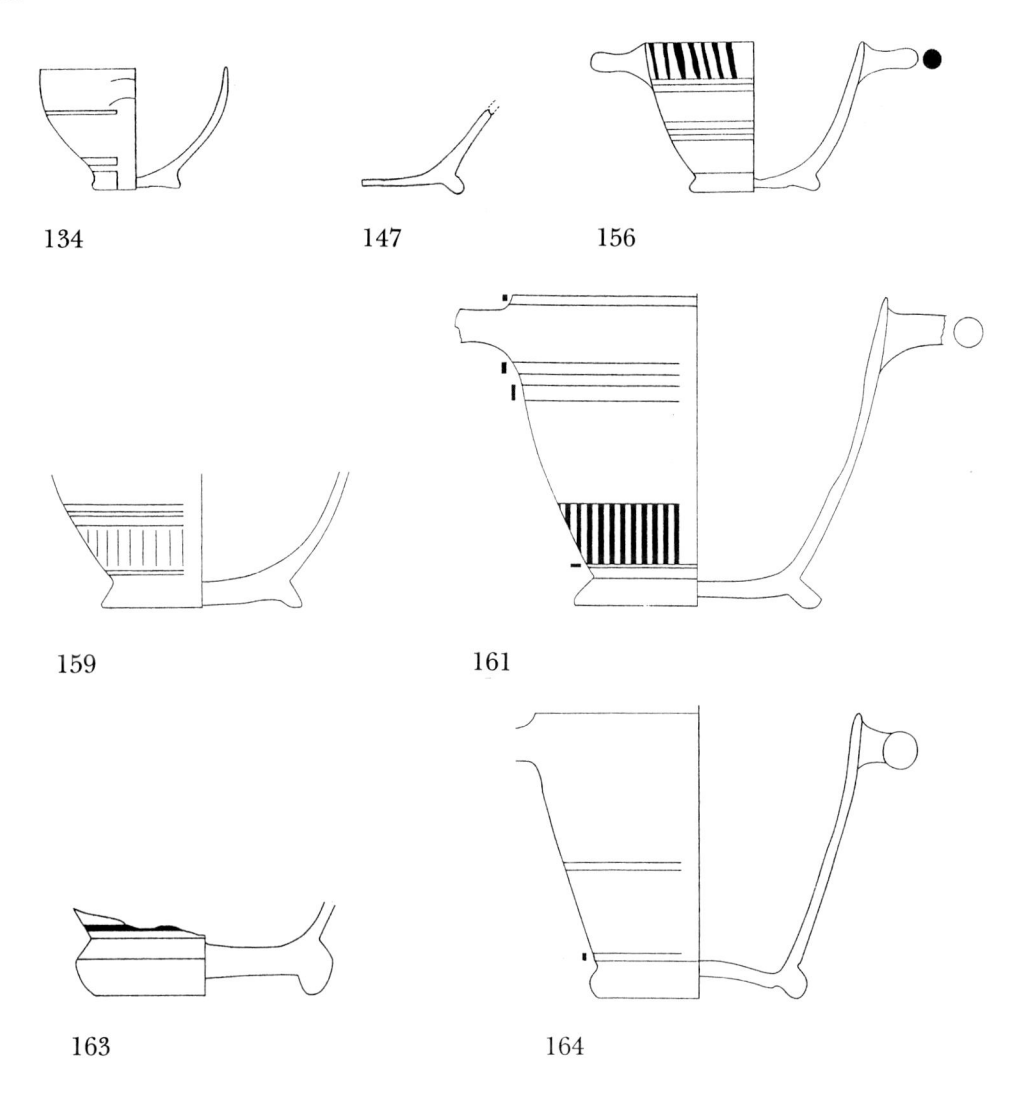

134 147 156

159 161

163 164

Kylix

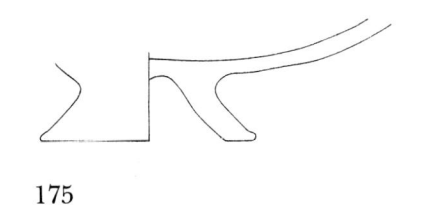

175

Bowls

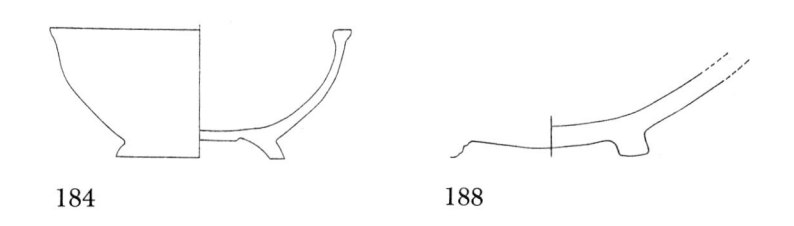

184 188

Figure 2

Plates

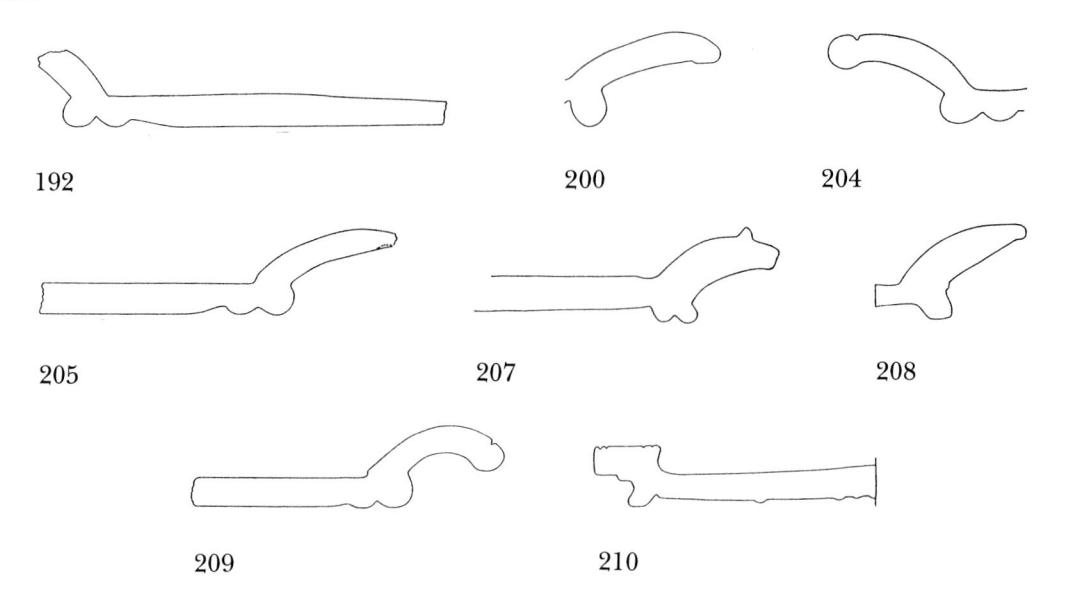

192   200   204

205   207   208

209   210

Krater

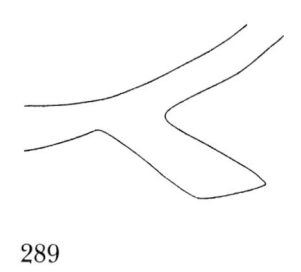

289

Miniature Vases

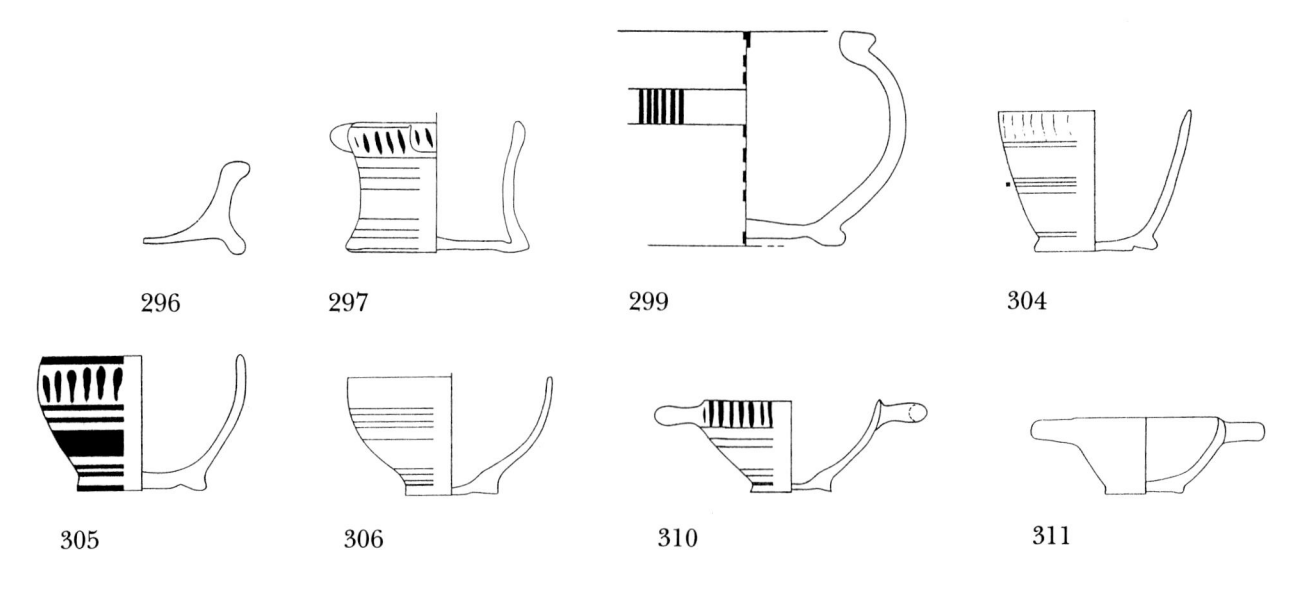

296   297   299   304

305   306   310   311

1:2

Figure 3

Miniature Vases (continued)

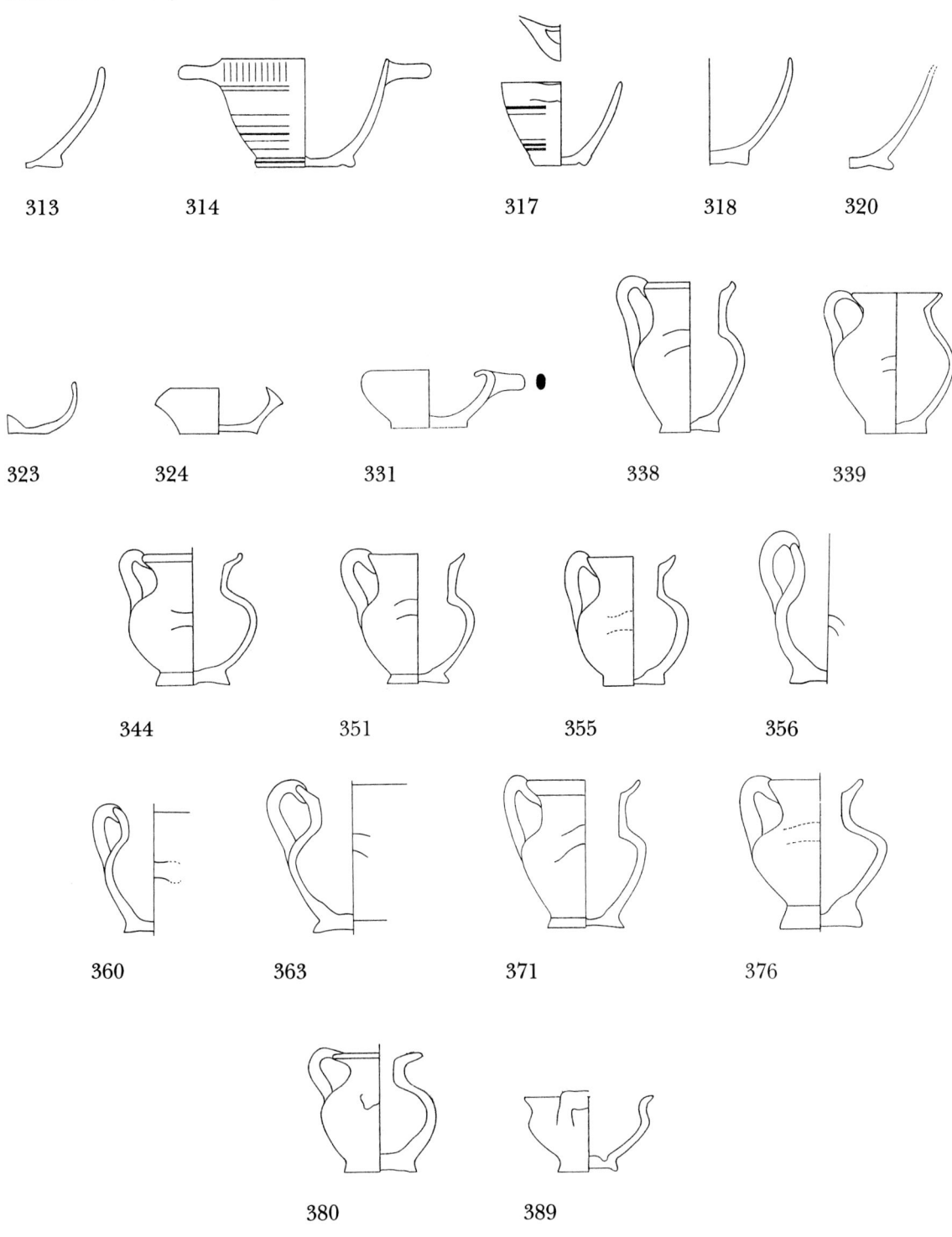

313 314 317 318 320

323 324 331 338 339

344 351 355 356

360 363 371 376

380 389

1:2

Plates

Alabastra Plate 1

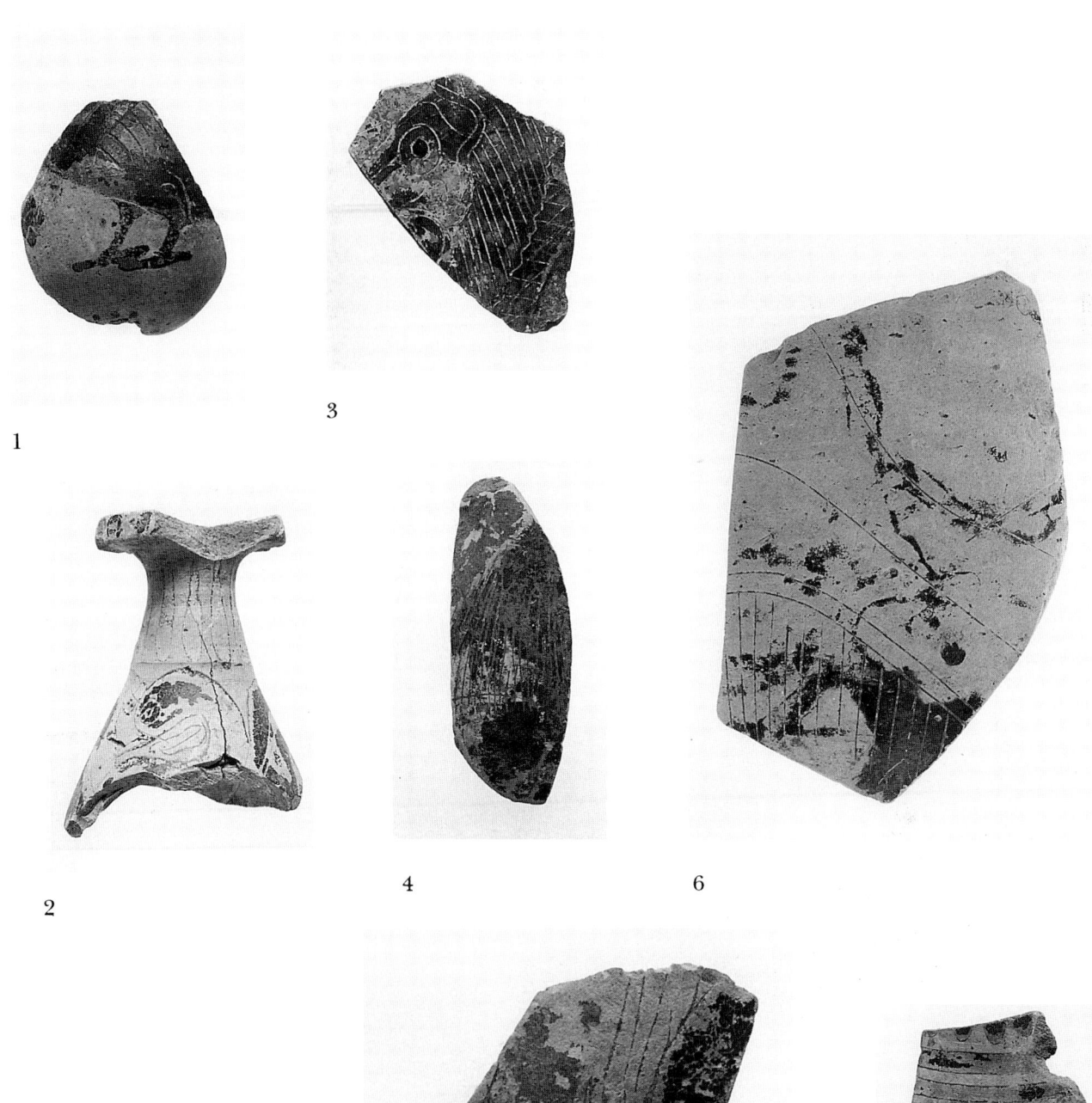

1

3

2

4

6

5

7

1:1
5 - 2:1

Plate 2   Alabastra

a

b

8   c

9

1:1

Alabastra Plate 3

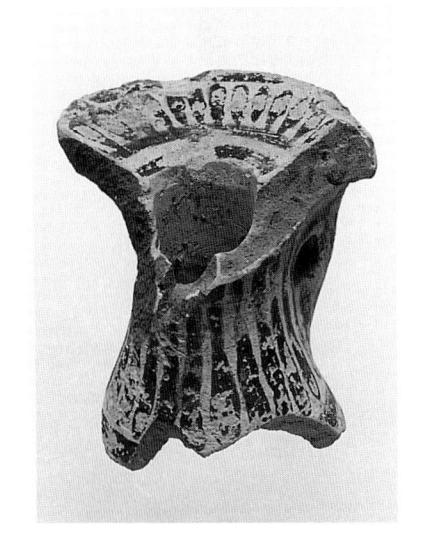

10

11

12

13

14

1:1

Plate 4   Aryballoi

15

16

17

18

19

20   21

1:1

Aryballoi Plate 5

22   23 a   b

24   26

25   27

1:1

Plate 6 Aryballoi

28

29

30

31

32

1:1

Aryballoi Plate 7

34

35

37

36

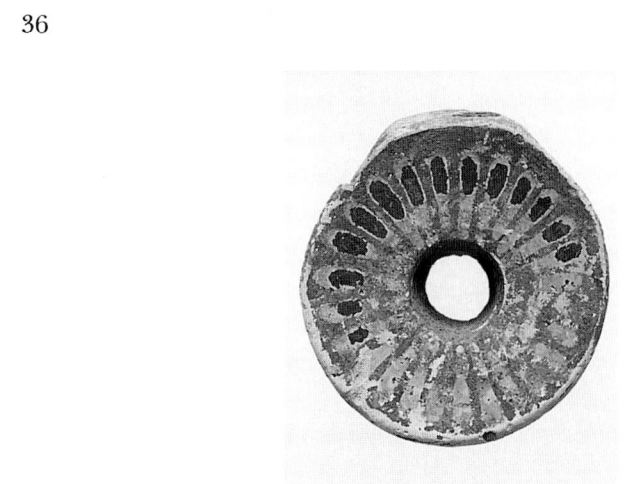

38  39

1:1

Plate 8   Pyxides

40

41

42

43

44

45

40, 42, 43 - 1:1
41, 44, 45 - 1:2

Pyxides Plate 9

46

47

48

49

50

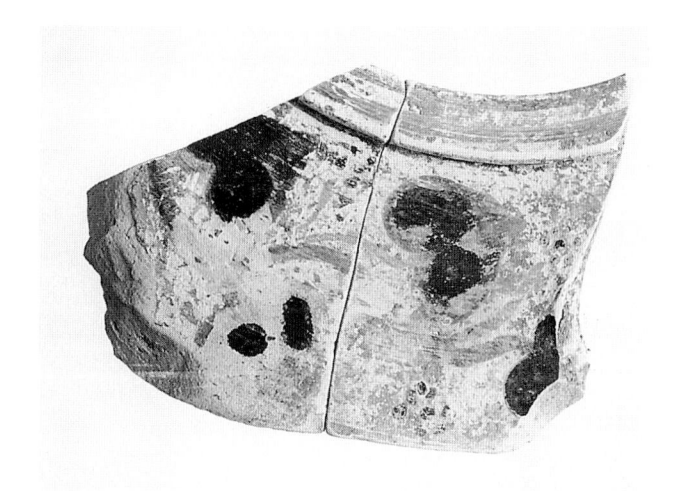

51

1:1
47, 48 - 1:2

Plate 10 Pyxides

52

53 a

53 b

54

55

56

1:1

Pyxides *Plate 11*

57

58

59

60

61

62 b   a

1:1

Plate 12   Pyxides

63

64

65

66   67

1:1

Pyxides Plate 13

68

69

70

71

72

73

1:1

Plate 14											Pyxides

74

75				76

77				78

1:1

Pyxides Plate 15

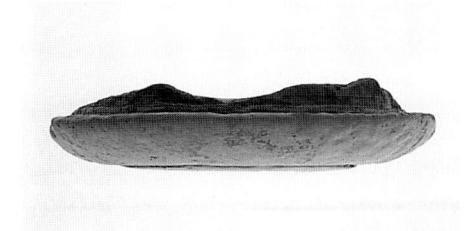

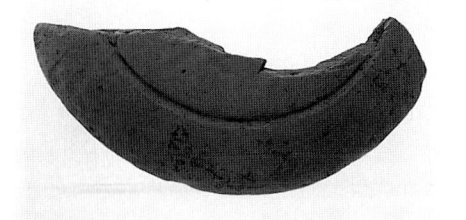

79

80

81

82

1:1
79 - 1:2

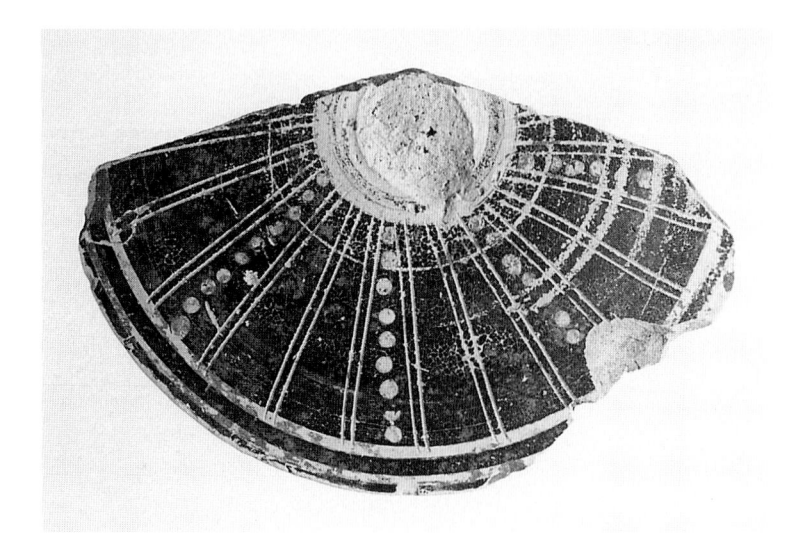

Plate 16   Lids

83

84

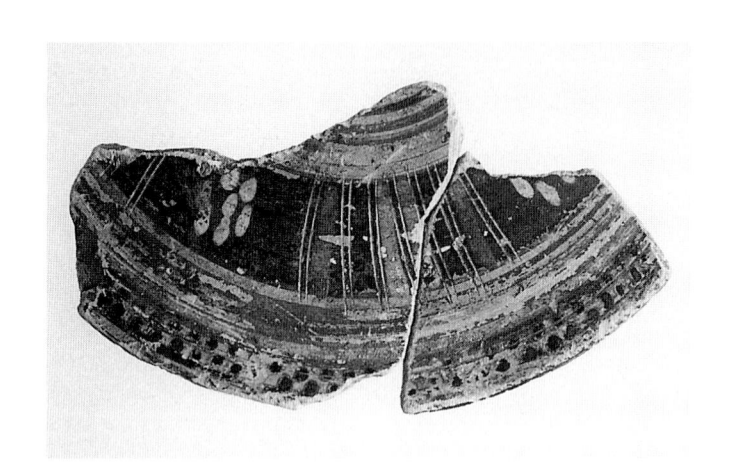

85

87

86    88

1:1

Lids
Plate 17

89

90

91

92

93

94

95

1:1
92, 94 - 1:2

Plate 18 Lids

96

97

98

99

100

101

102

1:1
98 - 1:2

Lids *Plate 19*

103

104

105

106

107

108

109

1:1

Plate 20 — Kotylai

110

111

112

113

115

114

116

1:1
110, 113 - 2:3
112 - 1:2

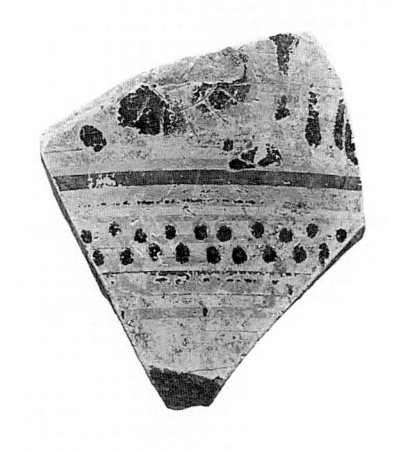

Kotylai   Plate 21

117

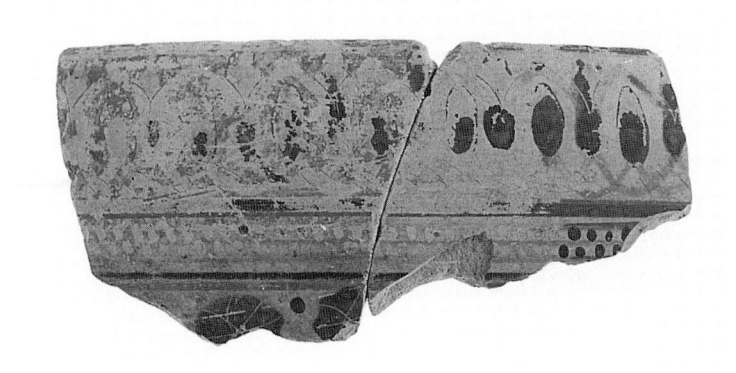

118

119

120

121    122

2:3
117, 118 - 1:1
122 - 1:2

Plate 22 Kotylai

123

124

125

126

127

128

129

130

1:1
123 - 2:3

Kotylai Plate 23

131

132

133

134

135 136 137

1:1

Plate 24 Kotylai

138

139

140

141

142

143

144

145

146

147

1:1
140, 141, 142, 145 - 1:2

Kotylai *Plate 25*

148

149

150

151

152

153

154

155

156

1:1
153, 154 - 1:2
156 - 2:3

Plate 26 *Kotylai*

157

158

159

160

161

162

163

164

157 - 2:3
1:2

Kylikes
Plate 27

165

166

167

168

169

170

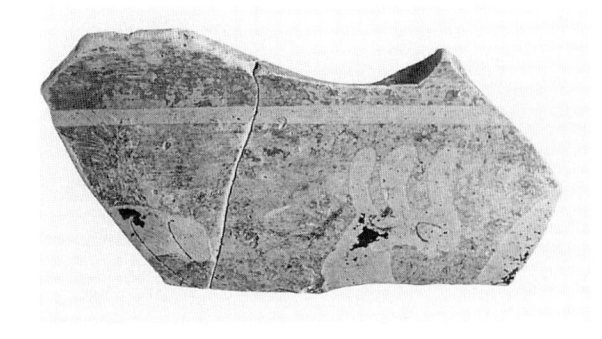

171

1:1
168, 170 - 2:3

Plate 28

172

173

174

175

176

1:1
174, 175 - 1:2

Bowls and Related Open Shapes Plate 29

177

178

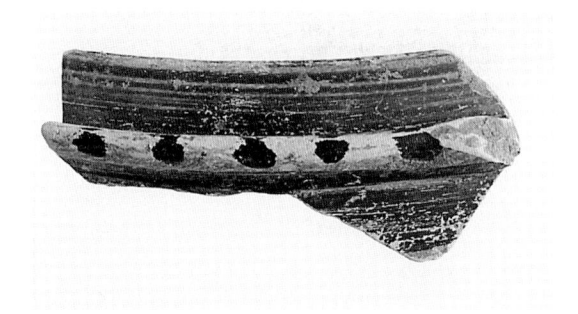

179

180

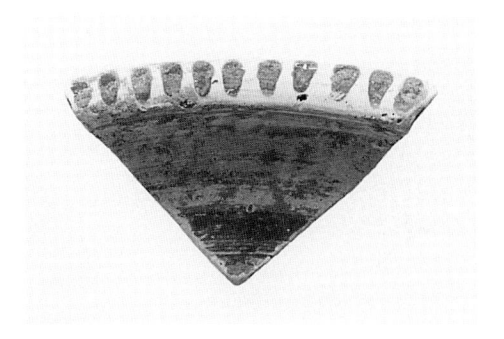

181

182

183

1:1

Plate 30　　　　　　　　　　　　　　　　　　　　　　　　　　Bowls and Related Open Shapes

184

185　　　　　186

187

188　　　　　　　　　　189　　　　　　　　　　190

1:2
184, 185 - 1:1
186 - 2:3

Plates *Plate 31*

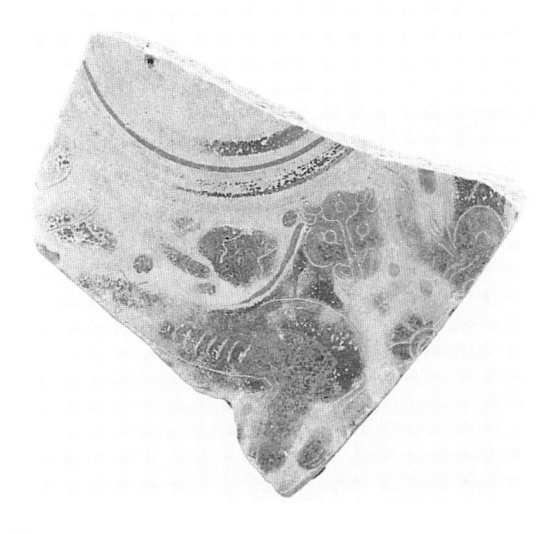

191

192

193

191 - 2:3
192, 193 - 1:2

Plate 32

a

b

194

195

196

1:1

Plates   Plate 33

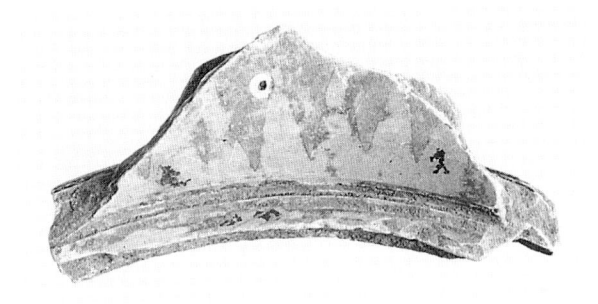

197

198

199

200

201

1:1
200, 201 - 1:2

Plate 34

202

203

204

205

206 a   b

1:2

Plates *Plate 35*

207

208

209

210

208 - 1:1
1:2

Plate 36　　　　　　　　　　　　　　　　　　　　　　　　Kothons

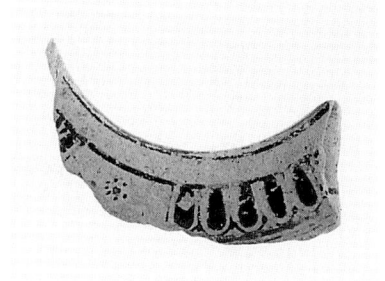

211　　　212　　　　　　　　　213

214　　　　　　　　　　215

216　　　　　　　　　217

218　　　219　　　220

1:1
211, 213, 216, 218, 220 – 1:2

Kothons   Plate 37

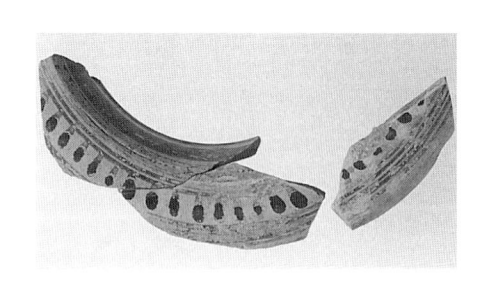

221

222

223 a   b   224

225

226   227

1:1
221, 223, 227 - 1:2

Plate 38	Oinochoai

228

229

230

231

232

233

234

235

236

1:1
230, 232, 235, 236 - 1:2

Oinochoai *Plate 39*

237

238

240

241

242

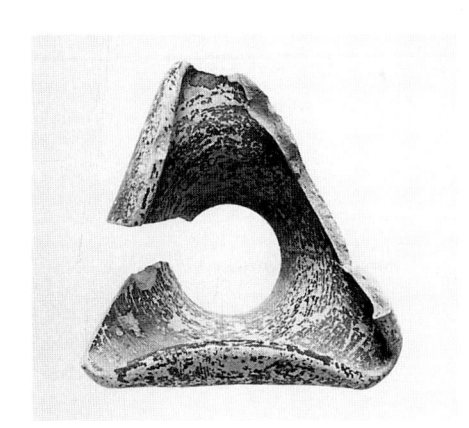

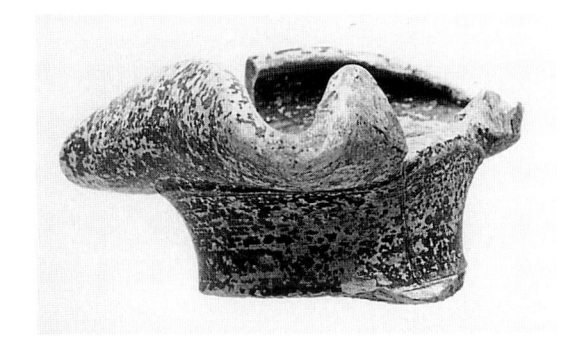

243

1:1
237, 238 - 1:2

Plate 40　　　　　　　　　　　　　　　　　　　　　　　　　　　　Oinochoai

244

245

246

247

248

249

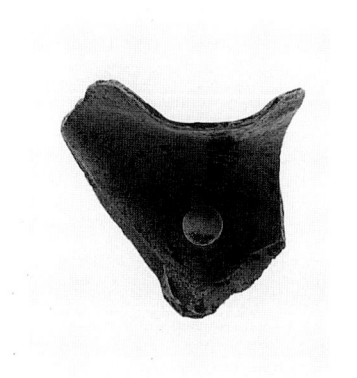

250

251

1:1
246, 250 - 1:2

Amphoriskoi Plate 41

252

253

254

255

256

254, 256 - 1:1
1:2

Plate 42　　　　　　　　　　　　　　　　　　　　　　　　　　Closed Shapes

a

b

c

d

e

257

1:1
a - 1:2

Closed Shapes	Plate 43

f

g

h

i

j

257 continued

258

259

1:1

Plate 44 Closed Shapes

260

261

262

263

264

265

266

1:1

Closed Shapes *Plate 45*

267

269

268

270

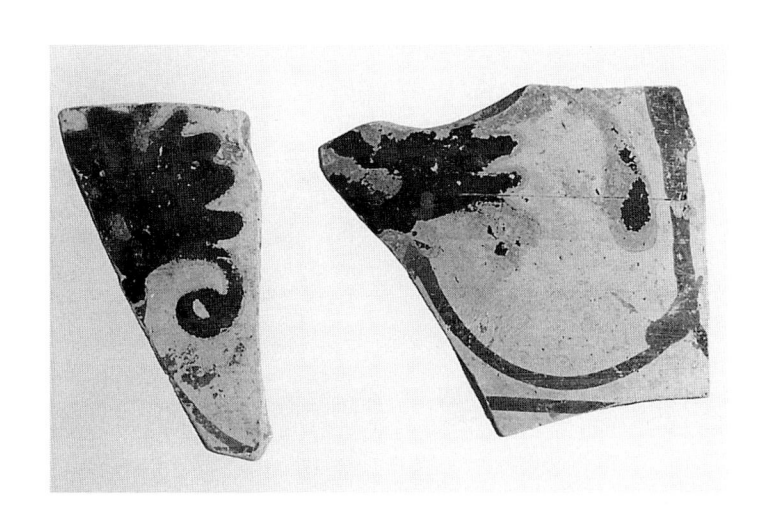

271

272

1:1
269 - 2:3
270 - 1:2

Plate 46   Closed Shapes

273   274

275   276   277

278   279

1:1
274 - 277 - 1:2

Kraters *Plate 47*

280

a
281

b

c

282  283  284

1:2
284 - 1:1

Plate 48 Kraters and Ring Vase

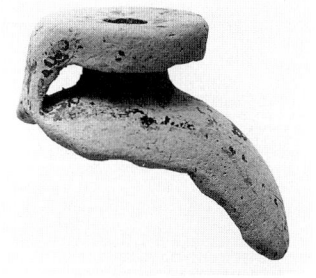

285

286 a   b

287 a   b   c

288

289

290

291

292

1:2
287, 291, 292 - 2:3

Minature Vases: Aryballoi and Pyxides Plate 49

293

294

295

296

297

1:1

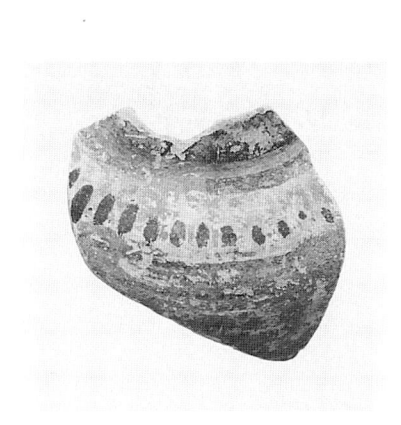

Plate 50 Minature Vases: Pyxides and Lids

298

299

300

301

302

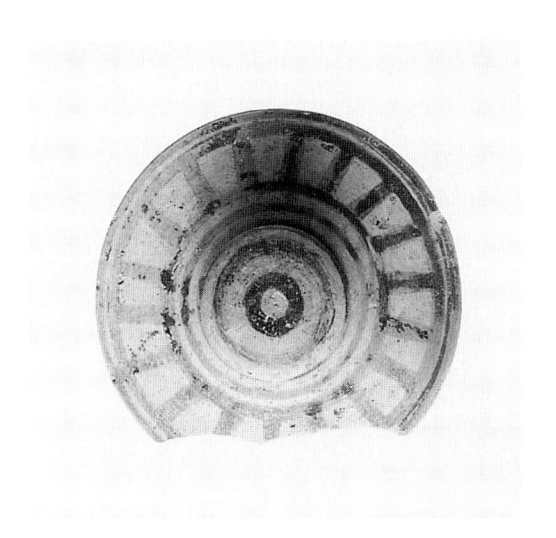

303

1:1

Minature Vases: Kotylai   Plate 51

304

305

306

307

308

309

310

1:1

Plate 52 Minature Vases: Kotylai

311

312

313

314

315

316

317

1:1

Minature Vases: Kotylai, Kylix, Phliale Mesomphalos Plate 53

318

319

320

322

321

323

1:1

Plate 54   Miniature Vases: Bowls, Kana, Kothons

324

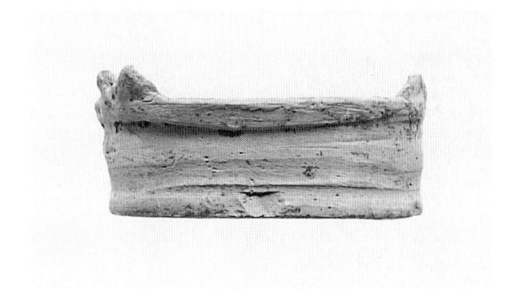

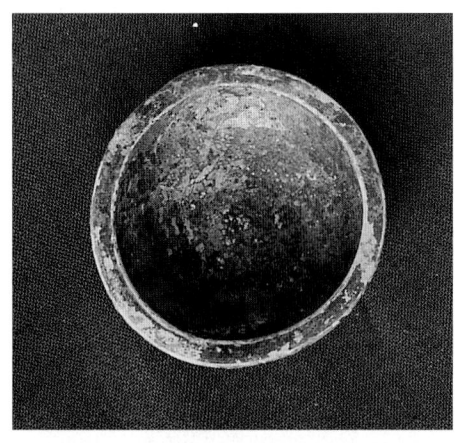

325

326

327

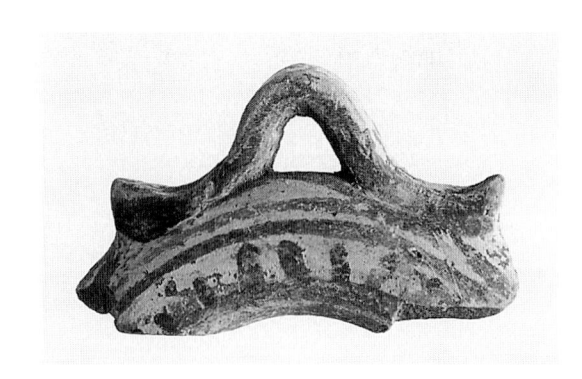

328

329

1:1

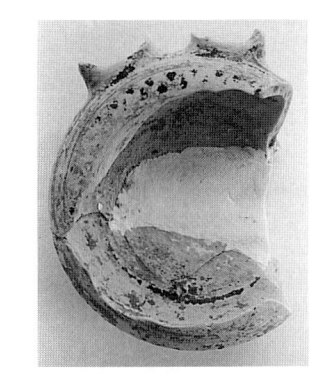

Minature Vases: Kothons, Oinochoe, Olpe, Hydriai Plate 55

330

331

332

333

334

335

336

337

Plate 56　　　　　　　　　　　　　　　　　　　　　　　　Miniature Vases: Hydriai

338　　　　339　　　　340

341　　　　342　　　　343

344　　　　345　　　　346

1:1

Miniature Vases: Hydriai Plate 57

347

348

349

350

351

352

353

354

1:1

Plate 58   *Miniature Vases: Hydriai*

355

357

356

358

359

360

361

1:1

Miniature Vases: Hydriai Plate 59

362    363    364

365    366

367    368

1:1

Plate 60 — Miniature Vases: Hydriai

369

370

371

372

373

374

375

377

1:1

Miniature Vases: Hydriai Plate 61

378

379

380

381

382

383

384

385

1:1

Plate 62　　　　　　　　　　　　　Miniature Vases: Hydriai, Kraters and Krater-Cups, Plastic Vases

386

387

388

389

390

392

391

393

394

1:1

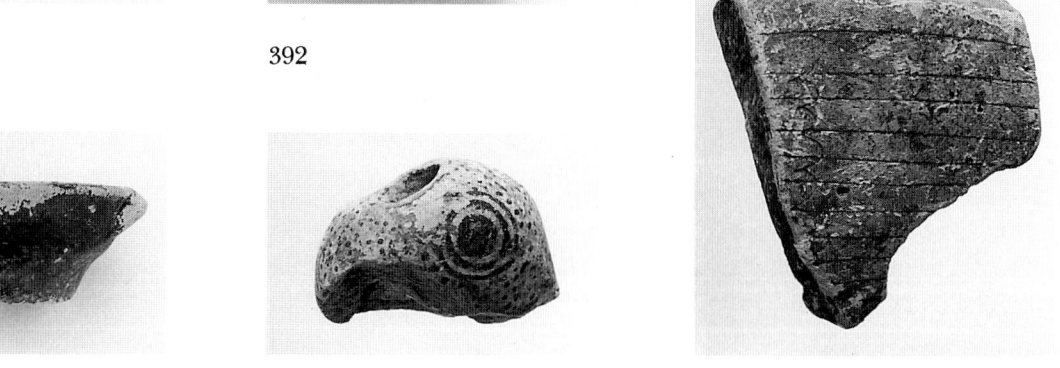

Miniature Vases: Hydriai Plate 61

378

379

380

381

382 383

384 385

1:1

Plate 62   *Miniature Vases: Hydriai, Kraters and Krater-Cups, Plastic Vases*

386    387

388     389

390    392

391    393    394

1:1